ISAAC ROSENBERG

The Making of a Great War Poet

A New Life

JEAN MOORCROFT WILSON

Weidenfeld & Nicolson
LONDON

First published in Great Britain in 2007
by Weidenfeld & Nicolson

1 3 5 7 9 10 8 6 4 2

A CIP catalogue record for this book
is available from the British Library.

ISBN-13 978 0 297 85145 5

Typeset by Input Data Services Ltd, Frome

Printed in Great Britain by Mackays of Chatham plc, Chatham, Kent

The Orion Publishing Group's policy is to use papers that
are natural, renewable and recyclable products and made
from wood grown in sustainable forests. The logging and
manufacturing processes are expected to conform to the
environmental regulations of the country of origin.

Weidenfeld & Nicolson

The Orion Publishing Group Ltd
Orion House
5 Upper Saint Martin's Lane
London, WC2H 9EA

To Cecil
and in memory of Isaac Rosenberg's sister, Annie Wynick

Contents

List of Illustrations

Black and white illustrations
Isaac Rosenberg with his parents and sister (*Bernard Wynick*)
Early family group (*Mrs Gerda Horvitch*)
Jubilee Street, Stepney (*Cecil Woolf*)
Stepney Green Arts and Crafts School (*London Metropolitan Archives*)
Narodiczky's shop in the Mile End Road (*Joseph Cohen*)
87 Dempsey Street, Stepney (*Tower Hamlets Libraries*)
Oil painting of Rosenberg by J.H. Amshewitz (*Private collection*)
Rosenberg's pencil self-portrait (*Private collection*)
Rosenberg's black chalk and pencil portrait of his mother (*Mrs Betty Silver*)
Rosenberg's oil portrait of his father (*Private collection*)
Slade picnic of 1912
Minnie's marriage to 'Wolf' Horvitch (*Mrs Gerda Horvitch*)
Rosenberg aged c. twenty-three (*Bernard Wynick*)
Rosenberg's oil painting of his uncle (*Private collection*)
'Betty' Molteno and Alice Greene
Rosenberg in his army greatcoat
Rosenberg with his younger brother Elkon (*Imperial War Museum*)
Rosenberg in army uniform with Elkon (*Bernard Wynick*)
Rosenberg from an autographed postcard (*Tower Hamlets Libraries*)
Rosenberg's gravestone (*Bernard Wynick*)

Colour illustrations
Self-portrait, 1910/11 (*Tate 2008*)
People on the Seashore (*Private collection*)
The Road (*Imperial War Museum*)
Highgate (*Mrs Betty Silver*)

The Fountain (*Imperial War Museum*)
The Artist's Father, oils (*Mrs Betty Silver*)
Sacred Love, composition in oils for the Slade (*Private collection*)
The Murder of Lorenzo
Head of a Woman 'Grey and Red' (*Imperial War Museum*)
Self-portrait (with raised hand) (*Mrs Betty Silver*)
Self-portrait (in red tie) (*Mrs Betty Silver*)
Self-portrait (in pink tie) (*Imperial War Museum*)
The Artist's Sister (*Private collection*)
The Artist's Father (*Private collection*)
The Artist's Brother-in-law (*Mrs L. Kellman*)
Self-portrait (in green hat looking left) (*Mrs Gerda Horvitch*)
Self-portrait (without hat, rounded shirt collar) (*Doron Swade*)
Cape Coloured Woman (*Garson family*)
Cape Coloured Man (*Garson family*)
Cape Coloured Girl (*Mrs Gerda Horvitch*)
Portrait of Clara Birnberg (*UCL Art Collections, University College London*)
Portrait of Sonia Cohen (*Joan Rodker*)
Self-portrait (hand in lapel) (*Private collection*)

Author's Note

I have taken all poetry quotations, unless otherwise specified, from the only complete edition of Rosenberg's verse in print, *The Poems and Plays of Isaac Rosenberg*, edited by Vivien Noakes (Oxford University Press, 2004). Unfortunately there is no complete edition of Rosenberg's letters and prose now in print. However, since Ian Parsons's edition of *The Collected Works of Isaac Rosenberg* (Chatto & Windus, 1979) is still available in libraries and from second-hand sources, I have taken quotations for all but the most recently discovered letters and prose from it. Like Parsons, I have for the most part silently corrected obvious mistakes of spelling, punctuation and grammar where I felt they would distract or hinder ease of reading.

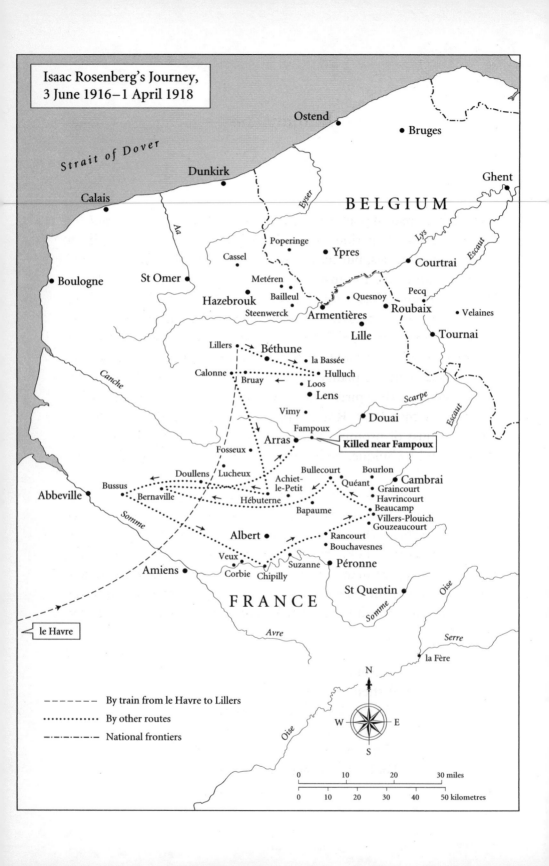

Isaac Rosenberg's Journey,
3 June 1916 – 1 April 1918

Strait of Dover

Ostend
Bruges

Dunkirk
Calais

Aa

Yser

BELGIUM

Ghent

Boulogne
St Omer

Cassel
Poperinge
Ypres

Météren
Bailleul
Steenwerck

Hazebrouk

Armentières

Quesnoy
Pecq
Roubaix

Courtrai

Lys

Escaut

Velaines

Lille

Tournai

Lillers
Béthune
la Bassée

Calonne
Bruay
Hulluch
Loos
Lens

Vimy

Fampoux

Arras

Fosseux

Doullens
Lucheux

Bussus
Bernaville

Abbeville

Canche

Scarpe

Escaut

Douai

Killed near Fampoux

Bullecourt
Bourlon

Achiet-
le-Petit
Quéant
Cambrai
Graincourt
Havrincourt
Beaucamp
Villers-Plouich
Gouzeaucourt

Hébuterne
Bapaume

Somme

Albert

Rancourt
Bouchavesnes

Veux
Suzanne
Péronne

Amiens
Corbie
Chipilly

FRANCE

St Quentin

Somme

Oise

le Havre

Avre

Serre

la Fère

N

W   E

S

Oise

– – – – – By train from le Havre to Lillers
· · · · · · · By other routes
– · – · – · – National frontiers

0   10   20   30 miles

0   10   20   30   40   50 kilometres

Introduction

'Who *is* the greatest poet of the First World War?' Most biographers and teachers of the period are familiar with the question. I have been asked it many times, but find it impossible to answer. How can one begin to compare, for instance, the lyricism and compassion of Wilfred Owen's 'Was it for this the clay grew tall?' with the biting understatement of Siegfried Sassoon's 'And the Bishop said: "The ways of God are strange!"'? Or the universal vision behind Edward Thomas's 'men strike and bear the stroke / Of war as ever, audacious or resigned' with the plangent insight of Ivor Gurney's 'Out of the heart's sickness the spirit wrote'? What I do know without doubt, however, is that Isaac Rosenberg belongs among these poets. In terms not just of promise, but of achieved originality of language, thought and technique, he is perhaps the most outstanding poet of the Great War.

Yet even now, ninety years after his death on 1 April 1918, Private Rosenberg lacks the rank he deserves and his work demands. He has certainly not been absorbed into the national consciousness in the way that Rupert Brooke, together with Sassoon and Owen, have. How many people can quote, or even identify one line of Rosenberg's verse? Yet this is the poet who wrote some of the most devastating and at the same time humane words about front-line experience ever penned:

> A man's brains splattered on
> A stretcher-bearer's face;
> His shook shoulders slipped their load,
> But when they bent to look again
> The drowning soul was sunk too deep
> For human tenderness.[1]

It is not that Rosenberg has lacked his admirers. But there has often been a condescending, slightly grudging or at least qualifying note to the praise. Laurence Binyon, for example, while thinking it worthwhile to help produce an edition of his poems in 1922, described him guardedly as 'not the least gifted' poet and thought it necessary to apologize for the 'difficult[y]' and 'obscur[ity]' of his writing, 'because he instinctively thought in images and did not sufficiently appreciate the limitations of language'.[2] And Edward Marsh, though a generous and consistently loyal patron, was too much a traditionalist to measure the scale of Rosenberg's achievement. Like his fellow Georgians Gordon Bottomley and Lascelles Abercrombie, he admired isolated phrases, occasionally whole passages, but looked for a more regular verse-form and more conventional imagery. As a recent critic, Deborah Maccoby, has put it, 'to a "policeman in poetry" like Marsh, whose main interest was in form, Rosenberg's agonised struggles with ideas would always be baffling.'[3] Long after his death Marsh would continue to refer to him as 'poor little Isaac Rosenberg'.[4]

But the best example of condescending praise has to be Ezra Pound's, who wrote to his friend Harriet Monroe, editor of *Poetry* magazine in Chicago: 'I think you may as well give this poor devil a show. . . . He has something in him, horribly rough but then "Stepney, East". . . . We ought to have a real burglar . . . ma che!!!'[5] And yet if anyone might have been expected to understand Rosenberg by 1915, when these words were written, it was Pound, or his fellow innovator T.S. Eliot, with whom Rosenberg has sometimes been compared.[6] For Rosenberg was a Modernist before his time, something of an exception among First World War poets, and not only with regard to his technique. He differed widely in terms of race, class, education, upbringing and experience from almost all the other well-known names of the period.

His Jewishness alone gives him a unique position among them. Sassoon, it is true, was half-Jewish, but on his father's side, and he was brought up as a Christian. And though many of Rosenberg's friends from the East End – David Bomberg, John Rodker, Joseph Leftwich, Stephen Winsten, Abraham Abrahams – wrote verse during the First World War, they will certainly not be remembered among its greatest poets. While Sassoon, like most of his fellow war poets, drew largely on the Christian and Classical mythology he had absorbed through his traditional public school education, Rosenberg's different cultural heritage distinguishes his work in a number of ways, lending to it, as Sassoon himself claimed, 'a racial quality – biblical and prophetic. Scriptural and sculptural ... '[7]

The fact that Rosenberg had also been exposed to an English education and would eventually read widely among the English poets only adds to his interest, his work displaying, as Sassoon again argued, 'a fruitful fusion between English and Hebrew culture'.[8] T.S. Eliot, who by 1953 believed Rosenberg to be 'the most remarkable of the British poets' killed in the First World War, considered that his work 'does not only owe its distinction to its being Hebraic: but because it is Hebraic it is a contribution to English Literature. For a Jewish poet to be able to write like a Jew in Western Europe and in a western European language, is almost a miracle.'[9]

William Plomer, who believed that 'the Jewish strain' was the more pronounced, said this showed itself 'especially in Rosenberg's choice of themes and colours, his sensuousness and eroticism' and that it provided 'a particular richness and warmth not to be matched among his contemporaries'.[10] For his part Rosenberg claimed that Jewishness gave him and his fellow Jewish artists 'that which nothing else could have given'.[11] 'The travail and sorrow of centuries' he wrote in a review of two Jewish painters 'have given life a more poignant and intense interpretation, while the strength of the desire of ages has fashioned an ideal which colours all our expression of existence.'[12]

Rosenberg's working-class origins and deprived upbringing in Bristol and the East End of London also mark him out from the mainly middle-class public schoolboys who make up the war poets. Like one of his earliest and most enduring models, Blake, he was largely self-made, a fact which helps account in both for their fierce originality as well as occasional clumsiness. Rosenberg himself saw no advantages in his situation, writing bitterly to an older, more privileged friend towards the end of his apprenticeship to an engraver which even Blake's example could not sweeten:

It is horrible to think that all these hours, when my days are full of vigour and my hands and soul craving for self-expression, I am bound, chained to this fiendish mangling-machine, without hope and almost desire of deliverance, and the days of youth go by ... I have tried to make some sort of self-adjustment to circumstances by saying, 'It is all *experience*'; but good God! it is *all* experience, and nothing else. ... My mind is so cramped and dulled and fevered, there is no consistency of purpose, no oneness of aim; the very fibres are torn apart, and application deadened by the fiendish persistence of the coil of circumstance.[13]

Someone who got to know Rosenberg during his apprenticeship, the painter Frank Emanuel, remembered how 'very bitter and despondent' his circumstances had made him.[14]

His reasons for enlisting, unlike the visions of valour, patriotism and sacrifice which motivated poets such as Brooke and, initially, Sassoon, were economically driven. He freely admitted to Marsh that he 'never joined the army from patriotic reasons'.[15] It was simply because he could not get work and needed to earn some money to send home to his struggling mother. She, like his father, who had had to leave Lithuania to avoid conscription in the Russian army, was a pacifist and their son had understandably no desire to fight on the same side as the hated Russians. Many of his Jewish friends of similar origins became conscientious objectors.

Moreover, when Rosenberg eventually arrived in France in summer 1916 he almost certainly found conditions there less harsh than men from more privileged backgrounds, though life for a private on the Western Front was undoubtedly tougher than for an officer. He was used to sharing his bedroom with the lodgers his mother was obliged to take in, and army food must have come as less of a shock to someone whose idea of a 'banquet' was 'salted herring, boiled potatoes, bread and butter and coffee'.[16]

On the other hand, and this is where the difference most clearly affects his work, his background did mean that he was automatically enlisted as a private, rather than an officer, unlike most of the other war poets. So that when he recalls, in the lines quoted earlier, how 'a man's brains splattered on / A stretcher-bearer's face', he *was* the stretcher-bearer. And when, in the same poem, he records how 'the wheels lurched over sprawled dead', he was the driver of the limber-carriage referred to, not the officer ordering or witnessing the incident. In other words, his position as a private gives an even greater immediacy and authenticity to his account of the war. Certainly it is more grittily realistic. Who else among the war poets could have written the grotesque account of 'Louse Hunting', which brings out so sharply the obscenity of war?

> Nudes—stark aglisten
> Yelling in lurid glee. Grinning faces of fiends
> And raging limbs
> Whirl over the floor one fire,
> For a shirt verminously busy
> Yon soldier tore from his throat
> With oaths
> Godhead might shrink at, but not the lice.[17]

And which other war poet has been able to convey so vividly and so convincingly at first hand the sensation of soldiers on the march?

> My eyes catch ruddy necks
> Sturdily pressed back,—
> All a red brick moving glint.
> Like flaming pendulums, hands
> Swing across the khaki—
> Mustard-coloured khaki—
> To the automatic feet.[18]

Both 'Louse Hunting' and 'Marching' highlight another distinguishing feature of Rosenberg, his training as a painter as well as a poet. In addition to noting the vivid use of colour in 'Marching', for example, it is tempting to suggest the influence of the Futurist artists here in the machine-like effect created by the 'flaming pendulums' and 'automatic feet', though Rosenberg himself largely resisted their message. While this does not make him unique – David Jones was both painter and poet – it does lend extra force to his vision on many occasions. In some cases the link between his two disciplines is completely explicit: it is clear, for instance, that his charcoal drawing 'Hark, Hark, the Lark' helped inspire the visually intense lines of stanza three in 'Returning, We Hear the Larks':

> But hark! joy—joy—strange joy.
> Lo! heights of night ringing with unseen larks.
> Music showering our upturned list'ning faces.[19]

The same is true of 'The Troop Ship' and 'Louse Hunting', both of which he had attempted to depict visually. As in Jones's case, Rosenberg's artistic apprenticeship appears to have made him more adventurous in poetry, though his development as a painter was almost certainly arrested because he failed to respond to the challenge of new movements in art. (At least that was what his close friend and fellow student at the Slade, David Bomberg, told his own student, Frank Auerbach.)[20] Jon Silkin argues that Rosenberg's 'capacity as a painter, as a thinker in images, impelled him into regarding the "idea" as the crucial component in the "made thing"'.[21]

Rosenberg's dual role as a poet and painter is significant in another respect: it reflects his position in general, caught between two worlds, the 'rootlessness' Silkin has identified in both life and work. Not only was he poised between the Jewish culture of his family and the English one of his education, or between the Yiddish language his parents spoke and the English he learnt when he started school, but his training at the Slade brought him into contact with a class and expectations quite different from those of his working-class beginnings. To heighten this conflict he was trapped between two very distinctive selves. There was the uncertain, stammering, undersized, almost clownish figure whom people like Marsh pitied, yet also the defiant, independent character who stares coolly out from his many self-portraits. Joseph Leftwich, who has described his first meeting with Rosenberg in 1911, was puzzled yet clearly fascinated by the apparent contradictions of the twenty-year-old:

> I wonder whether Rosenberg will be a friend [he wrote in his diary].
> He seems to be hardly capable of friendship. He is very self-absorbed

and there is no light-heartedness in him. He did not smile once the whole evening. I think he rather awed Simy [Stephen Winsten], awed him and depressed him, like something heavy and solemn. He is short and awkward, and his features are very plain – he has no personality. . . . He stutters, and his voice is monotonous.[22]

'Self-absorbed', 'no light-heartedness', 'heavy', 'solemn', 'hardly capable of friendship', 'short and awkward', 'very plain', 'no personality', 'stutters', 'voice . . . monotonous' – the list of negatives is extensive.

Yet there was another side to Rosenberg, as his friends – for he *was* capable of friendship, despite Leftwich's doubts – also testify. John Rodker, a fellow member of what became known as the 'Whitechapel Group', thought him 'remarkable', though 'semi-literate', and insisted that a younger friend, Lazarus Aaronson, must meet him.[23] Aaronson remembered being introduced to 'an uncouth little fellow, bandy-legged', yet with striking eyes, 'greenish with a red fleck'.[24] He too noted the 'taciturnity'.[25] Rosenberg himself was well aware of the poor social figure he cut, writing to Ruth Löwy about 1912: 'I have a dread of meeting people who know I write, as they expect me to talk and I am a horrible bad talker. . . . in absolute agonies in company . . .'[26]

But the shyness, embarrassment and social ineptness of this unprepossessing figure were balanced by a total dedication to art which turned him at times into the mysterious, Romantic figure of his self-portraits and those painted of him by others. As Leftwich noted, he could talk passionately and persuasively of his work, especially to a sympathetic listener. And in the pursuit of his vocation he could be as bold, if not more so, as his flamboyant fellow painter friend, David Bomberg. He would, for instance, even argue on occasions with the Slade's Professor Frederick Brown, and no one, as Bomberg noted, 'not Augustus John, William Orpen or Sir William Rothenstein, would ever presume to argue with Professor Brown'.[27]

Likewise, though his impoverished upbringing made him feel sorry for himself at times and socially inferior, fully prepared to ingratiate himself with potential patrons, he could be highly independent. He could also display unexpected stoicism and resilience in the face of setbacks. Determined to waste nothing of his experience, he even managed on occasion to be positive about the war: 'One might succumb[,] be destroyed' he conceded, '– but one might also (and the chances are even greater for it) be renewed, made larger, healthier.'[28]

And though he was both self-absorbed and forgetful – he had a habit of failing to address letters before he posted them – he was capable of great sensitivity and also of compassion towards others. Despite suffering enormously himself on the Western Front, even when not in the line, he genuinely felt that 'the chaps to pity' were those actually in the trenches.[29]

Perhaps the least predictable side to Rosenberg's character, and the most endearing counterbalance to the solemn, awkward figure whom Aaronson and his friends found so boring on one occasion that they left him to pay the bill at the Café Royal, is his whimsicality and humour. He loved small children and had his own collection of little toys he had bought in the street. And the painter John Amshewitz, who admired his work and encouraged him all he could, remarked on his humour: it was like Rosenberg's work, he remembered, 'original' and often self-directed.[30] One day, for instance, Rosenberg rushed into his studio and said: Mr Amshewitz, I have got a poem here' – feeling in his pockets the while – 'I think it is a good idea' – the search in his pockets getting more frantic – and then disappointedly, 'I must have forgotten it somewhere' – and then he collapsed, shaking with laughter – 'Great snakes! But I have forgotten to write it!'[31] As Amshewitz, who knew him well, expressed it: 'He was a strange mixture . . . '[32]

Rosenberg's conflicts of character and circumstances account for a great deal of the impact of his poetry, which appears to be both involved and detached at the same time. When in 'Break of Day in the Trenches', for instance, he addresses the 'queer sardonic rat' he spies there, he explores one of the central themes of the war, the indifference of Nature to distinctions of nationality, in a way which suggests first-hand understanding of the subject:

> Droll rat, they would shoot you if they knew
> Your cosmopolitan sympathies.

> Now you have touched this English hand
> You will do the same to a German
> Soon, no doubt, if it be your pleasure
> To cross the sleeping green between.
> It seems, odd thing, you grin as you pass[33]
> Strong eyes, fine limbs, haughty athletes,
> Less chanced than you for life,
> Bonds to the whims of murder,
> Sprawled in the bowels of the earth,
> The torn fields of France.[34]

Is it too fanciful to believe that Rosenberg identifies with the rat at this juncture?

This poem in particular, organized as it is round two of the most familiar features of trench life, rats and poppies, and ending with a breathtaking vision (in both senses of the phrase) of man's mortality –

> Poppies whose roots are in man's veins
> Drop, and are ever dropping,
> But mine in my ear is safe—
> Just a little white with the dust.[35]

– demonstrates that Rosenberg's distinctiveness from his fellow war poets is not simply a matter of class, education, artistic training or army rank. Not only is his technique very different from any of them, but his whole attitude towards the war is unique. Though he shares the views of Sorley, Graves, Sassoon, Owen and others that there is nothing ultimately 'heroic' about war, unlike them he is not entirely anti-war. The most consistent impression, as I have suggested, is one of involved detachment. His attitude encompasses almost every possible response to war, from seeing it as a potential purge ('On Receiving News of the War'), through patriotic ('The Dead Heroes') and neutral ('Marching', 'Break of Day') to negative ('Dead Man's Dump') then back to positive ('Daughters of War').

The distinctiveness of his technique is less easy to pin down, but it is undoubtedly a vital element of his greatness. Denys

Harding, who edited the second collection of Rosenberg's work in 1937, believed that its complexity arises from the fact that 'he brought language to bear on the incipient thought at an earlier stage of development. Instead of the emerging idea being racked slightly so as to fit a more familiar approximation of itself, and words found for *that*, [he] let it manipulate words almost from the beginning, often without insisting on the controls of logic and intelligibility.'[36] This was probably what Rosenberg meant when he told Winifreda Seaton that any apparent 'blindness or carelessness' in his work was 'really a result of the brain succumbing to the Herculean attempt to enrich the world of ideas'.[37] On a first reading of the final stanza of 'In War', for instance, his imagery seems confused to the point of obscurity, especially in its combining of concrete and abstract:

> What are the great sceptred dooms
> To us, caught
> In the wild wave?
> We break ourselves on them,
> My brother, our hearts and years.[38]

There are so many images packed into these few lines – sceptres, dooms, entrapment, wild waves, broken hearts and years.[39] Yet from this very welter of partially, if at all developed metaphors there emerges a powerful sense of the unbearable grief brought about by Fate. How 'great sceptred dooms' relates to the 'wild waves' is not exactly clear. But both images have become symbolic of the violent and merciless yet majestic nature of war. As Edwin Muir notes, Rosenberg uses language 'as only the great poets have used it; as if he were not merely making it serve his own ends; but ends of its own as well, of which it had not known'[40] – almost as though language were paint.

Perhaps the words that take us closest to understanding Rosenberg's technique are his own praise of the American poet Ralph Waldo Emerson, in whom he detects 'That ebullition of the heart that seeks in novel but exact metaphor to express itself, the strong but delicate apocalyptical imagination that startles and suggests, the inward sanity that controls and directs – the mainspring of true poetry'.[41]

We need go no further than the words 'novel' and 'apocalyptical' to understand why charges of obscurity and difficulty have been levelled at Rosenberg from Marsh and Binyon onwards. Yet for those unfettered by set expectations and open to experiment his poetry has always repaid the effort to understand it. As early as 1932 the great iconoclast F.R. Leavis dared to suggest that, though 'Wilfred Owen was really a remarkable poet, and his verse . . . technically interesting', Rosenberg was 'equally remarkable, and even more interesting technically'.[42]

It was Leavis, again, who first suggested that what Rosenberg saw as his disadvantages in life may have, in reality, been advantages, a claim his friend Leftwich repeated. After pointing out perceptively that he 'thought Dr Leavis had tried to make too much of Rosenberg as a *conscious* pioneer' of Modernism, he continued: 'Especially after he had said very truly that Rosenberg had probably been saved by his lack of systematic education and that public school and university would most likely have killed him as a poet. They would certainly, to my mind, have made him conventional.'[43]

It is an area that needs further exploration, one of many reasons I believe a new life of Rosenberg is called for. Rosenberg's strikingly original approach to language seems to me to spring from a related, apparently even more severe disadvantage of his upbringing – the fact that English was, in effect, his second language, that he spent his earliest years speaking nothing but Yiddish. Its effect on his technique must surely have been significant, yet apart from some pioneer work by Diana Collecott and Chris Searle,[44] this has not been seriously investigated. As Gordon Bottomley, one of Rosenberg's greatest admirers when he was alive, wrote to his fellow editor Harding about reviews of their 1937 *Complete Works of Isaac Rosenberg*: 'No one makes the point that used to strike me most – that Rosenberg was of a first generation to use our tongue, and so had no atavistic or subconscious background with regard to it – and that must have conditioned his freshness of usage.'[45]

It was in a review of the *Collected Works* that Leavis would make an even greater claim than his 1932 one, identifying 'genius' in Rosenberg, whose interest in life he believed was 'radical and religious in the same sense as D.H. Lawrence's'.[46] He also saw in Rosenberg 'an extraordinarily mature kind of detachment' which he argued Lawrence lacked.[47] Sassoon, in his foreword to the 1937 edition, was less theoretical but equally admiring of Rosenberg's war poetry: 'Sensuous front-line existence is there, hateful and repellent, unforgettable and inescapable.' One of Rosenberg's greatest promoters, Silkin, who helped organize the next landmark in Rosenberg studies, the Leeds Memorial Exhibition in 1959, would argue that his strength as a war poet arises partly from the ability to 'particularize' the powerful physical horror alluded to by Sassoon, and take it 'without losing its presence, to a further stage of consciousness'.[48] Silkin's chapter on Rosenberg in *Out of Battle* (1972) undoubtedly contributed to the placing of him in the hierarchy of First World War poets, as did the three full-length biographies that followed, simultaneously, in 1975.[49] The last twenty-five years of the century produced a number of important essays, including pieces by C.H. Sisson, Charles Tomlinson and Martin Seymour-Smith, and an extremely helpful account of the poet from the Jewish perspective.[50]

In spite of which Rosenberg has not yet received full recognition and acceptance. There is still a tendency to regard him as somehow flawed, a poet who might have achieved great things had he lived longer. (This is not to undervalue the promise of his last, unfinished drama, *The Unicorn*.) But how many poets, of whatever period, can boast work of such finished achievement as 'Break of Day in the Trenches', 'Dead Man's Dump', or 'Returning, We Hear the Larks', among others? Rosenberg himself believed sufficiently strongly in what he called his 'Trench poems' to plan their publication, though he was also convinced that the war retarded his development as a poet: 'Seeing with helpless clear eyes the utter destruction of the railways and avenues of approaches to outer communication cut off?', he told his friend Sydney Schiff, he felt he had 'no more free will than a tree'.[51] He had always tried to 'wait on ideas', letting 'as it were, a skin grow naturally round and through them'.[52] On the Western Front he found himself, 'when the ideas come hot', having to 'seize them with the skin in tatters raw, crude, in some parts beautiful in others monstrous'.[53]

Unlike many of the other First World War poets, Rosenberg was already a poet nearing the peak of his powers when he enlisted in October 1915. Yet it could be argued that the war 'made' him as a poet as it did Sassoon or Owen. At the most basic level it forced him to choose between his two vocations, since the sheer practical difficulties of carrying on with his art in such a situation inclined him to concentrate on his verse. And in the appalling conditions of the Western Front he rejected the last vestiges of the derivative Romanticism which had marked his poetry as late as mid-1915. The harshness of his own and others' existence there undoubtedly focused his perception and gave his work an immediacy and edge it had previously lacked. Walt Whitman, whom Rosenberg greatly admired, has written that the poet 'must flood himself with the immediate age as with vast oceanic tides',[54] and in France Rosenberg vowed to do just that: 'I will not leave a corner of my consciousness covered up,' he told Binyon, 'but saturate myself with the strange and extraordinary new conditions of this life, and it will all refine itself into poetry later on.'[55]

The time has now come for a reassessment of Rosenberg. His poetry is nearer to our own age, in terms of both its themes and technique, I believe, than almost any other of the war poets, including Owen and Sassoon. It was Robert Graves who labelled him a 'born revolutionary'[56] and his work certainly reveals a poet trying, as Tomlinson put it, 'to realise new potentiality in life by saying "This *is* and I accept the fact"'.[57] Moreover, attitudes towards important areas of Rosenberg's life, such as his race and class, have changed greatly since the last major biographies were written thirty years ago. And we are now far more inclined to understand and identify with the ordinary 'Tommy' in the First World War than with his officers.[58] Leone Samson made an important point in her recent examination of Rosenberg's war poetry when she wrote: 'Only by shifting the framework of the body of First World War poetry to include the voices of the lower ranks can the full experience of the trenches be revealed.'[59] Conceding that many of the letters and diaries written by private soldiers are 'in literary terms, mundane in thought and language', she argues that:

> it is more important, therefore, that the voice of the eloquent private be heard for, [quoting Martin Stephens] 'In poetic terms, the true voice of the infantryman is hard to find.' ... In the articulate and creative poetry of Rosenberg the ordinary men of rank and file can, at last, take their place alongside the work of their superior officers.

Additionally, interest in that war, rather than diminishing, is ever-increasing. And openness to inter-disciplinary studies, which has grown considerably since the mid-Seventies, means that we are now more prepared than ever to evaluate the profound effect of Rosenberg's training as a painter on his poetic vision and technique.

Fortunately we now, for the first time, have a definitive edition of the poet's work, gathering together all but the most recent of the fresh manuscript material which has appeared over the past three decades, including that published in Ian Parsons's invaluable *Collected Works* of 1979.[60] Work on other related areas of Rosenberg's life, such as an excellent study of the attitude of immigrant Jews and their families towards the First World War,[61] and new biographies of significant figures in his life (David Bomberg and Mark Gertler, for instance) have also been written. And, since Rosenberg was involved in some of the most interesting cultural movements of his age – Imagism and Modernism as well as Georgianism; Post-Impressionism, Vorticism and Futurism as well as Impressionism – a fresh look at his life involves a different approach to the period. As I wrote of Sassoon, a study of his life is a study of an age.

Most excitingly of all, I have unearthed a significant body of new material about Rosenberg himself, including a detailed unpublished description of him by a close friend, possibly lover, at a crucial stage of his development, unpublished information from another close friend about a largely uncharted period of his life, and fresh evidence of his activities in South Africa between 1914 and 1915. The Cape Town material includes a hitherto unknown self-portrait of Rosenberg and several extraordinary letters from him to Olive Schreiner's close friend Betty Molteno, also a friend of Gandhi, to whom she may have introduced Rosenberg. Last but not least, just as I was completing this work I was fortunate enough to learn of new material recently discovered at the British Library, consisting mainly of letters from the Front, and to which I was given access, enabling me to incorporate it into my text.[62]

A re-evaluation is clearly needed, if only to send readers back to Rosenberg's work itself. And I can think of no more appropriate words to recommend it than those he himself has written, again in praise of Emerson:

> We have here no tradition – no tricks of the trade. Spontaneity, inspiration, abysmal in its light, is the outer look these poems have to the eye. The words ebulliate and sparkle as fresh as a fountain. But we are always near a brink of some impalpable idea, some indefinable rumour of endlessness, some faint savour of primordial being that creeps through occult crevices and is caught back again.[63]

Chapter 1

'My Wild Little Pick-a-Back Days in Bristol'

1890–1897

This day I cry day and night, my eye drops a tear
  on my dearest, my heart's loveliest Isaac the Levite,
    blessed be his memory.
Fell on the field of battle . . .
In half of his life, he was only twenty-seven and a half . . .[1]

These grieving words, written by an aspiring Hebrew and Yiddish poet, Barnett Rosenberg, for his English poet son, Isaac, and intended for his tombstone, never appeared there. Nor, indeed, was Rosenberg's body ever found for them to commemorate. Instead, with an irony and misfortune which had largely dogged his life – and which certainly characterized his death on 1 April 1918 in one of the last great German offensives of the First World War – the headstone above his empty grave bears only the official words, 'Artist and Poet'.[2]

Yet his father's epitaph seems in many ways the more fitting. Though Isaac Rosenberg was born in England, he started life in an almost completely foreign world. His first exposure to language was to Yiddish, the Jewish lingua franca spoken by his family and their neighbours. He even learnt a little Hebrew before he mastered English, a language to which he was not fully introduced until he began school at the age of seven or eight. Moreover, his parents and their friends continued to address him in Yiddish throughout his life.[3] It is true that after starting school he would reply to them in what one of his contemporaries, Selig Brodetsky, has called 'a gradually improving English';[4] that his conversation with friends his own age and siblings would likewise be in English; and that he never learnt to write Yiddish. Nevertheless his linguistic habits were significantly affected by this distinctive start, as I shall show.

16

The eldest son of orthodox Russian Jews, Rosenberg's way of life was very different from that of his English contemporaries, even if his speech came eventually to resemble theirs. By the time he was born in 1890 his parents, with Isaac's one older sibling, Minna ('Minnie'), had travelled a long way from their home near Devinsk in Lithuania, one of the Baltic provinces of Russia;[5] but they still gravitated to Jewish ghettoes similar to those they had abandoned in their flight from the pogroms of Eastern Europe. These were at their worst in Russia, where they were aggravated by the anti-Jewish policy of the Tsarist autocracy. After more than a generation of earlier attempts at enforced Westernization the Russian government had settled down to a regime of calculated oppression, and all Jews were confined within the Pale of Settlement.[6] The breaking-point for Isaac's father, like so many of his fellow emigrants, had been reached when the threat of conscription into the Russian army became unavoidable.

So in 1885 Barnett, leaving his wife Anna and their baby daughter behind, set off alone by land to Hamburg, intending to sail for the United States. His limited funds took him only as far as Hull, however, where he made at once for the nearest large established Jewish community at Leeds. There he settled down with Jews from his own district, possibly also an older brother,[7] in the Leylands, an area of narrow streets and unsanitary conditions. Rather than work in a Jewish sweatshop, like most of his compatriots, he became an itinerant trader, or pedlar. Too clumsy for manual work, he in any case preferred the independence and freedom of travelling to the relative security offered by the two main outlets for immigrant Jews, shoemaking and tailoring.[8] His eldest son, Isaac, would later show similar preferences when deciding on a career, and in both cases the result would be material hardship.

This was not a problem for Barnett at the start, since it was only he who suffered, but once his wife and young daughter joined him in 1888 it became a serious issue, one more reason for a growing discontent on Anna Rosenberg's part. By the time she caught up with him he had moved on to Bristol either with or following two of his brothers, Peretz and Max Jacob. He may also have been attracted by the milder climate of the West Country, where his trade

Isaac Rosenberg's three homes in Bristol (all now destroyed): **1** Born at 5 Adelaide Place, Cathay, 1890 **2** Victoria Square, Temple **3** Harford Street, Cathay (? No. 2) Unnamed streets on this plan have all disappeared.

route for the next forty years would run through Devon and Cornwall to the Isle of Wight, places his son would also visit. Bristol had had a Jewish community in medieval times, reinstated after Cromwell allowed Jews back into England in the seventeenth century, and it was in the Jewish quarters near the ancient church of St Mary Redcliffe in the old city centre that Barnett and his family settled at 5 Adelaide Place.[9]

It was there that Isaac Rosenberg was born on 25 November 1890.[10] Minnie was about seven at the time,[11] but already, if contemporary photographs and later accounts of her can be trusted, a responsible, helpful child. She needed to be, since her mother gave birth to two sons, not one, in 1890. The younger of the twins, Isaac was the sole survivor, a fact which Joseph Cohen believes marked him for life: 'He seems to have been forever in search of the other side of himself, forever in need of making himself whole, forever aware that he had to cram two lives into his single existence.'[12] More prosaically, one concomitant of his twinship was an extremely low birth weight; like his dead brother he was so small that, as his mother never tired of telling her family, 'you could have put him in a jug'.[13] It needed her constant care and attention to keep him alive. (Possibly as a result of this unpromising start, he would suffer from a weak chest throughout his life.) Yet Anna, who could not support her family on the pittance Barnett was able to send home each week,[14] was obliged to take in lodgers, as well as her neighbours' washing, and to spend long hours on the fine needlework she also sold. She was determined as well as hard-working, however, and Isaac not only survived, at a time when the infant mortality rate was high, but looks positively plump in the photograph taken of him a few months after birth. The death of his twin may have made him even more precious to Anna, for she made no secret of her adoration of him: 'Isaac was his mother's God' was how one friend expressed it.[15]

As the eldest son Isaac had, in any case, a special position in an orthodox Jewish family, signified by his name. When his father was away peddling his goods round the West Country, as he did for at least six months every year, his son became symbolically the head of the household. It was sons, not daughters, who were consecrated to God and allowed to participate fully in religious rites once they reached adolescence. They alone were qualified to say Kaddish, mourning prayers, for their father after his death. Anna, who seems to have quickly tired of a husband she considered ineffectual and idle, a daydreamer, unquestionably cared more for Isaac than for Barnett, probably more than for any of the five other children born to her. Fortunately Isaac's older sister, Minnie, and the two younger ones who followed him – Anna ('Annie') in 1892, Rachel ('Ray') in 1894 – appear not to have resented this. Even his two brothers – David ('Dave'), born in 1897, and Elkon, born in 1899 – seem to have accepted Isaac's elevated status in the family as his natural due. 'We looked up to him as a genius,' his second sister remembered.[16] At home his needs were always paramount, an awareness he carried with him into the outside world and which may account for his apparent arrogance at times, curious in someone otherwise so diffident.

The close relationship between Isaac and his mother undoubtedly affected his attitude towards life and towards women in particular, though this should not be exaggerated. It has been suggested that his experience of growing up with a dominating mother and ineffectual father convinced him that the real wielders of power were women, and that the image which most obsessed him in his poetry was 'the all-powerful feminine principle', with his poems 'The Female God' and 'Daughters of War' cited as evidence.[17] But it is useful to remember that there is truth behind the stereotype of the 'Jewish momma' and that mothers are traditionally the dominant figure in the orthodox home, making Anna Rosenberg little different from other Jewish mothers of her time. Jewishness, after all, technically passes through the female not the male line. It must also be remembered that Isaac spent the first years of his life in a female-dominated world, with a father absent for half the year, an older sister and two younger ones. He was already six when his first surviving brother was born.

Anna herself would probably have been surprised to be thought 'dominating'. She simply wanted practical solutions to problems – in this as in so much else the polar opposite of her husband. Before marriage she had helped her parents, the Davidovs, run an inn near Devinsk. (Another daughter had married a well-to-do builder, Boris Eidus; a brother had started up a department store in Moscow; they were clearly an enterprising family.) So it was natural enough for her to take in lodgers when Barnett's earnings proved inadequate. Later, after the family moved to London in 1897 and Isaac was growing up, she would open a sweet shop, which she stocked with her own confectionery and ice cream made from recipes given her by neighbours. And when that failed she, too, turned to peddling. With young children still at home her travelling would be limited to North London, where she sold her fine needlework to wealthy Jewish ladies. Shrewdly, she would often take one of her children with her, and at least two of them, Isaac and Annie, would benefit from the advice and patronage that ensued. Isaac's introduction to the Amshewitzes and their painter son John, for instance, would be crucial in his development both as an artist and a poet. Later still, when Isaac enlisted and complained of army food, she deluged him with edibles, even managing to get eggs, butter and borscht to the Western Front.

Not only did Anna continue to cook her native food all her life, but she also grew her own produce as she had in Lithuania, planting vegetables, strawberries, apple trees, even a vine, in the small back-yards of the succession of tenement houses the family inhabited. Likewise she cultivated herbs and established a reputation among her neighbours for her healing remedies. The fact that she also grew flowers points to a more sensitive, artistic side, revealed too in her exquisite embroidery. She even wrote verse occasionally, though the one example I have seen suggests that it was not from his mother that Isaac inherited his poetic gift,[18] whereas the gardens she created in his childhood almost certainly influenced him, opening his eyes to nature at an early age. In this respect his was not a typical East End upbringing. A friend who grew up in Spitalfields, not far from Isaac, said that there '[hadn't] been a tree there in 200 years', yet Isaac would spy 'a tree in a deserted area and would stand there and dilate on it – how it lives in spite of the mud, fog, filth, etc.'[19]

Even in Anna Rosenberg's creation of gardens, however, it is her practical side that stands out. When she wanted a pond, she made it herself; when she found a garden bench selling cheap at a market, rather than miss a bargain she would carry it home herself, small as she was.

Determination ruled. She taught herself to read English, for example, progressing as far as the newspaper headlines. (Yiddish she read fluently, and entertained her less educated neighbours daily with serializations from the local Yiddish paper.) Everything about her in the photographs we have of Anna as a young woman looks firm and resolute. Not unattractive, though no great beauty, she has a fairly full face, slightly curved nose and dark eyes. Neither fat nor thin, she is shapely and looks boldly out at life. A lively woman, who grew to dislike Bristol because 'she didn't find men after her fancy' (her husband claimed),[20] she would still be trying to execute a Russian dance for one of Isaac's friends in her eighties. The same friend, Joseph Leftwich, remembered her as 'very vivacious, a bubbling, self-assertive woman who was much given up to her family'.[21]

It is not difficult to understand why Anna's family depended so much on her, though not all of them were as close to her as Isaac.[22] Her nephew's description of her as 'the anchor of the family' is wholly believable.[23] There was nothing she would not have ventured in her children's interests, especially Isaac's.

What does not seem totally credible, however, is her husband's claim that Anna came 'from an aristocratic family, no longer monied'.[24] After his first visit to the Rosenberg home, Leftwich, who knew her until her death in 1947 at the age of eighty-four, commented specifically on the lack of refinement in her face.[25] He believed she came of peasant stock.[26] And when Isaac told him of his longing to live in the country after the Great War, Leftwich attributed this directly to Mrs Rosenberg's influence.[27]

Leftwich also remembered Anna's frequent presents of home-grown vegetables and was not the only family friend to comment on her generosity. Joe Rose, whose family lodged with her in his childhood, when he attended the same school as Isaac, recalled how kind-hearted she was.[28] For example, the main reason her sweet shop had failed, according to her daughter, was that 'she gave most of her stock to children in the neighbourhood'.[29]

Barnett's picture of his wife, however, suggests another side to Anna. He thought her something of a shrew, describing her among other things as 'strong-willed' and 'sharp-tongued'.[30] Reading his account of their courtship and eventual marriage, it is no surprise to learn that their relationship was not a success: *she* had been in love with someone else, *he* had been promised a dowry that failed to materialize.[31] He was an aspiring scholar, she was an innkeeper's daughter. The early years in Bristol were more or less tolerable, especially since Barnett was away travelling for months at a time. But as Isaac grew up the situation deteriorated. By the time the Rose family lodged with them, when Isaac would have been about ten, it was very bad indeed. 'They wouldn't speak for long periods' Joe Rose recalled, and Barnett would go out for protracted walks because the atmosphere was so unpleasant at home. Rose was convinced that 'their constant bickering and estrangement weighed heavily on Isaac' and that 'he always worried about it'. He could remember Isaac appealing to them to settle their differences, 'but to no avail'. When details of this unhappy relationship were given by Joseph Cohen in 1975, however, the critic C.H. Sisson pointed out in *The Times Literary Supplement*: 'Sir, – Joseph Cohen calls the marriage of Isaac Rosenberg's parents "disastrous". But it produced Isaac Rosenberg ... '[32] In fact, it very nearly did *not*, since Anna had applied for a separation from Barnett shortly after Minnie's birth and only relented after several years of fending for herself and her daughter. Though Sisson's point is valid, what must not be overlooked is the amount of conflict this unhappy marriage created in Isaac's life.

He himself makes no mention of the trouble between his parents, though his younger sister Annie spoke frankly about it. The most likely explanation is that it upset him too much for him to be able to discuss it. Perhaps he felt that if he suppressed it, it would cease to trouble him. His silence on the subject suggests that he was more like his father, a 'very silent man' according to Leftwich,[33] than his outgoing mother. And that, in itself, must have been a further source of conflict to their son. Though he undoubtedly adored his mother, writing to her regularly whenever he was away from home and trying, as Annie recalled, to cheer her up 'in the direst of circumstances', often saying to her 'Don't worry Ma, when I have something good – *you* will know it',[34] even joining the army later on, he claimed, so that his mother would get the separation allowance,[35] he was also close to his father.

The fact that there are not as many letters to Barnett as to Anna may simply reflect the practical difficulties of contacting his father on the road. The single full-length letter which has survived shows that they had at least one crucial thing in common, their love of poetry. Whereas to his mother Isaac writes mainly of practical matters such as his living conditions in the army, or the need for more food, with his father he discusses literature. And from the way he writes, it is clear that they have similar views on the subject and that this is not the first time they have talked of it. However infrequently Barnett's peddling allowed them to see each other, it clearly did not prevent them sharing something that mattered greatly to them both. Though Barnett wrote Hebrew and Yiddish verse whenever possible, he was not a poet in any formal sense. Nevertheless his poetic aspirations almost certainly influenced his eldest son. Leftwich remembered translating some of Isaac's poetry into Yiddish, at his request, so that his father could appreciate it more fully.

Isaac drew or painted his father far more often than his mother, which also suggests a greater closeness. And though this too may have a practical explanation – that his father, when home during the winter months, was more readily available than his overworked mother – the portraits themselves reveal a sympathy, understanding and admiration of their subject. If the surviving examples can be regarded as evidence, Isaac's perception of his father was quite different from his mother's. The face that emerges from these portraits indicates a strong, serious, far-seeing man who, while remote, even isolated, has a determined look, rather than the weak, irresolute, naive, inept, self-centred person of Anna's version. The only point at which the two interpretations meet is that Isaac's portrayals hint that there is something of the dreamer in Barnett, a characteristic Anna called escapism. (Unlike many of her contemporaries, she was not prepared to accept the Jewish tradition in which men devoted themselves to Talmud Torah, while their wives kept the family going.)

The more objective eye of the camera shows a small, slightly-built man of brooding aspect, not unlike Isaac in later photographs. Rather than a pedlar Barnett looks more like the scholar he claimed to have been and longed to be again. (His third child, Annie, described him as 'a student, a "Yeshivah Bochur"', coming from a 'bookish family'.)[36] The only indication of his trade is the walking-stick he rests between his knees. Though Isaac himself would cherish no scholarly ambitions, which in any case his limited education would have ruled out, he was to educate himself in the English poets with great determination after leaving school. Temperamentally he was much nearer to his introverted, rather isolated father than to his lively, extrovert mother. (When he made friends later on, they would note first his reserve.) For Barnett, it was essential that he should be able to bear, even enjoy solitude for long stretches: a more gregarious man might not have been able to endure the often lonely life of the pedlar. For Isaac, the ability to study, write or paint for many hours alone must have contributed significantly to his development as a poet and painter.

This aspect of father and son must not be exaggerated, however. Barnett's seriousness, like Isaac's, would be punctuated by unexpected bursts of humour. (Zangwill refers in *Children of the Ghetto* to the 'flashes of freakish fun found in the most earnest of Jews'.)[37] It was their absorption in art and learning that would make them both appear preoccupied, even self-centred at times. Yet Barnett, whatever Anna believed, was a dutiful father – and son, as Isaac would be. If Barnett's earnings alone were not enough to support his family, it was not just that peddling had become less lucrative by the end of the nineteenth century, or that he was lazy, as his wife claimed; he was also sending money to Lithuania to help his own father, an activity Anna tried to curtail by hiding Rosenberg senior's pleas from her husband.

In addition, and strange as it may seem nowadays when the term 'traveller' has largely negative connotations, further traits Barnett shared with his son were his pride and independence. According to his daughters his choice of occupation had been made not just because he loved solitude and the countryside, but from a scorn of shoemaking and tailoring. Though his situation, like Isaac's later on, allowed him few opportunities to exercise this pride and independence, yet both of them had that 'self-reliance' and 'jealous independence of spirit' noted by Laurence Binyon in the son.[38]

Anna accused her husband of being 'gullible', 'lacking in ambition' and 'weak and resentful',[39] and these are all charges that would at times seem true of Isaac. He was to have few worldly ambitions, and would gleefully leave a secure but dull job at the age of twenty to devote himself to the precarious pursuit of art and poetry, where his *naïveté* would make his life even more difficult. And when frustrated in his aims, largely through lack of education and money, he could, like his father, appear self-pitying, however understandably.

Which if any of these characteristics came down from father to son is impossible to say with any accuracy. Less speculative is Barnett's influence on Isaac with regard to poetry. He must have devoted both time and energy to his passion, especially during the winter months at home. Since he taught himself with some effort to write English later on, so that he could send letters to his children, he was clearly a communicator. It seems natural therefore that he would have continued his dialogue with them at home. And the fact that Isaac loved poetry from a small child suggests that he was introduced to it by his father. This would account for that anxiety 'to establish an understanding between his father and his poetry' referred to by Leftwich in relation to his translation of some of Isaac's poems into Yiddish.[40]

It is also very likely that Barnett told his children stories of his escape from Russia, events he wrote about in an autobiographical fragment.[41] Though at least two of his daughters suspected that his account was exaggerated, it was bound to have a powerful effect on the imagination of a child of Isaac's heightened sensibility. He referred on several occasions in later life to his Russian roots, which formed such a strong contrast to the world in which he grew up.

Isaac spent the first seven years of his life in or near the small house in Adelaide Place where he was born. His family moved at some point, first to Victoria Square in the Temple district, then back to the Cathay district of his birth, to Harford Street, but all well within the Jewish ghetto. The area is, in effect, an island created south of the Floating Harbour by the New Course of the River Avon, and a first glance at a contemporary map suggests a situation as romantic as the names Cathay and Temple evoke. But by the time the Rosenbergs took up residence there, a large railway bisected the area, ending in a grimy, teeming station, arrival place of further floods of immigrants as poor as, or poorer than themselves. The reality, therefore, was an overcrowded area of numerous alleyways and narrow, irregular streets which would, over the next century, be redeveloped by the city council and nearby businesses, or destroyed by bombs. These were Isaac's surroundings during his first impressionable years.

It was not all depressing, however. Bristol itself was a lively, bustling city. Though it had declined by the end of the nineteenth century from its peak of commercial prosperity before the revolt of the American colonies, the abolition of the slave trade and the rise of Liverpool as a larger, more active port, it was still a thriving centre of industry. With the enlargement of its docks between 1877 and 1880 in the decade before the Rosenbergs' arrival, there had been a rapid increase in the population. Its industries covered a wide area, ranging from shipbuilding and all its associated trades to chocolate, shoe and tobacco factories, as well as coal mining.

None of these appealed to Isaac's father, apparently, who carried on work as a pedlar, the only difference being that he now hawked his wares in the more congenial climate of the West Country. Close parallels have been drawn between Barnett Rosenberg and Zangwill's fictional sometime pedlar Moses Ansell, in *Children of the Ghetto*.[42] It is true that Barnett, like Moses, was a 'passionate student' of Hebrew literature and experienced the 'strenuous inner life' of Zangwill's deprived 'travellers'. But while Moses lived chiefly on dry bread and black tea on the road, to avoid breaking Jewish dietary laws, the less strictly religious Barnett was prepared to eat non-kosher food when travelling.[43] In addition, he seems to have preferred reading the Bible and other Hebrew poetry to that elaborate body of Jewish lore pored over by Moses, the Talmud, and would eventually present his eldest son with the King James's version of the Bible – which included of course the New Testament – because of the poetry of its language. These are important points, because Barnett's lack of strict orthodoxy helps to explain Isaac's own later attitude towards Judaism.

There is no mention of Barnett in the records of the local synagogue, though this was conveniently close to him in Temple Street. (Newly arrived Jews often preferred to gather at much smaller meetings – chevras – with their fellow immigrants.) But more importantly, as far as Isaac's life is concerned, Barnett did keep a kosher home and observe all the main religious festivals of his faith. Each week would end with the celebration of the Jewish Sabbath on Friday evenings, when, if Barnett was not on the road, the whole family would gather round to enjoy the ritual food and drink prepared for the occasion. Similarly the Rosenbergs' year, like that of their Jewish neighbours from whatever country, would be punctuated by the major festivals of Pesach (Passover), Yom Kippur and Rosh Hashanah, marking respectively the liberation of the Israelites from Egyptian bondage, the Jewish New Year and the Day of Atonement, 'high holidays' occupying a role roughly equivalent to a traditional English family's Easter, Christmas and New Year.[44]

Since Isaac was 'fervently religious' as a child according to his eldest sister, there is no doubt that these rituals and festivals of his traditionally Jewish family made a deep impression on him.[45] And at the age of about five he was also introduced to another facet of an orthodox Jewish upbringing, Hebrew classes, one of only two activities he refers to from his Bristol years. ('I have some vague faraway memories of the name of Polack in connection I fancy with Hebrew classes and prize-giving' he wrote to a friend from the Western Front.)[46] He would continue to find his race's observances and language culturally significant long after their religious impact had been lost to him, writing nostalgically to his father in 1917, for instance, of 'a beautiful poem [by Heine] called "Princess Sabbath" ... where the Jew who is a dog all the week, Sabbath night when the candles are lit, is transformed into a gorgeous prince to meet his bride the Sabbath'.[47] And at relevant times of the year his thoughts would turn towards his Jewish upbringing, prompting him to a rare use of Hebrew phrases: 'I hope you admire my Yomtov [holiday] energy' he wrote to his father as Yom Kippur approached in October 1917; and to his brother Dave in March 1918: 'I do hope you get your leave for Pesach.'[48] Both references occur long after he had rejected orthodox Judaism.

The effect on his work is even clearer. Two of his earliest extant poems, written at the age of fifteen, are religious in content and, judging from a letter written to his father about them by a helpful local librarian, so were the verses which accompanied them (now lost): 'I trust,' the librarian, Morley Dainow, wrote, 'you will use your influence over him (which I think is profound) to emancipate him from the bonds of tyrannical orthodoxy.'[49] Whether as a result of Barnett's response to this plea or not, his son's poetry during the next decade would become largely secular in theme. But towards the end of his short life, as the war encroached more and more on his imagination, he would return to the Jewish mythology of his childhood in his struggle to give form to his ideas.

Apart from being 'fervently religious' in his Bristol days, Isaac is also described by his older sister as 'sad and discontented'.[50] She portrays an isolated, introverted little boy whose main outdoor activity was drawing on the city pavements.[51] Yet Isaac's own description of his time in Bristol as 'wild little pick-a-back days'[52] conjures up a more congenial picture of him rushing round the streets clinging to Minnie's obliging shoulders. It is a contradiction his friends would note in later years, one that suggests a less limited personality than is often depicted. And his habit of collecting small toys when he grew up implies not just a lack of them as a child but someone, too, with a sense of fun and love of play. Though he was not yet attending regular school by the time his family left Bristol in 1897, it is reasonable to assume that he was joining in the boisterous street games of children everywhere, however poor.

What can be said with certainty is that Isaac passed a far from isolated childhood. Apart from his parents and three sisters, he had his paternal uncles Peretz and Max Jacob with their families living nearby. And his later reference to his cousins (Peretz's boys')[53] and their liveliness indicates both familiarity and involvement with them. Another reference to 'our Russian cousins'[54] shows a similar sense of family connections.

Both Peretz and Max Jacob Rosenberg would finally take their families on to South Africa, however, and it may have been their decision to do so which prompted Isaac's own parents' resolve to leave Bristol. Barnett himself had originally intended to move on to America from England but had never been able to save sufficient money for the fare. Instead, he and Anna settled on London. Their neighbours the Levines had recently moved there and sent back glowing reports.

But as the retired Chief Rabbi of England, Nathan Adler, had written less than a decade previously concerning the impossibility of supporting all the impoverished Jews who flocked to the capital: 'There are many who believe that all the cobblestones of London are paved with precious stones, and that it is the place of gold. Woe and alas, it is not so . . .'[55] Ironically, the Rosenbergs' living conditions in London, where they hoped to improve their situation, would be worse than in Bristol for at least the first few years. Bristol council had been particularly active during their seven years there, building playgrounds, parks and public baths, opening libraries, museums and hospitals, improving the city's sanitation system and generally making it a less unhealthy place for the poor.

Yet there was noticeable unrest among Bristol's workers towards the end of this period. Strikes took place among shoemakers, bargemen, dockers and factory-hands, and may ultimately have affected even Barnett's itinerant trading. The Malago Vale Colliery had to close down in 1896 because of persistent demands for increased wages by the miners. Coinciding with a severe winter when coal was desperately needed, this caused great suffering among working-class families such as Isaac's. The birth of a fifth Rosenberg child, David, in February 1897 can only have added to their difficulties. The most pressing reason of all for Barnett and Anna's decision to move, however, concerned Isaac. He was already in his seventh year and, as the eldest son, they felt it particularly important for him to have a 'good' Jewish education, which they believed they would find in London.[56]

So later that same year, as all of England prepared for Queen Victoria's Diamond Jubilee, the Rosenbergs uprooted themselves from Harford Street, their current home, and took the train from nearby Temple Meads Station to the capital. It was the last time Isaac was ever to see his birthplace.

Chapter 2

Lost in Translation: an East End Education

1897–1904

*You mustn't forget the circumstances I have been brought up in,
the little education I have had. Nobody ever told me what to read,
or ever put poetry in my way. . . .*

*Whenever I read anything in a great man's life that pulls him
down to me, my heart always pleads for him, and my mind
pictures extenuating circumstances.*

— IR to Winifreda Seaton, 1911[1]

Isaac Rosenberg's first experience of London was of being lost. His
father had travelled ahead of Anna and their five children to find
lodgings,[2] but when he arrived, late, at Paddington Station to meet
them, he found his wife searching frantically for their elder son, who
had been missing for at least an hour. Isaac's first train journey, he
had evidently found it an exciting experience and had wandered off
to play among the railway carriages. His failure to find his way back
to his family suggests that, at the age of over six, this future English
poet was still unable to communicate adequately in the language.
Selig Brodetsky, whose siblings would become friends of the Rosenbergs, has described how on his own family's journey from Ukraine
in 1893 they nearly lost his older brother altogether on the train
through his inability to speak anything but Yiddish.[3] When one
considers that other major First World War poets, such as Brooke,
Owen, Graves and Sassoon, were reading and writing English fluently at the same age and, in Sassoon's case at least, being encouraged
to write creatively in the language, it makes Rosenberg's eventual
achievements in English poetry all the more remarkable. In addition
it would be yet another year before he started to learn English at
school. When Barnett met his family at Paddington in a hired horse

and cart to drive them across London to Tower Hamlets, his wife was already exasperated with him for his lateness, but she would think him even more ineffectual when he failed to get their eldest son into the 'good' Jewish school they had planned for him.

That problem lay in the future, however. Anna's immediate concern on arrival in London was Barnett's choice of lodgings, which she found characteristically ill-judged. For the seven of them he had rented a single cramped room behind a rag-and-bone shop at 47 Cable Street in St George's-in-the-East, a stone's throw from the docks.[4] Backed by a noisy railway, the room had the further disadvantage of providing sole access to the loft, where the shop-owner, Eli Bernstein, and his family lived. The only lavatory, a privy in the yard, was shared not just with the Bernsteins and their shop assistants but also with the scavengers who came to deposit rubbish collected from local refuse dumps.

The location itself was equally sordid. The Jewish East End was an area concentrated most densely between those two great eastern arteries, Whitechapel Road and Commercial Road, and by 1897 its rapidly expanding population had spread south, east and, less vigorously, north from what Lloyd Gartner calls its 'historic moorings' round Duke's Place and Petticoat Lane.[5] By the time Isaac and his family arrived there were already about 115,000 Jews living in the overcrowded East End. But even the most desperate of them kept their distance from the dock area, which was occupied mainly by Anglo-Irish labourers. Cable Street was the southernmost limit of the Jewish East End, an uneasy, unsafe district, full of 'squalor and misery' according to one contemporary observer.[6]

It was a far from ideal place to bring a wife and young children. Isaac's sister, Rachel, though only three at the time, distinctly remembered the 'sleaziness' of the neighbourhood.[7] And his second-eldest sister, Annie, gave a vivid account of it: 'Instead of gold, the streets were lined with drunks, prostitutes, thieves, swarthy sailors from Africa and the Orient, beggars, cripples, stevedores and derelicts.'[8] She still remembered, sixty years later, the terror these caused the Rosenberg children, and it does not require much imagination to realize the violent effect they might have had on a child of Isaac's extreme sensibility. The grotesque imagery of much of his later poetry may have been one tangible result. Even in his early work there are signs of its effect:

> Dim, watery lights gleaming on gibbering faces.
> Faces speechful, barren of soul, and sordid.
> Huddled and chewing a jest, lewd, and gabbled insidious;
> Laughter born of its dung, flashes and floods, like sunlight ... [9]

The fact that Isaac attached these lines to his one known sketch of the area, 'The Wharf', suggests that he was thinking of the docks and their sleazy denizens. According to one of the few people to have seen this picture, the three men in the foreground 'huddle' together, as in the poem, with 'brutalized' faces. The warehouse, barge and river in the background, quite apart from the title, make it clear that this is a dock scene, though the poem itself was called (possibly later) 'In the Workshop'.[10]

One of the most memorable images in Rosenberg's poetry which may have originated from this time is the rat. Annie maintained that it was the 'huge rats' from the docks and river that the Rosenberg children found most menacing, though by the time Isaac introduced the creature into his war poetry in 'Break of Day in the Trenches' he had clearly become less terrified of it, converting a nightmare figure into a 'droll' fellow, a 'queer sardonic rat' with 'cosmopolitan sympathies'.

A more objective but equally grim picture of the area is drawn by Charles Booth in his contemporary account of London's poor of the nineteenth century. He argues that of all the districts of the deprived 'inner ring' of the East End, that occupied by the Rosenbergs, St George's-in-the-East, was 'the most desolate':

> The other districts have each some charm or other – a brightness not extinguished by, and even appertaining to, poverty and toil, to vice, and even to crime – a clash of contest, man against man, and men against fate – the absorbing interest of a battlefield – a rush of human life as fascinating to watch as the current of a river to which life is so often likened. But there is nothing of this in St George's, which appears to stagnate with a squalor peculiar to itself.[11]

Less than a decade earlier St George's own MP (and Cabinet minister), Charles Ritchie, had written to the prime minister, Lord Salisbury, warning that the flood of Jewish immigrants to his constituency was becoming the most urgent problem the government faced. And nearly forty years later Cable Street would achieve lasting notoriety as the scene of the 'battle' that took place there when left-wing parties and locals successfully prevented Sir Oswald Mosley's Fascists entering the street on their march through the East End. Anna Rosenberg's anger with her husband over his choice of lodgings is understandable, though his options were probably severely limited by his poverty. One main effect of this move was to widen the gap between the couple further, a situation almost certainly worsened by Barnett's failure to get Isaac into the Jews' Free School.

The lure of this famous establishment, founded in Spitalfields in 1732 and enlarged considerably in 1883, had been the strongest motive for the Rosenbergs' move to London in Isaac's seventh year. Education has always loomed large in Jewish culture, a religious duty passed down by Moses, and the schooling of the eldest son is of special importance. So although at least seventy-eight state schools had been opened in the East End by the late nineteenth century, and sixteen of them catered almost exclusively for the Jewish population, most orthodox Jews wanted to send their children to a specifically Jewish school. Added to that was the outstanding academic record of the Jews' Free School. And since the school, in the words of its most famous head teacher, Moses Angel, 'imposed no selection process, and did not accept only the brightest children', recognizing the claim of any child who was both 'Jewish and poor', there was theoretically no bar to Isaac's own admission by 1897. In reality there were hundreds of other Jewish parents anxious to get their own children admitted by that date, as a reporter for the *Windsor Magazine* witnessed when he visited the school in 1898:

It must not be imagined that all the poor Jewish children find admission within the portals of the building in Bell Lane. Although 'first come, first served' is the rule, there are hundreds clamouring for admission, and the sight on a day when vacancies are filled is one not easily forgotten. Crowds of anxious parents with equally excited children fill every available place in the street, besiege every entrance until the regular pupils find it impossible to get in [and] the assistance of the police is invoked to keep the crowd in order.[12]

Barnett Rosenberg's naive description of his own attempts to enrol Isaac shows that he had failed completely to grasp the situation. He had applied to the 'two large gates' of the Jews' Free School in Spitalfields as soon as the family arrived in London.[13] When challenged by an equally 'large' doorman, he was told to 'enter with [his] child'.

But imagine my surprise when the man in charge told me politely to leave and take my boy with me as they had no room for him. Confused and scared, I argued that this was my only reason for moving to London, the need of my child now denied. After I got outside I thought there must be some mistake, so I returned. But when I opened the door, the big doorman blocked my way, showed me out, and slammed the door in my face.

Barnett and Anna then applied to various Jewish charities for help in gaining entrance to the school, but all appeals failed. Their arrival in London had coincided with the peak of the Jews' Free School's popularity. Isaac's contemporary and fellow artist David Bomberg was almost certainly the victim of the same shortage of places.[14] Ironically, only a year after the Rosenbergs were turned down the school would enlarge its intake to over 4,000 pupils, and less than a quarter of a century after that, when its vacancies rose to 1,300, would be in danger of closing.

The Rosenbergs' failure had significant consequences. Lloyd Gartner claims that once the 1870 Education Act had been introduced, safeguarding Jewish children from exposure to Christian religious instruction, 'it made little difference to Jewish parents where they sent their child to school'.[15] But this was clearly not the case for Isaac's parents and even less so for Isaac himself. Had he attended the Jews' Free School he could not, for example, have written, with (understandably) some self-pity, of the 'little education' he had had. He would unquestionably have received a superior education at the

Jews' Free School, which boasted among its alumni men like Selig Brodetsky, who became Senior Wrangler at Cambridge and President of the Jewish University. The proportion of students passing examinations in all subjects rarely fell below 95 per cent. Another disadvantage for Rosenberg was that, while genuinely regretting his lack of a 'good' education and frequently apologizing for his poor grammar and patchy knowledge of English literature, this also made him defiant at times and difficult to help.

Whether it would have made him a better or more interesting poet is another matter. Ernest Lesser, secretary of the Jewish Education Aid Society, believed that Rosenberg was 'handicapped by his defective education and an environment ever at war with his inner being': 'Who knows what he might have given us?', Lesser wondered, 'had the Fates been kinder!' Joseph Leftwich on the other hand, echoing F.R. Leavis's statement in 1937 that Rosenberg had been 'saved by his lack of systematic education', believed that 'public school and university would most likely have killed him as a poet'.[16] And though it is unlikely that a classical education would have had such a fatal outcome, it would possibly have made him more 'conventional', as Leftwich also claims: 'He admired the classic poets and would have wished to work like them, but he stopped short because he lacked the training and the result was more interesting.'[17]

The argument has been well rehearsed, frequently citing Blake, one of Rosenberg's strongest role models, as evidence that originality is often strongest when least exposed to traditional education. Another great original, Yeats, in referring to his own lack of the 'classical foundation to be found in public schools and universities', argued that 'lacking sufficient recognized precedent, I must needs find out some reason for all I did'.[18] And above them all towers Shakespeare with his 'small Latin, and less Greek'. All that can be said with certainty on the question of Rosenberg's education is that a more traditional one would have made him a very different poet, incapable perhaps of both the daring originality and the obscurities of poems like 'Daughters of War'.

After their first strenuous efforts to get Isaac the Jewish education they wanted, his parents appear to have given up completely. And

St Paul's School, Wellclose Square, London, EI (1898–99)

when he did eventually start his formal education in the summer of 1898, at the prompting of the local schools' inspector, it was at a Church of England school. His mother seems to have chosen St Paul's, in Wellclose Square, simply for its proximity, but she was fortunate in her choice.[19] When Rachel was registered with Annie in the Infants department and Isaac in the Mixed on the floor above, they entered a well regulated school of clearly defined academic standards. It was also enlightened for its time: school rules forbade staff to 'strike' a child 'on any account'.[20] Though directly affiliated to St Paul's Church, Dock Street, there was no attempt made to convert the increasing number of 'Hebrews', as the staff called them. (Gentile pupils and staff were obliged to attend church regularly.) Their absence on Jewish holidays was accepted and they were allowed home early on Fridays in winter to prepare for the Sabbath before dark fell.

Isaac, who entered the school at Standard I in 1898 unable either to read or write English and probably innumerate, passed all three required subjects, Reading, Writing and Arithmetic (the so-called 'three Rs'), in just over a year. In addition he was given 'Object Lessons', which seem to have been geared towards the children who entered the school from a non-English culture. These began, intriguingly, with 'A Beehive', ending more pedestrianly (perhaps a little insensitively for the Jewish children) with 'The Pig'. And despite Isaac's later complaints that no one ever told him what to read, his lessons included 'Poetry' as well as 'Grammar'. 'Drawing', which had become optional for elementary schools by the 1890s, was also taught in Standard II.

Just as he appeared to be settling down and could look forward to at least one subject that interested him, however, he was uprooted. Eighteen ninety-nine, which was the lowest point in his family's fortunes, ended with their move away from the fringes of Jewish society in Cable Street nearer to its centre. The year had started badly, with Anna's discovery that she was expecting another child to add to their overcrowded room. With improvements in transport and the opening of village shops, hawking was on its way out and Barnett was earning less than ever. Anna's family intervened, begging him to go to America, that country which, as Emanuel Litvinoff testified, had become 'a dream ... that obsessed poor men all over Europe'[21] by the end of the nineteenth century. Anna's sister and husband, already established in New York, sent money for Barnett's crossing and, once he arrived, more money for his wife and children to follow. But they were destined not to do so and Isaac remained in England, to the benefit of English poetry.

The crisis concerned Minnie, now in her mid-teens. Though a studious girl and a keen scholar, she had been forced to leave school at an early age to earn money and to look after the younger children. She had been helping support the family for some time with her needlework by 1899, occasionally finding a job in a draper's shop. But it was fine work carried out generally in poor light, and a great strain on her eyes. Shortly after Barnett's departure she had been diagnosed with glaucoma, and a heavily pregnant Anna had to take her for daily treatment to Moorfields Eye Hospital some distance away. Unable to afford a private cure, too proud to accept help and about to give birth to her sixth child, Anna despaired and gave up all thoughts of America. Though Minnie's sight was eventually saved, it was at a heavy cost. Anna laid the blame entirely on Barnett and, when he rejoined his family shortly after the birth of Elkon, made it clear that the marriage was to all intents and purposes over. No more children followed and Isaac grew up in a completely divided household.

The only positive result of the whole debacle was a move to better lodgings. Whether Anna spent the money intended for a transatlantic crossing on them, or received more money from her family, by November 1899 she had taken the whole of the ground floor and basement, with garden included, at 58 Jubilee Street. A long terraced thoroughfare of modest two-storey houses, Jubilee Street ran north-south between the Mile End Road, near its junction with Whitechapel High Street, and Commercial Road. Fermin Rocker (son of the great East End radical, Rudolf) described it as a place of 'unrelieved monotony' with a skyline of 'storage cylinders and smoke stacks of gas works, breweries and factories'.[22] But to Isaac and his family it must have seemed welcoming after the sinister dockside area. For Barnett and Anna, whose language remained Yiddish, it was like coming home, since Jubilee Street was almost entirely Jewish. (Though they were to move twice more in the next seven years, they would do so within the street.) Joe Rose, whose family occupied the flat above the Rosenbergs at Number 58, remembered it as a 'friendly', 'neighbourly' if rather noisy place, where the grocery shop opposite their house allowed its customers to buy goods on credit and settle the bill at the end of each week. There was a Jewish dairy next door to them and a kosher butcher just down the street where Anna bought meat when she could afford it. She herself would open her sweet shop there, though it rapidly failed. Since she now had a garden, she was able to start growing her own vegetables and some fruit. Together with the absence of a sooty railway, and wharf rats, Jubilee Street was undoubtedly a healthier place for Isaac, whose constitution had almost certainly been undermined further by conditions in Cable Street. The one overcrowded room there was now replaced by a separate kitchen, sitting-room and several bedrooms, however tiny, and offered slightly more privacy.

Isaac even had his own room briefly, until Anna had to let part of it to a lodger to bring in some money. Throughout his childhood and adolescent years, quite apart from his time as a private in the army, he would be forced to work in circumstances that might have stifled a less powerful creative urge. When, shortly after the move to Jubilee Street, he began to draw and paint in earnest, his only studio, as Leftwich could testify, was in the kitchen, 'a small, stuffy, crowded room at the end of a long passage, which was the family living room. The dresser, crammed with crockery, occupied most of the space; the table, at a corner of which Rosenberg sat sketching, was rickety and littered with cups and plates.'[23] Later still, when he started to write poetry, finding a place where he could concentrate at home would prove virtually impossible, but by then he would have discovered the Whitechapel Library and Art Gallery.

Following the move, Whitechapel High Street became his new centre of gravity. By the end of the nineteenth century it presented a striking contrast to at least one thoughtful observer. 'The most spacious, most picturesque, and most impressive of the great streets of the metropolis', according to the Religious Tract Society worker Henry Walker, it also carried 'an air of historic London', with its 'gabled houses of the time of Defoe, of Thomas Cromwell, of Strype ... and old inns, with the relics of galleried yards of the stagecoach period ...'[24] Despite the Englishness of the architecture, however, Walker felt that he was 'practically in a foreign land, so far as language and race [were] concerned'.[25] Israel Zangwill, brought up as a child partly in Bristol like Rosenberg and arriving in Whitechapel aged eight, was even more conscious of the dichotomy between the English setting and the foreigners who mostly inhabited it. They struck him as 'strange exotics in a land of prose, carrying with them through the paven highways of London the odour of continental ghettoes'.[26] And for Russell and Lewis in their 1900 study *The Jew in London*, the area seemed like 'a great living picture gallery of the street scenery of our Eastern Babylon'. Its foreign, half-oriental air was similar in many ways to that found in Brick Lane today, despite the difference of nationalities, with the flowing, colourful robes of its crowds and the strong smells of food unfamiliar to English nostrils. In 1900 the food itself – garlic sausages, pickled herrings, onion bread and other Eastern European delicacies – was kosher, the language Yiddish. And the population came from different but almost as distant towns, with strange names like Kishinev, Kharkov, Odessa or, in the Rosenbergs' case, Devinsk. As Brodetsky recalled, there was 'much talk of Russia, of the troubles there and the pogroms, and there was a great deal of nostalgia for the "old home", for the intensely Jewish life of the Russian Pale of Settlement, that vast ghetto'.[27]

There was also talk of Poland and other countries of exile, but Whitechapel was united by its Jewishness. Numerous synagogues, Jewish burial grounds, charitable bodies, cafés and restaurants dotted the area. There was even a special ward for Jews in Whitechapel's London Hospital. Yiddish dailies were published, and in 1906, when Isaac was fifteen, the first of several Yiddish theatres would open. Instead of the Gentile MP of anti-alienist tendencies of St George's-in-the-East, Whitechapel was represented more appropriately – and sympathetically – by Samuel Montagu, one of the first Jews to sit in Parliament.[28]

In her authoritative account of East End Jewry, Beatrice Webb found life at its most exotic in Whitechapel's 'chevras', associations which combined the functions of a benefit club for sickness, death and the solemn rites of mourning with that of public worship and study of the Talmud. Many Jews preferred the chevra to the more formal synagogue, and the Rosenberg family are likely to have attended their local branch, probably with people from their own area of Lithuania. Isaac would certainly have been familiar with the institution. Webb was particularly fascinated by the strong contrast between their outer sordidness and inner richness, which mirrored Isaac's own existence closely. Picking your way between 'broken pavements' and 'household debris', she noted, you arrived at a rickety wooden building which resembled the numerous sweatshops surrounding it:

You enter; the heat and odour convince you that the skylight is not used for ventilation. From behind the trellis of the 'ladies' gallery' you see at the far end of the room the richly curtained Ark of the Covenant, wherein are laid, attired in gorgeous vestments, the sacred scrolls of the Law. ... Scarves of white cashmere or silk, softly bordered and fringed, are thrown across the shoulders of the men, and relieve the dusty hue and disguise the Western cut of the clothes they wear. A low, monotonous, but musical-toned recital of Hebrew prayers, each man praying for himself to the God of his fathers, rises from the congregation, whilst the reader intones, with somewhat louder voice, the recognized portion of the Pentateuch. Add to this rhythmical cadence of numerous voices, the swaying to and fro of the bodies of the worshippers ... and you may imagine yourself in a far-off Eastern land.[29]

Isaac grew up amid such scenes. Though he nowhere refers to them directly, he did describe Whitechapel in one of his early poems, and if poetry can be relied on as autobiographical evidence, his attitude towards it was critical, even hostile. His 'Ballad of White-chapel' portrays it as both grim and depraved, its 'merry glare of golden whirring lights' illuminating a 'monstrous mass that seethed and flowed', its 'warm lights' gleaming on 'shrunk faces pale'.[30] Even allowing for a youthful tendency towards melodrama and possibly because of his relatively late arrival, his response was very different from that of fellow inhabitants such as Brodetsky. For Brodetsky Whitechapel's streets 'were home, its architecture was to me just what architecture should be – I had no other standards and we were not particularly conscious that we were poor, especially as my mother managed to keep the house going, and even sweeten existence on an income that was below the Whitechapel minimum.'[31] Though circumstances had forced Rosenberg, like Brodetsky, to regard the streets as 'home', there is nothing at all homely about his description of them as 'a gliding chaos populous of din'.[32] More significantly for his future development, and again unlike Brodetsky, he was very conscious of his poverty, which he would grow to resent deeply. Temperament probably goes some way towards explaining the difference in their attitude. So, too, must Brodetsky's happier home life and his solid educational foundation at the Jews' Free School.

By contrast the institution Isaac entered when he moved from Cable Street was a run-of-the-mill London Board School which offered such basic fare that few of its pupils went on to higher education. Most, like Isaac, left at fourteen, an age at which more privileged middle-class boys, such as Brooke and Graves, were just beginning their public school education in preparation for university.

Since Baker Street School, where Isaac enrolled, catered for local children, its intake was almost wholly Jewish. Like the Jews' Free School, it observed Jewish holidays, released its pupils early on Fridays, offered Hebrew lessons and taught the Old Testament rather than the New in Scripture classes. It was, in effect, a Jewish school operating within the state system and funded by local rates.

There the resemblance to the Jews' Free School ended. Baker Street's syllabus was far less ambitious and expectations much lower. Entering the school at nine at Standard II, Isaac was already several years behind the predicated English norm and by the time he left had still not reached the top standard. Yet he was no exception, performing if anything slightly better than many of his classmates and winning several prizes.

One problem in such schools was the large class sizes: sixty boys to one teacher on average. An even greater handicap was that most of the pupils were still not fully at home in English by the time they moved up from Infant School,[33] so that far too much energy had to be devoted to handwriting and spelling, not very successfully, as Isaac's adult efforts show. This left less space for topics that would have interested him more, like literature and art. He was drawing more than ever and, as his literacy increased, had begun to love reading. It is clear from Isaac's letter to Winifreda Seaton – quoted at the beginning of this chapter – that he was most conscious in later life of what was *not* included in his education. There were, for instance, no languages beside English taught, an omission he would regret keenly when he was sent to France in 1916 and unable to speak the 'infernal lingo'.[34] Music, too, was virtually absent from the syllabus, a little singing and marching being the only nod towards it. 'I know nothing about music' he would write apologetically to Miss Seaton later, though it emerges in the rest of his letter that he did not lack a musical sensibility.[35] When he discovered that his family's friends from Bristol, the Levines, had a phonograph, for instance, he would listen to it with great pleasure. Furthermore, subjects that *were* in the curriculum, such as history, geography and arithmetic, were made duller than need be by the rote learning then in fashion. Multiplication tables were chanted aloud, historical dates, rivers and bays of Britain learnt by heart.

Another disadvantage from Isaac's point of view were the Hebrew classes ('cheder') offered twice a week and on Sundays, which in the case of Baker Street School were held on the premises, with heating and lighting paid for by the council. Officially optional, it was virtually impossible for a Jewish child at the school to avoid them. At least three of the staff – Henry Hart, Jacob Simons and Joseph Jacobs – were devout Jews, and the head of Hebrew studies, Jacobs, would stand at the classroom door in the morning to confront any absentees from the previous day. An otherwise pleasant man and popular teacher, he would point menacingly at boys who had missed the class, then send for them half an hour before the end of regular school to make sure they attended the next one. According to Sidney Scott, a fellow pupil, Isaac disliked Hebrew lessons so much that he continued to play truant even after repeated canings from Jacobs.[36] 'We would cut the class many a time,' Scott remembered, 'to go for a lovely walk through Blackwall Tunnel leading to Greenwich, with Greenwich Hospital, a place with lovely grounds.' While Hebrew mythology would continue to fascinate Isaac and ultimately provide fruitful content and themes for his poetry, the language itself and all the surrounding traditions and observances began to bore him. Still as 'intensely religious' as he had been in early childhood, he nevertheless moved ever further away from orthodoxy as he approached his teens. His bar mitzvah at thirteen, a ceremony his parents would have found it unthinkable to omit according to Leftwich, appears to have left no lasting impression on their son. Another childhood friend, David Dainow, recalled that Isaac 'never talked about God, but Nature':

> He was also very sensitive to colours. Colours fascinated him, and he almost worshipped the force that brought colour in to the world. He would say how terrible it would be if we were not conscious of colour. To him colour was not only that which you saw through the eyes, but that which he felt in the consciousness. Colour did something to him internally. 'Colour could make,' he said, 'a man happy or unhappy.' ... It was his feeling of perpetual wonder of nature and life which kept him alive and vital in the midst of the most unhappy economic circumstances.[37]

Scott confirmed Dainow's theory: Isaac preferred the picturesque Greenwich pensioners in their red coats and the grass and trees of the Hospital grounds to Jacobs's lessons: 'He simply was not interested in Hebrew.' Scott's suspicion that Isaac 'had enough Hebrew forced on him by rote for his bar mitzvah and then forgot everything afterwards' was corroborated by Isaac in a letter to a later friend: 'We Jews are all taught Hebrew in our childhood but I was a young rebel and would not be taught, unluckily now. I read Hebrew like a parrot without knowing the meaning.'[38]

Another activity Isaac disliked, according to Scott, was organized games. It was one thing to play in Greenwich Park, quite another to accompany boys to the much nearer Victoria Park to watch or take part in football. Instead, when his schoolfellows made for the park on Friday afternoons, he would go off by himself to read or draw.

Art dominated his life even at school. He is unlikely to have been offered anything very sophisticated in the subject, certainly not a specialist teacher. But he was very fortunate in one respect at Baker Street – in having Mr J. Usherwood as his headmaster. Though not Jewish himself, Usherwood had a great deal of sympathy for his largely Jewish pupils. A kindly, humorous but firm man, nearing retirement age, he was something of a progressive, valuing artistic gifts as much as strictly academic ability. When Isaac's talent was brought to his attention – boys were often set to copy pictures from their history books – he encouraged him as best he could. Where once the budding artist had to use the pavement as his canvas, with chalk when available, Usherwood now supplied him with paper, crayons, even paints. He sometimes took Isaac out of formal lessons to allow him to draw in his study undisturbed. Joe Rose, Isaac's fellow lodger who also attended Baker Street, remembered seeing him in the headmaster's room holding a picture he had drawn, possibly of the Lady of Shalott: 'It was of a woman in a long flowing robe looking in a mirror, with the reflection showing in the mirror.'[39] The sensuousness of the later work is hinted at in Rose's concluding comment: 'She had just got out of bed or out of the bathroom at the time.'

Isaac's total absorption in his work, essential in any serious artist, impressed Rose, as it did all who knew him. Minnie had noted it in him as a small child. Now, worried by his refusal to tell his family anything about school life, she went to see Mr Usherwood, who told her that Isaac was 'very capable, but seemed to take little interest in anything but in drawing'.[40] At playtime, when all the other children were outside, he would sit in the classroom drawing, the head told her: 'He did not make friends with the other children, and seemed much too serious for his age.' Rachel believed that her brother had no interest outside art. According to her he had nothing in common with any of the family: 'None of us ever saw him or knew anything of him.'[41] Exaggerated though this may seem, it was the impression Isaac's schoolfellows also gained. Rose, for instance, never saw him with friends: 'He would be on his own either reading or writing.' Absorbed in his work for hours together, he gave little trouble outside Hebrew classes and was awarded a medal for Good Conduct in 1902.

Isaac's need to draw whatever caught his imagination led him to sketch complete strangers on street corners, according to his sisters. Rachel, who attended a different school after the move, occasionally sat for him and was astonished when someone from his school recognized her from her portrait, which had been displayed on the wall by the headmaster. By the age of eleven Isaac was painting in watercolours, and Usherwood thought his illustration of 'Caxton and Edward IV' so good that he sent it to a children's exhibition. Probably copied from a history book, it is nevertheless extraordinarily skilful for his years, particularly in its rendering of faces and bodies.

That was in 1901, shortly after his eleventh birthday, by which time he had already made his longing to be an artist plain. His mother, still desperate to supplement Barnett's income, had started her peddling of needlework to wealthy Jewish ladies in North London by then and turned to one of them, Mrs Amshewitz, for advice.[41] Like Anna Rosenberg, Mrs Amshewitz had a son who wanted to be a painter, despite his father's opposition. But, eight years older than Isaac, John Amshewitz was already studying at the Royal Academy on a scholarship by the time Anna consulted his mother, and he very kindly invited her young son to show him his work.

A photograph of the Rosenberg children taken at about this time confirms Amshewitz's recollection of Isaac as diminutive – he was

Caxton and Edward IV 1901. Watercolour on canvas. Inscribed 'I. Rosenberg Standard VII 18.12.01 Baker Street School'. (*Mrs Gerda Horvitch*)

noticeably small for his age and would never grow beyond five feet two inches – and 'elf-like in visage'.[43] The camera shows a solemn little boy in his best clothes (knickerbockers and a bow tie) with a rather long, narrow face and protruding, slightly pointed ears. When Amshewitz came to paint Rosenberg almost a decade later, it was the elfin quality he conveyed, together with his delicacy and sensitivity.[44] It is a romanticized but not entirely false portrayal, which Rosenberg himself, in a review of Amshewitz's work in 1912, would describe as 'the portrait of a young poet, gazing as if out of "dreamdimmed" eyes, holding the pen in his hand, apparently waiting for inspiration'.[45]

At their first meeting, however, it was Isaac's graphic skills and extreme sensitivity that stood out, though poetry also came into it. Nearly forty years later Amshewitz could still vividly recall the small boy's extraordinary reaction to his help: 'I advised him as best I could and awkwardly purchased a drawing with a poem attached for half

47

a crown whereat he burst into tears and rushed from my presence.'[46] Joseph Cohen believes that this response was because Isaac 'did not want charity, he wanted instruction',[47] but it might equally well have stemmed from a feeling of gratitude for this first meaningful recognition of his work. As Amshewitz noted, Rosenberg was 'a strange mixture of extreme modesty and assertiveness – factors which made him difficult and led to the estrangement of many of his best friends and to disaster as a student'.[48] One thing is clear, that he had already begun to link his art with literature, though whether the poem that accompanied the drawing was written by himself is not stated.

Isaac's interest in literature certainly dates from this period. Annie remembered her brother writing poems while still at school, generally in bed at night by the light of a candle and often interrupted by the series of lodgers who shared his room. As his competence in writing as well as reading increased, so did his need to express himself verbally as well as visually.

Art was still uppermost, however, and in 1902 Mr Usherwood was able to send him one day a week to the borough council's Arts and Crafts School in Stepney Green. An imposing Georgian building behind elegant cast-iron railings, the Stepney Green Crafts School was his first step away from his heavy Victorian redbrick school and the drab streets surrounding it. Though his training was, of necessity, vocationally based, it was his introduction to professional art teaching. (A Mr Cook taught him in art metalwork.) It also led to his first contact with boys and girls of similar talents and aspirations to his own. Still shy and withdrawn, he nevertheless made friends there with a student from an equally difficult background, Morris Goldstein.[49]

Goldstein, who was two years younger than Rosenberg, had been born in Warsaw but emigrated to London with his Jewish parents and two younger sisters at the age of eight. He lived near Isaac, in Redmans Road, in similar poverty and their families would also become friends. Importantly, Goldstein understood the conflict between dreams and reality. Though studying Pure Art at the Stepney Green School, he knew that the need to earn a living at fourteen would prevent him from pursuing it full-time. Like

Rosenberg, he would be obliged to take up an apprenticeship in commercial art, in his case marquetry. More practical than his friend, he would persuade Rosenberg to continue his art studies alongside his wage-earning and, more outgoing, would introduce him to other like-minded young people in their district. Talented, hard-working and determined, Goldstein would eventually succeed in winning a scholarship to the Slade, which he attended during the same period as Rosenberg. But he would eventually be forced to give up full-time art when his father died shortly after the First World War, leaving him the main breadwinner in the family. Isaac was by no means the only aspiring artist who fought against heavy odds in the East End.

Rosenberg was lucky to meet Goldstein when he did, just as he had been fortunate in having Usherwood as his headmaster. Whether or not, as Cohen argues, Usherwood 'accelerated his movement towards the main corpus of English writing and art and away from strictly provincial, ethnic concerns',[50] it is true that, unlike the Jewish teachers at Baker Street School, Usherwood took Isaac's sketching seriously.[51] And in this respect alone he was vital to the development of his pupil's talent. Perhaps it really was as a result of Usherwood's 'gentle tutelage' that Isaac's priorities were transposed, with art and literature from this time on becoming far more meaningful to him than religion or politics.

Even Mr Usherwood could not prevent the inevitable, however, and within two years of starting at Stepney Green Arts and Crafts School, Isaac had to leave school altogether on 23 December 1904 to earn his living.

Chapter 3

'The Days of Youth Go By': Apprenticeship

1905–1910

*It is horrible to think that all these hours, when my days are full
of vigour and my hands and soul craving for self-expression, I am
bound, chained to this fiendish mangling-machine, without hope
and almost desire of deliverance, and the days of youth go by ... I
have tried to make some sort of self-adjustment to circumstances
by saying, 'It is all* experience'; *but, good God! It is* all *experience,
and nothing else ...*

– I R to Winifreda Seaton, before 1911[1]

Rosenberg entered the job market in January 1905, aged fourteen
years and one month, a situation graphically described by a fellow
East End Jew as being 'dressed up like a man of forty sawn off at the
knees'.[2] His timing, as so often in his short life, was unfortunate. By
1905 the flood of immigrant Jews was at its peak and native hostility
towards the newcomers so strong that the anti-alienists were able to
force through the Aliens Act that same year. With its various controls
on immigrant life, and not just on their entry into the country, it
was a regrettable break in Britain's liberal tradition. In the East End,
where by far the largest percentage of immigrants were Jews, anti-
alienism generally meant anti-Semitism and was particularly strong
in the labour market. As Rosenberg quickly realized, like Emanuel
Litvinoff after him, the choices for young Jewish school-leavers were
'few and gruesome'.[3] Litvinoff's list of the limited possibilities facing
most fourteen-year-olds in the East End makes depressing reading:

I could boil a glue-pot and sweep up wood shavings, carry a tailor's
sack from workshop to retailer, learn to baste a hem, press out a seam,
nail a fur, lather a chin, weigh sugar into one-pound bags, or diss a
stick of lead type with average competence. During my first week I'd

be sent on errands for pigeon's milk, rubber nails and elbow grease, be ordered to take my hands out of my pockets and stop playing pocket billiards and might well be held down while boot-blacking was smeared on my penis. At the end of the week I'd buy my first packet of fags and have nothing to hope for but the Revolution.

Though Rosenberg adopted none of these trades, he came to regard his own job as equally grim. Unlike Litvinoff he had at least been asked by his family what he wanted to do before leaving school. His honest but completely unrealistic reply had been that he 'wished to become an artist'.[4] Since, as Minnie pointed out, 'such an expensive career was impossible' for her brother 'because of our poverty', a compromise was sought. His mother, who made all the financial decisions in the family, again consulted Mrs Amshewitz. And once more Mrs Amshewitz turned to her artist son.

John Amshewitz had continued to encourage Isaac after their first meeting. His brother remembered the boy visiting their house frequently 'before he was bar mitzvah' at the age of thirteen,[5] which meant that Rosenberg had been seeing Amshewitz regularly for several years when his mother returned for more advice. Since Amshewitz still saw 'promise' in her son's work, he believed that he should be found a job at least connected with the art world.[6] The only feasible way to do this without money was to find a suitable apprenticeship, and to that end he put them in touch with a brother who worked for the Jewish Board of Guardians. This was the most important of the many charitable institutions run by established English Jews for poor Jewish immigrants which spread like a safety-net over the East End.[7] Set up in 1858, the Board received generous support from the whole Jewish community. One of its many functions was to find appropriate apprenticeships for children leaving school. Though Anna Rosenberg's pride had previously prevented her from accepting charity, even during the crisis over Minnie's eyes – she was more likely to dispense it than receive it – in Isaac's case she was prepared to apply to the Board. Amshewitz's brother suggested that the nearest approach to art would be engraving, and an apprenticeship was found with a firm of process-engravers, Carl Hentschel of 182–184 Fleet Street.[8] After a satisfactory trial period Isaac's inden-

tures were drawn up, his premium advanced by the Board of Guardians,[9] and an agreement signed to repay the loan in weekly
instalments. Only in cases of extreme poverty was money given
outright, since the Board believed it bad for the recipient's moral
fibre.

Carl Hentschel's location in Fleet Street meant that one of the
firm's main activities was supplying half-tone blocks to the publishers
and newspaper owners who dominated the area at that time. This
involved plate-making and engraving, a procedure Rosenberg had
to learn from scratch. If he had made any conscious connection with
another, more famous apprentice engraver, William Blake, before
starting at Hentschel's, he would have been quickly disillusioned.
Engraving had changed radically since Blake's time, from the largely
creative to the largely mechanical. The 'process' of Hentschel's title
was the word loosely applied to the photo-procedures which had
mainly replaced the need for skilled draughtsmanship in engraving.
Whereas Blake had drawn his designs directly onto a copper plate,
the most required of Rosenberg by 1905 was a little 'touching-up'.
Working at Hentschel's made him more, not less frustrated at not
being able to take up art professionally. It was a dissatisfaction almost
certainly not helped by Hentschel's production in 1907 of plates for
a book on the Slade School of Art, beautifully illustrated with work
by Augustus John, William Orpen and others, which he would have
seen.[10]

It is unlikely that Rosenberg was consciously emulating Blake,
but the parallel is a striking one. Like Blake he was involved in two
different arts and, though the two men had dissimilar racial origins,
both came from deprived social backgrounds and grew up in poorer
districts of London. Each was forced to work for a living at the same
trade and, while Rosenberg did not actually engrave his own books
as Blake had, he would bring out at his own expense the only three
collections of his work published during his lifetime. Like Blake, he
was to create virtually his own mythology, including the concept of
a tyrannic Male God and powerful Female counterpart. The violent
energy, terse aphoristic clarity yet lyric grace of Rosenberg's later
work has clear links with Blake's. And besides sharing the eighteenth
century poet's love of the Bible, Rosenberg, too, had leanings towards

the symbolic and mystical. Later on, when he grew to admire Blake greatly, both as a painter and a poet, these similarities would become even more evident as he began consciously to model his work on the earlier artist.

With no real outlet for his artistic talent provided by his work, Rosenberg quickly tired of his apprenticeship. Though Hentschel himself – the original for Jerome K. Jerome's 'Harris' in *Three Men in a Boat* and founder of the First Nighters' Club – was undoubtedly a humorous man, the work he offered his apprentices was anything but fun. The working hours were gruelling, starting at 8 a.m. or earlier and ending as late as 11 p.m., with only one day off a week – Saturday in the case of a Jewish firm like Hentschel's. Process-engraving itself was unpleasant, and Rosenberg had to spend long hours bending over vats of corrosive acids, an activity that may help to explain his lung trouble later on. Laurence Binyon in his Introductory Memoir to the 1922 edition of Rosenberg's poems, which was based partly on a 'sort of autobiography' written by Isaac himself in 1911,[11] refers to him 'hat[ing] the trade', feeling 'in bondage' and being made 'bitter and despondent by his circumstances'.[12] As Binyon also notes, Rosenberg's letters reveal 'fits of the deepest depression' at this time, and it was almost certainly during his apprentice years that Rosenberg wrote a prose fragment revealing strong suicidal tendencies:

> If I could die and leave no trace, ah, that thought of mine must live, incomplete and imperfect, maimed. Could I destroy all I have ever thought and done ... You the world, will sneer: 'Young fool – mad ...' But my quiet undisturbed serenity rebukes your despairs and vexations and the joys that pass. I go to meet Moses who assuredly was a suicide, and the young Christ who invited death, I who have striven to preach the gospel of beauty—[13]

Though some of this might be dismissed as a young man's posturing, Rosenberg was undoubtedly beginning to understand the Yiddish phrase so common in his East End upbringing, 'Schwer und bitter is dos Leben.' [14]

53

Two pen and wash drawings
by Rosenberg, c. 1910. (*Tullie
House Museum and Art
Gallery*)

His greatest consolation at this period was poetry, which he wrote during his meal breaks, the only free time he got. And it is in this early verse that his unhappiness and frustration emerge most clearly. One of the first of these poems hints not only at his sense of isolation but also at his boredom, in the line 'Cold time shall drag the weary hours'.[15] Another poem, ominously entitled 'Death', refers to 'the gloom/That life spreads darkly like a living tomb/Around my path'.[16] A third, 'In the Workshop', describes his harsh working conditions – 'Dim, watery lights gleaming on gibbering faces'.[17] To his jaundiced eyes Fleet Street, whose bustle and activity can still seem so positive, appears as 'a shrieking vortex', where 'the stony buildings blindly stare/Unconscious of the crime within', underlining his sense of the indifference of the outer world to his plight.[18]

It is ironic that Rosenberg's family's effort to find him a job connected with art should have turned him so rapidly to poetry. While he had shown promise as a writer at school, winning an essay prize in his next to last term there,[19] his main interest had remained art. But on starting at a firm with at least some links, however tenuous, to the art world, most of his spare time was devoted to literature. Besides writing verse in his short breaks, submitting at least one of them to a London monthly, *The Jewish World*,[20] he also combed the stalls in the nearby Farringdon Road market for inspirational reading matter. Family legend has it that one day he bought a book either by, or about, Thackeray for a halfpenny and discovered, on showing it to the ever-helpful Amshewitz, that it was a valuable first edition containing a drawing either by Thackeray, or of him. When Amshewitz took it to a bookseller it fetched forty pounds, an enormous sum to Isaac, who was giving money to his parents as well as repaying his loan to the Board of Guardians from his meagre wages.[21] But this was an exception; his main purpose in visiting Farringdon Road market was to find new reading material.

Minnie wrote that her brother was 'fairly happy' at Hentschel's,[22] but it was probably wishful thinking. She could hardly have failed to notice the frustration, gloom and yearning in his poems, which she certainly read. Sharing his literary interests, she was the only member of the family who could fully appreciate his efforts at that time. An exceptionally sweet-natured girl, according to her sisters, she had at an early age become something of a second mother to Isaac. Not only had she visited his school for progress reports and accompanied her mother to ask advice of the Amshewitzes, but as he grew older she had also encouraged his love of literature. As a younger child she had taken him to the West End to see plays:[23] now she found him advice on his poetry-writing.

A slight, pretty but earnest and bespectacled young woman in her early twenties by the time her brother joined Hentschel's, Minnie had already embarked on her own strenuous course of self-education. One main resource for her was Toynbee Hall, opened in 1884 in Commercial Street by the great social reformers, the Rev Samuel Barnett and his wife Henrietta. Rev Barnett had come to the East End as vicar of St Jude's, Whitechapel, with his wife in 1873 and they had both been appalled by the deprivation they found there. Toynbee Hall formed part of their effort to educate local people, especially the young, so that they could escape their situation.[24] Staffed mainly by idealistic graduates from Oxford ready to offer their services free, the centre ran courses ranging from elementary Arithmetic and Ambulance Drill to English Literature, Art and Economics. In spite of its Church of England founder and in defiance of more orthodox Christians, Toynbee Hall also ran courses on Sunday, to cater for the largely Jewish population. Minnie was a regular attender, together with her neighbours and friends the Brodetskys.

The Barnetts had also been largely responsible for the opening of a Whitechapel Public Library in 1892, five years before the Rosenbergs' arrival in London, and Minnie regularly borrowed books there as well as using its Reference Room. It was to the library she turned for help with Isaac. It was almost certainly at the weekly Reading Circle that she met the librarian concerned, Morley Dainow, who had founded it:

One day [Dainow wrote] I was approached by a Jewish young lady who asked me whether I could help her young brother whose aim in life was to be a poet. The next day a fragile Jewish boy was brought to me by this lady. This boy was Isaac Rosenberg. I took young Rosenberg for walks, and discovered him to be perfectly convinced

Drawing of the proposed Whitechapel Art Gallery. The Whitechapel Library can be glimpsed in the right-hand margin. (*Toynbee Hall*)

that his vocation in life was that of a poet and a painter. I was much impressed by his confidence and sensitivity.[25]

Dainow was about thirty when he first met Isaac in 1905, a fellow Jew from a well-known local orthodox family, though not religious himself.[26] He would leave the library not long afterwards, take a degree in Psychology at London University and write books of his own on his subject later. But it was his knowledge of poetry, rather than his interest in psychology, which had convinced Minnie that he was the person to advise Isaac. A 'down-to-earth' man, according to relatives who knew him,[27] he set about it at once and his responsiveness marked another turning-point in Isaac's life. Just as Amshewitz's praise had given him the confidence to carry on with his art, so Dainow's now encouraged him to continue with his poetry.

Their first meeting probably occurred shortly after Isaac left school in December 1904, since by 26 September 1905 Dainow is writing enthusiastically to him about his first extant poem (almost certainly a second or third draft revised with the librarian's guidance): 'Ode to David's Harp'. The letter suggests that the 'Ode' was only one of a number of poems Isaac had shown him and comes with a word of caution as well as encouragement:

Dear Rosenberg,

Thanks for greetings, which I heartily reciprocate and extend to your sister. I should not advise you to write so much. Only write when you feel inspired and then [arise] such poems as 'The Harp of David' [i.e. 'Ode to David's Harp'] and 'The Charge of the Light Brigade'. Am very sorry to have disappointed you last Saturday. I am extraordinarily busy just now, but hope to visit some galleries with you in the near future. Shall be pleased to see you in the library, if you call early,

with kindest regards,
Morley Dainow[28]

It is clear both from Dainow's letter and from one written by Rosenberg to a friend later that, beside the promise to take him to 'some galleries', Dainow had been advising him on which poets to read. Though there is little evidence that Dainow's admiration for Tennyson influenced his disciple strongly,[29] he was almost certainly responsible for the fact that, as Rosenberg told his friend, he 'galloped through Byron when [he] was about fourteen'.[30] Admitting that he had read Byron 'more for the story than for the poetry', he continued: 'I used to try to imitate him.' He also refers to his enjoyment of Keats and Shelley. The influence of these three great Romantics, not unusual in an imaginative, aspiring poet, is apparent in his early verse. Though the theme of 'Ode to David's Harp', for example – a Zionist longing for a reawakening of 'the zeal in Israel's breast'[31] – could have arisen naturally from Rosenberg's Jewish background, his own reading of the Old Testament[32] and his longing to escape his sordid surroundings into an ideal world, he could also have taken the subject matter and much of his poetic diction from Byron's 'The Harp the Monarch Minstrel Sweeps' in *Hebrew Melodies*.[33] Likewise the distinctive metre is reminiscent of Shelley's 'To a Skylark', a poem that also lies behind his later, more famous poem 'Returning, We Hear the Larks':

> Hark—the harp is pouring
> Notes of burning fire,
> And each soul o'erpowering
> Melts the rousing fire,
> Fiercer—shriller—wilder far
> Than the brazen notes of war ... [34]

This first surviving poem of Rosenberg's is interesting for its Jewish subject-matter, its emphasis on the power of music (a recurrent theme in his later verse) and its prophetic reference to war. In poetic terms, however, his 'Ode' is an unremarkable if fairly fluent apprentice work.

Another poem, 'Zion', almost certainly one of a number of religious poems written at this time, also reveals Byron's influence and suggests that Rosenberg had been reading two other poems from *Hebrew Melodies*, 'She Walks in Beauty Like the Night' and 'Oh! Weep for Those'. He may have been directed to *Hebrew Melodies* initially by the Jewish Dainow, but it was their strong sense of desolation, mirroring his own, that probably inspired his imitation of them a second time. This feeling of loss is even more apparent in Keats, especially in *Hyperion*, which 'ravished' Rosenberg at this time.[35] Whereas his initial passion for Byron would quickly cool, his love of Keats would inform a great deal of his early work. (He did not know what 'real poetry' was, he wrote, till he read Keats.[36]) Keats's belief that 'Beauty is truth, truth beauty', his sensuousness and his preoccupation with death struck a chord in Rosenberg, who would also live his life with the threat of tuberculosis hanging over him. The 'hill-ensceptred Queen' and her fall from 'virtue' in 'Zion', together with the personification of twilight's 'drowsy, half closed eyes' are reminiscent of the splendour but desolation of the fallen gods in *Hyperion*.[37]

Keats was not a conventionally religious poet, and Rosenberg did not remain one for long. It is possible that he was encouraged to explore other subjects by Dainow, whose own rejection of orthodoxy emerges in a letter to Rosenberg's father. After spending a day with Isaac – presumably the visit to an art gallery deferred on 26 September 1905 – he tells Barnett on 6 October what a 'real pleasure' it was for him: 'I have rarely met a lad of his age displaying such love for Art and Literature.'[38] Then comes that curious warning already quoted: 'I trust that you will use your influence over him (which I think is profound) to emancipate him from the bonds of tyrannical orthodoxy.' Yet Isaac's cutting of Hebrew lessons at school alone shows that he had little time for orthodox religion. Perhaps, as Joseph Cohen suggests, he had complained to Dainow that his parents did not understand his artistic aspirations and Dainow had inferred that 'a rigid orthodoxy was the reason for their inadequate response' to their son.[38]

Whatever the explanation, Isaac's next poems are less conventionally religious, though their theme is still religion of a kind. It is his belief in the 'pure realm of art' that now forms the subject. Just as Keats had longed for ten years to 'overwhelm / [Him]self in poesy' in 'Sleep and Poetry', so Rosenberg yearns to devote himself to it, however arduous the path. In 1906 he writes, in words which suggest that he had recently been reading Keats's 'On First Looking into Chapman's Homer':

In art's lone paths I wander deep
And slowly, slowly, onward creep.
I seek, I probe each deep recess
To reach the secret of success.
In vain, 'tis hidden from my gaze
I still must hail its glowing rays.

Cold time shall drag the weary hours
And slowly tint the blooming flowers;
The flowers shall fade, the flowers shall bloom,
Yes many a time shall fade to gloom,
Ere I can burst thro' the wild bounds
That the pure realm of art surrounds.[40]

Rosenberg's sense of frustration, isolation and despair, after only one year of an occupation that was preventing him from pursuing his true interests, emerges clearly in the concluding verse:

I see of art its dazzling star
In glorious splendour shining far;
It dims my eyes, but year by year
To enter in its flaming sphere
I wildly try; 'tis vainly tried
For e'en its drudgery I'm denied.

Rosenberg's dependence on the Romantic poets at this period of his life is hardly surprising. They offered him, Keats especially, an escape from his uncongenial circumstances. Though forced to spend his days (to quote Wordsworth) 'in populous city pent', he could glimpse in their poetry an ideal and attempt to recreate it for himself in his own work. And, as Diana Collecott has pointed out, 'even in the city he is granted, by a trick of the light, a Wordsworthian vision of "buildings glorified, / Whose windows shine / And show the heaven".'[41]

However consoling poetry-writing proved, it was an essentially lonely pursuit. Even the rather solitary Rosenberg found that 'isolation ... preyed on [his] spirits' and made him long for company.[42] He welcomed his visits to Amshewitz, his 'only friend' at this period, he claimed.[43] A sympathetic, sensitive man, and shy himself, Amshewitz was able to see through Rosenberg's awkwardness. He recognized that beneath his 'strange mixture of extreme modesty and assertiveness' he was 'terribly sincere ... in his enthusiasms'.[44] His 'apparently uncouth manner and lack of appreciation of his true friends', Amshewitz believed, 'were his reaction to circumstances he had not always chosen', the Hentschel apprenticeship being a prime example. His conviction that Rosenberg had 'a soul far above the ordinary both as an artist and a poet' enabled him to ignore his protégé's failings and concentrate on his achievements. 'It is wonderful' he would write to a friend after a decade's knowledge of Rosenberg, 'when one remembers that his education has been that of an east-end board school and incomplete at that – and that these poems [i.e. *Night and Day*] were written under the most grinding poverty.'[45] There were probably occasions when Amshewitz had to remind himself of Rosenberg's disadvantages in order to keep his temper and there would eventually be something of a break between the two,[46] but during Rosenberg's apprentice years he was undoubtedly his greatest support.

His help came in a number of ways. When Rosenberg needed somewhere less crowded than the family kitchen to draw and paint, Amshewitz would lend him his studio. He also interested the successful academician and fashionable painter Solomon J. Solomon in his work, a link which would prove extremely useful later on. But it was Amshewitz's introduction to another established painter, Frank Emanuel, that was of greater help to Rosenberg during this period.[47] Emanuel was twenty-five years older than Rosenberg but still exhibiting widely in Paris and London when they met, possibly as early as 1906, the year Rosenberg wrote the poem he copied out for him, 'In Art's Lone Paths I Wander Deep'. Whether in direct response to the frustration expressed in Rosenberg's poem or not, Emanuel at once took a fatherly interest in his life as well as his work. As he explained to Binyon when he was writing an Introductory Memoir, he had been his guardian (from the Jewish Board of Guardians) during Isaac's apprenticeship.

He remembered how 'the poor chap always chafed against being in trade' and how he had 'pointed out to him how difficult it was for an artist – even provided with certain means – to earn a living as a painter'.[48] Emanuel urged Rosenberg to persevere with Hentschel's – 'to learn an art trade – to fall back upon' – but also encouraged him 'to push forward his art on all *available* occasions so as to reach a point at which he would be justified in abandoning trade and launching out'.[49]

One tangible way in which Emanuel helped Rosenberg was by inviting him to become a member of 'The Limners', a group of artists and art teachers who met at his studio and 'who were trusting enough', as he put it to Binyon, 'to listen to my criticism':

> I gave them prizes of prints and such like – found little jobs for some of them now and then and had exhibitions to which the public came and purchased in my studio and elsewhere – I felt that it was an opportunity to bring East and West end together and under the mutual interest of art to foster such social intercourse as would lessen class feeling. For Rosenberg whose circumstances had rendered him very bitter and despondent I felt to become a member would be a good thing . . . [50]

It was a great honour to bestow on a mere novice and one that suggests a high opinion of his potential. It gave Rosenberg the opportunity of meeting other artists apart from Amshewitz and exchanging ideas with them. It must also have helped his technique, since he won at least one of The Limners' monthly prizes for his 'Head of a Barrister', a red chalk drawing Emanuel thought 'very beautiful'[51] and bought, partly to help Rosenberg, when he was 'hard up'.[52]

Emanuel's friendship was very important to Rosenberg during his apprentice years, but whether it ultimately benefited him is debatable. Trained at the Slade under Legros and at the Académie Julian in Paris, he was probably a little more open to change than the Royal Academy-trained Amshewitz, but he had his limits. Perhaps that was what Leftwich (presumably echoing Rosenberg) meant when he described Emanuel as 'academically-minded'.[53] While his training

Head of a Barrister, 1910
(*University of South Carolina*)

must have persuaded him of the importance of Impressionism, he was very dismissive of what he called 'mad, modernistic styles'[54] and his attitude almost certainly influenced Rosenberg's own cautious reaction later on to Post-Impressionism, Cubism, Vorticism and Futurism. Nevertheless his kindness and charm – Gordon Bottomley, who met Emanuel in 1937 when working on the *Collected Works* of Rosenberg, described him to his fellow editor, Denys Harding, as 'delightful ... old but gorgeous now' and felt sure Harding would 'enjoy him'[55] – made him welcome company for Rosenberg in those early years.

Emanuel thought Rosenberg 'a remarkably clever young fellow', and a good artist, but came to believe that his 'greater strength' lay in his poetry.[56] Rosenberg was already longing to break into the literary world, and in this respect too, Amshewitz helped. Comfortably established in a circle of cultured middle-class friends who met at his Parkhill Road studio in Hampstead, the older man was able to write letters of introduction to at least two of these. One, Holbrook Jackson, the then editor of *T.P.'s Weekly*, would be enthusiastic but not much help in placing the poems Rosenberg sent him. The other, Dr David Eder, was to be more helpful, though not quite in the way Rosenberg expected. As a cousin of Zangwill, whose *Children of the Ghetto* had made him famous far beyond the East End and a role model for many young Jewish writers, Rosenberg probably thought of Eder more as a means of approaching Zangwill (with whom he lived in Guilford Street) than useful in himself. But after Rosenberg's first letter to Zangwill, enclosing some of his early poems, elicited little more than 'one word of perfunctory praise',[57] according to David Bomberg, Dr Eder stepped into the breach. A psychiatrist by profession, one of the earliest practitioners of Freudian analysis in England and a friend of D.H. Lawrence, Dr Eder was both shrewd and cultured. It was Eder who would introduce Rosenberg to the work of a highly experimental Imagist poet, F.S. Flint, for example, long before the significance of that group was widely recognized. And his assessment of Rosenberg's early poetry is not just the tactful response of an older, wiser person, but also perceptive as well as charming in its foreign English:

> . . . Much I like very much. You are young, and your verse shows that much. My own counsel would be not to think of publishing yet awhile . . . You have the artist's feeling for expression and for words. I should say you have not yet developed your own technique. That is not meant as a fault – [to] the contrary. But there is a fault. And that is, you have so far not given utterance to your own personality and it is all too reminiscent. I think you want courage to strike out into a line of your own. I should not write thus to anyone whom I did not respect for what he had done. We have all done a little versifying in our green days and hence these counsels.[58]

'I know [Eder's] right' Rosenberg admitted to another of Amshewitz's friends, Miss Winifreda Seaton,[59] though adding defensively that 'of course, his criticism does not refer to the latest things I showed you'. His inability to accept criticism would reveal itself just as plainly in his relationship with Miss Seaton, whom he also got to know at Amshewitz's studio.[60] A middle-class, middle-aged schoolmistress from Highgate, there was no question but that her education and experience were superior to his, yet he was unable to accept even the mildest of her comments without trying to defend his views on poetry and art generally, greatly to posterity's benefit:

> Now I see your argument and cannot deny my treatment of your criticisms, but have you ever asked yourself why I always am rude to your criticisms? . . . I think anybody can pick holes and find unsound parts in any work of art; . . . It is the unique and superior, the illuminating qualities one wants to find – discover the direction of the impulses. Whatever anybody thinks of a poet he will always know himself: he knows that the most marvellously expressed idea is still nothing; and it is stupid to think that praise can do him harm.[61]

To begin with, however, Rosenberg seems to have been more appreciative of Miss Seaton *and* her criticism. Her eagerness to help him remedy his poor education saw him exploring writers of whom he had almost certainly never heard, such as the eighteenth-century novelist Laurence Sterne. While indicating a reader of some sophistication, Miss Seaton's choice of *Tristram Shandy* suggests that she had great faith in his abilities. For a youth of his background to read and evidently enjoy Sterne's quirky approach to the novel, so far ahead of his time, is further proof of Rosenberg's extraordinary literary sensibility. 'My brains, as Sterne says, are as dry as a squeezed orange' he writes to Miss Seaton, showing off with pardonable pride the speed with which he had seized Sterne's idiom:

> . . . but I've got your letter to answer; and my conscience wouldn't let me sleep if I didn't do that. Not that I don't enjoy writing to you (writing to and hearing from you is a real treat), but even enjoyment is a laggard at times with the end in view, and must be spurred by conscience. 'Gee up,' says conscience, cracking his whip. 'Where?' cries enjoyment with dancing heart but empty head. 'To Mademoiselle Seaton, of course, you noodle!' 'But how? I don't know the road; besides my feet are heavy though my heart is light.' 'That matters not,' says conscience, 'Up, and look for it; be sharp about it too,' and here, giving a cut of the whip, enjoyment comes galloping delighted but astounded at the wide prospect of white fields of blank paper; and here I am groping for what to say . . .[62]

Sterne's influence also lies behind those occasional humorous out-bursts Rosenberg's friends recalled and the innuendo of apparently innocent prose pieces by him, such as 'On Noses' and 'On a Door Knocker'. His appreciation of Sterne suggests that his choice of words and phrasing, once he had developed his own literary voice, was a deliberate one and not the haphazard affair his patrons would often condescendingly imply.

In addition Rosenberg's letter shows, beneath all the jokiness, how much he valued Miss Seaton's friendship, which was considerable. She copied poems to send to him, knowing that he could rarely afford to buy books. And when he reciprocated with poems of his own copying, she joined in the joke, realizing that they were sent to test her own literary knowledge. After his death one such unsigned poem in Rosenberg's hand was assumed by one of the compilers of the 1922 edition of his work, Binyon, to be by Rosenberg himself. In fact, it was Coleridge's 'Sole Positive of Night', which he had evidently admired. (The other compiler, Bottomley, afterwards claimed that he had doubted Rosenberg's authorship, but for at least fifteen years it gave scholars something to debate.) They lent each other books, when Rosenberg was in a position to do so, though he was not always very gracious about her offerings, telling her quite bluntly, for instance, that he did 'not feel inclined to open' the slim collection of German verse she had sent.[63]

The volume of letters from Rosenberg to his 'Egeria', as she evidently regarded herself,[64] together with their content makes it clear that she was genuinely sympathetic towards his problems. His outpouring of misery over Hentschel, with which this chapter opened, his relief when he finally leaves the firm, his anxiety about finding another job, all are related to her in detail. Incomplete as they are – Miss Seaton herself insisted on a selection only for publication – these letters provide an invaluable picture of the rather shadowy period of his life between 1905 and 1911. He confided in her in a way that might have surprised his family and other friends, who found him mostly taciturn, even secretive. For example, he admits to a tendency towards self-pity and his attempts to resist it in a manner which is both forthcoming and highly revealing:

One conceives one's lot (I suppose it's the same with all people, no matter what their condition) to be terribly tragic. You are the victim of a horrible conspiracy; everything is unfair. The gods have either forgotten you or made you a sort of scapegoat to bear all the punishment. I believe, however hard one's lot is, one ought to try and accommodate oneself to the conditions; and except in a case of purely physical pain, I think it can be done. Why not make the very utmost of our lives? ... I'm a practical economist in this respect. I endeavour to waste nothing ... waste words! Not to talk is to waste words.[65]

These letters are not limited only to personal matters. however. Miss Seaton's interest in art as well as literature encouraged Rosenberg to report on a Blake exhibition at the Tate, for instance, in addition to poets she had suggested he read. His references to Donne, whom he initially found difficult, are particularly interesting, not just because we have Miss Seaton's later gloss on them but also because of Donne's obvious influence on Rosenberg's own poetry:

He grew to care for Donne [Miss Seaton wrote in 1919] almost as much as I do – like Jonson I put him first in the world for some things – and I remember a note of his beginning 'You cruel girl, what have you done with my Donne?' when I kept an old and rather curious copy he picked up somewhere, and was in the habit of looking into every day.[66]

Though unfortunately her letters to him have not been found, it is clear from his response that she asks him his opinion on a whole range of topics, music included. 'Do I like music, and what music [do] I like best?' Rosenberg responds:

I know nothing whatever about music. Once I heard Schubert's 'Unfinished Symphony' at the band; and – well, I was in heaven. It was a blur of sounds – sweet, fading and blending. It seemed to draw the sky down, the whole spirit out of me; it was articulate feeling. The inexpressible in poetry, in painting, was there expressed. But I have not heard much ... [67]

Despite such disclaimers, Rosenberg's poetry is full of musical metaphors and his confidence to Winifreda Seaton a useful one. There were many others.

At first glance it seems a curious friendship for a working-class teenager and a middle-class, middle-aged schoolteacher to strike up. His uncouthness and apparent lack of appreciation, as Amshewitz testified, made him a difficult person to help, and her own lack of confidence could cause her to be rather prickly. She was offended, for instance, when his offer to draw her failed to materialize. Rosenberg's response, beside showing the quickness with which he wants to rectify the situation, demonstrates an almost comical lack of tact towards an ageing spinster, as he tries to lighten the atmosphere with a joke: 'I don't suppose you have aged much since I saw you,' he writes, 'although it seems ages ago; because I don't seem to be in sympathy with old heads. I am seldom successful.' The extract ends with one of those many insights into his methods of working that fill these letters: 'You must be prepared to sit about two hours as I draw slowly.'[68]

Another letter displays him in an unusual reversal of roles, as he tries to reassure her about her 'powers as a critic', which she had 'deprecated'.[69] Having benefited frequently from her response to the many poems he sends her, he 'most emphatically disagree[s]' with her verdict on herself and in doing so evidently enjoys repeating back to her words she must often have used to him to reassure him:

Before a less prejudiced court you are found guilty of that most heinous crime of modesty. You are convicted (the jury has all agreed) of having vilely slandered your critical abilities; of having perjured yourself by forswearing and denying the 'gifts the gods gave you'.

The playfulness and wit of passages like these give quite a different picture from Edward Marsh's 'poor little Isaac Rosenberg'. And the gallantry with which he tells her 'I'm not going to flatter or say anything, (though I could hardly flatter)' shows an unexpected confidence for someone in his position. Perhaps it was created partly by her belief in him as well as by his own belief, which he repeats in closing his letter: 'I'm sure if anyone's got anything in one it will out, in spite of everything.'

Some of Rosenberg's friends were very critical of Winifreda Seaton. Bottomley, for example, found her bossy and managerial,[70] as she suspected. ('I've no doubt he thought I was the usual irritating female trying to get prominence by clinging to the tails of Mr Rosenberg's Pegasus' she wrote wryly to Binyon.)[71] But whatever her faults may have been, she was an important player in Rosenberg's life. She extended his reading considerably, stretched him intellectually with challenging writers, and provided not only a perceptive audience for his poetry but a sympathetic ear for his troubles. Above all she elicited from him some of the most interesting statements that have survived about his attitude towards poetry. Asking her to return some poems he intends to revise, for instance, he agrees that the 'emotions' in them 'are not worth expressing' but defends them on the grounds of 'an idea or so I rather liked':

I believe we are apt to fix a standard (of subject) in poetry. We acknowledge the poetry in subjects not generally taken as material, but I think we all (at least I do) prefer the poetical subject – 'Kubla Khan', 'The Mistress of Vision', 'Dream-Tryst' [both by Francis Thompson]; Poe, Verlaine. Here feeling is separated from intellect; our senses are not interfered with by what we know of facts: we know infinity through melody.[72]

Miss Seaton, as Rosenberg always addressed her, would remain a friend to the end of his life, despite difficult personalities on both sides. When he complained of army food later she would send home-baked bread and chocolates to the Front. His last letter to her was written less than a month before he died and in circumstances that cost him great effort. Winifreda Seaton, for her part, was devastated by his death:

He died too soon, which cannot be said of Sir Philip Sidney or Keats with the same deep regret [she wrote to Binyon a year later]. Had he had Rupert Brooke's advantages he might have expressed himself more perfectly, but when you compare the environment of the two, Isaac Rosenberg is a wonder.[73]

The case was quite different with another member of Amshewitz's circle and even more generous patron, Michael Sherbrooke. An actor of Polish origin,[74] Sherbrooke was a close friend of Amshewitz, who was interested in the theatre. Sixteen years older than Rosenberg, Sherbrooke had established a reputation for himself in Ibsen's plays by the time they met. His main point of interest for Rosenberg, however, would be his dramatic renderings of poetry, which he would later celebrate.[75] 'Frank' and 'good-humoured' though Rosenberg claimed to have found him,[76] and generous with both his time and money towards him ('a modern Roscius'), their relationship would come to an abrupt end in 1912, and in circumstances which suggest that Sherbrooke's interest was not entirely altruistic. Until then Sherbrooke would be one of a number of people introduced to Rosenberg by Amshewitz who would keep him going in the dark days of his apprenticeship.

Rosenberg expressed his appreciation of Amshewitz in a sonnet ('To J. H. Amschewitz') which is worth consideration despite its heightened rhetoric and derivativeness. Not only does it underline his continuing frustration with his situation, but the imagery of the first four lines, alternating as it does between 'night' and 'day', is an interesting anticipation of his first published work, *Night and Day*. And the last six lines of the sonnet point to the almost godlike role Amshewitz played in Rosenberg's life during this period:

> ... Life holds the glass but gives us tears for wine.
> But if at times he changes in his hand
> The bitter goblet for the drink divine,
> I stand upon the shore of a strange land.
> And when mine eyes unblinded of the brine
> See clear, lo! where he stood before, you stand.[77]

Chapter 4

'Art Is Not a Plaything': Bolt Court and Birkbeck College

1907–1911

> *I really would like to take up painting seriously; I think I might do something at that; but poetry – I despair of ever writing excellent poetry. I can't look at things in the simple, large way that great poets do. My mind is so cramped and dulled and fevered, there is no consistency of purpose, no oneness of aim; the very fibres are torn apart, and application deadened by the fiendish persistence of the coil of circumstance.*
>
> – IR to Winifreda Seaton, before 1911[1]

Rosenberg's visits to Amshewitz's studio quickly revived his own ambitions as a painter. And it was Amshewitz once more who came up with a solution. Having himself attended evening classes at Birkbeck College, he suggested that Rosenberg should do the same, to qualify him for the Royal Academy or the Slade.[2] The fees were modest enough even for Rosenberg, but the standards were high. In the autumn of 1907 Rosenberg duly enrolled.

At the same time, according to Morris Goldstein, he started evening classes at Bolt Court School of Photo-Engraving and Lithography, a London County Council institution catering mainly for apprentices and journeymen in those and related trades.[3] The most likely explanation is that Rosenberg was sent there for further training by Carl Hentschel, who donated an annual prize in 'Screen Negative Making' to the school, in which case there would have been no fees to pay. But Goldstein claimed that it was at his suggestion that they attended and that Rosenberg, like himself, studied painting under Cecil Rea. Whichever it was, Rosenberg does not appear to have taken Bolt Court very seriously, despite its august literary location in Dr Johnson's old haunts.

Drawing of
Rosenberg by H.C.
Hammond at Bolt
Court Art School in
early 1914 (*Berg
Collection/New York
Public Library*)

Yet there were some good artists in the making at Bolt Court during Rosenberg's time there, Paul Nash, for one, who would go on to the Slade and wider fame.[4] The two do not appear to have met, but someone Rosenberg did get to know, also of great promise, was H.C. Hammond, a half-tone etcher.[5] They would remain friends long after Isaac left Bolt Court, and in 1914 Hammond would execute a fine Indian ink and brush portrait of his friend.[6] Lost sight of for many years, it recently resurfaced in the New York Public Library's Berg's Edward Marsh Collection. More flattering than any of his self-portraits, and drawn with bold, confident lines, it presents someone of exotic appearance whose long eyelashes conceal down-turned eyes and whose pointed ears – that elfin impression gained also by Amshewitz – give him a slightly fantastic air. However romanticized it may be, it is skilfully executed and reveals how at least some of Rosenberg's friends perceived him. A second portrait of him by another student – 'Character Drawing on Brown Paper' – has not survived but was seen by David Bomberg, who thought it 'very good work'.[7] Bomberg's standards in art were already high when he formed this opinion, together with his claim that 'Isaac ... did excellent work at Bolt Court'.[8] But his proviso – that 'its standard was high in relation to the printing trade but not to painting' – helps to explain Rosenberg's reticence about his time there: it was hardly ideal for someone who was hoping to become a serious painter. As Nash observed, 'the whole purpose of the school was avowedly practical. You were there to equip yourself for making a living.'[9] Different as his more privileged middle-class upbringing was from Rosenberg's, Nash could have been speaking for him when he added that: 'Instead of profiting by the commercial art training of Bolt Court and becoming a slick and steady machine for producing posters, show cards, layouts and other more or less remunerative designs, I fell under the disintegrating charm of Pre-Raphaelitism, or rather of Dante Gabriel Rossetti' – and, though he does not say so here, of Blake. Rosenberg would not read Blake till later, but it would be one of his teachers at the less vocationally driven Birkbeck who would introduce him to the artist-poet, inspiring in him a lifelong devotion.

Birkbeck College, conveniently situated a stone's throw from Hentschel's in Fetter Lane,[10] was quite different from Bolt Court School. It ran no trade classes, but offered a wide range of courses in scientific, commercial and humanist subjects. It made its first application to become part of London University in 1907, the year Rosenberg joined it, and though this would not be granted until 1920 the standard of teaching was high. The type of student came on the whole from a different social stratum from most of Bolt Court – most of them were clerks, teachers and candidates for the Civil Service – and the college had a reputation for earnestness and high-mindedness. As a contemporary observer put it: 'No one goes to Birkbeck for any other purpose than that of serious study. There is a quiet thoughtful air about the place that would quickly frighten away those intent on pleasure.'

This created no problem for Rosenberg, who welcomed his first real chance to study seriously. He was at last entering the 'pure realm of art' for which he longed. Not only would he be encouraged to approach drawing professionally with expert teachers, but for the first time he would be allowed to sketch from the nude. He would write tenderly, later, of the 'sacred, voluptuous hollows deep' of the human body.[11] (The only fully authenticated works known to have survived from this period are a few life-class sketches.)[12] He also learnt to paint in oils and took classes in portraiture. His two known portraits in oil from this period, one his earliest surviving self-portrait of 1910, the other of a fellow student at Birkbeck, also at Bolt Court, Henry Dixon,[13] were almost certainly Birkbeck assignments. Another self-portrait, showing his head in full profile (a difficult pose he seldom adopted later), probably dates also from this period. A fine pencil drawing of unadorned honesty, it was dated 1910 by his brother David, who owned it until his death in the late twentieth century, when it disappeared from view.[14]

Rosenberg's 1910 self-portrait in oils shows an assurance and skill that explain the confidence his teachers quickly developed in him. More romanticized than later self-portraits – he dresses himself in an 'artist's' pink cravat and sports a brown velvet collar on his coat – it lacks their forcefulness. It is also distinguished from them by the fact that Rosenberg gazes directly at the viewer, rather than with the sideways glance of later paintings. But the look is a wary, rather tentative one, with none of the defiance hinted at in many of his subsequent works. Overall it has an old-fashioned air, revealing little sign of influence from more modern movements in art.[15] Nevertheless, it is an impressive start.

Rosenberg won a number of awards during his three years at Birkbeck, including a book prize in the National Competition of December 1908 for the study of a head in charcoal (almost certainly his 'Head of a Monk'), the Mason Prize for some nude studies also in 1908, and the Pocock Prize for his '3 hours' study from the nude in oils in 1910.[16] He said nothing of these successes to his family, who learnt of them only through Amshewitz.

Less predictably, he also made friends at the college, despite the class differences from the majority of the other students. His working-class mannerisms must in any case have been softened by his contact with Amshewitz and his middle-class friends, though as Amshewitz noted he retained an 'appalling Cockney accent to the end'.[17] David Bomberg, in a long, unpublished account of his friendship with Rosenberg which has only recently come to light, accused

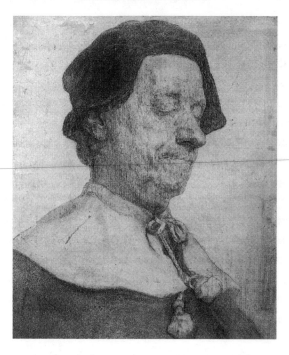

The Monk, almost certainly a Birkbeck College assignment of 1908 (*Imperial War Museum*)

him of being 'a snob',[18] but Rosenberg appears to have got to know his fellow students for less class-motivated reasons, as his close friendship with one of them shows.

Mitchell, the young man in question whose first name is unknown, was half British, half Japanese and had left his family behind in Japan. Rosenberg, still living with his own family in Stepney, took Mitchell home to meet them shortly after the autumn term started in 1907. His mother had just uprooted the Rosenbergs once again and transferred them round the corner to 159 Oxford Street (renamed Stepney Way in 1938). It is not known when this move took place, but the chances are that the family was still living in Jubilee Street when the young Joseph Stalin stayed in lodgings there at No. 77 on a visit to London to attend the Fifth Congress of the Russian Social Democratic Workers Party in 1907. The home of a Russian Jewish cobbler, who would undoubtedly have been known to his fellow immigrant Russians, the Rosenbergs, 77 Jubilee Street was almost certainly the meeting-place, however briefly, of one of the most intriguing quartets in modern history – Stalin, Lenin, Trotsky and Gorky, all of whom attended the 1907 Conference. It is more than likely that Isaac, who like most of his fellow Jews in the East End, had socialist leanings in his youth, would have known of Stalin's stay, possibly even met him.[19]

The Rosenbergs' move from Jubilee Street, whenever it occurred, was their fourth in eight years, two of them within Jubilee Street itself, but appears to have been more satisfactory than previous ones, since they would remain there until 1912. Their new house at 159 Oxford Street was not shared with other tenants and was evidently large enough for Anna to be able to take in Mitchell as a lodger.

The son of a Glasgow ship's engineer who held a high-ranking post in the Japanese government, and a mother who came from Japan's ruling class, Mitchell was a colourful figure, according to Bomberg, with 'muscles like a Gladiator and a body like teak'.[20] He had received a good education which culminated at Tokyo University. Once he had left the university, however, he had been faced with the threat of military service rather than the career in painting he wanted. Probably as a result of Japan's recent war with Russia from 1904 to 1905, he had found no way of avoiding conscription despite his privileged background, except by leaving the country and taking up his British citizenship. In order to be independent of his parents, he had found a day job in a music-publishing business in Oxford Street in central London, while attending Birkbeck College at night, but was looking for lodgings when he and Rosenberg first met. Annie remembers him replacing an even more exotic lodger who had shared her brother's tiny bedroom in Jubilee Street, a Pakistani named Haronof, who drove Isaac mad by cracking nuts and eating them until well into the night, undoing any effort to focus on his work.[21] With Mitchell it was quite different and, if Bomberg is to be believed, they took turns at painting self-portraits in the small, cracked bedroom mirror they shared. Mitchell was clearly close to the family, with whom he would remain until after the First World War, using Rosenberg's father, sisters and brothers as models on the rare occasions they were free to sit to him.

More importantly, Mitchell exerted a significant influence on

Rosenberg's literary development. Widely read in English, French, German and Japanese literature, he became a conduit for Rosenberg to French writers in particular. Though his spoken French was poor, he read it fluently and subscribed regularly to magazines such as the *Revue des Deux Mondes*. It was Mitchell, Bomberg claimed, who 'kept Isaac in touch with what was happening in current French literature'.[22] This explains why Rosenberg, who never learnt French, was able to refer confidently to writers as varied as Balzac, Verlaine, Baudelaire, Zola, Flaubert, Stendhal and others. Mitchell was also the 'first person Isaac consulted regarding anything he wrote', apparently,[23] even though their tastes differed as widely in English literature as they did in art. Rosenberg would continue to send copies of his poems to Mitchell until army service made it too difficult.[24] He formed other friendships at Birkbeck,[25] but Mitchell's was the most important, and a significant formative influence on his literary development during this period.

Rosenberg also got on well with the Birkbeck staff, a sign of his contentment there, since he was not always the easiest of students. His family recalled that he made a good impression on the head of the institute, Dr Norman Bentwich, 'a very understanding man' according to Minnie.[26] She claimed that Bentwich, alerted no doubt by the head of the Art department, Alfred Mason, took a great interest in Isaac. One way he tried to keep his impoverished student was to provide him with a free pass allowing him to copy masterpieces in the National Gallery on private viewing days, a practice that would eventually lead to the fulfilment of at least one of his dreams.

There are no surviving letters from Rosenberg to Bentwich, but Birkbeck's staff was handsomely represented in the second edition of Rosenberg's work by Miss Alice Wright, who was able to produce a dozen letters and five poems sent to her by Rosenberg, together with two sketches from the nude.[27] The close relationship which developed between them reinforces the impression that he got on better with older women than with those of his own age at this period.

Rosenberg's family failed to locate Alice Wright in the mid-1930s when his *Collected Works* was being prepared, but its editors managed to trace her in North London and her reply to their request for material, written in a firm, educated hand, suggests that she was still fairly young when she became Isaac's teacher at Birkbeck nearly thirty years earlier.[28] We know that she was living with an unmarried sister, Lilian, who also taught in Birkbeck's Art department as well as writing poetry. Alice herself edited an anthology of *English Nature Poems* for Grant Richards in 1908, shortly after Rosenberg first met her. So that, not only could she direct his art studies but she could also respond knowledgeably to his literary efforts, a combination that must have appealed particularly to the divided Rosenberg. His letters to her make it evident that her encouragement was important to him. It is also clear that she put him at his ease, bringing out his humorous side as Winifreda Seaton occasionally did. He feels able to joke with Miss Wright, for example, about a model he is using for part of a large painting: whilst acknowledging that 'Miss Grimshaw' was a 'very good sitter', he complains that 'her figure was too scraggy for my purpose – I practically finished the drapery, and the upper part I will do from some more *titanic* model if I can get the type'.[29]

Though Rosenberg would fail to visit Alice Wright immediately after leaving Birkbeck as he had intended, he would send the sisters two copies of his first (self-published) booklet, *Night and Day*, in 1912, the second at their request. As a result they would invite him to visit them at their North London flat, hence the letters to Alice. While these show that he still valued her response to his art – it is thanks mainly to her that we know as much as we do about the painting referred to above, and now lost, *Joy* – the advice of both sisters on his literary output was equally important to him, as his gift of his poems indicates. And their gift to him of works by Shelley and Blake, particularly the latter, would exert some influence on the direction his own poetry took.[30]

It is possible that the Wright sisters also introduced Rosenberg to Swinburne and the Nineties poets, still a daring read in the first decade of the twentieth century. Youngish, well-read and highly emancipated for their day, they are far more likely to have done so than Morley Dainow, whose ideal was Tennyson. Whoever made the introduction, Rosenberg's debt to these writers is clear in the poems of the Birkbeck period. The most powerful of these initially was Swinburne; the title of Rosenberg's 'Dawn Behind Night' suggests that he had been reading 'Songs Before Sunrise' when he wrote it in about 1909, the year the older poet died. The compulsive rhythms of its long, alliterative hexameters, the revolutionary spirit of its theme and its preoccupation with death all bear this out, though the despair appears to be Rosenberg's own:

> In the golden glare of the morning, in the solemn serene of the night,
> We look on each other's faces, and we turn to our prison bar;
> In pitiless travail of toil and outside the precious light,
> What wonder we know not our manhood in the curse of the things
>   that are?[31]

Long after Rosenberg had rejected Swinburne for other models, he would still find him 'gorgeous' and consider his ballads a significant contribution to nineteenth-century literature, in which he argues that:

> art somehow had lost touch with nature and lay simpering, cosy and snug, propped up by sweet anecdote and delicious armchair comfort. It was the day of Dickens' slime and slush. Then Baudelaire published 'The Flowers of Evil', Swinburne his ballads, and Meredith 'Modern Love'.[32]

Rosenberg attempted two ballads of his own during this period, one of them, 'A Ballad of Time, Life and Memory', heavily indebted to Swinburne not just in its form and heavy alliteration but also in its dependence on allegory and personification. He had first come across these devices in Keats and Shelley and they are evidently still strong influences when he writes his own first ballad some time before 1911.[33] 'A Ballad of Time, Life and Memory' is also full of echoes of the Nineties poets, whose laments for the brevity of 'the days of wine and roses' are beginning to appeal to him. As life drops her flowers in the procession, Time crushes them and Memory, of course, picks them up:

And by her side, whose name is Memory,
The ghosts of all the hours,
Some smiling as they smiled within the sun.
Some stained and wan with tears.
To those she gives the roses as they fall,
And bids them tune the praises of their prime.
To these their tears and dust.[34]

The Nineties poets, heavily influenced by Baudelaire as Swinburne himself was, also wrote ballads, often about the seamier side of city life. Rosenberg's debt to them at this time emerges in another poem written during his Birkbeck years, 'A Ballad of Whitechapel'. Here he attempts to achieve 'the sort of poetry that appeal[ed] to [him] most' in his early years and which he found in one of the greatest of the Nineties poets, Francis Thompson, that is, 'richly coloured without losing that mysteriousness, the hauntingness which to me is the subtle music – the soul to which the colour is flesh and raiment'.[35] He was later to find Thompson 'too fond of stars'[36] and to dismiss the rest of the Nineties poets as 'morbid' and 'perverse',[37] perhaps because he suspected that their vision of the hopelessness and ephemerality of life was in most cases an affectation, but his debt to them in 'A Ballad of Whitechapel' is considerable.

Like their forerunners the Pre-Raphaelites, whom Rosenberg would quickly come to prefer and whose influence – Dante Gabriel Rossetti's in particular – is already apparent in 'A Ballad of Whitechapel', the Nineties poets favoured the theme of prostitution. Most of their poems on the subject fail to avoid the danger of sentimentality or melodrama inherent in such a subject and Rosenberg falls into a similar trap. After painting a 'lurid' picture of the haunts of sin, the narrator describes an encounter with 'a girl in garments rent', who 'peered 'neath lids shamed, / And spoke to me and murmured to my blood'.[38] Predictably, she is not really wicked but 'sadly spiritual', having been forced into prostitution by the death of her parents and the threat of homelessness to herself and her dying brother. Rosenberg attempts to bring the scene to life by having the narrator fall in love with the girl, but she remains a cardboard figure. Yet there is interest in the poem, especially in the narrator's identification with another socially deprived figure from the East End, his night-marish vision of the area, which appears to reflect Rosenberg's own, and his awakening to sex and its relation to love. The poem ends somewhat unconvincingly with the union of the narrator and pros-titute in true love:

> Love's euphony
> In Love's own temple that is our glad hearts,
> Makes now long music wild deliciously,
> Now Grief hath used his darts.
>
> Love infinite,
> Chastened by sorrow, hallowed by pure flame,
> Not all the surging world can compass it,
> Love—love—Oh! tremulous name.
>
> God's mercy shines.
> And my full heart hath made record of this.
> Of grief that burst from out its dark confines
> Into strange sunlit bliss.[39]

Rosenberg may have been in love himself when he wrote these words. His family and friends talked of his closeness at this time to a young Jewish woman, Annetta Raphael, a shadowy figure at best. She lived near the Rosenbergs with her mother apparently, was slightly older than Isaac, a dressmaker by day and art student at night. She was also musical and would often visit Jubilee, later Oxford Street, to give the children music lessons, according to Annie, which may partly account for Rosenberg's interest in the subject. Joseph Cohen believes that she was 'the most likely person to have initiated [him] into sexual experience'.[40] The fact that she kept in touch with him till his death, that it affected her very badly and that she would remain unmarried for many years after the war bears this out.[41] In the absence of firm evidence, however, I am more inclined to believe that his sexual initiation came later.[42]

A similar temptation to interpret Rosenberg's verse autobiographically is presented by another of his apprentice poems, 'Death', in which he claims 'Death's gift is best, not worst'.[43] The narrator's despair is convincing, but it is a theme common to most of the poets who constituted Rosenberg's favourite reading at this time. It is also a familiar young man's pose. (Siegfried Sassoon, for example, wrote frequently on the subject in his youth, partly from admiration of Shelley's *Queen Mab*, partly to impress his mother, he admitted.) Rosenberg may simply have been trying to emulate those poets who, in his own words, 'delight in the morbid, for whom life always is arrayed in crepe whose very vigour and energy find its outlet in a perverse and insistent plucking at the wings of death'.[44] 'Death' may be a largely literary exercise deriving from his reading of Keats and the Nineties poets in particular. Its melodramatic imagery, much of it paradoxical, is full of living tombs, cursed lips, cankered flowers, Life pregnant with Death's offspring, Death poisoning Life's 'warm lips' with his 'pale mouth', the 'world's blood' dripping away.[45]

On the other hand 'Death' may be proof of continuing suicidal tendencies on Rosenberg's part when it was written around 1910, five years into his apprenticeship, particularly when taken in conjunction with a letter he wrote to Miss Seaton not long afterwards: 'All one's thoughts seem to revolve round to one point – death. It is horrible, especially at night, "in the silence of the midnight"; it seems to clutch at your thought – you can't breathe.'[46]

Yet Rosenberg's years at Hentschel's were not entirely negative. Full of activity and progress in both poetry and art, they also saw him developing from a shy, introverted youth singularly lacking in confidence into someone capable of making friends of his own age. And one of the most significant of these both in personal and artistic terms was David Bomberg, whose meeting with Rosenberg in late 1907 would lead a few years later to the emergence of the Whitechapel Group.[47]

The two first met in the reference room of the Whitechapel Library where Rosenberg frequently went to read or write poetry. One of the librarians, F.B. Bogdin, remembered him there, 'an extremely slightly built young man, very shy, softly spoken and with somewhat dreamy eyes', whose 'almost only reading was the works of the poets: Tennyson, Shelley, Keats (*Keats* for weeks)'.[48] He also remembered Rosenberg reading Shakespeare's sonnets and Laurence Binyon's poems, though this may have been slightly later. A large, glass-panelled area, the reference library was lighter than Rosenberg's room at home, much warmer in winter and open until 10 p.m. every day of the week including Sundays: like a friend, Joseph Ascher, whom he met there, he probably found it a real refuge. Isaac's Birkbeck friend and family lodger, Mitchell, went there daily after work, not to consult its numerous art reference books but to take advantage of the light and some free models to practise portraiture. It was his surreptitious attempt to draw Bomberg's head that led, first to their friendship, then to Mitchell's introduction of Bomberg to Rosenberg. Mitchell could hardly have failed to recognize the similarities in their backgrounds, though he may not have known their full extent.

Only ten days younger than Rosenberg, Bomberg had also been born in the provinces to Jewish immigrant parents but moved to the East End as a child and was brought up in Whitechapel.[49] Like Rosenberg he had gone to a local Board School rather than the Jews' Free School his father favoured, had left at fourteen to earn a living but was desperate to escape his apprenticeship. Both had started drawing and painting at an early age, encouraged by strong, devoted mothers. In Bomberg's case this had led to the luxury of his own studio, a vacant room next to the family flat in Tenter Buildings, St Mark Street, which Rebecca Bomberg rented for him. Not too far from the Rosenbergs in Oxford Street, it also became a retreat for Isaac, who would later paint part of his most ambitious picture, *Joy*, there while Bomberg worked on the same Slade assignment, which he called *Island of Joy*.[50]

No photograph of Bomberg's studio survives, but it can be glimpsed through an open door in his *Bedroom Picture* (1911–12). 'Isaac ... knew that bedroom as I knew his,' Bomberg wrote, 'for when there was a Domestic disturbance at home' – a not infrequent occurrence – 'I took as my "refugio" the hospitality of his mother and father and family.'[51] It is possible that some of Bomberg's early self-portraits were executed from the same small cracked mirror

Rosenberg shared with Mitchell in their crowded bedroom studio. It is even more likely that the three of them discussed poetry there, since Bomberg himself was attempting to write it at the time and for some years afterwards.[52] He was also relatively well-read, his older siblings having introduced him to the nineteenth century novelists and poets. Particularly fond of Swinburne – he knew 'miles and miles' of him according to his younger sister[53] – he is another possible candidate for introducing his work to Rosenberg.

Another aspect of Rosenberg and Bomberg's early life that links them is their reaction to Jewishness. Both rejected orthodoxy, in Bomberg's case with the active encouragement of his mother. But after an almost mandatory flirtation with politics, in which they both joined the Young Socialist League, neither found in it a substitute for religion. It is clear that each of them identified in his own way with their heritage, though it is Bomberg's early work as a painter that shows his fondness for Jewish themes, while it is mainly in Rosenberg's later work as a poet that his is revealed.

In their individual ways Rosenberg and Bomberg would live their lives as outsiders of a kind. It is significant that those who write about Rosenberg all point to the well-known photograph of the Slade School picnic of *c.* 1912, where he kneels to one side apart, as evidence of his outsidership, and that Richard Cork uses the same photograph to point out that 'Bomberg stands quite apart from' the other students.[54]

Cork appeals to the same photograph, however, to highlight the difference between the two, contrasting Rosenberg's 'conspicuous correctness' of dress with Bomberg's 'rough-and-ready' clothes and defiant air, and it is the disparities that dominate. The most obvious ones early on were those of appearance and character, though later it would be their contrasting approaches to art that would stand out, including Rosenberg's eventual choice of poetry as opposed to Bomberg's of art. One of Bomberg's nicknames, for instance, was 'Bomb', highlighting his noisy, extrovert approach to life, while Rosenberg's lack of any nickname suggests that he was too remote for such intimacies. Leftwich, who knew both of them well, said that 'Bomberg appeared to be supremely confident, full of himself and completely different from Rosenberg who was taciturn'.[56] And Sonia Cohen, who describes her close relationship with both in her unpublished memoirs detected an even greater contrast:

> ... No two men could have less resembled one another in outward manner than Isaac and David. Although Isaac's poems have a declamatory and passionate emphasis, in speech he was low-toned and unemphatic. He seemed prudent of using his voice as if he wished to preserve it.
>
> David, on the other hand, was above all articulate and his speech was forceful ... [He] had an intensity in his approach to ideas and indeed to all around him which made him utterly impervious to whatever might be outside his immediate interest.[56]

Sonia remembered one particularly characteristic remark of Bomberg's to her, made regardless of the crowds milling around them at a fashionable art exhibition, in response to her carefully chosen Liberty-influenced outfit: 'Why do you wear abominable brown? It's the colour of dung.'[57] Rosenberg would never have uttered that remark. He is, in any case, unlikely to have shared Bomberg's reaction, since his own clothes at the time included the brown velvet-collared jacket of his 1910 self-portrait. Sonia claimed that he 'held to the romantic tradition', whereas Bomberg aimed at a deliberately 'anti-romantic' look 'by dressing in the clothes of the East End "tough"'.[58]

The differences went deeper than appearance. Where Isaac was cautious and reticent, Bomberg was audacious, at times aggressive, 'a stocky little bombastic person' according to one female friend who had probably been pursued by him.[59] Though not much taller than Rosenberg, he was more powerfully built and had far more presence. Having learnt boxing from an older brother to defend himself in the Whitechapel streets, he loved the gyms and wrestling-halls of the East End, which inspired some of his early art. With his fiery red hair, which reflected his personality apparently, he was, literally, pugnacious. Leftwich's word for him, 'blasty', best sums up his whirlwind personality and defiant attitude towards life in general.

Full of Jewish 'chutzpah', he never hesitated to push himself forward. When, partly as a result of this, he was admitted to the Slade, his teachers would eventually find his lack of 'modesty' and 'humility' a problem.[60]

It would be misleading to portray Rosenberg as his complete opposite in all these respects, however, since he too could be defiant and assertive at times. It was expressed in a quieter, less obvious way, but it stemmed from the same source, a reaction to the many obstacles which threatened to prevent both of them from realizing their ambitions. The similarity of their circumstances helped to cement their friendship in 1907 and brought them very close for the next four years. So, too, did their different temperaments, which complemented each other usefully. When the unassertive Rosenberg was bullied for being Jewish, Bomberg would come to his rescue. But when Bomberg, in hot pursuit of a girl, needed a softer approach, it would be Rosenberg who wrote a romantic poem to her on Bomberg's behalf. Morley Dainow's brother David, who knew Isaac at this time, remembered that Bomberg was 'one of his few friends'[61] and Sonia Cohen refers to the 'close friendship' that still existed between them as late as 1912.[62] Even after a certain amount of rivalry grew up between them at the Slade, she said, 'One was seldom seen without the other.' Bomberg's pencil portrait of Rosenberg, 'Head of a Poet', which won the Henry Tonks Prize at the Slade in 1913, shows tenderness as well as insight. Years later, after Rosenberg's death, Bomberg would talk warmly about him, describing him fondly as 'the poet laureate less the title and the retaining fee'.[63] He would join forces with Leftwich in 1937 to honour Rosenberg with a retrospective exhibition and would undertake a great deal of the work himself.

In the years following 1907 their closeness had at least one practical result in Rosenberg's first serious attempts at landscape painting.[64] It was an area of art he appears not to have explored either at Birkbeck or Bolt Court. Diana Collecott has argued with some truth that, unlike Bomberg, who would become increasingly concerned with form over subject-matter, Rosenberg, as an 'expressionist painter, remained romantically preoccupied with the subject, and in the hope of a livelihood, ... apprenticed himself to the traditional arts of portraiture and landscape-painting'.[65] It is ironic,

'Head of a Poet' by David Bomberg, 1913

therefore, that he appears to have made his first real attempt at landscape with Bomberg's encouragement. Their immediate surroundings, with the exception of Victoria Park and the Thames, offered them little scope, and Bomberg remembered how 'together Isaac and I got our painting equipment' and went to the nearest available open spaces, Epping Forest, Chingford and Hampstead, 'on the off day Sunday'.[66] It was with Bomberg beside him, therefore, that Rosenberg painted many of his landscapes, since the bulk of them were executed during the height of their friendship. His three seascapes of 1910 are proof of just how close the relationship was, since they were painted during a holiday they took together on the Isle of Wight that year.[67] Bomberg vividly recalled staying at Shanklin with Isaac, at the house of Barnett Rosenberg's employer in the Pioneering Cotton Goods Company, whose wares he peddled.

Though one of Rosenberg's seascapes, *Shanklin. Oils. 1910*, has vanished since its appearance in the 1937 Whitechapel Art Gallery Exhibition, the other two, *People on a Seashore* and *Sea and Beach*, have survived[68] and strongly suggest the influence of the Impressionists, those of the *plein air* school in particular. And since Bomberg was taking lessons from Walter Sickert at the Westminster School of Art by 1910, this was almost certainly filtered through him. (Roger Fry's revolutionary first Post-Impressionist Exhibition would not take place until a few months later and Bomberg was still happily experimenting with his own brand of Impressionism.) There is evidence in Rosenberg's two surviving seascapes of the Impressionist interest in colour and light and a similar absence of firm outline round objects. As in many Impressionist works the paint is applied in small, brightly coloured dabs, especially in *People on a Seashore*. *Landscape with Three Figures, 1910*, executed in a similar manner, was almost certainly a product of the same holiday.

Unfortunately Bomberg destroyed most of his work from this period, making it impossible to prove the likely affinity between their art at this time. In addition some of their Isle of Wight efforts were probably seized by the local police when, at Bomberg's suggestion to the less adventurous Rosenberg, they tried to paint Sandown's military fortifications. Both were arrested and detained until their landlady, a Mrs Haydon, managed to persuade the police of their harmlessness.

Yet the holiday was a success overall. 'We did good painting and enjoyed the bathing though Isaac was no swimmer' Bomberg recalled. 'It became great fun when Father [presumably Barnett Rosenberg] joined us who could swim.' At this stage the advantages of their friendship are clear. Not only was Rosenberg encouraged by daily contact with someone of his own age with similar ambitions facing similar obstacles, but the bolder, more confident Bomberg was already introducing Rosenberg to newer theories and movements in art. He also, directly or indirectly, made Rosenberg believe that the Slade was a future possibility. Having himself received encouragement from John Singer Sargent by the time they met, Bomberg would break his indentures with the lithographers, Fischer's in 1908 to devote himself wholly to art.

Bomberg's example was reinforced by that of another young painter Rosenberg met during this period, possibly through Bomberg, Mark Gertler. A year younger, Gertler shared their background in almost every other respect. Born in Spitalfields to Austrian Jewish parents, he had been taken back to Galicia before he was one but brought back to the East End in 1896 and educated at his local Board School in Deal Street.[69] He was then apprenticed much against his wishes to a firm of stained-glass makers, Clayton and Bell of Regent Street, in December 1907. His outstanding talent was already so evident, however, that with William Rothenstein's support he applied successfully to the Jewish Education Aid Society in 1908 for a grant to the Slade. He was either in the process of doing this, or had just started at the Slade in the autumn of that year, when he and Rosenberg met.

Blessed with a more charming appearance – that of a 'Jewish Botticelli' according to Paul Nash[70] – and of a less volatile temperament than Bomberg, Gertler was also less revolutionary in his approach to his art, which Rosenberg would come to prefer to Bomberg's audacious experiments. He would value Gertler's opinion from the time they met till the end of his painting life. And Gertler, despite his somewhat dismissive description of Rosenberg as 'a funny little man',[71] would be generous with his help, inviting Rosenberg to the studio he acquired in 1910 and introducing him to potential patrons like Edward Marsh and Sydney Schiff. Rosenberg's gifts of a poem, 'The One Lost', and his 1915 booklet *Youth* suggest that Gertler responded enthusiastically to his poetry, though there is (perhaps significantly) no record of Gertler's opinion of his art. None of their mutual friends ever detected the closeness they did between Rosenberg and Bomberg, but there was undoubtedly affection.[72]

Goldstein, still determined to become a painter himself, places Rosenberg's (and his own) first meeting with Gertler in late 1908 at the Whitechapel Art Gallery.[73] It is unlikely, however, that young men of such similar interests gathering, as they all did by 1907, in Whitechapel Library would not have met sooner, once the gregarious Bomberg entered the scene. Morris Goldstein's recollections of this period are invaluable but his memory for dates is not always reliable. Nevertheless his reference is useful because it indicates that Rosenberg was drawn to the Whitechapel Art Gallery just as much as his fellow painters were. For poor Jewish artists to appreciate free access to fine art was exactly what Samuel and Henrietta Barnett had hoped for when they planned the gallery at the end of the nineteenth century. It was as a result of their own art exhibitions at Toynbee Hall that they had set about raising money for the 'East End Gallery' as it was originally called. Opened next door to the Whitechapel Library in 1901, it housed some valuable paintings, though Rosenberg's letter thought to be to Winifreda Seaton does not make it clear whether he is referring to a permanent collection or, as seems more likely, to one of the many exhibitions it mounted from 1901 onwards:

> The paintings are in the upper gallery. Some wonderful Reynolds and Hogarths. There is Hogarth's Peg Woffington, the sweetest the most charming, most exquisite portrait of a woman I've ever seen. A Rossetti drawing – fine and a lot of good things.[74]

Another frequent visitor to the Whitechapel Art Gallery and Library was Mark Wayner (born Weiner), who would follow Gertler to the Slade in 1909.[75] His most vivid memory of Rosenberg was of meeting him on the festival of Yom Kippur and being dismayed to learn that 'when all good Jews were in the synagogue', Rosenberg was 'hurrying to the library to get a poem down'.[76] It may have been Wayner's own orthodoxy at that time which prevented them becoming closer friends.

Wayner, nevertheless, played a significant, if minor role in Rosenberg's life, since his own entry to the Slade in 1909, following Gertler's the previous year, encouraged Rosenberg to continue hoping and fighting for the same. He had first applied to the Jewish Education Aid Society (JEAS), which funded Wayner as well as Gertler, in December 1908, at the end of Gertler's first term. But his application was 'ordered to stand over'[77] and it is not until he has completed his third successful year at Birkbeck that he returns to the Jewish Education Aid Society in November 1910 with a more convincing application, put together, no doubt, with the help of his sponsors, Amshewitz's friends Solomon J.

Solomon and Marion Spielmann, who 'strongly recommended the case'.[78] Reading the report, and allowing for a little exaggeration on his part, it is not difficult to see why Rosenberg was desperate to leave Hentschels:

> This applicant aged 19, was at present working as a photo-etcher in the employ of Messrs. Carl Hentschel and Co., his weekly earnings varying between 30/- [shillings] and 35/- [shillings], the hours being abnormally long, as he seldom reached home before 11 o'clock at night. He had attended the evening classes at the Birkbeck School of Art, but the long hours at his work prevented him continuing to do this. He was ambitious to become an artist.

The committee decided to adopt the case and, with his employer's cooperation, to send him to yet another evening art school to qualify him either for the Royal Academy or the Slade. But the affair dragged on, even after Frank Emanuel had been brought in as Rosenberg's 'case-guardian'. Then, at the beginning of 1911, when the committee finally received a response from Carl Hentschel, it was to the effect that 'this youth', whose talents he believed 'were being practically wasted' in photo-engraving, 'had been suddenly dismissed from this firm'.[79] Jobless, and still without the coveted JEAS grant, Rosenberg faced a bleak future in January 1911. Yet it was the start of a miraculous year for him, and a turning-point in his fortunes both as a poet and as a painter.

Chapter 5

The Whitechapel Group

---

*Youth is still childhood. When we cast off every cloudy vesture
and our thoughts are clear and mature; when every act is a
conscious thought, every thought an attempt to arrest feelings;
our feelings strong and overwhelming, our sensitiveness
awakened by insignificant things in life ... When the skies
race tumultuously with our blood and the earth shines and
laughs, when our blood hangs suspended at the rustling of a
dress ... Our vanity loves to subdue – battle, aggressive ...
How we despise those older and duller – we want life, newness,
excitement.*

– Prose fragment by IR[1]

Rosenberg's chance meeting with Joseph Leftwich and Stephen
Winsten on Monday 2 January 1911 changed, however slightly, the
course of history, both his own and others'. Even without the detailed
diary account Leftwich wrote, setting out more clearly than anyone
before or after him Rosenberg's character with all its contradictions,
it would have been an important moment. For in becoming friends
with the aspiring authors Leftwich, Winsten and the third member
of their little circle, John Rodker, Rosenberg was creating a bridge
between the artists and writers of Whitechapel. In his dual role as
both painter and poet he became in effect a catalyst for the Whitechapel Group, which had existed previously only in separate cliques.

The Whitechapel Group, like its predecessors the Pre-Raphaelites,
and near-contemporaries the Bloomsbury Group, was a coterie that
straddled the arts. As well as writers and painters, both the Whitechapel and the Bloomsbury Group would also include a publisher
and a dancer as they developed, and were distinguished from the
Pre-Raphaelites in yet another way: they had no common artistic
creed, though both groups tended towards Modernism.[2] Quentin
Bell's statement about Bloomsbury could equally well have been
written of the Whitechapel Group:

It had no form of membership, no rules, no leaders ... it can hardly be said to have had any common ideas about art, literature or politics, and although it had a common attitude to life and was united by friendships, it was as amorphous a body as a group of friends can be.[3]

United not just by friendship but by a love of the arts and a reverence for beauty, the main purpose and activity of both Blooms-bury and Whitechapel as groups was the interchange of ideas. Though Rosenberg and his friends were not quite as frank as Bloomsbury, particularly in relation to sex, it is evident from Left-wich's diary that they found support in talking about their private lives as well as their artistic aims. 'We were all dreamers,' wrote Emanuel Litvinoff, attempting to pinpoint what brought him and his fellow East Enders together, 'each convinced it was his destiny to grow rich or famous, or change the world into a marvellous place of freedom and justice.'[4]

And just as Bloomsbury did not acquire its full flavour until the young men who met in Cambridge in 1899 – Lytton Strachey, Leonard Woolf, Clive Bell, Saxon Sydney Turner and Thoby Stephen – had joined Thoby's sisters, the writer Virginia and the painter Vanessa, in London in 1904, so the Whitechapel Group became most truly itself when complemented by the artist Clara Birnberg and the dancer and actress Sonia Cohen. In addition, when the Great War came both groups would be predominantly pacifist.

It is in its differences from Bloomsbury, however, that the character of the Whitechapel Group most fully emerges. Although both were identified by their whereabouts in London, those locations presented a stark contrast socially. To at least one contemporary critic 'art like life [was] more exciting' in the East End 'than in Piccadilly'.[5] But to Rosenberg and his East End friends the West End of London implied a far more privileged existence, and for the majority of Bloomsberries this held true. Most of them had been educated at public school or by private tutors before proceeding (if male) to Cambridge, lived on private incomes and inhabited pleasant, spa-cious houses in garden squares. Only one member, Leonard Woolf, was Jewish and the group was on the whole anti-Semitic. By contrast the Whitechapel Group, all Jewish, came from far poorer backgrounds, had been educated at Board Schools and forced to work long hours at menial jobs. Unable to offer each other much in the way of hospitality, they met in public places – the Whitechapel Library and Art Gallery, Toynbee Hall, the South Place Ethical Society (which later became Conway Hall), and on public holidays the National Gallery and British Museum.

When Rosenberg did take Leftwich, Winsten and Rodker home to see his paintings and drawings, even Leftwich was shocked by the squalor of his surroundings: 'It is hardly an artist's home.'[6] Later, the more socially mobile of the group would form links with Bloomsbury, but in 1911, with the exception of Gertler, their worlds were quite separate, almost reverse images of each other. While the Bloomsbury Group held 'civilized' luncheons, dinners and evening 'At Homes' in Gordon Square, the Whitechapel boys walked the streets, which were free.

It was on one such occasion that Leftwich encountered Rosenberg:

I first met Rosenberg along the stretch of road that leads from Whitechapel, which was our home, to the by-day teeming and by-night deserted Piazza of the Bank of England and then further to the Thames Embankment or round home again by the Tower of London and the Dockyard walls – the nightly promenade of my boyhood coterie and of other closely-knit groups of Whitechapel youths, though not all bound by our own interests – many of them frankly engaged in the adolescent flirtation that gave the promenade its name of 'Monkeys' Parade'.[7]

Rosenberg is introduced to Leftwich by Winsten, whom he has met a few days previously, and immediately starts to talk to them about Poetry (Leftwich's capital 'P'). He then 'pulls a bundle of odd scraps of paper out of his pocket and reads [them] his poems under a lamppost'.[8] They both recognize an unusual gift as well as a kindred spirit. 'The fellow writes good poetry' Leftwich concludes.[9] There is no doubt in his mind that it is 'real' poetry and Rosenberg a 'genius', nor in Winsten's, who is 'awed' by Rosenberg yet at the same time 'depressed' by him 'like something heavy and solemn'.[10] Their only doubt, as they invite the 'very self-absorbed' young man to meet them again, is whether he is 'capable of friendship'. Leftwich who, as a diarist, is somewhere between Pepys and Pooter, with a dash of Boswell thrown in, brings out the striking contrast between Rosenberg's unprepossessing appearance and manner ('short and awkward', 'very plain', 'he stutters and his voice is monotonous') and his poetry. Two poems in particular impress Leftwich, the first, 'In the Workshop', because in January 1911 he, too, is working long hours in poor conditions, the other, 'A Ballad of Time, Life and Memory', because of its elaborate language and allegory.

Rodker's approval is quickly won – he too finds Rosenberg 'remarkable'[11] – and Rosenberg becomes a member of the little group. But it is clear from Leftwich's detailed account of the year which follows that Rosenberg remains always an outsider, too bound up in his own creative efforts to be close to anyone for long. When, after a month of meeting them sporadically, he tells the trio that 'he is glad he has gained [them] as friends' and that 'he has never been in close contact before with boys of his own age',[12] it is a rare burst of confidentiality. But it is also a puzzling contradiction of Bomberg's vivid memories of Rosenberg's intimate friendship with Mitchell and himself from at least 1907 onwards. Yet by February 1911 Rosenberg is insisting – convincingly as far as Leftwich is concerned – that 'his only really intimate friend for a very long time has been Amshewitz'.[13] Did he truly believe that? Or was it a way of ingratiating himself with his new friends? Or did he genuinely see himself as essentially isolated? The answer may lie in that extreme self-absorption noted by Leftwich: because Amshewitz had recently painted his portrait and was encouraging him to paint his self-portrait for the Royal Academy Summer Show, he may have been the only person impinging on Rosenberg's consciousness at that time. Helpful as Amshewitz was, however, he was hardly an 'intimate' friend. Nor would Rosenberg become very close to his three new acquaintances, though they each played a part in his development during this crucial year of his life.

Jacob Leftwich (born 'Lefkovitz') was eighteen when he met the twenty-year-old Rosenberg, a small, dark, serious young man in glasses. Born in Holland to Polish Jews, Leftwich had lived in Cologne until his parents moved him to London when he was seven.

An only child, he nevertheless had had to leave school at fourteen to help support the household and had been in a number of menial jobs since then, his current one in a furrier's sweatshop. He was determined to be a writer and his efforts at self-education, which included the conscientious keeping of a diary and joint attempts at essay- and novel-writing with Winsten and Rodker, were to encourage Rosenberg, who joined in with group projects, including the joint novel and an essay 'On a Door Knocker'.[14]

Leftwich's love of literature included drama. He had no difficulty in persuading Rosenberg, who had been introduced to West End theatre as a child by Minnie, to accompany him on several occasions to plays. Once they saw Laurence Irving in an adaptation of Dostoevsky's *Crime and Punishment (An Unwritten Law)*, and although Rosenberg did not go with him to see Maeterlinck's *The Blue Bird*, which was playing in London throughout 1911, Leftwich's admiration for the Belgian dramatist and poet almost certainly influenced his friend, who would later argue that Maeterlinck was superior to Donne, seeing his 'Orison' as 'a most trembling fragile moan of astonishing beauty'.[15] Rosenberg's decision to write plays of his own later on may have been partly prompted by Leftwich's enthusiasm for the genre.

Leftwich had already rejected his parents' orthodoxy by 1911. Like Rosenberg he had been exposed in Stepney to the strong Eastern European revolutionary tradition among the immigrant intelligentsia and thought of himself primarily as a socialist.[16] Though almost as quickly disillusioned by organized politics as Rosenberg, he remained passionately interested in political questions, which he debated endlessly with his friends on their nightly walks. In a time of growing social unrest, there was a great deal to discuss: the hunger marches of the previous year (on one of which Leftwich had first met Winsten); the infamous Sidney Street siege, which occurred almost on their doorstep the day after Rosenberg joined the group; the hotly fought Bethnal Green by-election of July 1911; the epidemic of strikes that broke out in August, involving at least 200,000 dockers, bus-drivers, railwaymen and other vital workers; the anti-Jewish riots in Wales that same month; and the strike of 12,000 taxi-drivers in November. Even the schoolchildren went on strike in 1911.

By 19 September it would seem to Leftwich that there was: 'Revolt abroad. Rebellion everywhere. Strikes, Revolutions ... '[17]

Rosenberg's reaction to the political situation was less direct than his new 'friends''. Leftwich could not remember him once speaking at a public meeting, 'yet the rest of us always did' he remembered.[18] But then, Leftwich argued, Rosenberg was 'not a speaker at all, he was a mumbler, a fumbler and he needed poetry to articulate himself'.[19] Proof that Rosenberg was infected by the group's political concerns emerged indirectly in 1911 in his sonnet 'An Incitement to Action', which he sent to the *Young Worker* magazine. He also started another called 'The City of All Dreams'. Though neither has survived, both were clearly polemical, written under the influence of his little circle's intoxicating midnight debates. Significantly it was Leftwich to whom Rosenberg first showed these poems on 12 March 1911.[20] It was Leftwich, too, who recorded Rosenberg's decision to rejoin the Young Socialist League three weeks later.

When Leftwich himself decided to rejoin the Young Socialist League later still in July, it was largely in the hope that socialism would help fight anti-Semitism. For despite his rejection of his parents' orthodoxy, he continued to identify first and foremost with Jewishness, unlike Rodker and Winsten, who would try to leave their backgrounds behind them. Leftwich, who wrote Yiddish as well as speaking it fluently, was interested in Yiddish theatre and would later introduce Rosenberg to a circle of Yiddish poets. Under Rosenberg's influence he began to write English verse,[21] but he would make his name not as an English poet but as a translator and anthologist of Yiddish literature. He would, however, always remain proud that his poem on Rosenberg, 'Killed in Action', would be mistaken for one of Rosenberg's own.[22]

Despite a certain prudishness, lack of humour and slightly self-righteous attitude towards human frailties, Rosenberg found Leftwich a good friend. He was happy to supply 'Lines Written in an Album to J.L.', a romantic piece of occasional verse which shows not just his increasing assurance as a poet but also the lingering influence of one of Leftwich's own favourites, Swinburne. It is thanks to Leftwich that we know that Rosenberg was still reading Keats and Shelley in 1911 and was beginning to admire Dante Gabriel

Rossetti, who would influence his work heavily for the next few years. His diary is full of such information on Rosenberg's development as a poet, as well as his character. On one occasion, for instance, Leftwich records that while he and Rodker passed Winsten's bowler hat to each other to punish him for sneering at their hatlessness, Rosenberg 'took no part at all in our little dispute':

He shuffled along very taciturn at one side, talking about Rossetti's letters and Keats and Shelley. He mumbles his words very curiously. Poor Rosenberg! His people are very unsympathetic to him. They insist on treating him as a little out of his mind. They consider him as an invalid, somewhat affected mentally. But he goes on in his own way, running away to the libraries whenever he can, to read poetry and the lives of the poets, their letters, their essays on how to write poetry, their theories of what poetry should be and do – everything he can find about poets and poetry. Poetry is his obsession – not literature, but essentially distinctively poetry. In novels, in drama – other than poetic drama, in which he is concerned with the poetry, and with the drama only as the vehicle for poetic expression – he says that his taste is very poor and he enjoys boys' magazines and his sisters' novelettes. It is only in poetry that he feels himself worth something.[23]

As Leftwich concluded, Rosenberg's 'strange awkward earnestness and single-mindedness' had its effect on him, as it had on the poet's family. But rather than dismissing him as mad, as Rosenberg implies, his family could hardly have been more supportive of his artistic aspirations; by this time possibly made overconfident by his new friend's belief in his 'genius', he had already been discharged from Hentschel's and they are supporting him fully. His claims smack of self-pity but may simply have arisen from unawareness of anything except his work.[24]

Leftwich also enables his reader to follow Rosenberg's development as an artist in 1911. When Rosenberg takes his friends home to see paintings and drawings, most now lost, Leftwich gives a careful description of them:

There is ... a painting of himself – a self-portrait and an excellent likeness.[25] His drawings are of women mainly, big heavy women with very plain features – all the faces are alike – almost one face in all of them and that a heavy, coarse, ugly face. There are also a few drawings of old men – with heavy, puffed faces and bald heads. All the drawings are in carbon [charcoal?] or red chalk. There is one drawing which I liked best; he calls it 'Dreams'. It represents a young girl sitting back apparently in deep reverie. It is simply drawn, with few lines, hardly any masses ... It is very striking ... He says he is going to write a few lines of poetry to accompany it ... [26]

It is thanks also to Leftwich that we know that Rosenberg was painting another self-portrait in February 1911 to submit to the Royal Academy, and that in trying to follow Amshewitz's advice he spoilt it. Once again Leftwich finds it an 'excellent likeness', noting that the painting is 'bold and outstanding':

The face is in shadow. The pose is very striking. It is a three-quarter length – quite a big canvas. He is standing up, wearing his overcoat with the collar turned up and his huge broad-brimmed Tyrolean hat on his head.[27]

The hat, 'violently green' apparently, had replaced Rosenberg's bowler as a sign of his emancipation from Hentschel's and his complete dedication to the arts. (The otherwise rather shy Amshewitz wore a flamboyant sombrero.) Such details bring Rosenberg vividly to life, and it seems appropriate that, when Leftwich is remembered in English literature at all, it is for his friendship with Rosenberg, his 1911 diary in particular.[28]

Leftwich had been introduced to Rosenberg by Stephen Winsten (still 'Samuel Weinstein' in 1911, nicknamed 'Simy'), who was the first to declare Rosenberg a genius. His awe of Rosenberg may partly account for the lack of closeness between the two. Of Russian-Jewish origin, Winsten had been born in England several years after Rosenberg. A student teacher at Isaac's brother's school in Dempsey Street by 1911, he was preparing to go to teacher-training college. His expectations were, therefore, less bleak than those of either

Leftwich or Rosenberg, but this appears to have made him over-confident and rather domineering. Even the charitable Leftwich, to whom he was closest, regretted 'Simy's' constant sneering, especially at Rodker whom he taunted continually. Small and dark like Leftwich but more solidly built, he belonged, Leftwich noted, to 'the swarthy Jews, yet hardly the Eastern Jews; he is too restrained for their passionate thought.[29] His deliberateness, slowness and lack of 'easy brilliancy' sometimes gave the impression of flat-footedness, Leftwich conceded, but loyally attributed these qualities to his scholarliness. Winsten's repeated failure to get a grant from the Jewish Education Aid Society, however, suggests that his was not an outstanding talent. His repeated attacks on the more gifted Rodker probably stemmed from jealousy and occasionally included the still more talented Rosenberg. Winsten's 'nasty foolish remarks' about Rosenberg's pictures, which Leftwich thought deliberately provocative, may also help to explain the lack of intimacy between the two.

The only real connection between Winsten and Rosenberg in 1911 was their decision to rejoin the Young Socialist League together. 'Simy' came from a highly political family; the eldest Winsten had been leader of the Bund (the Jewish Social Democratic Party) in Russia and had Marxist sympathies, which his son shared.[30] (His most violent arguments with Rodker would concern politics.) Since Rosenberg quickly lost interest in the subject in any formal sense, their initial bond did not last. Nor did their friendship, though it survived long enough for Rosenberg to paint Winsten's future wife, Clara Birnberg, in 1915.[31]

Winsten, who went on to write poetry of his own and to become a friend and biographer of George Bernard Shaw, was proud of having known Rosenberg, describing him fulsomely after his death as 'cultured in his conversation, a very encyclopaedia of literary knowledge, an artist of ability, a poet of rich and profound imagery, a gentleman in the best sense of the word'.[32] His description of the 'frank conversation' and 'liberation of the spirit' which the four of them enjoyed in 1911 shows at least one way in which being a member of this group affected Rosenberg:

My friend became quite voluble. See those young people walking round the gloomy gas-lit streets, talking quietly, laughing loudly at a sudden epigram, stopping suspiciously under a lamppost while one fumbled in all his pockets for his latest poem. He read and they criticised, and then they returned to their unsympathetic homes to write a little more while sleep could be conquered. There was a club [Toynbee Hall] which drew them together. An artist or critic would sometimes lecture, and he little knew that his ideas were discussed after the meeting in long walks. Epping Forest was less than ten miles away, splendid for an all-night walk, an all-night talk on life and death, youth and love.[33]

These four young men seem to have been at their closest on such marathon walks to Epping Forest – '*our* Epping Forest' as Leftwich called it.[34] On one occasion Rosenberg took his oils and painted the bridge over the river at Chingford. But it was on this walk that 'Simy' made his sneering remarks about Rosenberg's picture, causing him to go home separately with Rodker.

Leftwich's descriptions of 'Jimmy', as Rodker was known to friends (he had dropped 'Simon' and replaced it with the less Jewish 'John'), reveals his own preference for the more 'solid' Winsten. Though ostensibly of very similar background – born in Manchester in 1894 to Polish-Jewish parents and brought to the East End at the age of six – Rodker and his family seemed disturbingly irregular to Leftwich's conservative mind. There was a rumour of mental instability in the mother and Rodker's stepmother cared little for domestic duties, lending a rather bohemian air to the household. In addition Rodker's father, a skilled corset-maker, who had a shop in the Mile End Road, where the family lived, and two others in Hackney, earned more money than most in the area, so that 'Jimmy' was able to contemplate a university education, though he was working as a clerk in the Civil Service in 1911. He was also much taller than the rest of the group, a fact that seems to have irritated Leftwich more even than his unconventional approach to life. After describing Rodker as 'superficial', Leftwich continues in his diary:

He is tall and thin like a garden-hose and squirts out a lot of water. His hair is straw-coloured and neutral. His complexion is pale and pasty and he is always punning and making brilliant remarks – but there is nothing solid in anything he says – beautifully coloured bubbles. His phrases move round, whirl round rather effectively, but they get nowhere ... I think he is weak and easily influenced by anything which appears effective. He loves razzle and effect. He should make a good tinsel and paste actor. He is a poseur.[35]

Whether Rodker had already taken to wearing one gold earring, larger reputedly than that worn by the flamboyant Ezra Pound, is not noted, but it may explain Leftwich's term 'poseur'.

Leftwich was also highly disapproving of what he considered Rodker's lax attitude towards sexual morality, though he suspected that 'Jimmy' was as innocent of sexual experience as he believed Winsten and Rosenberg to be. It was inevitable that, when Winsten started to pick quarrels with Rodker regularly, Leftwich would, however reluctantly, side with Winsten. The effect on Rosenberg seems to have been to draw him closer to Rodker. As Leftwich noted, while he and Simy took walks together in Victoria Park, Rosenberg would often be closeted with Jimmy. On one occasion, calling at Rodker's house for him, he found Rosenberg drawing him, another picture unfortunately lost, though a superb oil painting of Rodker by Bomberg has survived.[36]

Leftwich had wondered at first what Jimmy would think of Rosenberg, but it is clear that Rodker recognized his genius as much if not more than his friends, and he was the most qualified of the three to appreciate Rosenberg both as a poet and a painter. Possessed of what his daughter remembers as 'an incredible feel for the English language',[37] an adventurous character and a growing interest in art and all 'New Art' movements, he understood Rosenberg's aims possibly more clearly than Rosenberg did. Rodker would himself go on to write Modernist verse and prose. After starting his own small press he would publish work by many of the best-known names in Modernism, including Ezra Pound, T.S. Eliot, James Joyce, Wyndham Lewis, Henri Gaudier-Brzeska and Edward Wadsworth.[38] Pound believed that the young Jewish boy – Rodker was only sixteen when he met Rosenberg in 1911 and not much older when he got to know Pound – had 'more invention and guts' than many of his contemporaries and would go further.[39] In this and a number of other ways he resembled Bomberg. Both had what one friend called an 'electrical quality';[40] both were daring experimentalists, risking security and a safe life for the sake of their artistic vision; and neither would be very successful in a worldly sense. (It seems appropriate that when Rodker published his first book, *Poems*, in 1914 he should ask Bomberg to design its cover.) Rodker would die at sixty-one a 'disappointed man', according to his daughter, who suggests that this was because Gertler and Rosenberg, and to some extent Bomberg, had been recognized by then whilst he felt he had not. Significantly, Rodker, Bomberg and Gertler would be the only members of the Whitechapel Group in whom Rosenberg remained interested after the war started.

Rodker had already begun writing verse by the time he met Rosenberg, but he was encouraged to increase his efforts by Isaac's example. His reasons for choosing poetry may throw light on Rosenberg's own compulsion towards it: 'When I wrote poetry,' he noted in his introduction to his *Collected Poems* (1930), 'I was, as it were, hanging in the void, and these poems [i.e. between 1912 and 1925] are my effort to establish contact.'[41] The rootlessness to which Rodker alludes was something Rosenberg, too, undoubtedly experienced and his poetic imagery is full of it, as Jon Silkin has pointed out, most memorably in the reference to Absalom hanging by his hair.[42] Whilst it reflected the situation of many of their Jewish contemporaries, it was not true of them all. Leftwich and Winsten, for all their rejection of orthodoxy, were still rooted in Jewishness in 1911. Rosenberg and Rodker, however, had already started to move away into a different cultural world. And it would be Rodker who introduced Rosenberg to, for instance, a more cosmopolitan circle of writers at Harold Monro's West End 'Poetry Bookshop'.[43] Rodker also suggested he read T.S. Eliot and other Modernist poets. (Rosenberg would write to Rodker a month before he died: 'I'd like to read Elliott's [*sic*] work but I hardly get a chance to read letters sent to me.')[44]

Leftwich believed that it was Rosenberg who influenced Rodker, particularly in his 'love of [the] macabre'.[45] He found Rodker's work 'unhealthy', especially his fascination with prostitutes, about which Rosenberg had already written in 'A Ballad of Whitechapel'. Rodker's association of the morbid and the erotic is a feature of his early work and not unlike Rosenberg's own later exploration of it in, for instance, 'Daughters of War'. These concurrences may simply be a case of two like-minded young men developing along similar lines, but there is no mistaking the importance of Rodker's personal intervention on Rosenberg's behalf during the years that followed their meeting. His close friendship with Pound makes him the most likely person to have interested Pound seriously in Rosenberg's work, though it was Yeats who first drew Pound's attention to his verse. And when Pound, as London literary scout for Harriet Monroe's *Poetry* magazine in Chicago, sent some of Rosenberg's poems to her it was probably at Rodker's urging that he suggested she publish them, albeit in a typically laconic fashion, as I have shown:

> I think you may as well give this poor devil a show ... I think you
> might do half a page review of his book [i.e. *Youth*], and that he is
> worth a page for verse ... He has something in him, horribly rough
> but then 'Stepney, East' ... We ought to have a real burglar ... ma
> che !!![46]

Later still Rodker himself would send two of Rosenberg's poems to Monroe and, when she appeared to be dragging her feet over her promise to publish one of them, would write again to remind her of her commitment. His belief in Rosenberg would also lead indirectly to Binyon and Bottomley's first edition of Rosenberg's work in 1922.[47]

It was therefore a fruitful friendship that grew up between Rodker and Rosenberg at a crucial stage in the latter's poetic development, one that opened his mind to experiment in literature as Bomberg's theories would fail to do in art. This may be because Rosenberg's visual awareness and training began far earlier than his linguistic one: his attitude towards language is demonstrably less academic than towards art. His friendship with Rodker, together with Leftwich and Winsten, certainly increased his confidence as a poet. Leftwich, who frequently comments in his diary on Rosenberg's shyness socially, also describes several occasions when he spontaneously read his poems out loud to virtual strangers as though he was beginning to have real faith in his work. This increased confidence as a poet is apparent in the poems written during this period, which form a significant part of his first publication, *Night and Day* (1912). Though still derivative, with Rossetti joining Keats and Shelley as the main influences, Rosenberg's own voice is now sometimes heard.

The least individual of the pieces, not surprisingly, are the group of occasional verses written by Rosenberg for his growing circle of friends: the Swinburnian 'Lines Written in an Album to J[oseph] L[eftwich]' the Keatsian sonnet 'To J.H. Amschewitz' and a few other polite exercises written almost certainly to please an important new patron he met in 1911, Mrs Henrietta Löwy ('To Mr and Mrs Löwy on Their Wedding Anniversary', 'Birthday Song' and 'Summer in Winter').[48]

The last three of these poems reveal the growing influence of his latest 'ideal',[49] Rossetti, who seemed to him, especially in 'Monochord' and 'The Song of the Bower', the 'keynote' in contemporary verse: 'in the first all poignancy – a richness and variety, a purity of imagination – a truth, far beyond wit, or thought'.[50] Rossetti's painter's eye for visual detail in his poetry, his frequent use of personification, his heightened awareness of death and his idealization of the beloved all reinforce aspects of the Romantic poets which had attracted Rosenberg originally. His conclusion to his fragment on Rossetti shows how he views his role as a poet by 1911 and helps to explain why Leftwich thought some of his work 'macabre' at this time. Referring to the 'poets who delight in the morbid' (already quoted), Rosenberg continues: 'The poet is not so because he is weak but because he is perverse. His life is a paradox – he does not live if what other men do is life. This poet would make a song out of sorrow, and find in a tear a jewel of delight.'

Rosenberg's earlier admiration for Francis Thompson and Verlaine, together with his recent introduction to the verse of Edgar Allan Poe, made such a conclusion all but inevitable for him. It also throws light on one other occasional poem he wrote in 1911, 'In the Heart of the Forest', written for Amshewitz's sister, which otherwise seems an odd choice for a young lady's autograph album, particularly since it was written within what Leftwich described as 'a space shaped like a tombstone'.[51] The first of its three stanzas gives the flavour of the whole:

> In the heart of the forest,
> The shuddering forest,
> The moaning and sobbing
> Sad shuddering forest.—
> The dark and the dismal
> Persistent sad sobbing
> Throughout the weird forest.[52]

Apart from its autobiographical interest – it sounds similar to a passage from Leftwich's diary describing a visit to Epping Forest[53] – this fascination with the 'perverse' anticipates an important facet of Rosenberg's later poetry, the grotesque underbelly of life.

His morbid vein is evident in the three other poems known to have been written this year, 'The Dead Past', 'My Days' and 'The World Rumbles By Me'. Part of the pessimism in them may have been a natural reaction to his situation in the first half of 1911. While he had longed to leave Hentschel's, his sudden dismissal in mid-January 1911 left him jobless and dependent on his family, which worried him greatly. His first reaction had been jubilant and upbeat. He wrote to Miss Seaton:

> Congratulate me, I've cleared out of the [bloody] shop, I hope for good and all. I'm free – free to do anything, hang myself or anything except work. ... I'm very optimistic, now that I don't know what to do, and everything seems topsy-turvy.[54]

But reality quickly intervened. Soon afterwards he wrote to Miss Seaton again:

> I'm out of work. I doubt if I feel the better for it, much as the work was distasteful, though I expect it's the hankering thought of the consequences, pecuniary, etc., that bothers me ... all one's thoughts seem to resolve round to one point – death.[55]

Busy with his new friends, buoyed up by their belief in his 'genius', he had perhaps half-invited his dismissal, but the consequences depressed him greatly. His efforts to get a job in advertising, or with the greeting-card magnate Sir Adolph Tuck, increased his desperation and he turned once again to Zangwill. But even Zangwill, who was clearly much readier to help than Bomberg's negative report of his response to Rosenberg's earlier letter suggests, failed to change his friend Hentschel's mind, despite his persuasiveness:

> Elm Bank, Little Baddow, Essex
> Aug. 22/11
>
> Dear Hentschel,
>
> If you recognize the enclosed pencil-sketch it will be a proof of the artistic powers of the sketcher – a young man who claims to have been apprenticed to you for five years and then dismissed 'for slackness' – yours, I presume, not his own.
>
> This Isaac Rosenberg of 159, Oxford Street, Mile End, E. now finds it difficult to get work and has people dependent on him. He has sent me a batch of compositions in prose and verse, besides his sketch, all showing artistic faculty, so that he ought to be more valuable in your work than the average apprentice. As he has appealed to me, may I take the liberty of asking you whether there is any chance of your employing him again. Of course I hope you can, unless there are circumstances which he has not divulged to me.
>
> With kind regards to yourself and Mrs Hentschel – I meet Olga sometimes in her new role –
>
> Yours sincerely,
> Israel Zangwill
> P.S. please return the sketch.

Regret is the keynote of 'The Dead Past', nostalgia for his 'life's dead Springtime',[56] which Isaac though not his family remembered himself as experiencing. Like Browning's thrush he longs to 'recapture' that 'first fine careless rapture', yet he also needs to believe that the greater awareness age brings is preferable, despite the suffering:

You too are dead, the shining face that laughed and wept without
    thought
Uttered the words of the heart, wept or leapt as was right.
O were you taken to heaven by God in a whirlwind caught,
I do not know yours was best, you not conscious of your delight.[57]

However clichéd 'The Dead Past' is in parts, it was probably a
genuine expression of Rosenberg's feelings for most of 1911 and not
simply a poetic exercise. His state of mind is suggested most forcibly
in an additional verse cancelled perhaps precisely because it was too
personal:

I in this workaday world, little joy do I know—
Books, pictures and sometimes friends, a girl's sweet sight and voice
Many sorrows have I, but each pleasure or pain is a throe
I can witness my own delight.[58]

A similar sense of someone fluctuating between delight and
despair is conveyed in 'My Days' and 'The World Rumbles By Me',
both of which show a new influence at work in his verse. 'My Days',
with its particular take on the sonnet and its theme of time versus
the immortality of art, confirms what Leftwich noted – Rosenberg's
great admiration in 1911 for Shakespeare, whom he echoes very
clearly in his concluding couplet:

They only live who have not lived in vain,
For in their works their life returns again.[59]

'The World Rumbles By Me' suggests that Rosenberg was also
reading Yeats, in particular his 'rose' poems. Though Yeats's Modernist experiments were still relatively unknown in 1911, Rodker
might have alerted Rosenberg to them.[60] Rosenberg certainly knew
Yeats's early Pre-Raphaelitish work, as several poems of this period
reveal, the last line of 'Nocturne', for instance, containing both words
and imagery from 'The Lake Isle of Innisfree': 'Dropping from the
night's blue walls in endless veils of loveliness'.[61]

The most interesting poems of 1911, however, are a series of love lyrics written to a young woman whom Rosenberg met this year, since it is in these that his own voice emerges most clearly.

Chapter 6

'Lady, You Are My God': Romance, Frustration and Fulfilment

1911

> *He was an artist and a dreamer. . . . But day after day of unrequited endeavour, of struggle and privation, brought depression, and in the heaviness of his spirit the futility of existence was made manifest to him. Often inspiration was dead within, and all his aspirations and ideals seemed to mock at his hollow yearning. In his social and spiritual isolation, in his utter desolation he felt as if he was God's castaway, out of harmony with the universe, a blot upon the scheme of humanity. Life appeared so chaotic, so haphazard, so apathetic – O! it was miserable. He – a spark struck from God's anvil, he – who could clasp the Heavens with his spirit – to whom Beauty had revealed herself in all her radiances – and to what end? What purpose was there in such wasted striving – and supposing success did come would it be sufficient recompense for the wasted life and youth, the starved years – the hopelessness of the barren Now?*
>
> – Isaac Rosenberg, 'Rudolph'[1]

It may have been Sonia Cohen, as she was called, who inspired the final sentence in this attempt to define the poet's role some time during 1911: 'Love is his theme, life is the background, and the beauty of woman stands to him as the manifestation of the beauty of spiritual nature and all outer aspects of the workings of nature.'[2]

Sonia's background was even more deprived than his own. Her parents were Russian Jews and 'old-time revolutionaries', to use her own phrase.[3] When her father died in her second year her mother, who never learnt to speak English, was unable to cope with both Sonia and her younger brother, and Sonia had been taken into care at the age of five. Sent to a Home for Christianizing the Jews, she remained there until leaving school at fourteen. While her education had been reasonably good, fostering in her, for instance, a great love of poetry, it had left her, in her own words, 'extraordinarily innocent about life',[4] also virtually unqualified. When she first met Isaac she was working long hours in a dressmaker's sweatshop but struggling to escape the grimness of her situation. When work ended she would go to the reference room of the Whitechapel Library, determined to qualify herself for something better. It was there, in the spring of 1911, that she first met Rosenberg. He had come, as usual, with Bomberg for a little unorthodox study of their own. A naive girl in her mid-teens, Sonia had been deeply struck by this meeting, in particular the ingenuity of their advances. Though she mistook Rosenberg's newly acquired dark-green hat for black, her recall of detail is otherwise entirely convincing and brings the aspiring artist, Rosenberg, and the recently enrolled Slade student, Bomberg, vividly to life:

... both ... wore large-brimmed black hats and neither had the bow or tie usual with this particular headgear. In fact the taller of the two [Bomberg] wore an apple-green or sometimes a yellow tie which invariably had a red stone pinned onto it; and his companion [Rosenberg], he of the slow upturned smile, favoured pink ties.[5] This last mentioned young man once had a whole neckcloth of pink.[6] Seldom, if indeed ever, did they as much as glance at the books forced upon them by library regulations. Plodding study from indexes and text-books or quotation copying into blue-lined notebooks was not for them. They made no attempt to conceal the fact that the plodders themselves were the material for their study.

Before they entered the reference library, they peered through the glass panes of the entrance and having made a preliminary survey of the objects seated at the long polished table, he of the yellow and apple-green tie pushed the door, plunged through the opening and then stood examining the subject matter that so obligingly was present for his purpose. If he approved of what he saw, with a large swoop he removed his black hat and placed it on the available table space before him, summoned his companion with a circular 'all's well' signal.

The notice 'Silence please' was not for them, at least not for the young man who favoured yellow and apple-green ties. He discussed this one and that among us, while his friend who seldom initiated conversation, smiled or listened with his head lowered and tucked down inwards as if he wished to prevent what he had in his head escaping. At last they sat. And after further scrutiny of the figures before them, each lifted a pencil or crayon and, having levelled it against his nose or contracted eye muscles, first one young man and then the other lowered a right hand and swished it in curves, verticals and diagonals across large sheets of paper they had brought with them.[7]

Though neither Bomberg nor Rosenberg wore the floppy black satin cravats Sonia expected of artists, she quickly realized that both of them were drawing her. She was probably not prepared, therefore, for the wooing of her that followed to take poetic form:

Soon it became their habit to sit directly opposite my table and I was made very aware of being the subject of whispered comments of the one and of the smiles these provoked in the other. The smiles of this young man in pink ties were cautious. They spread slowly from eyes that were aslant to his full upturned lips. Sometimes he smiled as if in spite of himself and from a cause secret to him alone. The slips of paper the taller of the two laid in front of me I allowed, at first, to remain on the spot where he had placed them and when he put them on the very page – often on the very paragraphs – I was reading, I thrust them aside with a gesture I considered elegantly scornful.

Then one evening, having surreptitiously glanced sideways, I noted that not only were the terms of address most gratifying but that the writing itself was in poetry which of course elevated the communications to a place too high for me to ignore. Isaac Rosenberg's 'Lady, You Are My God' was one of these poems ...[8]

'Lady, You Are My God', which Bomberg ordered Rosenberg to write on his behalf, appears to have been the duo's first offering, an elaborate and witty compliment that suggests the influence of

Elizabethan and Jacobean poets. Rosenberg may not have been so altruistic in writing it as Bomberg imagined:

> Lady, you are my God—
> Lady, you are my heaven.
>
> If I am your God
> Labour for your heaven.
>
> Lady you are my God,
> And shall not love win heaven?
>
> If love made me God
> Deeds must win my heaven.
>
> If my love made you God,
> What more can I for heaven?[9]

An early anticipation of Rosenberg's later preoccupation with a Female God, this poem hints that Rosenberg himself was powerfully attracted to Sonia, which she confirmed. She also remembered that 'Lady, You Are My God' was one of a number of poems written to her by Rosenberg, ostensibly on Bomberg's behalf. One which neither she nor Leftwich (who also recalled the situation) mentioned but which Sonia almost certainly inspired is 'So Innocent You Spread Your Net', possibly even 'The Nun'. 'I was unaware of sex in any way' Sonia claimed,[10] partly to explain her terror when Bomberg, following up in a more practical fashion on Rosenberg's poems, tried to seduce her. Though Sonia supposed that 'in his way [Bomberg] was in love with [her]', she found it 'all horrible'.[11] She preferred the romantic idealization of love presented in Rosenberg's verses and his far more 'diffident' approach.[12] She knew from Bomberg that Isaac was attracted to her: 'He used to have this look when he came to see me when I was alone.'[13] They started to take long walks together, stopping in doorways when it grew cold, and talking endlessly. Sometimes they visited the Tate, where Rosenberg taught her to love Blake. Sometimes she was invited to his house, a sure sign of his commitment, she felt, when she caught the look in his mother's eye. Strolling among the spring flowers in Kensington Gardens, there was 'even a first kiss in the April sunlight'.[14] That, according to Sonia, was the full extent of their physical relationship. Isaac continued to place her on a pedestal and kneel at her feet. Whether it was shyness or, as Sonia suspected, 'high-mindedness' that prevented him attempting like Bomberg to seduce her, she could not say, but she believed that the result was 'a lot of suppression'.[15] Yet his poetry, she observed, was so 'voluptuous'.[16]

There is certainly evidence of a conflict between physical and spiritual love in the poetry of this period. 'Lady, You Are My God' and 'So Innocent You Spread Your Net' are not alone in their exploration of female magnetism and power. Images of entrapment dominate the love poetry of 1911 and early 1912: the cage and prison bars of 'The Cage', the chains and lock of 'The Key of the Gates of Heaven', the tomb of 'Now the Spirit's Song Has Withered' and the ensnaring net again in 'Like Some Fair Subtle Poison', which also demonstrates the voluptuousness Sonia detected in his verse:

> Like some fair subtle poison is the cold white beauty you shed;
> Pale flower of the garden I walk in, your scent is an amorous net
> To lure my thoughts and pulses, by your useless phantom led
> By misty hours and ruins with insatiate longing wet.
>
> To lure my soul with the beauty of some enthralling sin.
> To starve my body to hunger for the mystic rapture there.
> O cruel; flesh and spirit your robe's soft stir sucks in,
> And your cold unseeing glances, and the fantasies of your hair.
>
> And in the shining hollow of your dream-enhaunted throat
> My mournful thoughts now wander and build desire a nest,
> But no tender thoughts to crown the fiery dreams that float
> Around those sinuous rhythms and dim languors of your breast.[17]

There is a plethora of erotic imagery in this early love poetry which Rosenberg's unfulfilled longing for Sonia may help to explain. His attempts to square his physical desire with the need to idealize the beloved lead to poems that could almost have been written at the height of the courtly love vogue, and the results are full of echoes from the Elizabethan lyricists. 'Heart's First Word' (I), one of the poems Sonia remembered him writing for her, is almost comical in its striving to keep his 'Lady' on her pedestal:

> Her hair, her eyes, her throat and chin;
> Sweet hair, sweet eyes, sweet throat, so sweet,
> So fair because the ways of sin
> Have never known her perfect feet.[18]

The conflict between physical and spiritual love emerges most clearly in the concluding stanzas of 'In November':

> As we stood talking in the porch
> My pulse shook like a wind-kissed torch,
> Too sweet you seemed for anything
> Save dreams whereof the poets sing.
>
> Your voice was like the buds that burst
> With latter spring to slake their thirst,
> While all your ardent mouth was lit
> With summer memories exquisite.[19]

Yet Rosenberg's imagination is not stifled by such preoccupations. The net that ensnares can also become a symbol of his vain attempt to capture 'lovely thoughts forgot in wind', a poem he presented to Sonia soon after they met, 'Twilight' (II). Though derivative in parts (Yeats again), it contains some original touches; the concept of twilight as 'dusky panic', for instance, is an early example of Rosenberg's ability to combine the concrete and abstract to powerful effect.

It is not just in his use of imagery that Rosenberg's originality begins to show itself in 1911. His handling of language itself reveals the same apparent disregard for normal rules in his search for the precise result. For instance, he opens an otherwise conventional love poem displaying all the signs of Pre-Raphaelite and Nineties' poets' influence – elaborate imagery of birds with 'jewelled quivering feet',

Right:
Isaac Rosenberg
with his parents
and sister
Minnie, c. 1891

Below:
Early family
group showing,
l. to r., Ray,
David, Annie,
Isaac and Elkon
Rosenberg

Below: Jubilee Street, Stepney, where Rosenberg lived from c. 1899 to 1907

Right: Stepney Green Arts and Crafts School

Above: Narodiczky's shop in the Mile End Road

Left: 87 Dempsey Street, Stepney, Rosenberg's home, c. 1912 onwards

Oil painting of Rosenberg
by J.H. Amshewitz, 1909

Rosenberg's pencil
self-portrait, c. 1910

Rosenberg's black chalk and pencil portrait of his mother, 1911

Opposite:
Slade picnic of 1912, with Rosenberg kneeling apart far left: front row l. to r.: Dora Carrington, unknown, C.W.R. Nevinson, Mark Gertler, William Roberts, Adrian Allinson, Stanley Spencer, unknown; back row, 3rd from l., David Bomberg, 4th from l., Prof. Fred Brown, 5th from l., C. Koe Child, Slade Secretary

Opposite:
Photograph taken at Minnie's marriage to 'Wolf' Horvitch, August 1913: seated l. to r.: Barnett, Minnie, 'Wolf' Horvitch, Anna, Elkon (kneeling); standing, Ray, Annie, David, five unidentified figures, then Isaac far r.

Rosenberg's oil portrait of his father, 1911

Rosenberg
aged about
twenty-
three

Rosenberg's
oil painting
of his uncle,
Peretz
Rosenberg,
?1914

'Betty' Molteno and her partner, Graham Greene's aunt, Alice Greene

Left: Rosenberg in his army greatcoat

Below left: Rosenberg in 'the family suit' with his younger brother, Elkon, September 1917

Below right: Rosenberg in army uniform with Elkon

Rosenberg from an autographed postcard, 1917

Rosenberg's gravestone, row D, plot 5, Bailleuil Road Cemetery

which land on a 'gold branch' in 'the woods mysterious' of the poet's heart, then fly to 'dark pools of brooding cave' and 'blinding wastes of loneliness' – with a striking, slightly ungrammatical first line: 'God looked clear at me through her eyes'.[20] The use of the adjective 'clear' rather than the strictly grammatical adverb is essential to the effect: that of the directness, clarity and divine nature of his beloved's eyes, the reader being allowed to attribute 'clear' both to God's gaze and to her eyes.

The poet Lazarus Aaronson, who came from a similar background to Rosenberg and got to know him in the Whitechapel Group, recalled: 'One day Jimmie [Rodker] said, you have to meet someone who is remarkable. Is semi-literate ... He was a little fellow and what I saw then were the eyes, ... greenish with a red fleck. Very quiet, with a guttural. Much taciturnity.'[21] He saw that it was Rosenberg's foreign background that enabled him to 'fertilize' the English language, as well as helping to explain the apparent awkwardness of his verse at times: 'A good deal of the stress and strain' he argued 'was due to the fact that English was new for him. The whole language was therefore fresh, even the clichés.'[22] Gordon Bottomley, a very different poet from Rosenberg, but a great admirer of his work, was struck most in reading it by the fact that he was 'of a first generation to use our tongue'.[23] His lack of 'atavistic or subconscious background' in English, Bottomley believed, 'must have conditioned his freshness of usage'.[24]

Leftwich went further, maintaining that Rosenberg remained highly aware of his Jewish beginnings, even after he began to use English regularly:

> They were always in his mind and they are everywhere in his work. His father's and mother's talk at home was rich with it, and I recall how often he spoke to me of his trying to recapture in his work some of their Yiddish tales and their Yiddish idiom.[25]

Another Jewish critic, Edouard Roditi, writing of Rosenberg and two other Whitechapel poets, Aaronson and Abraham Abrahams, refers to 'certain poetic traits' in their work 'which can nowhere else be found in contemporary English poetry'.[26]

Whilst it is impossible to prove a direct connection between Rosenberg's Yiddish and English, as Jon Silkin has tried to do (linking Rosenberg's 'bunches of harsh, obtruding consonants' with the guttural nature of Yiddish, for example),[27] there is little doubt that his late introduction to English had a distinct effect on his poetry. He himself was very apologetic about his 'desperate attempts to murder and mutilate King's English beyond all shapes of recognition' and what he saw as his limited vocabulary.[28] But Diana Collecott, among others, sees a direct relationship between his difficulties with English and the effectiveness of his poetry. Pointing to the discrepancy between the fluency of his letters and his hesitant, often stammering speech in face-to-face encounters, she attributes the latter to his 'limited experience of oral English' more than to shyness or introversion.[29] She then links this to the way his poetry emerges (in Binyon's words) in 'clotted gushes and spasms', concluding that for Rosenberg, more than most, 'Expression [was] difficult, fought for but extremely original', as the final stanzas of his poem on the subject both acknowledges and illustrates:

> Expression
> ... Can this be caught and caged?
> Wings can be clipt
> Of eagles, the sun's gaudy measure gauged,
> But no sense dipt
>
> In the mystery of sense.
> The troubled throng
> Of words break out like smother'd fire through dense
> And smouldering wrong.[30]

Chris Searle, a teacher in the East End fifty years after Rosenberg died, reinforces the point from his own experience with foreign children there. When he set his first generation of Indian, Pakistani and Bangladeshi schoolchildren the task of writing poetry, he observed: 'Sometimes raw, visionary images flashed out of their new English words and meshed with the reality around them.'[31] As Leftwich wrote in *The Golden Peacock*, his anthology of Yiddish poetry (which includes a piece by Barnett Rosenberg on his son), 'there is much to be said for bilingualism.'[32]

Rosenberg's linguistic background may go some way to explaining his far greater originality in poetry where, for whatever reason, his approach is less conventional than in painting, increasingly so throughout his dual careers. (His first mentors in art, of course, had been conservative painters like Amshewitz, Solomon and Emanuel.) It was perhaps for this reason that, by the time he met Leftwich, Winsten and Rodker in January 1911, the Jewish Education Aid Society had still not agreed to lend him the money for a full-time art course, whereas only two months later they would agree to send the strikingly original artist Bomberg to the Slade.

Yet Rosenberg carried on painting and drawing determinedly throughout the year, and by October would finally see his hopes realized, joining Bomberg at the Slade that same month.

Rosenberg's creative output in 1911 was prodigious. Equally divided between poetry and art, like his current 'ideal', Rossetti, he showed no sign of choosing between the two. No sooner had he read a new poem to Leftwich, Winsten and Rodker than he was taking them home to see his latest paintings and drawings. His dismissal from Hentschel's in January, while it had given him more time for his own work, had presented him with an urgent need to find a new job, a situation that might have discouraged a less dedicated person. Its effect on Rosenberg was to drive him on to greater creative efforts. For he was still determined to earn his living by either his poetry or his art.

When his attempts to place his poems failed completely – Leftwich reports him as 'very melancholy and dispirited ... about them' by 16 July[33] – he redoubled his efforts to succeed with his art. Besides the paintings and drawings shown to his new friends, and some illustrations for Keats's *Hyperion*, he executed several other portraits.[34] There were numerous drawings for his job application to Sir Adolph Tuck, ten or twelve landscapes and plans for illustrations to his own poems which he hoped to have published as a book. Though no longer attending Birkbeck College, he had evidently kept his pass to the National Gallery and was also copying at least one of the Old

Masters there. And in late March he told Leftwich that he was enrolling at the Lambeth School of Art.[35]

The Jewish Education Aid Society may have been partly responsible for this frantic activity. Its decision to 'adopt' him in late 1910 had increased his confidence in himself as a painter, though it had not yet led to anything tangible by the beginning of 1911. The Society's discussion with Mr Hentschel about the possibility of Rosenberg attending art school full-time may even have contributed to his dismissal, since it would have grown clear to Hentschel in the course of it that his apprentice was not happy in his firm.[36] When the JEAS's efforts to find Isaac a job in advertising or greeting-card design failed, and encouraged by his sponsors, Solomon J. Solomon and Marion Spielmann, the Committee decided on 22 February 1911 'that this boy should compete for a Royal Academy Scholarship'.[37] It agreed to fund a further six weeks of instruction to that end, but only on condition that he 'obtained suitable employment at once'.[38] Rosenberg's own increasingly desperate efforts to interest Sir Adolph Tuck in his drawings came to nothing however – Tuck preferred his poetry – and the self-portrait of early 1911 may well have been his independent bid to gain entrance to the Royal Academy. When the painting was ruined in the process of trying to improve it,[39] he again appealed to the Society, and at the end of March they resolved to approach the Slade's Professor Frederick Brown for his opinion. The timing could not have been more cruel; at the same meeting at which Brown was reported as 'advising against taking up' Rosenberg, £30 was voted to David Bomberg, who had 'entered the Slade . . . as a student'.[40]

Since Rosenberg, always secretive, reported none of this to Leftwich, we have no record of how he felt about Professor Brown's report. His continued artistic efforts suggest that, in spite of his extreme shyness and lack of social confidence, he had that crucial component for a self-made artist, enormous self-belief. And in any case, by the end of April there were other prospects in sight.

Ironically, it was Rosenberg's least original painting, his copy of Velázquez's *Philip IV of Spain*, that helped turn his fortunes, as well as leading to a meeting with the British king, George V. The exercise was yet another attempt to impress the Royal Academy, Rosenberg told Leftwich, and to show the Jewish Education Aid Society that he was 'in thorough earnest about taking up art as a life-work'.[41] He had already started his copy on 9 March, the day the King opened some new rooms at the National Gallery. While other students crowded into a passage to watch George V pass, Rosenberg loftily went on with his work, but was rewarded by the King stopping to watch him paint. Fortunately, he was not quite so aloof with the next person to inspect his picture, Mrs Lily Delissa Joseph.[42]

Mrs Joseph, a moderately successful painter of interiors and city-scapes by the time Rosenberg met her on 17 March, made a habit of visiting the National Gallery weekly to paint her own impressions of the Old Masters. The sister of Solomon J. Solomon, she had been trained largely in the same academic tradition but was slightly more experimental than her brother, showing evidence of the influence of the Impressionists in, for example, her looser handling of paint. She had failed repeatedly to convince her more famous brother of the efficacy of a curious 'method' she had developed of painting in a few colours only, white, cobalt, and orange- and rose-madder. Another limitation, imposed on her by her Jewish orthodoxy perhaps, was her unwillingness to paint recognizable faces in her interiors. According to at least one critic she ruined many of her best pictures, such as *The Family Group*, by changing the faces of her sitters, presumably to avoid breaking the second commandment, 'You shall not make for yourself a graven image'.[43]

Born in 1863, Lily was nearing fifty when she and Rosenberg met, but still as bold in life as she was timid in her art. An early suffragette who had been in prison for her beliefs, she was one of the first women to ride a bicycle (in bloomers) and drive an electric brougham. In her late fifties she would learn to fly and would also set out alone with car and caravan for Palestine. (The car broke down in Italy and she had to complete the journey by rail and ship.)

The most reliable version of Rosenberg's first meeting with her is related conscientiously by Leftwich, based on Rosenberg's account to him the same day.[44] As Rosenberg concentrates on finishing his Velázquez, Mrs Joseph comes up to him and speaks about his work. After explaining her own 'method', she hands him the three colours involved and asks him to paint her something in it. When she also gives him her address and invites him to call, he resolves not only to experiment with a landscape of Hampstead Heath, but also to show her his poems. Two days later, despite heavy rain, he is out on the Heath painting the view towards Highgate Pond, a rather subdued landscape which reflects Mrs Joseph's insistence on a limited palette.[45] (Two other paintings in similar style, *The Pool of London* (1911) and *Blackfriars Bridge* (1911), were almost certainly further attempts at Mrs Joseph's 'method'.)[46] When he calls to show Mrs Joseph his picture, he is invited to dinner. After Leftwich read Rosenberg's short story 'Rudolph', based loosely on his friendship with Mrs Joseph, he asked Rosenberg whether Rudolph's attendance at the dinner in borrowed clothes was 'real' and 'was not satisfied with his denial': the 'whole thing' seemed to him to have 'the nature of fact, and not of an invented tale'.[47] Given that the Rosenberg males shared a 'family suit and hat',[48] it is more than probable that Leftwich was right.

Accurate as Leftwich's account probably is, however, it misses out a number of factors of which neither he nor Rosenberg was necessarily aware. While it is just possible that the sister of Solomon J. Solomon should not have been aware of his sponsorship of a promising young Jewish painter by the name of Rosenberg, it is highly unlikely that she could have resisted Amshewitz's earlier efforts to interest her personally in his plight. This had involved Amshewitz persuading his actor friend Sherbrooke to read Rosenberg's poetry to her, which would explain why Rosenberg resolved to show her his verse as well as his paintings on his first visit to her.[49]

Rosenberg's own version of events in 'Rudolph' makes no reference to the possibility that Mrs Joseph was 'set up', as it were. Nevertheless, disguised though some of the facts are in 'Rudolph', it is revealing. (Rosenberg may have been referring to his short story when he wrote to Binyon in 1912: 'I am sending a sort of auto-biography I wrote about a year ago.')[50] Bottomley, though doubtful about including 'Rudolph' in the 1937 edition, because he thought it was 'of intrinsically small value' as prose and 'would too cruelly give away the innocent, mournful, unhappy youth who wrote it', finally decided to do so, since he believed that the main character, Rudolph, was 'clearly a hundred per cent [Rosenberg] and what he says is nearer to [his] *credo* than anything else we have'.[51]

Bottomley's dismissal of 'Rudolph's' style is a little harsh. It was only Rosenberg's second attempt at a sustained piece of prose. (His first, 'On a Door Knocker', had been written in February 1911 for Leftwich and his little group.) Both works suggest that he felt more relaxed in prose, perhaps because it was not his chosen discipline. There is some effective humour in both, 'On a Door Knocker' displaying the fancifulness of Sterne in its use of the mock heroic. In the more autobiographical 'Rudolph', the humour is often self-directed, as in Rosenberg's letters. Commenting on society's apparent 'desire to elevate [Rudolph] to a higher and still higher – garret', a thinly disguised Rosenberg continues: 'Though a nearer view of heaven and though a poet, he would have preferred a less lofty dwelling place to preserve, what he facetiously termed his ancestor's remains, from the chill November weather . . .'[52]

Both pieces also show, as Bottomley conceded, some passages of 'mature and shapely and energetic writing',[53] suggesting that Rosenberg's reading of Lamb, Macaulay and Dickens, among others, has been influential.[54] The finest passages in 'Rudolph' occur when, laying aside the farcical plot he has set up – a young man going to dinner in borrowed, outsize clothes which turn out to belong to the butler who serves him coffee – Rosenberg voices Rudolph's and, according to Bottomley, his own artistic beliefs and aims. After the 'pleasant-faced lady', whom Rosenberg tactfully makes over a decade younger than Mrs Joseph, in a reversal of what actually occurred shows *him her* picture, she confesses defiantly to thinking 'Van Eyck the greatest artist that ever lived . . . because he makes the commonplace so delightfully precious'.[55] To which Rudolph replies, in words that could apply to Rosenberg's poetry as much as his painting:

'I think a picture should be something more . . . Van Eyck is interesting to me just as a pool reflecting the clouds is interesting, or a landscape seen through a mirror. But it is only a faithful transcript of what we see. My ideal of a picture is to paint what we cannot see. To create, to imagine. To make tangible and real a figment of the brain. To transport the spectator into other worlds where beauty is the only reality. Rossetti is my ideal.'[56]

'Rudolph' is also interesting because it appears to describe Rosenberg's state of mind, at a time when he, like Rudolph, faced almost insurmountable social as well as financial barriers in early 1911:

'When one has to think of responsibilities [Rudolph tells the Mrs Joseph figure 'bitterly'], when one has to think strenuously how to manage to subsist, so much thought, so much energy is necessarily taken from creative work. It might widen experience and develop a precocious mental maturity, of thought and worldliness, it might even make one's work more poignant and intense, but I am sure the final result is loss, technical incompleteness, morbidness and the evidence of tumult and conflict'[57]

Rosenberg's awareness, both of himself and of the effect his background had had on him, emerges most impressively in a passage that summarizes his character even better than his friends could do, though many of them tried:

Brought up as he had been: socially isolated, but living in spiritual communion with the great minds of all the ages, he had developed a morbid introspection in all that related to himself, and a persistent frivolousness in relations with others ... The development of temperament had bred a disassociation from the general run of the people he came in contact with, that almost rendered him inarticulate when circumstances placed him amongst those of more affinity to himself, from disuse of the ordinary faculties and facilities of conversation. Naturally these circumstances would be such where his vanity suggested he had a reputation to sustain, and he would be perpetually on the strain to say something clever. He was totally lacking in the logic of what might be called common sense, but had a whimsical sort of logic of his own which was amusing till it became too clever ...[58]

'Rudolph' ends on a positive note, with the protagonist experiencing a dizzy sense of new possibilities, which Rosenberg himself undoubtedly felt in the face of Mrs Joseph's sympathy and interest:

> His past – what a horrible waste of God's faculties – unused. If he had only been taken up and moulded; but life had been cruel to him. Now she showed signs of remorse and atonement. He was young, upon the threshold of life. Life would hold the doors for the golden stairs.[59]

'Rudolph' was written in April 1911, only a month after Rosenberg met Lily Delissa Joseph, and there were still times when its author felt as hopeless and cast out as his main character initially had. As late as June he would feel desperate enough to contemplate taking a cattle boat to America.[60] A poem written at about this period, 'Spiritual Isolation', expresses his despair forcibly, as well as showing that he was following Miss Seaton's advice on reading-matter carefully. Evidence that he has been studying Donne, especially his religious sonnets, emerges in almost every line, together with echoes from another metaphysical poet, George Herbert, and the eighteenth-century poet William Cowper's 'The Castaway'. As with all these poets, it is the relationship between God and himself that concerns him, and at this early stage it is a largely benign deity he portrays. It is the human being who is (to use Jon Silkin's word) 'defective',[61] a state reflected in the imagery of disease that dominates the opening stanza:

> My Maker shunneth me.
> Even as a wretch stricken with leprosy
> So hold I pestilent supremacy.
> Yea! He hath fled far as the uttermost star,
> Beyond the unperturbed fastnesses of night,
> And dreams that bastioned are
> By fretted towers of sleep that scare His light.[62]

By October 1911, however, Rosenberg's mood had swung back to optimism with the advent of another dramatic change in his fortunes this roller-coaster year. Mrs Joseph, married to a successful architect, was moderately well off, and her first attempt to help Rosenberg had been to ask him to become art tutor to her two young sons. Soon he was leading the boys and their cousins, the daughters of Lily's sister, Mrs Henrietta Löwy, for lessons to Kensington Gardens, which he painted on at least one occasion.[63] Judging from poems written to Mr and Mrs Löwy and their six daughters, he became quite close to the Löwy family and showed some affection for them, particularly the children. According to Winsten he 'did quite well as a painting coach',[64] though neither the Josephs nor the Löwys could afford to pay him enough for a full-time course at either the Royal Academy or the Slade. But Mrs Joseph and her sister remained impressed by his ability and approached their wealthier friend Mrs Herbert Cohen, who agreed to supply both the fees and a living allowance for the Slade.[65]

Mrs Herbert Cohen was one of the most powerful of the West End Jewish ladies who dispensed charity in the East End to their fellow Jews. There are stories which suggest that in doing so she was rather managerial and condescending towards the people she helped. And her relationship with Rosenberg would indicate that she always expected to have her own way: 'patronizing' was how he viewed her.[66] Her portrait by the successful Jewish portraitist Alfred Wolmark suggested to at least one viewer 'a large, rather formidable woman with a somewhat arrogant expression, dressed opulently in a satin gown, furs and jewellery'.[67]

Mrs Cohen was well-meaning, however, and there is no doubt as to the value of what she did, nor her kindness of heart, as Rosenberg would come to realize. Nor can she be dismissed simply as a female 'do-gooder'. Besides painting herself, in a conventional Royal Academy style, she was a poet in her own right, producing at least one volume of poems and several plays, one of them quite successful.[68] Rosenberg would send her copies of a number of his own poems and several paintings and drawings during their relationship.[69] Though he would eventually rebel against his benefactor when she became too overbearing for his liking, in the autumn of 1911, as he prepared to enter the Slade with her sponsorship, she must have seemed to him his saviour.

Chapter 7

An Introduction to the Slade

1911–1912

I am studying at the Slade, the finest school for drawing in England. I do nothing but draw – draw –
                                                  – IR to Miss Seaton, 1912[1]

'The Slade marks an era in the history of Art' Rosenberg wrote after entering it himself in October 1911.[2] But by the time of his arrival there, it seemed as if that era might be nearly over. For the Slade had reached a crisis in its history, a situation that would affect his own career as a painter. While he came of age a month later, the Slade was already starting to look as if it was past its peak, the avant-garde threatening to become the old guard. Ironically this drama was played out when the school was at one of its greatest periods of vitality, producing between 1908, when Mark Gertler arrived, and 1914, when Rosenberg left, a host of outstanding artists – Stanley Spencer, David Bomberg, C.R.W. Nevinson, Paul Nash, Dora Carrington, William Roberts and Adrian Allinson, among others.

Founded in 1871 with a generous endowment from the collector Felix Slade as a School of Fine Art at University College London, by the turn of the century it had already acquired a reputation for daring and innovation, based largely on the enthusiasm for the French Impressionists of its leading teachers, Frederick Brown, Henry Tonks, Philip Wilson Steer and Ambrose McEvoy. But in 1910 Post-Impressionism had exploded on London, and its effects on the Slade were being felt by both staff and students alike, Rosenberg's close friend Bomberg chief among them.

After his own three years at the Slade witnessing at first hand the seismic shock of this new movement, Rosenberg would write in words that apply equally well to the parallel disruptions caused by

Modernist movements in literature – and that reflect his fascination with torn-up roots, corrosion and a decaying civilization:

> Art is now, as it were, a volcano. Eruptions are continual, and immense cities of culture at its foot are shaken and shivered. The roots of a dead universe are torn up by hands, feverish and consuming with an exuberant vitality – and amid dynamic threatenings we watch the hastening of the corroding doom.[3]

There is sympathy here both for the old and the new in their violent collision, though the sentence that follows shows that Rosenberg's own inclinations, in art at least, were for the tried and tested: 'But we believe that [Leonardo's] Gioconda will endure, and Albrecht Dürer will never be forgotten, and that the reign of Blake is yet to begin.'[4]

Post-Impressionism had first become popularly known as a movement in Paris during the opening years of the twentieth century following a series of large retrospective exhibitions of Eighties and Nineties painters such as Gauguin, Cézanne and Van Gogh. These shows, in turn, stimulated a new wave of developments, including Fauvism from 1905, with Matisse its chief exponent, and Cubism from about 1907, with Picasso and Braque to the fore. Yet more revolutionary developments ensued, a similar ferment in Germany giving rise to Kandinsky's abstract paintings in 1910. The tradition of naturalistic, representational painting, which had lasted for several hundred years in Europe, was seriously under threat.

The British art world tended to the insular and knew very little of developments in France and Germany. It was only just beginning to accept the Impressionists of the 1870s when the art critic and painter Roger Fry introduced it to the Post-Impressionists in 1910. The reaction to his large exhibition of their works at the Grafton Galleries, London, at the end of that year was explosive.

It was a furore Rosenberg probably witnessed, since there is little doubt that he accompanied Bomberg to this show. Of the students who attended the Slade between 1910 and 1912, when Fry's First and Second Exhibitions took place, the majority of those who went on to achieve fame were profoundly affected by Post-Impressionism.[5]

This may explain Frank Emanuel's otherwise puzzling reaction to Rosenberg going to the Slade. Though he had studied there himself, he had evidently found the students' largely positive response to Post-Impressionism regrettable. Describing the Slade's atmosphere at the time as 'extremely nasty and unhealthy', he continued:

> The art produced there was morbid, artificial and unclean and that influence has not yet dissipated itself. The influence was bad for any young artist and doubly so for the already socialistic East End boys, who really required fresh air and sunshine let into their work and their lives to make their lives and their achievements healthier and happier. At the Slade stage scenery was preferred to nature, ugliness, sordidness and disease were preferred in its models – to beauty and health and cleanliness.[6]

Fry had almost certainly prepared Slade students for his bombshell during his lectures on the history of art to them, which started this same year. But Rosenberg's views evidently remained neutral, neither as enthusiastic as most of his fellow students, nor as hostile as his teachers and the art world at large. 'Post-Impressionism' he argued:

> was an attempt by men of the deepest culture, and reverence for art, to see nature as a child might see it. However profound their ideas, however mixed with the multiplexity of modern life, their presentation of that idea must be a sort of detachment from all they know – it must be purely that one thing.[7]

While Rosenberg's art, with a few exceptions, shows little influence from the Post-Impressionists, his description of their technique sounds similar to his own later achievements in poetry.

The British public, however, and even its most respected artists and critics, almost universally rejected what they clearly could not grasp. The eminent art critic of the *Daily Telegraph*, Sir Claude Phillips, for instance, according to Paul Nash, 'threw down his catalogue upon the threshold of the Grafton Galleries and stamped on it'.[8] Fry had expected them to make the leap from Impressionism to Post-Impressionism to abstract art too quickly.

That the Royal Academy, bastion of the traditional and conventional, should have rejected the new movements is understandable. That the Slade should also have done so is more surprising. For its staff prided itself on its revolutionary reputation and, to a large extent, despised the Academy. In the Nineties it had produced artists such as Augustus John and William Orpen, whose work had shocked and delighted the art world. As the first British art school to accept the Impressionists' innovations, its rejection of Post-Impressionism seemed ironic, especially since it was being introduced into England by its current guest lecturer, Fry. The Slade's leaders felt their position threatened, yet were too established as Impressionists themselves to be able to reconsider their creed. Deeply disturbed by the Post-Impressionists' rejection both of naturalistic representation and of the belief that art and beauty were necessarily connected, they were even more upset by the notion that a long course in drawing might not be essential for a painter. The Slade's chief drawing master, Tonks, told his old friend George Moore that all the 'talk about Cubism' was 'killing' him and ordered his students to boycott Fry's exhibitions.[9]

It was not just Tonks who felt strongly; the Slade as a whole laid great emphasis on the importance of draughtsmanship, as Rosenberg's letter to Miss Seaton quoted at the head of this chapter shows. According to him, 'the young men [had] been taught by John that a sharp contour means more than the blending of tone into tone'. His own training would be dominated by an insistence on a knowledge of anatomy – Tonks had started his career as a surgeon – and the importance of line. Unlike the Royal Academy and the London County Council schools Rosenberg had previously attended, and which made their students spend months producing an elaborately finished drawing, the Slade encouraged its students to work fast at different poses in the Life Room, to train them to search quickly for the essential 'bones' of their subject. Tonks believed that elaborate tone and shading were often a cover for poor draughtsmanship. At the same time, his students were warned against fixing their outline too soon: the drawing must be kept 'open' as long as possible. This training in the necessity for a sharp, clear, economical line was one Rosenberg needed to learn in October 1911 and would affect his poetry as well as his art. (He would write in his 1914 essay on 'Art' that it should have 'the concise pregnant quality of poetry'.)[10]

Rosenberg clearly embraced the Slade's insistence on the importance of draughtsmanship, so much so that even one of his most recent 'ideals', Blake, would be criticized for lack of it. He wrote in 'Art':

> Blake was not a good draughtsman ... It was a great pity he had Flaxman for a teacher instead of Dürer. I here mean drawing as we understand it in the classic sense. ... The unbroken tradition that runs right from Egypt through Da Vinci, Dürer to John, passed by him; there were none to hand it on to him.[11]

Rosenberg, on the other hand, had Tonks to pass on what, echoing his teacher, he described as the 'science' of drawing.[12] Tonks never let his students forget his career as a surgeon, which seems to have led him to claim a more 'scientific' approach to art. In his late forties by the time he taught Rosenberg, he had been at the Slade nearly twenty years, for his medical life had ended early.[13] Despite training as a doctor, his real interest lay in art, and at the age of twenty-six he had begun to attend evening classes run by Frederick Brown, an action that was to change the course of his life. For when Brown was appointed head of the Slade in 1893, he offered Tonks a post there and Tonks accepted. But his medical training remained with him, particularly in his emphasis on the skeleton framework in drawing the human figure, a method generations of students called 'Tonking'.

Tonks quickly eclipsed Brown at the Slade, both as a personality and a teacher. As one of his students put it: 'Tonks was the Slade and the Slade was Tonks.'[14] The artist William Rothenstein related how 'young ladies of the best families were known to weep at Tonks's acid comments on their work; yet young ladies of the best families flocked to the Slade to throw themselves before Tonks's Jaganath [juggernaut] progress through the Life Rooms'.[15] And it was not only women who suffered at his hands. Gertler, for instance, may have told Rosenberg and his other East End friends of his initial, searing experience with Tonks. On showing him his first hard-won effort in the life class, he was asked sarcastically, 'Is that the best you can do?'

and was further humiliated when his humble nod of assent earned Tonks's, 'Then why do it?'[16]

Despite his daunting manner and appearance – 'he was very tall and grim with a faint resemblance to the "Iron Duke"' – Tonks seems to have been basically quite kind.[17] His fierce criticism was undercut by humour and directed at those he believed could take it. He showed great loyalty to his students and sympathy for those who most needed it. Stanley Spencer, for example, whose family were not well off, was allowed to take up a scholarship for which he had not, strictly speaking, qualified only after Tonks's intervention and support.[18]

It was this side of his teacher that Rosenberg evidently experienced. He felt nothing but respect and admiration for Tonks, describing him after a few months in his class as 'a most remarkable man'. Far from complaining of his sarcasm he tells Winifreda Seaton that 'he talks wonderfully, so voluble and ready, crammed with ideas – most illuminating and suggestive – and witty'.[19] Even those who became the unfortunate targets of his scorn acknowledged that Tonks was a brilliant teacher. Bomberg, for instance, despite rebelling against many things at the Slade, said that he had learnt more from Tonks than from any previous teacher, Sickert included. It was a view Rosenberg shared. He may also have identified with Tonks's dual career and would certainly have agreed with a statement Tonks made in his lecture on the artist's role, that 'the painter who is not a poet ought to be put in the stocks'.[20]

Whatever the reasons, it is clear that Tonks had a strong influence on Rosenberg's art. His pencil self-portrait of 1911, one of his first assignments for the Slade, shows a greater interest in line and sensitivity of approach than any previous work. And his portrait of Ruth Löwy, drawn in red chalk in 1912, exhibits a strong, firm line, especially in the profile. 'Marda Vanne', a later, black chalk drawing, still demonstrates the same interest in line, though it is a softer, more delicate one. As a well-trained Slade student Rosenberg would come to demand a great deal from a picture:

Can I read it? Is it clear, concise, definite? It cannot be too harsh for me. The lines must cut into my consciousness; the waves of life must

Self-portrait in pencil, 1911. (*University of South Carolina*)

be disturbed, sharp, and unhesitating. It is nature's consent, her agreement that what we can wrest from her we keep. Truth, structural veracity, clearness of thought and utterance, the intelligent understanding of what is essential.[21]

Though neither of the two drawings of women under discussion achieves this counsel of perfection, they are nearer to it than most of the paintings. The line in both is 'clear, concise, definite', while at the same time managing to convey an impression of feminine softness and delicacy.

Many of Rosenberg's later drawings would be of female heads, but there are also two delicate pencil drawings of his father's head executed in 1913 and 1915, and two later drawings of himself in the trenches, all of which confirm that Tonks's forceful teaching would have a lasting effect. And a chalk drawing given by Rosenberg to the poet Gordon Bottomley in 1916, 'The First Meeting of Adam and Eve', displays all the benefits of having attended Tonks's life class, as well as reflecting his belief that the artist needs also to be a poet. (Bottomley always associated this drawing with two of Rosenberg's own poems, 'I mingle with your bones' and 'If you are fire and I am fire'.)[22]

In pursuit of his high ideals, Tonks, like the other members of the Slade's staff, had evolved a rigorous programme. There was for many students a preliminary training with casts in the Antique Room, during which they were sent for the last hour of the day to practise quick pose changes in the Life Room. After a few terms they would spend most of their time there. Bomberg characterized his three years at the Slade as 'sitting on a low donkey stool from ten till four drawing worm's eye views of the nude'.[23] When a student's drawing was judged acceptable, he or she was allowed to progress to painting under Wilson Steer and his assistant, McEvoy. The nude was central to both disciplines, but portraiture and composition were also important aspects of the syllabus, as Rosenberg's Slade pictures indicate. Prizes were awarded annually in all three areas.[24]

The more advanced classes were limited to about thirty students and made great demands on them. Gertler remembered working, even in his holidays, from ten in the morning to eight-thirty at night, with only a short break for lunch and tea.[25] Even for those who – like Rosenberg, unable to afford more than an occasional trip to a café – left at 5 p.m. to take their evening meal at home, the workload was heavy. Morris Goldstein, who joined Rosenberg and Bomberg at the Slade in 1912 and made the long walk to and from it daily with them to save money, described it as a 'full-time job'.[26] There was always homework, which included sketching set subjects for composition and studying the history of art. Though the books for the latter could be borrowed from the college library and taken home, Isaac 'often went to the Whitechapel Library', Goldstein recalled, since the Rosenberg house 'was not peaceful'.[27]

It says much for Rosenberg's ability, as well as the training given to him at Bolt Court and Birkbeck, that he was allowed to bypass the Antique Room and go straight to the Life Class. His own description of his first day at the Slade shows how central this room was. It also underlines the fact that, enlightened as the school had been in providing its male students with female models for nude studies, there was still strict segregation between male and female students in this class. Rosenberg's account suggests that this would

Slade study by Rosenberg in
black chalk, c. 1912 (*Trustees
of the British Museum*)

have been a great relief to him. Most of the other ex-students who
have written of their first day at the Slade concentrate on how
intimidating they found the staff, Tonks and Brown in particular.
But Rosenberg, painfully shy and socially insecure, especially with
women, tells how he experienced extreme discomfort even before
entering the building. It was not so much confusion at having
mistaken the 'stately imposing edifice' of University College's porters'
lodge for the more modest entrance to the art school that threw him,
as the sight of 'girls in painting overalls' in the women's Life Room
on the ground floor.[28] 'Oppressed by an uncomfortable feeling of

being watched by numberless eyes from rows and rows of windows',
it takes him all his courage to enter. Then, after doing so, he spends
'the whole day in trying to find my way out without being seen'.
Succeeding only in getting himself grabbed by a student – 'a male
luckily' – in search of a newcomer to take the place of the Life Room
model, who is ill, he manages to escape but ends up in the Life
Room anyway by following some 'stray waifs of youthful males ...
to the lower regions', where the tobacco-laden atmosphere becomes
mercifully 'more masculine'.

Rosenberg is unlikely to have felt quite so lost for long, since he
had both Gertler and Bomberg there to smooth the way for him.
Gertler had probably warned him what to expect during Rosenberg's
visit to the attic studio he had acquired in Commercial Street in 1910
and may have offered his support. But his attendance during the 1911–
12 session, his final year, became more erratic and it was Bomberg who
was of most immediate help. Appointed Isaac's 'unofficial guardian',[29]
his reputation in itself was a protection of sorts. While neither
Bomberg nor Rosenberg had Gertler's good looks, irresistible charm
or social mobility to help them combat the anti-Semitism he had
suffered as the first working-class Jew to enter the Slade, Bomberg
had his aggressiveness and early training in boxing. He had already
blacked the eye of the worst offender, Alvaro Guevara, for his anti-
Semitic taunts and was ready to do so again on his meeker friend's
behalf. (Rosenberg's parents were pacifists and had discouraged
fighting at home.) So was another Jewish student, Jacob Kramer.
When the Chilean Guevara continued to bully Rosenberg, Kramer,
too, came to his aid. Tired of watching Guevara picking on Rosenberg, who endured it philosophically, Kramer attacked Guevara with
his fists and the taunting stopped.[30]

There is no doubt that Guevara's behaviour stemmed largely
from anti-Semitism, but it was probably not the only factor. By
the time Rosenberg had been one term at the Slade, there were
at least nine other Jewish students there.[31] It was only the working-
class East Enders who were singled out so unpleasantly, however.
Slade students came mainly from the middle or upper classes, and
while Rosenberg's friendship with Amshewitz and his circle,
together with his time at Birkbeck, had gradually accustomed him

to social differences, it could hardly have prepared him for the Slade, with its predominance of wealthy, privileged young people. He was entering new territory. Many of the men had been educated privately; in fact the Slade reminded Paul Nash, who came to it fresh from St Paul's at this time, of 'a typical English Public School seen in a nightmare'.[32] George Charlton, who arrived the year Rosenberg left, compared it to a 'rich man's club'.[33] The women were equally if not more privileged on the whole and included three members of the aristocracy – Lady Diana Manners, the Hon. Dorothy Brett and Lady Violet Charteris. Lady Diana Manners confessed that she was simply unaware of Rosenberg's existence at the Slade.[34] But the aristocrats were outnumbered by students from the middle classes, who were most typical of the Slade at that time, women almost equalling the men in number among this social group. Among them were Dora Carrington, later famous, like Dorothy Brett, for her connections with Bloomsbury, Lytton Strachey in particular; Iris Tree, the flamboyant daughter of the actor-manager Beerbohm Tree; and Phyllis Gardiner, a professor's daughter with flaming red hair.

Whereas Gertler welcomed what he called his 'nice friends among the Upper Class ... so much nicer than the rough "East Ends"' that he was used to,[35] and practised copying their accents, Rosenberg's voice remained unchanged, his accent still 'barely intelligible' to some of his middle-class contemporaries.[36] It was not that he was unaware of the social discrepancies between himself and his fellow students: Leftwich remembered him saying that the new company he found at the Slade 'worried him considerably'.[37] This apprehension would be justified on at least one occasion when he lent the studio he had acquired in 1912 to a middle-class student, Redmond, the son or nephew of a well-known Irish politician. When Redmond with some of his friends smashed up the studio in a fit of high jinks, Rosenberg would complain bitterly:

It is all very well for them to play the Bohemian. They can afford to run riot for a couple of years and then go back to their roots; the old life is waiting for them, good home, family, connections. But we poor Whitechapel boys have nothing to go back to, we dare not let go.[38]

On the whole, however, he was tolerant of, even amused by the excesses of others. But he could not join in, either unable or unwilling to acquire social graces.

In addition, and again unlike Gertler, Rosenberg was an unprepossessing figure, described even by a close friend as 'very short [and] rather pathetic-looking'.[39] His small stature alone would have guaranteed him a certain amount of teasing, if not bullying. His equally diminutive contemporary Stanley Spencer, for instance, had been tied up in a sack, left in the Slade's boiler room and forgotten by his tormentors on one occasion. Though Rosenberg reported nothing of that kind, there is little doubt that of those students who registered his existence at all, some thought him a figure of fun. George Charlton remembered him reading his poems aloud in the Life Room in his 'husky' voice. 'The recitals were not popular' Charlton said; 'indeed the other students used to bombard him with pellets of paper, and sometimes even chase him out of the room.'[40] According to Charlton, Rosenberg 'took this in good part' and 'would look back with pleasure on his time at the Slade'.[41]

Rosenberg was regarded as something of a 'loner' at the Slade, conscientiously attending the school daily, including Saturdays, often on his own. While the Slade picnic photograph shows how this reputation might have arisen, however, it is important to note that he had more friends there than at any other time of his life, including army service. His friendship with Bomberg, for example, continued at the Slade, despite their rapidly diverging aims in art. It seems unbelievable that an art gallery would later confuse Rosenberg's work with Bomberg's, addressing him as 'Isaac Bomberg'.[42] While Bomberg's increasing concern with form would lead him to experiment in a variety of Modernist techniques ranging from Cubism to Futurism – 'the new life' he believed 'should find its expression in a new art, which has been stimulated by new perceptions'[43] – Rosenberg's more literary approach to art and his attachment to Romanticism would make him reluctant to abandon the subject. Though he would have the importance of form drummed into him daily by Tonks and others, he appears to have paid only lip-service to it. Judging from his writing on the matter, it is doubtful whether he really accepted Tonks's argument on the importance of form for Ingres and Degas in particular.[44]

It was not simply his need to earn a living that made Rosenberg concentrate on the more traditional arts of portraiture and landscape-painting, though that played a part. He found Bomberg's experiments (to quote Rosenberg's own words in 'Art') 'too purely abstract and devoid of any human basis to ever become intelligible to anybody outside the creator's self'.[45] The symbols used by the Futurists seemed to him merely 'symbols of symbols' and their pictures gave him the sensation of 'a house falling'.[46] Bomberg on the other hand felt that to concentrate on Nature 'while [he] lived in a *steel city*' was absurd: 'My object is the construction of Pure Form' he declared in the foreword to his one-man exhibition catalogue at the Chenil Gallery, London, in July 1914.[47] To Rosenberg the importance of Nature and the 'human basis' in painting were never in question. It is as evident in the compositions he executed at the Slade as in his portraits and landscapes. The tenderness between his young lovers in *Sacred Love* (1911–12) and 'The First Meeting of Adam and Eve', for instance, is as important to him as the design as a whole.

Sacred Love, in particular, one of his earliest Slade assignments, suggests that Rosenberg's greatest gift as a painter – and the quality that distinguishes him most clearly from Bomberg – is his visionary quality, encouraged by his growing interest in Blake. Christopher Hassall's description of *Sacred Love*, which would be bought by the art connoisseur Edward Marsh in 1914, recreates the intense effect it had on him as it hung in Marsh's guest bedroom:

The new acquisition was a small oil-painting of curiously dry texture and pallid tone, like a pastel. In the foreground, a green clearing in a wood, a youth was kneeling by a girl who sat on a rock, and in an attitude of adoration he lifted her hands to his lips. In the background naked figures seemed to be scattering in alarm through the tilted trees. It glowed with a strange, dreamlike intensity, reminiscent of Blake – a lovely vision which ... confronted on their waking all the guests in this little room.[48]

Though Rosenberg lacked Bomberg's outstanding ability and his audacity and originality as a painter, the power of his imagination is rarely in doubt. It has been suggested that it was not to Rosenberg's advantage to be at the Slade at the same time as Bomberg, that Bomberg's far greater talent completely overshadowed his friend's more modest artistic gift. Bomberg himself always maintained that Rosenberg was a much better poet than painter, entitling his pencil portrait of Rosenberg which won the Henry Tonks Prize in 1913 'Head of a Poet'.[49] Nevertheless Rosenberg's training as a painter and his friendship with Bomberg would play a part in his development as a poet. There was inevitably a certain amount of jealousy and conflict between the two, but the relationship would survive and each would remain concerned about the other's welfare.

Rosenberg's other champion at the Slade, Jacob Kramer,[50] would also become a good friend. Two years younger than Rosenberg, Kramer arrived at the Slade slightly later in 1912. Born in the Russian province of Ukraine, his family had moved first to Poland then in 1900 to Leeds, where the young Kramer was eventually taken up by the cconnoisseur Michael Sadler, a professor at Leeds University, and sent to the Slade. Kramer was more admiring of Rosenberg's art than Bomberg, perhaps because he was something of an individualist himself. (He thought the training at the Slade 'very good' during his and Rosenberg's time there because 'they allowed for individuality of expression'.)[51] Just as he had discovered his 'religion through painting not through the synagogue', he claimed, so he believed that Rosenberg 'wasn't religious in an institutional sense but was as far as his poems [were] concerned'.[52] Kramer believed Rosenberg to be 'an exceptionally fine draughtsman' and found his compositions 'very creative'.[53] He also admired his poetry. Rosenberg would pass him verses written on scraps of paper in the Life Room, where they worked side by side, and Kramer got 'a helluva lot of pleasure' when Rosenberg recited them to him.[54] He was so inspired by one of them that he painted a picture, *The Sphinx*, to illustrate it. Rosenberg once took him to a poetry society meeting in the West End, where Rosenberg recited his own poems, an event not mentioned in his letters. But the venue was almost certainly Harold Monro's Poetry Bookshop in Devonshire Street, where poets were encouraged to perform. Rodker, who had introduced Rosenberg to Monro initially, was also present. (While Leftwich confirmed that Rosenberg did show his poems to Monro on at least one occasion, he felt that Monro was 'condescending' in conversation about Rosenberg in 1914.)[55]

Kramer was evidently very fond of Rosenberg, and as protective of him as Rodker was, referring to his 'frailty and delicacy' and later finding it a 'shame' to take someone so 'delicate' into the army.[56] Nevertheless, there was a balance in their relationship, created to a large extent by Kramer's respect for Rosenberg's poetry. Though their relationship would not continue much beyond the Slade years, Rosenberg felt sufficiently close to him there to compose a poem 'To J. Kramer'. A teasing affair of twelve lines, it shows that he was still writing occasional verse and that he was unable to resist treating his friend's tendency to loftiness with a dose of 'cod-liver-oil'.[57] Rosenberg also gave Kramer several of his poems, all of them unfortunately destroyed in the First World War.

Kramer, who was not interested in women himself, remembered that 'Isaac had an eye for the ladies'.[58] His allusion to 'an affair with one of them' may be a mistaken reference to the friendship with Sonia Cohen, whom both Rosenberg and Bomberg continued to see throughout 1911 and 1912. She often read to them from the Book of Job or Song of Solomon as they worked on Slade biblical assignments at Bomberg's Tenter Street studio. Sitting there with her after dark fell, with no money to feed the meter for the gaslights, could only have encouraged Rosenberg's romantic interest in her. Her own account of the period confirms Kramer's memory of Isaac undergoing 'a sex conflict' at this time.[59] Kramer was certain that it did not involve one of the Slade's female models, who were known for what was termed 'loose morals' in that period. 'We hardly talked to them' he recalled, though he would probably have known of the occasion when Rosenberg took one of them home and posed her, half-naked, in the family kitchen, to his mother's dismay. (Leftwich related this story with some relish.)

The 'affair', if it did take place, was almost certainly not with any of the numerous female students at the Slade. Many of them would, like Lady Diana Manners, have been unaware of his existence. And there is no evidence to suggest anything more than friendship with the two women, both Jewish, who did know him there, Ruth Löwy and Clara Birnberg. Ruth, whom he had tutored with her cousins, Lily Delissa Joseph's sons, in the summer of 1911, entered the Slade at the same time as he did, together with another cousin, Gilbert Solomon.[60] Rosenberg's description of Ruth in his poem to the six Löwy sisters –

> ... Ruth, joyous as a July
> Song-throbbing noon,
> And rosy as a newly
> Flushed eager rose in June ... [61]

– suggests that he thought her attractive. And his sensuous Pre-Raphaelite sketch of her as 'The Sleeping Beauty', which he planned to use in his composition *Joy*, hints at some sexual appeal. ('How really fine that drawing of the Löwy girl is' Gordon Bottomley would write.)[62] The poem he sent her as he painted *Joy* for the Slade Summer Competition of 1912 is romantic but keeps a respectful distance: in it sexual desire is tastefully buried under spiritual bliss. Nevertheless reading 'The Garden of Joy', an ingenious reversal of the Garden of Eden myth, the suspicion remains that its creator identifies far more with the sexual urges he dismisses – 'the fanged fire/Of hot insatiate pleasure', the 'pulsed chime/To summon to tusked orgy of earth's slime' – than the 'tranquil' contentment of the spiritually fulfilled.[63] Since this poem, unpublished in full till very recently, was sent to Ruth, we can be fairly sure that if Rosenberg did lust after her, he did not openly say so.

Sonia doubted that Ruth was 'ever loved by [Isaac]' at all.[64] What is more certain is that Ruth never thought of him in a romantic light. Interviewed by Marcia Allentuck about him sixty years later, she remembered vividly Rosenberg's 'poor physical equipment, muffled voice, bad adenoids and shocking teeth'.[65] And in any case, their class differences and his indebtedness to her family make it most unlikely. But she did respect him greatly as a poet. Normally 'silent and shy', when he 'spoke of his completed poems and his future prospects', she recalled, it was 'almost as if an angel of God put a finger on his lips'.[66]

Rosenberg's letters show that he valued Ruth's friendship at the

Ruth Löwy as the Sleeping Beauty. Sanguine. 1912

Slade and that he cared about her progress there as well as his own. In March 1912 he suggests a visit to a Pre-Raphaelite exhibition at the Tate: 'We would both learn.'[67] Hoping that she has been refreshed by her holiday in the summer of 1912, he encourages her to start work on a large canvas of her own for the 'Joy' competition. When he has problems with her mother's friend, Mrs Herbert Cohen, he writes a long letter of explanation to Ruth, clearly anxious not to lose her friendship. He recommends poetry to her, even from the trenches, and sends her his own experiments in prose as well as verse.[68] Though conscious of their class differences – he addresses her respectfully as 'Miss Löwy' to the end – he finds her a 'sympathetic listener' who puts him at his ease.[69] He also feels linked to her by race; his one reminiscence of early childhood, an unusual confidence on his part, emphasizes the Jewish element in it – his Hebrew classes. And later in the same letter he discusses a friend's idea that he should write 'Jewish plays'.[70]

With Clara Birnberg, who arrived at the Slade a year before Rosenberg, the links appear stronger at first sight. Though her background was middle-class, she had come to live in the East End after her family's fortunes had declined. (She described herself, perhaps bitterly, as a 'down start'.) A talented girl, and the only female painter in the Whitechapel Group, she had won a scholarship to study at the Central School of Art but was attending the Slade at her own expense. She could therefore identify with Rosenberg's money worries and his inability to pay for professional models, and they sat for each other.[71]

Their main connection seems to have been through their art. Clara shared Rosenberg's suspicion of the more extreme Modernist experiments and, like him, favoured portraiture at this time. She seems to have sat to him quite willingly in 1915 for what may have been his last oil painting, though she had been more reluctant to satisfy Bomberg in this respect. At the height of his passion for Michelangelo at the Slade Bomberg had decided that Clara personified the statuesque female figure of the Sistine Chapel and, with his usual persistence, urged her to model for him. Understandably suspicious of his motives – she would have witnessed his determined pursuit of Sonia, who was her friend – she had initially refused. Her final capitulation, she told Bomberg's biographer many years later, was because 'Tonks was a woman-hater and made [her] feel miserable'.[72] Bomberg's appreciation, of whatever kind, was evidently preferable to Tonks's misogyny.

There is no indication in Rosenberg's portrait of Clara (painted, incidentally, in the same blue dress in which she sat to Bomberg)[73] that Rosenberg found her either 'statuesque' or physically attractive. The main impact is one of character: he portrays a handsome, melancholy, rather withdrawn woman of obviously Jewish origin. His technique is quite different from that used for his portrait of Sonia, painted during the same period, being more impressionistic, less finished. His sensuous portrayal of Sonia, who was heavily pregnant at the time, underlines the greater detachment of his portrait of Clara, who was already committed to his friend Winsten by 1915. (She would spend the rest of her long life with him.)[74] Clara's two pencil portraits of him are similarly objective, demonstrating the 'fine delicacy and refinement of outlook' for which she would be recognized as an artist and sculptor.[75]

Drawing of Rosenberg by Clara
Birnberg (*British Library*)

Rosenberg's circle of friends at the Slade included some non-Jews among it. He became close for a time to William Roberts, for instance, a working-class boy from Hackney who had won an LCC scholarship to the Slade in 1910. By the time Rosenberg arrived, 'Bobby' had become friends with Bomberg, though he was five years younger, and the trio were for a period inseparable. All three had been unwilling apprentices in trades they disliked and relished the freedom to pursue their own ambitions. In Roberts's case this meant progressive experimentation, culminating in a highly idiosyncratic style. 'Roberts', Rosenberg would write later, ' ... is a remarkable draughtsman in a stodgy academic way, clear, logical, and fervent',[76] a remark which reveals both admiration and reservation. Perhaps because both, according to Sonia, were rather introverted, needing Bomberg to draw them out, their friendship did not survive after he and Roberts left the Slade.

Rosenberg was also friendly with Adrian Allinson who, though half-Jewish, did not identify himself as such. In fact, if Sonia is to be believed, he was positively 'anti-Semitic'.[77] An ex-medical student a year older than Rosenberg, he had been at the Slade a year when he arrived. Despite Sonia's charge of anti-Semitism, Allinson was a close friend of Gertler, who had probably introduced him to

Rosenberg. The son of the founder of Allinson's brown bread, he lived in a beautiful house in Manchester Square, where he had his own large studio and sometimes invited Rosenberg to tea. A tall, slim, elegant figure, who nevertheless enjoyed playing the buffoon, he exuded wealth and privilege and seems an unlikely friend for Rosenberg. (When he paid his first visit to the East End with Gertler, for instance, he 'felt [he] was going abroad'.)[78] It is a sign of Rosenberg's increased confidence that he not only accepted the invitations to tea at Manchester Square, but took Sonia with him. It may have been Allinson, determined like Rosenberg to rectify what he described as severe 'educational handicaps' despite his wealthy father, who helped broaden Rosenberg's intellectual horizons: 'A common need drew us together,' Allinson wrote with reference to his fellow students at the Slade, 'and through the pooling of our mental resources, each one of us benefited by the possessions of the others.'[79] While his reading in the German philosophers, with the exception of Nietzsche, appears to have passed Rosenberg by, his literary enthusiasms echoed and possibly even stimulated some of Rosenberg's own – Balzac, Flaubert, de Maupassant, Tolstoy, Gorky, Dostoevsky, Poe, Baudelaire and Verlaine.

Rosenberg makes no mention of Allinson in his list of outstanding Slade students, though Allinson would eventually become a successful caricaturist among other things. Nevertheless, it is safe to assume that anyone who had won the annual Slade scholarship on the grounds of his 'imagination'[80] would have earned Rosenberg's respect, especially since Allinson had won it jointly with Stanley Spencer. For Spencer was the artist Rosenberg most admired among his fellow students.

A year younger than Rosenberg, Spencer was known simply by the name of the Berkshire village he commuted from daily, 'Cookham'. His insignificant stature, unpolished manners, limited education and lack of worldliness, as in Rosenberg's case, had ensured that he was teased and bullied mercilessly when he had first entered the Slade, aged only seventeen, in 1908. By the time Rosenberg arrived three years later Spencer's outstanding talent had earned him great respect and the teasing had become more affectionate. But the memory of it probably made him more sympathetic to Rosenberg.

Though they overlapped by only one year they became good enough friends for Rosenberg to write to Spencer from South Africa at the end of 1914. (The letter, sadly, went astray perhaps because Rosenberg addressed it simply Cokeham' [*sic*].) He would also include Spencer among the few people he enquired after in his letters home.

Even without such evidence it is clear that Rosenberg identified closely with Spencer's artistic aims, despite Spencer's early leanings towards Cubism and the fact that he was one of the few British painters included in Fry's Second Post-Impressionist Exhibition of 1912. In his lecture on modern art Rosenberg reserves his greatest accolade for Spencer because he is 'too independent for contemporary influence',[81] a position he understood himself. Spencer, he argues, 'goes back to Giotto and Blake as his masters. He strikes even a deeper note than John, and his pictures have that sense of everlastingness[,] of no beginning and no end[,] that we get in all masterpieces.'[82] Maurice de Sausmarez claimed that Rosenberg's 'pictorial compositions show a sympathetic bond with Stanley Spencer' because his 'real aspiration was to produce imaginative works'.[83] Both young men, under the influence of Blake, displayed what Rosenberg defined as Blake's 'inspired quality':

> that unimpaired divinity that shines from all things mortal when looked [at] through the eye of imagination. Each touch is interpenetrated with sense, with life that breathes from the reachless and obscure heights and depths, deep, profound and all embracing.[84]

Like Blake, too, both young artists responded powerfully to the verbal as well as visual. Spencer's direct response to the Slade Sketch Club competition passage from Ecclesiastes in 1911 – 'Also when they shall be afraid of that which is high, and fears shall be in the way, and the almond tree shall flourish, and the grasshopper shall be a burden, and desire shall fail; because man goeth to his long home, and the mourners go about the streets'[85] – is a vivid rendering in paint of specific words in the text, 'Man Goeth to His Long Home'. His pencil, pen and wash sketch, showing a small, squat figure facing an arduous climb heavenwards through a delicately detailed landscape, has, as Richard Cork points out, 'a painstaking intensity that derives from the Pre-Raphaelites'.[86] Rosenberg, who was still in thrall to the chief of the Pre-Raphaelites, Rossetti, in 1911, would most definitely have approved. In his notes on the Tate's Pre-Raphaelite exhibition of 1911–12 he declared that the 'cream of the collection is Rossetti's pen-and-ink drawings from Tennyson, etc.'[87] What made them 'unique in art', he argued, was their 'wealth of design, the poetic exuberance of the idea, and the extraordinary dramatic and fervid execution of them',[88] all qualities Rosenberg detected in Spencer and aspired to himself. Rossetti clearly influenced his art as strongly as his poetry. *The Murder of Lorenzo* (1912), for instance, is indebted to Rossetti both in its technique and in its choice of subject matter from Keats's *Isabella*. And the title of another work from 1912, 'La Belle Dame Sans Merci', illustrating another of Keats's poems suggests Rossetti's influence, though the painting itself has unfortunately been lost.

Like the Pre-Raphaelites as a whole both Rosenberg and Spencer responded well to the biblical subjects often set by the Slade. Spencer, for example, concluded his career there by winning the 1912 Summer Competition on 'Joy' with a picture of the nativity, while Rosenberg was awarded a First Class Certificate for his entry based on the Garden of Eden myth.[89] Another of Rosenberg's oils which unlike 'Joy' has survived, is *Sing Unto the Lord*, where the importance of the biblical text is emphasized by its being attached to the painting.[90]

The most intriguing of all the friendships Rosenberg formed outside his Jewish circle, and the best-documented, was with C.R.W. Nevinson (known as 'Richard', not his first name 'Charles'). At first sight there seemed very little to unite the dandyish Nevinson, dressed by his own account in 'a large bowtie, bewaisted coat, socks and handkerchief of a delicate peacock blue' with 'a slight growth of whiskers *à la Rapin* about his ears'[91] and Rosenberg. Nevinson's upbringing in a cultured middle-class household and public-school education at Uppingham could hardly have differed more widely from the ghetto life of Rosenberg's youth and his Baker Street Board schooling. But at every point in Nevinson's life there had been conflicts, which may explain why (to quote Nevinson again) they 'got on together'.[92]

Nevinson's own explanation was tentative. To begin with, he

admitted, it was 'perhaps because I love the courage of a pariah jew'. The initial attraction for Rosenberg, he speculated, was that 'he enjoyed the contrast of what at least appeared birth and privilege compared to his life and lack of opportunity'. Their discovery of 'how wrong we both were', he believed, created a bond which lasted beyond their Slade days. When Rosenberg left for South Africa he would write regularly to Nevinson, letters which Nevinson, to his subsequent regret, would destroy, together with most of his other personal letters, when he thought he was dying.

There were other factors, Nevinson's parents for one. The only child of an eminent war correspondent, whose devotion to the army and the establishment was combined with a passionate belief in social reform, and a mother who was equally involved in progressive causes and an ardent feminist, Nevinson frequently visited White-chapel as a boy. Encouraged by the Barnetts, his father officered an East End cadet corps and his mother taught French to working-class students at Toynbee Hall. According to Gertler, one of the first friends Nevinson made at the Slade, and unlike Allinson, Nevinson had 'no English fear of the poor or the uneducated',[93] and claimed to despise snobbery. It may have been his experience at Uppingham, where he had been badly bullied, that accounted for his attitude, as well as helping to explain his bond with Rosenberg.

There are other possible explanations. Nevinson, with what Allinson described as his 'bulbous forehead, flat nose and crinkly hair', was nicknamed 'Buck nigger'.[94] And though he evidently had the confidence to rise above such a racist remark, it would almost certainly have made him more sympathetic towards Rosenberg. Temperamentally, too, there were some likenesses, Nevinson's moods fluctuating between jokiness and deep depression as Rosenberg's did. They also both loved literature far more than did most of their fellow students. And their achievements at the Slade were similarly modest, though Nevinson would later become far better known as an artist than Rosenberg. (It is worth noting that when Nevinson did achieve fame as a painter it would be, like Rosenberg, for his harsh depiction of war.) Surrounded by an exceptionally talented group of students between 1910 and 1914, neither of them would stand out. Nevinson won no scholarships or prizes and Rosenberg's greatest achievement would be a shared 2nd Prize for a Head Painting in 1912.[95] Nevinson had been very shocked indeed when Tonks told him during his first year that 'he had no talent and ought to abandon art as a career',[96] but had saved any rebelliousness for his art; by 1913 he would be painting overtly Futurist pictures and by 1914 was helping Marinetti write and publicize his *Futurist Manifesto*.

Rosenberg, on the other hand, appeared unadventurous in art, but when Professor Brown, doubtful of his abilities as a draughtsman, reputedly told Bomberg 'Rosenberg will have to leave',[97] he stood up to the professor, as I have shown. Perhaps he was still resentful of Brown's failure to recommend him for a Jewish Education Aid Society grant in April 1911. Whatever the reason, his daring in arguing with Brown was great. Bomberg, who was no coward, described it as 'an outstanding incident like Blasphemy in the Synagogue' and thought it 'a very courageous thing to do'.[98] Even allowing for exaggeration on Bomberg's part, it reveals a side to Rosenberg's character which emerges publicly only after he enters the Slade but which helps to account for his determination to realize his ambitions against all the odds. His independence was shown again in another incident at the Slade when Brown in one of his painting classes criticized Bomberg's work and the hot-tempered young man brought his palette down on his teacher's head. Rosenberg wrote to Ruth Löwy: 'I don't think the professor was at all fair to Bomberg. He may have been perfectly right from his point of view, but not to enter into Bomberg's at all I don't think was just.'[99] It is clear that neither Rosenberg nor Bomberg held their professor in quite the awe one might have expected for 1912.

In spite of Brown's more prominent position, he was a more shadowy figure at the Slade and something of a negative quantity in Rosenberg's experience there. On the surface a 'gruff, hard-bitten man', according to one student, those who got to know him well said that his military manner hid extreme shyness and 'great feeling'.[100] Rosenberg lists him in his 'Art' lecture among the English Impressionists, together with Tonks and Wilson Steer, though he does not single him out for praise. It may have been under Brown's influence that Rosenberg's own work at the Slade becomes noticeably more Impressionistic. When he arrived in 1911 his landscapes, thanks probably to Bomberg and Lily Delissa Joseph, were already tending that way, but by 1912 his portraits also begin to show signs of Impressionist technique. His *Head of a Woman 'Grey and Red'* (1912), for instance, and *Self-Portrait* (1912) (with oddly raised right hand) both look as though the paint has been applied more rapidly than in previous portraits. Details such as hair and clothes have received less attention, concentrating interest on the faces. The fullness of the woman's face has been brought out very simply by three dark broken lines, which contrast with the black angularity of her dress's neckline, and the steadfastness of her gaze by an equally simple light effect in the eyes. This is significantly absent from the eyes of the self-portrait, where the expression is consequently more brooding and restless. The nose here has been deliberately accentuated, almost to caricature, by one unbroken line from bridge to tip, which again conveys character – slight arrogance, even disdain. The mouth, save for the sensuous fullness of the lower lip, has been made little of but the shadows under the eyes have been emphasized, suggesting a rather neurotic young man.

This clear Impressionist influence could, of course, have come from any of Rosenberg's teachers, not just Brown, for Tonks, McEvoy and Wilson Steer were all leading exponents of the movement in England. And it is Steer whom Rosenberg singles out in this respect, not Brown: 'Steer is more lyrical and gay and has recaptured the golden splendour of Turner' he would claim in 'Art'.[101]

Yet Frederick Brown was an influential figure in his time, turning out generations of outstanding painters at the Slade. He was a founding member of the New English Art Club, set up originally in 1886 to counteract what Brown and his co-founders viewed as the stuffiness of the Royal Academy. By 1911 it had lost much of its freshness and pioneering spirit, but it was still an important place for a young painter to exhibit. Rosenberg should probably have been more grateful to Brown for the chance to do so, though it was Tonks and McEvoy who suggested it.

Rosenberg makes only one reference to Ambrose McEvoy, who had been brought in by Brown as a supplementary teacher of painting to Wilson Steer, but it is sufficient to show how encouraging McEvoy could be. Reporting on the fate of a drawing and painting Rosenberg had submitted to the New English Art Club in 1912,[102] he reassured his student that, though the painting had not sold 'it was liked very much, and hung half a dozen times'.[103] It was this sympathy with his students which made McEvoy, who had been a student at the Slade himself in the mid-Nineties, such a popular teacher there. His own students 'adored him and all wanted to be painted by him' according to Lady Diana Cooper (née Manners), who was one of the few to be granted that privilege. Though Rosenberg was not in that category, he would almost certainly have valued the help of a teacher who specialized in his own two interests, landscape and portraiture.

On the whole, Rosenberg appears to have had nothing but appreciation for those who understood his aims and his work. When they failed to do so, however, he could be as stubborn and assertive as he had been with Brown. It was a trait that would nearly cost him his place at the Slade only a year and a bit after gaining it.

Chapter 8

Serving Two Masters

1912

Going to the Slade has shown possibilities – has taught me to see more accurately – but one especial thing it has shown me – Art is not a plaything, it is blood and tears, it must grow up with one; and I believe I have begun too late.

– IR to Mrs Herbert Cohen, ? October 1912[1]

When Rosenberg wrote this letter to his patron towards the end of 1912, he was clearly having doubts about succeeding as an artist. As usual he blamed this on his circumstances. Yet his altercation with Mrs Cohen, which prompted the letter, and the main cause of it – his Slade Summer Competition entry for 1912, *Joy* – suggest that he failed to establish himself as a painter for quite other reasons. The incident also helps to explain why he would eventually succeed in poetry rather than art.

Rosenberg took the Slade project very seriously, starting work on it at the first possible moment in mid-July, thus allowing himself the whole of the summer vacation to complete it. Elated by finally acquiring his own studio, courtesy of Amshewitz's actor friend Michael Sherbrooke, he proudly headed his letter to his former Birkbeck teacher, Alice Wright, '32 Carlingford Road, Hampstead' and told her that he planned to paint 'a fairly big picture for the School Competition' there.[2] His respect for Miss Wright is evident in his invitation to view his efforts and make suggestions. (One of his problems with Mrs Cohen would be that, though she painted herself, he made no effort to ask her advice and, when she offered it nevertheless, rejected it completely.) His initial attempt, painted partly in Bomberg's studio where they could share models, did not satisfy him, possibly because it showed too much of his friend's Modernist influence.[3]

By 6 August Rosenberg is telling Miss Wright that he has taken a 'violent dislike' to his 'first design' and has made a new start: 'It is absolutely another thing now, though the literary idea is the same.'[4] His main problem at this stage appears to be matching his colour conception – 'a wonderful scheme of rose silver and gold' – with the reality, which he humorously admits is still a rather mundane affair of 'pink yellow and blue'.[5] He may have been aiming at something similar to the 'definite patterns of colour' in 'rose and green and pearl' which he admired in Cézanne for the 'beautiful harmonies' thus created.[6] A sympathetic Miss Wright immediately supplied him with a pearl and his thank-you letter makes it clear that he is striving for a visionary effect: 'I have not seen the pearl by day but it looks gorgeous by night – it is just that iride[sce]nce – that shimmering quality I want to make the whole scheme of my picture.'[7] His palette is now 'rose *pearl* and gold – a dream picture' (my italics) and is so successful in conveying his intention that his landlady asks him if it *is* a dream.[8]

Miss Wright is unable to solve his other pressing problem, however, that of models. He can afford very few and has to appeal to family and friends to sit for him. Two of his sisters, Annie and Ray, their friend Sarah Maunter, and Sonia Cohen and Ruth Löwy oblige, but he still has a problem, since decorum demands that he paints them clothed, especially as he is working alone in his studio. Yet most of his figures are to be naked. (Rosenberg's nephew, Bernard Wynick, who knew *Joy* well from his childhood, remembered it being a large picture, approximately 6ft x 4ft, full of nude figures, except, he tactfully added, that of his Aunt Ray. He might also have included Ruth Löwy, clothed as a sleeping beauty in the only known remnant of the picture to have survived as an initial sketch.)[9] The one model he can afford, Miss Grimshaw, is too scraggy for the 'titanic' forms he envisages. Nor can he find anyone suitable for his chief head, 'Joy'. And when he does come across the 'fine type' he needs for it, her father does not like the idea of her posing for him – 'I don't know what the man imagined I was going to do' Rosenberg writes despairingly to Ruth Löwy.[10]

By the end of September, after ten weeks' hard work mostly alone in his studio, his picture is 'as it were – in the frying pan – not quite raw – not yet quite done'.[11] Still not sure of its final 'arrangement', he hopes that another week will decide it. Judging from Mrs Cohen's reaction when she was finally allowed to see *Joy* in early October, it was still fairly 'raw' when he submitted it at the beginning of the Slade's autumn term:

> I am sorry if I have disappointed you [Rosenberg wrote stiffly, following her visit]. If you tell me what was expected of me I shall have the satisfaction of knowing by how much I have erred. You were disappointed in my picture for its unfinished state – I have no wish to defend myself – or I might ask what you mean by finish: – and you are convinced I could have done better. I thank you for the compliment but I do not think it deserved – I did my best.[12]

Ostensibly a letter of apology, the tone is far from apologetic and was hardly likely to mollify Mrs Cohen.

It is impossible not to sympathize with both sides in this disagreement, which ended with Mrs Cohen declining to pay any further fees for Rosenberg at the Slade. Her own more conservative approach to art had not prepared her for Rosenberg's Blakean experiment, and to her eyes, untutored in any of the more radical modern movements, *Joy* simply appeared 'unfinished'. She was already irritated by his failure to send her cheque for the autumn term's fees to the Slade, not realizing that it had been five shillings short and that Rosenberg, unable to make up the difference from his small allowance (which he had spent mostly on having his boots repaired), was saving up to do so. Meantime the Slade had written to Mrs Cohen. She was also offended by the badly smudged letter of explanation he had sent her about the mix-up, not realizing that most of his correspondence, due partly to his poor education, gave an impression of great carelessness. To her eyes it only confirmed her suspicion, which his picture would reinforce, that he was not making much effort or working hard. She also suspected that he was becoming arrogant and overconfident. He was, she concluded, 'rude, ungentlemanly[,] ungrateful'[13] and he needed to get into a 'more healthy' style of work.[14]

Rosenberg was understandably enraged. Mrs Cohen had started

sending her secretary round to inspect his work before he moved to Hampstead and, perhaps as a result of an unsatisfactory report, had already reduced his small allowance further. He had been working very hard indeed at *Joy* and, though his sister Minnie described it as being 'full of sadness',[15] he felt that he had realized something of his vision. Tonks seemed to confirm this by awarding *Joy* a First Class Certificate, saying it 'showed a hopeful future and had great charm', though he also appeared to agree to some extent with Mrs Cohen: Rosenberg, he believed, 'wanted more study'.[16] For someone used to crowded family life Rosenberg had not found it easy living on his own: 'I worked all day and walked about in the rain all evening until I was wet through and tired out' he told Mrs Cohen '– that was the only amusement I got.'[17] Her doubting him was the last straw and he defended himself vigorously:

You did ask me whether I had been working hard, and I was so taken back [*sic*] at the question that I couldn't think what to say. If you did not think the work done sufficient evidence, what had I to say? I have no idea what you expected to see. I cannot conceive who gave you the idea that I had such big notions of myself, are you sure the people you enquired of know me, and meant me[?] You say people I have lately come in contact with. I have hardly seen anyone during the holidays – and I certainly have not been ashamed of my opinions, not about myself, but others – when I have; and if one does say anything in an excited, unguarded moment – perhaps an expression of what one would like to be – it is distorted and interpreted as conceit – when in honesty it should be overlooked. I am not very inquisitive naturally, but I think it concerns me to know what you mean by poses and mannerisms – and whose advice do I not take who are in a position to give – and what more healthy style of work do you wish me to adopt?[18]

The tone of Rosenberg's letters continues to be brusque, almost provocative, rather than conciliatory right up to December, when he tells Mrs Cohen of his meeting with the secretary of the JEAS, Mr Lesser, to whom he applies for fees when hers run out: 'I told him I was very vague as to what you expected me to do, or in which way you wished me to show my appreciation of what you had done – and that I was accused of all sorts of things, and that I was put into a state of mind which made working very difficult."[19] Though not in any position to afford pride, Rosenberg had a great deal of it and was prepared to sacrifice his Slade career to satisfy it if necessary. As Laurence Binyon would quickly realize when he met him this same year, 'with his sensitive artist's pride and jealous independence of spirit, he was not always easy to understand'.[20] Binyon may actually have been referring to Mrs Cohen – though there were plenty of other candidates – when he admitted that Rosenberg's benefactors 'sometimes felt that their efforts did not seem to be appreciated'.[21]

Fortunately Rosenberg's Slade career did not need to be sacrificed to his pride. Mrs Cohen, whatever her other failings, was kindhearted and genuinely wanted to help talent in those less privileged than herself. A devout woman, she took her religious duties seriously. (She was also a committed Zionist, which by 1912 Rosenberg was not, another possible cause of friction between them.) Despite the impression Rosenberg gave to his friends, it was she, not he, who first approached the Jewish Education Aid Society about taking over payment of his fees, an important detail. For she must have known that the request, coming from such an influential member of the Jewish community, was unlikely to be refused. The JEAS had also been urged to help Rosenberg, should he approach them, by Professor Brown, who had written in July 1912 to say (a little ambiguously) that Rosenberg had 'surpassed expectations' in his first year at the Slade.[22] In addition, Mrs Cohen was ready to continue paying Rosenberg's maintenance allowance. In fact, once he was no longer fully dependent on her, their relationship improved and he would spend at least one holiday at her Bournemouth house.[23]

The whole affair, trivial though it may now seem, underlines just how ill fitted Rosenberg was to be a painter, given his character and background, and the conditions that prevailed in pre-war England. In 1912 the art world still operated on a system of patronage, whereby poor, aspiring artists were dependent on wealthy art-lovers or philanthropists to support them and commission work from them. Painting, which required a studio, canvases, oil paints and other expensive equipment, was far more dependent on patronage than writing. Only the most outstanding talents, such as Bomberg's, could afford to be independent, and even he would suffer for it later on. Lacking Gertler's charm and social ease, Rosenberg's one hope of succeeding as an artist would have him suppress his most basic instinct, the need for independence.

Another incident in autumn 1912 shows that he was quite unable to do this. Shortly after his row with Mrs Cohen he 'broke' with his other patron, Mr Sherbrooke,[24] even though this meant losing the studio Sherbrooke was renting for him. His own efforts to find a replacement he could afford were ineffectual and he would be forced to return home from October 1912 until early 1913, when he started renting a room, near Bomberg's current studio, at 1 St George's Square, Chalk Farm.[25] (His family moved from 159 Oxford Street to 87 Dempsey Street this winter and would remain there for the rest of his life.) He was, nevertheless, unrepentant.

Initially, Rosenberg had been bowled over by Sherbrooke, particularly by his dramatic rendering of poetry, he told Ruth Löwy early in 1912:

He took me home with him and almost made me delirious with delight at some of his marvellous recitations. His power is almost incredible – I have never seen anything like it and could hardly conceive anything so. He gave [Poe's] the Raven. The melancholy insistence – the perpetual recurring note of despair – the gradual tightening to the climax.[26]

His immediate response was to write Sherbrooke two poems.[27]

Rosenberg's explanation for his sudden break with Sherbrooke a few months later – that his patron's 'goodness became unendurable'[28] – if true, underlines how hard he found it to accept favours, even from people he admired. He realized that his pride had put him in a 'very serious situation', as he described it to Miss Wright in December 1912 while waiting to hear whether the Jewish Education Aid Society would take over the paying of his Slade fees: 'I have thrown over my patrons, they were so unbearable, and as I can't do commercial work, and I have no other kind of work to show, it puts me in a fix.'[29] On this occasion he was bailed out by the Society, but his problems with patronage remained. The JEAS's funds were limited, the money they paid out strictly a loan, and Rosenberg would still need a patron in the future.

The main reason Rosenberg was less successful as a painter than as a poet, however, lay more in the nature of his creativity than in his character. His reference (in his letter to Miss Wright) to the 'literary idea' behind his painting *Joy* is highly significant, suggesting that he needed the stimulus of words and narrative to set his imagination working fully. Before he even began to paint *Joy*, he had expressed his conception for it in poetry, so that the painting became more of a translation, or illustration, of an original idea than a primary expression of his vision.[30] It is perhaps fitting that, while the painting would be lost, the poem would survive. The first stanza of 'The Garden of Joy', which he sent to Ruth Löwy with the words 'live in the garden of Joy so that when you get back you will know what sort of expression to wear when I put you in my "garden of Joy"',[31] shows how clearly he had envisaged his concept verbally:

> In honey-essenced bliss of sleep's deceit
> My sense lay drowned, and my soul's eyes saw clear,
> Unstranged to wonder, made familiar
> By instant seeing, Eden's garden sweet,
> Shedding upon mine eyelids odorous heat
> Of the light fingered golden atmosphere
> Shaken through boughs whose whisperings I could hear.
> Beneath, within the covert's cool retreat
> Of the spread boughs stood shapes who swayed the boughs,
> And bright fruit fell, laughing to leave green house;
> While gleeful children dabbled with the sun
> Caught the strange fruit, then ran with smiles of love
> To earth, whose peoples as they ate thereof
> Soft sank into the garden, one by one.[32]

The dreamer-narrator, familiar to Rosenberg from Keats and other Romantics, and the conjuring up of the Garden of Eden are essentially literary devices. The influence of that most literary of poets, Milton, whom Rosenberg had just been reading, is also evident, not just in the many echoes of *Paradise Lost*, but also in the Latinate, often archaic diction.

Laurence Binyon, a connoisseur of both art and poetry, since beside being an established poet he was Assistant Keeper in Prints and Drawings at the British Museum, felt that, though Rosenberg was a 'capable draughtsman' and 'could conceive an interesting design', art was not his 'inevitable means of expression'.[33] And, of all the drawings and paintings Rosenberg showed him when they first met, it was *Joy* that confirmed Binyon's belief.

> [It was] a large ambitious composition – an oil-painting which I fancy was never completed. I cannot recall the nominal subject, but it was saturated with symbolism and required a good deal of explanation. I liked the mysteriousness of it, and the ideas which inspired the painting had suggested figures and groups and visionary glimpses of landscape which had passages of real beauty, though the whole work had grown impossibly complex with its convolutions of symbolic meaning. It reminded me of his poetry; and I think that represented his natural bent in art.[34]

Rosenberg himself recognized that there was a difference between imagination in art and imagination in literature. In a short prose piece on the Pre-Raphaelites he emphasized that 'By imagination in paint we do not encroach on the domain of the writer; we give what the writer cannot give, with all his advantages, the visible aspect of things, which the writer can only suggest . . .'[35] If Binyon was right, Rosenberg's imagination functioned most effectively as a poet, though enriched by his training as a painter.

Rosenberg had been writing a great many poems other than 'The Garden of Joy' in the summer of 1912. With a, by now, predictable swing of the pendulum, no sooner was he established at the Slade following his artistic ambitions in earnest, than his attention turned back to his writing. Other Slade students apart from Kramer and Charlton remembered his poetic activities there, Goldstein, for instance, who arrived at the Slade in 1912. Gertler, too, described how, 'while they were drawing side by side', Rosenberg would 'pass him a piece of paper with a poem written on it'.[36]

It was not the only occasion on which Rosenberg's poetry interfered with his art. Despite his indignant rebuttal of Mrs Cohen's accusations, he had not worked single-mindedly on *Joy*, admitting to Ruth Löwy that, when the summer rains had been at their worst, he had been 'writing doleful ditties'.[37] He was also sending poems and prose to Miss Seaton and Miss Wright, though his enthusiasm for prose was half-hearted at best, for reasons that point to the nature of his verse. 'Prose is so diffuse and has not the advantages of poetry' he would write to a later friend.[38] Though he could admire the 'terrific conceptions' of writers such as Balzac and Stendhal, he preferred Hardy's poetry to his novels: 'There is so much unessential writing one puts in a novel and yet which must be there, at the same time, that makes me regard novel writing as a mistaken art.'[39] (He had admitted to Leftwich in 1911 that he preferred his sister's cheap novelettes to those by serious writers in the genre.) Accomplished though his prose can be – his review of an exhibition of work by Amshewitz and another Jewish painter, Henry Ospovat, for instance, was thought professional enough for publication in the *Jewish Chronicle* in May 1912[40] – it lacks the distinctiveness of his verse, in particular its packed, explosive quality. He himself appears to have recognized this, for it was poetry not prose that he sent to Laurence Binyon this year by way of introduction.

'I cannot precisely fix the date' Binyon wrote in an 'Introductory Memoir' to his and Gordon Bottomley's 1922 edition of Rosenberg's verse:

> but it must have been some time in 1912, when one morning there came to me a letter in an untidy hand from an address in Whitechapel, enclosing some pages of verse on which criticism was asked, and signed 'Isaac Rosenberg'. It was impossible not to be struck by something unusual in the quality of the poems. Thoughts and emotions of no common nature struggled for expression, and at times there gushed forth a pure song which haunted the memory.[41]

Laurence Binyon by Sir
William Rothenstein, c. 1923
(*BACS*)

In approaching Binyon, Rosenberg was reaching out beyond his East End Jewish world to the establishment. Discouraged by Zang-will's apparent failure to respond to at least two letters, and despairing of Amshewitz's literary contacts, Austin Harrison and Holbrook Jackson, who made noises but did nothing, he was desperate to be recognized as a poet. (One of the first things he would ask Binyon would be 'if you could give me introductions to Editors'.)[42] He had acquired a small volume of Binyon's poems in 1911, which he 'always carried about with him' according to the Whitechapel librarian F. B. Bogdin.[43] Binyon, over twenty years older than Rosenberg and a 'Georgian' poet of conservative tendencies, may not seem to have been the most obvious choice for someone of Rosenberg's anarchic instincts in verse, but he had in fact some sympathy with the Modernist cause. It was he who had introduced the instigator of many of the new poetic movements of the early twentieth century, Ezra Pound, to another rebel, Wyndham Lewis, in about 1910.[44] In his capacity as a scholar of Oriental languages, he also helped Pound with his experiments in Chinese and Japanese literature.

Binyon's response to the 'few pages of verse' Rosenberg sent him was both immediate and positive, prompting an equally swift reply from Rosenberg, who enclosed a copy of 'a sort of autobiography' (possibly 'Rudolph') written a year earlier. 'You will see from that that my circumstances have not been very favourable for artistic production,' he wrote, 'but generally I am optimistic, I suppose, because I am young and do not properly realize the difficulties.'[45] Referring to his Slade training – 'I spend most of my time drawing' – Rosenberg makes a statement which suggests that he was still devoting the greater part of his creative efforts, if not the greater part of his time, to poetry: 'I find writing interferes with drawing a good deal, and is far more exhausting.'[46] The relative lack of tension in Rosenberg's graphic work as compared with his verse probably explains why he found writing poetry more tiring. 'At present' he told Binyon, he was 'practising portraiture, as it was necessary to earn a living', but aspired to do 'imaginative work'.[47]

Binyon's assessment of Rosenberg, whom he invited to visit him at the British Museum, is very different from Mrs Cohen's in her letters of complaint but probably comes close to her first impression of him before he began to react to her 'patronage':

Small in stature, dark, bright-eyed, thoroughly Jewish in type, he seemed a boy with an unusual mixture of self-reliance and modesty. Indeed, no one could have had a more independent nature. Obviously sensitive, he was not touchy or aggressive. Possessed of vivid enthusiasms, he was shy in speech. One found in talk how strangely little of second-hand (in one of his age) there was in his opinions, how fresh a mind he brought to what he saw and read. There was an odd kind of charm in his manner which came from his earnest, transparent sincerity.[48]

It may have been his meeting with such an obviously sympathetic person which decided Rosenberg shortly after this meeting to publish at his own expense his first volume of poems, *Night and Day*. Mr Bogdin, who was presented with a copy, gained the impression that Binyon 'helped financially to have the booklet printed'.[49] Though this was almost certainly not the case, Binyon did probably help Rosenberg with later publications. According to Morris Robinson, who became a close friend of Rosenberg's in 1914, Isaac 'always told [him] that Laurence Binyon would publish everything he produced as he had a great admiration for him and always spoke of him as the only man who understood great works'.[50] By 'great works' Rosenberg undoubtedly meant art as well as literature, for one thing that must have appealed to Rosenberg in Binyon was his commitment to both disciplines, epitomized for them both, it would seem, in the engraver-poet Blake. Binyon would bring out four books on Blake between 1902 and 1926 and in 1931 edit a collection of Blake's poems. His emphasis on Blake's 'isolat[ion] in his own age ... by warping circumstances', his 'range and inventiveness as a technician' and the relative lack of understanding and appreciation of his work 'chiefly because it is little known' sounds very similar to his response to Rosenberg.[51]

Rosenberg would remain in touch with Binyon until at least 1917, when the older man was still responding to the poetry he sent him 'with the paternal rod half raised in one hand and some sweets and chocolates in the other', as Rosenberg put it.[52] Binyon's first advice to the poet, which Rosenberg was not sure he had 'quite followed', was to be 'more concrete',[53] and the 'paternal rod' was probably justified on occasions. Normally very bad at accepting criticism, he was surprisingly ready to accept Binyon's, which he thought 'very good'.[54] Even when Binyon described his poetry as emerging 'in clotted gushes and spasms',[55] he was ready to listen and would always be grateful for his interest in his work.

Although Binyon would not be of as much practical help as the next establishment figure Rosenberg met, Edward Marsh, he was a significant factor in his development. The first literary figure of any material consequence in Rosenberg's life, he encouraged him to continue with his poetry at a crossroads in his career. He would also be jointly responsible for the first edition of Rosenberg's work to be published after his death, when his sympathetic introduction to it, combined with his high reputation in 1922, ensured that Heinemann's small book was noticed in the literary world and Rosenberg's name remarked. It is ironic to think that nearly a century later, while Rosenberg's stock continues to rise, Binyon's own verse is virtually forgotten and the only lines of his known to most people nowadays are those which were inspired by deaths similar to that of his young protégé in the First World War: 'At the going down of the sun and in the morning / We will remember them.'[56]

Binyon's response to Rosenberg in 1912 probably encouraged him to publish *Night and Day* that same year, but there were others who were similarly positive. One of them was Ruth Löwy's cousin-in-law, a barrister called Cyril Picciotto, to whom she had shown his poems. Rosenberg's reaction to his praise shows just how uncertain he was feeling about his verse at this time. He wrote to Ruth Löwy:

> I feel very elated at Mr Picciotto liking my poems, as I was very anxious to know. Nothing is rarer than good poetry – and nothing more discouraging than the writing of poetry. One might write for pleasure but I doubt[,] if there is no stronger motive[,] whether one would be incited to ambitious work. Circumstances and other considerations have prevented me from applying myself assiduously, and also diffidence – so you can imagine what a rare pleasure it is to me when people appreciate my efforts.[57]

Another possible reason for Rosenberg's decision to publish his verse in 1912 is that he was beginning to realize at some level, among an exceptionally talented group of artists at the Slade, that he would never rise above the competent in art and that poetry was his true forte, as Bomberg believed. A poem written at this time throws an interesting light on this question. We know from Binyon that Rossetti still came 'first for Rosenberg among modern artists'[58] as late as 1912, and in choosing to write about a painter whom Rossetti and his fellow Pre-Raphaelites had reacted against – Raphael – Rosenberg may indirectly have been debating the possibility of a failure of imagination in himself as an artist. Though his poem 'Raphael' was modelled firmly on Browning's poem on a similar theme, 'Andrea del Sarto', Rosenberg attributes *his* chosen painter's failure not just (as Browning does) to his weakness for his wife and his need to provide her with a comfortable lifestyle, but also to an innate lack of greatness in the medium. (Raphael is made in Rosenberg's poem to envy the 'giant craggy heights' of one of Tonks's heroes,

Michelangelo.)[59] When Rosenberg puts the following words into Raphael's mouth, it is hard not to interpret them autobiographically as a reference to the far greater talent of friends like Bomberg, Gertler and Spencer compared with himself:

> What do I labour for if all is thus?
> I triumph, but my triumph is my scorn.
> 'Tis true I love my labour, and the days
> Pass pleasantly,
> But what is it I love in it – desire
> Accomplished? never have I reached
> The halfway of the purpose I have planned.[60]

Rosenberg also has Raphael declare towards the end of the poem: 'I would I were a poet – love – this once.' A pastiche of Browning, however skilful, 'Raphael' is interesting more for its content than its technique, though it does anticipate Rosenberg's later verse drama and indicates the direction his language was taking away from his early Romantic models towards Browning's more elliptical, less mellifluous style.

'Raphael' was not included in *Night and Day* when it came out in April or May 1912, possibly because it was written later in the year in response to Rosenberg's failure to win the Slade's Summer Competition with *Joy*. Still on reasonably good terms with Mrs Cohen when he decided to publish his little volume, he approached her for a loan of two pounds to cover costs. Binyon, who was presented with one of the fifty or so copies printed, thought that the twenty-four-page pamphlet was 'probably all that Rosenberg cared to preserve of his early verse',[61] but it is more likely that it was all he could afford. Two pounds represented a large sum of money to him in 1912, especially since he must have suspected how unlikely he was to be able to repay it from sales, as he had promised Mrs Cohen.

His problem was compounded by the length of his title poem, which he had been working on since 1910 or 1911. Though 'Night and Day' had some of his earlier verses woven into it, its 370 lines consisted largely of new material and left little room for much else.

He had to limit himself to nine of his other efforts, and at least one of these, the sonnet 'To J.H. Amschewitz', was probably put in to please. The other eight – 'Aspiration', 'Heart's First Word' (I), 'When I Went Forth', 'In November', 'Lady, You Are My God', 'Spiritual Isolation', 'Tess' and 'O! In a World of Men and Women' – are a mixture of love lyrics and expressions of his yearning for spiritual and artistic fulfilment. As he wrote to Binyon this year, his muse, still a rather 'conventional' one, was 'far away and dreamy, she [did] not seek beauty in common life'.[62]

Despite the limitations imposed on *Night and Day*, Rosenberg was fortunate in finding someone to print it so cheaply. This had come about partly by chance, when he met Reuben Cohen, who worked for a printer, Israel Narodiczky, at 48 Mile End Road. Leftwich may have witnessed Rosenberg's first meeting with Cohen when he described them in his diary on 29 March 1911 as deep in conversation. Cohen clearly believed in Rosenberg: he undertook the printing of *Night and Day* in 1912 and *Youth* in 1915, and in the same year he founded a magazine with him, *The Jewish Standard*. (Written mainly by Cohen, it would also contain the opening paragraphs of Rosenberg's first lecture on 'Art', but would fold after a single issue.) And in 1916, the year before Cohen returned to his native Russia, he would set up his own press, the Paragon Printing Works, for the sole purpose, apparently, of printing Rosenberg's third pamphlet, *Moses*. Nicknamed 'Crazy' Cohen, he was described by Leftwich as 'a kindly, fuddled fellow with literary pretensions who used to go about a lot with Rosenberg, trying to induce him to make changes in his text'. He also described him as 'queer' (not in the modern sense), but Rosenberg thought him 'superb'.[63] He would be especially grateful to him for his production of *Moses* – 'he's made quite an original thing of it'[64] – and be inspired by Cohen's 'million hints for new things'.[65]

Without Cohen's employer, Narodiczky, however, who allowed Cohen to use his printing machine for all these ventures, it is unlikely that *Night and Day* would have materialized. A far more practical man than 'Crazy' Cohen, he was equally idealistic and enthusiastic about literature. Well known for his willingness to produce the works of poor aspiring writers, anarchists and rebels at prices they could afford, he was not only responsible for the printing of all Rosenberg's publications, but also for the first twelve issues of the leading East End radical Rudolf Rocker's magazine *Germinal*, and the only issues of D.H. Lawrence and John Middleton Murry's pacifist magazine to appear before the police banned it.[66]

It seems appropriate that Narodiczky should be the printer of both Rosenberg and Lawrence, though Rosenberg would not necessarily have thought so. He admired Lawrence's 'power, but not his outlook' in his poems and declined the chance to read another book by him when it was offered.[67] Yet as F.R. Leavis pointed out, they had much in common, and not just their poor, working-class backgrounds and dual interest in painting and writing. However amateurishly Lawrence's vision in art was expressed by comparison with the professionally trained Rosenberg, they shared (to repeat Leavis's words) a 'radical and religious' interest in life which they struggled to express in their works.[68]

Rosenberg's quest for such a meaning shapes the title poem of *Night and Day*, linking it firmly to his role as a poet. In the prose 'Argument' which prefaces the piece, the poet looks to the stars for an answer but receives none. 'Night' having failed him, the poet next questions 'Day', 'walk[ing] through the city, out into the woods' where nature hopefully will provide an answer. Dreaming beneath the trees, he hears 'Desire sing a song of Immortality, / Hope, a song of Love, / And Beauty, a song of the Eternal Rhythm'.[69] But it is not until twilight, that period between day and night which Rosenberg loved for its mysteriousness and ambiguity, just as he would later love the dawn, that the poet arrives at the heart of things: 'for Beauty has taught him to hear, Hope to feel, and Desire, a conception of attainment'.[70]

The allegory is clear and already largely familiar to many readers from two of Rosenberg's continuing influences, Shelley and Keats. (Parallels with *The Triumph of Life* and *Endymion* abound.) Other main influences are the Milton of 'Il. Penseroso' and 'L'Allegro' and Blake's *Songs of Innocence and Experience*. There are signs of other minor influences but it is Francis Thompson who appears to exercise the strongest pull on him by 1912, when he tells Binyon of his 'immense admiration' for this 'tremendous' poet.[71]

Like Thompson a driven spirit, Rosenberg's narrator despairs of an answer for the greater part of 'Night and Day', though when he does find it eventually in the song of the evening star, it appears to lie nearer to the Romantics' faith in Beauty. There is an important distinction from the Romantics, however, and one which suggests that Rosenberg is gradually moving away from them towards a harsher view of life more in consonance with his upbringing. For his narrator, while searching as assiduously for Truth as his predecessors in literature, asks himself 'whether he is the scapegoat to bear the sins of humanity upon himself, and to waste his life to discover the secret of God' for all mankind.[72] The concept of the scapegoat, familiar to Rosenberg from orthodox Judaism, where it is an important religious symbol, transforms 'Night and Day' from a conventional Romantic quest allegory into something more akin to his own vision of life. Throughout his adulthood he would frequently return to the notion of the scapegoat learned in childhood, comparing himself on a number of occasions with the Christian embodiment of the man who 'b[ore] the sins of humanity upon himself', Jesus Christ. When his suffering and bewilderment in the First World War were at their worst, for instance, he would write (in a passage deleted by the army censor): 'What is happening to me is more tragic than the "passion play". Christ never endured what I endure.'[73]

Such insights into Rosenberg's character and outlook make 'Night and Day' well worth reading, despite some derivativeness and difficulty of form. His method of incorporating previously completed poems into it and adding separate short pieces, not complete in themselves but stages on the way to a longer work, almost certainly accounts for the not entirely satisfactory form of the finished piece. It was a method adopted partly through force of circumstances, his sister Annie remembered: 'He would wake up in the middle of the night, light his bit of candle and write down the lines that came to him.'[74] But possibly because of this early habit, when his situation improved a little and he had more time and privacy, he seems to have been unable to work any other way: 'that is the only way I can write, in scraps, and then join them together' he would tell Edward Marsh later.[75] And, though his 'method' was not entirely successful in 'Night and Day', in later works like 'Dead Man's Dump' it could result in a different kind of synthesis from that of traditional models, more akin to Pound and Eliot's experiments in poems like *Hugh Selwyn Mauberley* and *The Waste Land*, where the impression of fragmentariness is deliberate. For by then Rosenberg would, as he explained rather defensively in the same letter to Marsh, 'have the *one idea* in mind'.

Even 'Night and Day', for all its shortcomings, shows flashes of that ability to 'look at things in the simple, large way' that he had previously envied in all the 'great poets'.[76] There are also interesting anticipations in *Night and Day*'s title poem and supporting pieces of what will become familiar Rosenberg territory. Apart from his theme of the poet as 'one flower whose ardent fragrance wastes for all',[77] for instance, he is already dealing, as he will in many of his greatest poems, with the power of beauty but warning of the danger hidden within it. In one of his most effective passages in 'Day', for example, his description of the loveliness of nature is followed by hints at a hidden threat lurking there:

> Let me weave my fantasy
> Of this web like broken glass
> Gleaming through the fretted leaves
> In a quaint intricacy,
> Diamond tipping all the grass.
>
> Hearken as the spirit heaves
> Thro' the branches and the leaves
> In the shudder of their pulse.
> Delicate nature trembles so
> To a ruder nature's touch,
> And of peace that these convulse
> They have little who should much.
> Life is so.
> Let me carve my fantasy
> Of the fretwork of the leaves.
>
> Then the trees bent and shook with laughter,
> Each leaf sparkled and danced with glee.

On my heart their sobs came after,
Demons gurgling over me.
And my heart was chilled and shaken,
And I said thro' my great fear,
When the throat of tears is slaken
Joy must come for joy will hear.[78]

This is the same Rosenberg who, after describing the beauty of the larks' song to the weary soldiers returning from duty, warns that 'Death could drop from the dark / As easily as song', comparing it to the lure of 'a girl's dark hair for she dreams no ruin lies there, / Or her kisses where a serpent hides'.[79]

Likewise the fickleness of God, a powerful theme throughout his war poems, is already hinted at in *Night and Day*. For while the God of the title poem appears to be beneficent, bestowing kisses and the 'music of his smile' on the narrator, He 'gives no June, and Heaven is as a wall. / No symboled answer' to the poet's 'questionings'. In 'Spiritual Isolation', God becomes actively uncooperative, shunning the narrator 'even as a wretch stricken with leprosy' and, in a reversal of Thompson's 'The Hound of Heaven', flees from him as he seeks Him out. It is the start of an evolution in Rosenberg's concept of God that will bring him to reject the male God of both Judaism and Christianity as malignant and tyrannical in favour of a female God, who will be embodied first in a poem of that name, then most forcibly (and puzzlingly) in his favourite poem, 'Daughters of War'. This female God, hinted at in the mysterious figure of Twilight in 'Night and Day', will merge at times with his creation of an idealized female mate, bringing with it the theme of lack of fulfilment, either through timidity or circumstances:

Twilight's wide eyes are mystical
With some far off knowledge,
Secret is the mouth of her,
And secret her eyes.

Lo! she braideth her hair
Of dim soft purple and thread of satin.

Lo! she flasheth her hand—
Her hand of pearl and silver in shadow.
Slowly she braideth her hair
Over her glimmering eyes,
Floating her ambient robes
Over the trees and the skies.
Over the wind-footing grass.
Softly she braideth her hair
With shadow deeper than thought.

To make her comely for night?
To make her meet for the night?

Slowly she heaveth her breast,
For the night to lie there and rest?[80]

The sensuousness and voluptuousness of the language here will become a familiar feature of Rosenberg's later work, even of his war poetry. In 'Daughters of War', for instance, the Amazonians' grotesque yearning for the dead and dying soldiers is given physical embodiment as he describes 'the mighty daughters' giant sighs / In sleepless passion for the sons of valour, / And envy of the days of flesh'.[81]

Rosenberg's description in 'Night and Day' of another grotesque scene, 'the foul heat of painted faces', their 'lewd leer' and 'ribald breath' as they process in life's pageant towards death, links this sordidness with the city: his early lines 'In the Workshop' – 'Dim, watery lights gleaming on gibbering faces . . .' – are now incorporated as a lurid description of a city 'tavern'. But like Blake, Rosenberg already has a vision of the twofold potential in things and the sudden effect of the sun gleaming on the 'dim monstrous buildings' transforms them into 'buildings glorified, / Whose windows shine', giving the narrator a glimpse of heaven.[82]

Rosenberg's tendency to combine the concrete with the abstract, the literal with the figurative, is already evident in 'Night and Day', making his language dense and many-layered. His strong visual sense, as in so many later poems, enables him to bring his scenes to life; his city street glittering in the midday sun is as vivid and suggestive as the 'plunging' limber-carts full of barbed wire in 'Dead Man's Dump', which, 'Racketed with their rusty freight, / Stuck out like many crowns of thorns'.[83] He 'weaves his fantasy' in free verse, much readier to experiment in poetry than in painting, as I have pointed out. The work is held together by clusters of images which, again, anticipate his later verse. The most dominant of these is music. As Charles Tomlinson notes, 'Music seems to stand in Rosenberg's poetry for a kind of attitude of mind which can hear, as it were, the true melody of its own being and to which it had been previously deaf because insufficiently alive.'[84] Music often takes the form, now and later, of birdsong, both real and imaginary. And listening to it, the poet yearns to 'burst this trammel of my flesh', introducing another set of images dominant throughout Rosenberg's verse. Centring on the notion of imprisonment, they will include, as previously, the mesh, the web, the cage, and its bars, and relate back to the danger hidden in beauty, especially that of women's hair, their mouths, their kisses. The mirrors where they (and Rosenberg, the painter of many self-portraits) view themselves make frequent appearances in this 1912 volume, suggesting a fear that he is not experiencing life itself but only a reflection of it in his art. This obsession may also have been encouraged by Laurence Binyon's long poem 'The Mirror', which he read shortly after their first meeting this year.[85]

Rosenberg's fear that he is not participating directly in life is expressed forcefully in one of the most revealing poems in *Night and Day*, 'Aspiration', which opens with another image central to his verse, roots. The roots, which promise life, deceive, being 'roots of a dead universe'; and, like the mirror, the shadow and the ghosts, are illusory, expressing perhaps the poet's frustration at being unable to convey his vision of reality.[86] Like Tennyson's Lady of Shalott, who figures in one of Rosenberg's earliest paintings, the poet is unable to break through to the real world, or to convey, in his own words, 'what we cannot see'.

The frustrated longing expressed in 'Aspiration' is repeated in other poems, 'O! in a world of men and women', for example, and is the predominant emotion to emerge from Rosenberg's first public collection of verse. It was partly in response to such feelings that he had published *Night and Day*. By sending it to literary editors, as well as to friends and family, he hoped to be acknowledged as a poet. But while, as C.H. Sisson has written, the main impression on reading *Night and Day* is of 'a new and individual force' and though the response from well-wishers like Alice Wright and her sister was positive, prompting their request for a second copy to send to influential friends, the literary world ignored Rosenberg's little grey, soft-covered book. Even the aspiring intellectuals who bettered themselves nightly at Toynbee Hall rejected it. For when Leftwich loyally stood at its gate trying to interest them in *Night and Day*, he failed to sell a single copy. By September 1912 Rosenberg had given away the whole of his small edition with no tangible results. Ironically, it is now the rarest and most valuable of his three self-publications.

Chapter 9

'His Divided Self': John Rodker, Sonia Cohen and the 'Slot Meter'

1912–1913

The Poet (I)

The trouble of the universe is on his wonder-travelled eyes.
Ah, vain for him the starry quest, the spirit's wistful sacrifice.
For though the glory of the heavens celestially in glimpses seen
Illumines his rapt gazing, still the senses shut him in.
No fellowship of suffering to meet his tear-bewildered ways.
Alone he bears the burden of alienated days.
He is a part of paradise that all the earth has pressed between,
And when he calls unto the stars of paradise with heaven-
    sweet songs
To his divided self he calls and sings the story of earth's wrongs.

Himself he has himself betrayed, and deemed the earth a path
    of heaven,
And wandered down its sunless days, and too late knew
    himself bereaven.
For swiftly sin and suffering and earth-born laughter meshed
    his ways,
And caught him in a cage of earth, but heaven can hear his
    dewy lays.[1]

Rosenberg wrote this despairing account of the poet's role not long after his more positive analysis of it in 'Night and Day'. If, as seems likely, he had himself in mind, it was probably the failure of his little book to attract public recognition that explains his more negative attitude by autumn 1912, when he sent 'The Poet' (I) to Alice Wright. But there were other problems by then that could equally well account for his opening reference to 'the trouble of the universe'. Though able to return to the Slade in October for his second year, his difficulties with Mrs Cohen had not been resolved and he faced an uncertain future. His break with Michael Sherbrooke during the same period deprived him, as he had known it would, of his Hampstead studio. So, after abandoning the cheaper substitute he found near Euston Station as too noisy, he had to spend the whole winter at home. His family had recently moved to 87 Dempsey Street, not far from their previous house, but conditions were just as crowded and distracting. He found it difficult not just to work but even to show his pictures to people, and it is hardly surprising that he described his situation to Miss Wright as 'very unsettled'.[2] By Christmas things had grown even worse. Mrs Cohen having finally refused to pay any more Slade fees, on the chilling grounds that 'he could not easily be controlled',[3] his application for the JEAS to take them over had not yet been decided and he was having trouble with both his eyes and his lungs.

There were positive sides to his life, however. He was still attending the Slade daily and seeing friends there. Encouraged by Tonks and McEvoy to submit work to the New English Art Club, he had sold his 'Sanguine Drawing' for £4, though not his painting, and was generally, as Brown had reported, 'surpassing expectations'. Yet his mood remained dark. Despite the continued support and friendship of Amshewitz, Alice Wright, Winifreda Seaton, Bomberg, Mitchell, Gertler, Leftwich, Goldstein, Kramer and Ruth Löwy, his sense of isolation was very strong. Like 'The Poet' of his verse he appears to have experienced 'No fellowship of suffering to meet his tear-bewildered ways' and believed that 'Alone he [bore] the burden of alienated days'.

When he did for a moment feel connected to others, he appeared to think that he had betrayed his calling as a poet, which was to promote spiritual, not earthly truths; 'For swiftly sin and suffering and earth-born laughter meshed his ways, / And caught him in a cage of earth ...' He was, in his own words, a 'divided self'. His attempt to portray 'what we cannot see' in both poetry and art had, he believed, failed. *Joy*, his most ambitious painting to date, had been only marginally more successful in worldly terms than *Night and*

Rosenberg's pencil drawing of his father, c. 1913 (*Private Collection*)

Day. And neither discipline looked likely to earn him a living.

Yet he carried on doggedly, as much with his self-generated poetry as with his more externally organized art. In the middle stanza of another poem, composed a few months after 'The Poet' (I) apparently, he wrote:

> With fierce energy I aspire
> To be *that* Gods desire
> As the dreamy mountains are
> And no God can break or mar.[4]

Negligible as poetry, 'Peace' is nevertheless interesting as a record of two of Rosenberg's most valuable characteristics as a creative artist – and which helped to cancel out his occasional self-pity and defeatism – his determination and self-belief.

The need to convince the Jewish Education Aid Society that he was worthy of a grant in December 1912 made it essential for him to concentrate on art for a time. To show willing and to give the

Committee hope that any loan it granted him would stand a reasonable chance of being repaid, he promised to enter for the newly introduced Prix de Rome, a yet more prestigious annual competition than the Slade's Summer one. Open to those under thirty of British nationality, it guaranteed the successful candidate £200 per annum, renewable for three years, and the right to studio facilities in the British School at Rome. (Before entering, Rosenberg had first to be reassured by the JEAS's secretary, Mr Lesser, that he *was* a British subject, having been born in England, an indication of how un-British he sometimes felt.)

For as Sonia Cohen noted, when students' fees were being paid by the JEAS, 'results were expected from them apart from creative achievement in Art'.[5] Having seen Rosenberg regularly throughout 1912, she was aware that he had applied to the JEAS again, which probably explains the example she gave of the kind of 'tangible' results expected – 'the Prix de Rome or some similar token of school efficiency'.[6]

To Rosenberg, who was interested only in 'creative achievement in Art' as in poetry, the very nature of his Prix de Rome assignment was inimical. But he worked dutifully at it throughout late 1912 and early 1913. Several pieces were required and he needed somewhere of his own to work on them. Once he knew that his Slade fees were assured, he started looking for another studio in earnest, eventually finding the one at 1 St George's Square near Bomberg towards the end of 1912.[7] He worked intensely at his competition entries there, in spite of renewed eye trouble, but failed to win the Prix de Rome, or even to be placed.[8] Nevertheless, his work was exhibited, together with all the other entries, at the Imperial Institute, South Kensington, for a week in spring 1913. His work might not be winning prizes or selling well, but it was being seen.

None of Rosenberg's submissions for the Prix de Rome has been identified. In fact, there is no record of any surviving art work from 1913; the only possible exception is a fine pencil drawing of his father, one of his most sensitive portrayals of someone he evidently enjoyed drawing. Nor did he win any prizes at the Slade.

It may be that Rosenberg was affected, however indirectly, by Bomberg's departure from the Slade this year. By April 1913 Professor

Brown had reported to the JEAS of Bomberg that 'he thought it best if this student did not return to the Slade', since Brown believed that 'he would not profit by any further attendance'.[9] Tonks and Steer were 'quite agreed' with Brown that Bomberg was 'undoubtedly possessed of considerable artistic gifts' and that when he had 'learnt a little more modesty and humility and ceased to "theorise and analyse" quite so much he may well become a noteworthy artist', but they were worried about what Brown termed the 'disturbing influence' his views were having on other students.[10] Without Bomberg's daily encouragement Rosenberg's own enthusiasm may have flagged.

A further possible explanation for the distinct fall in his level of artistic production was being forced to leave his Spartan studio through further lung trouble in spring; he had to go home and be cared for by his mother once again. There was also a noticeable rise not only in the quantity but also the quality of his verse in 1913, another distraction from his art.

Prevented from writing poetry at the beginning of that year by the need to complete his Prix de Rome entries, he returned to it afterwards with what seems like renewed dedication and energy. His viewing of Blake's work at the Tate in late 1912 had convinced him that Blake's 'drawings [were] finer than his poems',[11] but it is clear from his own poetry of this period that Blake's verse had inspired him too. ('But how can God read human fear / Who cannot dry a human tear' he wrote in 'Walk You in Music, Light or Night', which despite its Byronic-sounding title, echoes Blake's aphorisms.)[12] Blake's dual artistic role, so evident in his art, may have reminded Rosenberg of his own commitment to poetry after an enforced absence from it. His change of allegiance is signalled in one of the poems he wrote at this time: titled originally 'The Artist', it was subsequently changed to 'The Poet'.[13]

His greatest incentive, however, may have come from his renewed contact with John Rodker. He had naturally seen less of his literary friends during his first strenuous year at the Slade, but in 1913 the situation changed dramatically when Sonia went to live with Rodker. If Rosenberg's love poems this year can be seen as evidence, he felt the loss of his muse very deeply. Though his own relationship with her had probably not progressed much beyond that 'first kiss in the April sunlight' and 'sedate' bus rides with her to study Blake at the Tate,[14] the thought of her in Rodker's bed cannot have been easy. The nature of his love poetry certainly changes from Romantically influenced generalizations about an idealized female to a harder, more direct approach more akin to Wyatt and the later Elizabethans and to Jacobean poets like Donne. Since Sonia herself claimed that 'Twilight' (II) was written specially for her, it is probably not too far-fetched to detect in its allusions to a 'proud heart' and a fading away of 'mortal loveliness' a reference to her.[15] He may also have had Sonia in mind when he wrote in 'A Warm Thought Flickers' of 'one forsaking face' which 'Hides ever – hides for our sighing',[16] and likewise when he wrote of 'a careless heart' in the poem of that name.[17]

It is notoriously difficult to date Rosenberg's poems, since he was, as his 1979 editor Ian Parsons points out, 'an inveterate re-writer and much given to incorporating lines and whole passages of earlier drafts in a later composition'.[18] But if Parsons is right to place 'Apparition' among the 1913 poems, it too invites speculation:

> From her hair's unfelt gold
> My days are twined.
> As the moon weaves pale daughters
> Her hands may never fold.
>
> Her eyes are hidden pools
> Where my soul lies
> Glimmering in their waters
> Like faint and troubled skies.
>
> Dream pure, her body's grace,
> A streaming light
> Scatters delicious fire
> Upon my limbs and face.[19]

The twining of the poet's soul into a woman's eyes and hair, the potential danger, signified in other poems by extending the metaphor to include a serpent hidden in the latter, suggest that Rosenberg was experiencing a strong sense of loss and deep frustration, and it is not impossible that it stemmed partly from Sonia's decision to live with Rodker. There is definitely a hint of Rosenberg's ambivalence towards women in this and other poems of the period, his need to idealize them ('Dream pure, her body's face') yet strong physical attraction to them ('her hair's *unfelt* gold' [my italics]).

Sonia, who was interested in politics, had met Rodker at the Young Socialist League. While Rosenberg had stopped attending shortly after rejoining it under Winsten's influence in 1911, Rodker was still an active member. (He would later become a Communist.) Exhilarated by her liberation from a religious charity home, Sonia aspired to be a 'liberated woman',[20] though she was not quite sure what this involved. Still 'extraordinarily innocent about life',[21] she had suspected enough of its dangers to fight off Bomberg's blatant attempts to seduce her. Rodker was a different matter. Handsomer than most of his friends and a great deal taller (Sonia was 'repulsed' by small men),[22] he had a gift with words, intoxicatingly idealistic views and a 'magnetic personality'.[23] When Sonia became interested in one of the most progressive of the 'little magazines' that flourished during the period, *The New Freewoman* (later renamed *The Egoist* under Pound's direction), 'Jimmie the poet', as she always referred to him, accompanied her to its meetings and they quickly fell in love. With a brass ring lent by an enlightened friend, they started to look for somewhere to live together and 'found sanctuary' at 1 Osborn Street, Whitechapel, over a stationer's shop.[24] All this seemed very high-minded to Sonia, who now considered herself emancipated. Even after a dangerous, botched, self-induced abortion and a second pregnancy that she dared not terminate, she would remain in the small, narrow room (christened the 'slot meter' by Bomberg)[25] until at least April 1915, when Rosenberg would paint her there.

Bomberg was furious at the union and refused to visit the daring couple initially, but Rosenberg, suppressing his jealousy as he suppressed so much else, was a regular visitor from the start. By comparison with his family home in Dempsey Street or his succession of poorly furnished, strictly utilitarian studios, Osborn Street must have seemed to him highly bohemian, since Rodker and Sonia were rebelling against the traditional in the arts as well as in morals. Apart from furniture made from wooden boxes and decorated in blue and scarlet and a bed without a headboard (the word 'divan' had an exotic ring in 1913), there were woodcuts by Rodker's recently acquired friend, one of the most revolutionary of the avant-garde, Percy Wyndham Lewis. (Rodker would later feature unfavourably and anti-Semitically as 'Ratner' in Lewis's *The Apes of God*.) There was also, pinned over the mantelpiece, a curious poem, printed and sold by the Poetry Bookshop and written by its owner, Harold Monro, 'Overheard on a Salt-Marsh' ('Nymph, nymph, what are your beads? / Green glass, goblin, / I stole them out of the moon').

This double allegiance to poetry and art was reflected in the friends who came to visit. Apart from the eventually mollified Bomberg, art was represented by William Roberts, who, like Rosenberg, listened attentively but rarely spoke, and (occasionally) Gertler, whose own studio was not far away in Spital Square. Literature was represented by Leftwich, Winsten, Rodker's ex-school friend Lazarus Aaronson, and the future editor of *The Sphere* following Clement Shorter, Jesse Heitner, who lived near the Rosenberg family off the Mile End Road. Rosenberg, with his usual ambivalence, fitted into both groups.

There were other friends, like Abraham Fineburg, who became a financial expert to the Soviet government, and Maurice Newfield, who was studying medicine, but the main interest was in the arts. The group, largely men, gathered nightly in Rodker and Sonia's narrow little room, and Sonia's vivid recollection of the scene gives a glimpse of Rosenberg's life at this time:

> They sat on the unsprung divan; balanced on the scarlet and blue boxes or squatted on the rush floormatting. With money that might otherwise have been spent on meals, I bought freshly ground coffee and served this with the almond cakes of the delicious variety baked in East End confectioners.[26]

But it was the talk that mattered. Ranging widely from art and literature to modern dance (Sonia's particular interest), it was unified only by its dedication to experimentation. For Rodker and Sonia, like many of their guests, were 'devotees of the New Age'.[27] Their central concern was how to renew what they regarded as the played-out language of both art and literature. Assailed by startling new theories in other fields – Freud's in psychology, Frazer's in anthropology, Einstein's in physics, for instance – and lacking their Victorian predecessors' sense of a settled, or at least reasonably predictable universe, they wanted to reflect what they saw as the contemporary 'reality', which they believed must include notions of relativity, irrationality and chaos. Traditional forms and techniques seemed no longer appropriate.

Rosenberg was already familiar with similar ideas from Bomberg's studio, where, as Sonia testified, 'prettiness and complacency in Art and Life were condemned. Down with romanticism and sentimentality was the cry.'[28] He would remain largely closed to such an approach in art, as his Slade assignments show, but he was beginning to respond to them in literature and his renewed contact with Rodker encouraged this process. In a sense it was the completion of a very full literary education, which had begun with Morley Dainow and the Romantics, expanded widely under Miss Seaton's guidance to include most of the great writers over the centuries, but stopped short at contemporary poetry. Rodker had already rejected the romantic idealism of his own 1911 verse, as his publication in defiantly Modernist organs like A.R. Orage's *The New Age* indicates. His more recent work, which he was preparing for publication, would also appear in *The Egoist*, which became one of the best-known of the new journals, shortly before his self-publication of them in *Poems* (1914). And this slim volume, as I have already noted, would carry a Modernist design by Bomberg, not the more conservative Rosenberg.

Richard Aldington, a close friend of Pound's who would be assistant editor of *The Egoist* for a time, described Rodker somewhat dismissively as 'a member of the school of affected revolutionaries' when *Poems* was published in 1914.[29] Yet there were several pieces in the collection that showed clear affinities with a movement Aldington himself had helped found only two years earlier, Imagism. The brainchild of Pound, like so much else in early Modernist poetry, Imagism focused, indeed, on the centrality of the image. It was based on three main principles agreed by Pound, Aldington and his future wife, Hilda Doolittle ('H.D.'), over cakes in a South Kensington teashop:

1. Direct treatment of the 'thing' whether subjective or objective.
2. To use absolutely no word that does not contribute to the presentation.
3. As regarding rhythm: to compose in the sequence of the musical phrase, not in the sequence of a metronome.[30]

Innocent though they sounded, these three aims would produce verse of apparent simplicity but underlying complexity and allusiveness which would challenge most of what the contemporary reading public had come to expect of poetry by 1912.

For Rodker, only eighteen at the time and yearning for change, Imagism was evidently a welcome and conscious break from tradition. Aldington labelled Rodker's work 'Futuristic' in his review of his poems in *Poetry* (Chicago) 1915, but 'Imagist' would have been a more accurate description of verses like the following (untitled):

> You said
> Your heart was
> pieces of
>> string
> in a
> peacock-blue satin
>> bag.[31]

For Rosenberg, however, Imagism, the most advanced poetic movement of the day, seems merely to have reflected his own natural development away from Romanticism towards the 'hard dry image' alluded to by one of Imagism's most famous (though least read) practitioners, the philosopher-poet T.E. Hulme.[32] Though not consciously aiming at the Imagists' goals of greater clarity of expression, concreteness and concision of language as well as imagery and freer rhythms in 1913, Rosenberg was already starting to question some of his own earlier assumptions in a way that brings him quite close to their practice. His nightly discussions with Rodker encouraged him to aim for even more precise imagery, less abstract language and a greater use of free verse. Another probable effect was to make him readier to handle subjects he had not previously considered strictly 'poetic', a development crucial to his future achievements as a war poet. His grotesque scenes of soldiers frantically hunting for vermin in 'Louse Hunting', for example, or carts lurching over the faces of corpses in 'Dead Man's Dump', a far cry from his early love poetry, convey the brutal reality of war in a way that his earlier concept of poetry could never have achieved.

It is clear that Rosenberg read some of the Imagists: apart from several references to Pound, he mentions F.S. Flint, for instance, whose 'Exultation' he admired 'very much' for the image in the last stanza of the

> birds, unrooted flowers of space,
> Shaking to heaven a silver chime of bells'[33]

There is also at least one complete poem of his own in the Imagist style:

> Green thoughts are
> Ice block on a barrow
> Gleaming in July.
> A little boy with bare feet
> And jewels at his nose stands by.[34]

Yet Rosenberg's comments on Flint also suggest that he found some Imagist poetry 'just experiments in versification'.[35] He was far more interested in other qualities, not specifically Imagist, in Flint's work, in particular 'the energy intensity and simplicity' with which one of his poems expresses 'that strange longing for an indefinite ideal; the haunting desire for that which is beyond the reach of hands'.[36] Consciously or not, he was here defining his own aims in poetry which the dry formalism and deliberately mechanistic, quasi-scientific approach of Imagism could not wholly satisfy. The same would apply to that other popular contemporary movement in poetry, Georgianism, as his meeting with its main promoter, Edward Marsh, in November this year would show.

Chapter 10

'It is All Café Royal Poetry Now:' Meeting Edward Marsh

Your criticism gave me great pleasure; not so much the criticism, as to feel that you took those few lines up so thoroughly, and tried to get into them. You don't know how encouraging that is. People talk about independence and all that – but one always works with some sort of doubt, that is, if one believes in the inspired 'suntreaders'. I believe that all poets who are personal – see things genuinely, have their place. One needn't be a Shakespeare . . .

I am not going to refute your criticisms; in literature I have no judgment – at least for style. If in reading a thought has expressed itself to me, in beautiful words; my ignorance of grammar, etc. makes me accept that. I should think you are right mostly; and I may yet work away your chief objections.

– IR to Edward Marsh, May–June 1914[1]

Rosenberg had been back at the Slade about a month when Gertler introduced him to Edward Marsh at the Café Royal on 10 November 1913. Gertler himself was no longer at the Slade but remained in touch and, as Marsh's biographer records, had 'the young Jewish boy . . . in tow'.[2]

The Café Royal, a French-style café-restaurant in Regent Street near Piccadilly Circus, was for several decades from the 1880s onwards the haunt of artists and writers. Predominantly bohemian in tone, its early habitués had included Oscar Wilde, Ernest Dowson and Max Beerbohm. By Rosenberg's day, as Sarah MacDougall nicely puts it in her biography of Gertler, 'anyone who was anyone in the arts passed through the Café . . . from Roger Fry and the "Bloomsberries" to Wyndham Lewis and the Vorticists . . . along with the philosopher T.E. Hulme and a host of glamorous, emancipated "new" women, such as Nancy Cunard, Iris Tree . . . and Lady Diana Manners . . .'[3]

Rosenberg was introduced to Hulme the same evening he met Marsh, but despite having friends in common (Rodker and Bomberg), they had little or no further contact. This may have been due to Rosenberg's lukewarm response to Imagism, or because, for all his frequenting of the Café, an underlying Puritanism made him suspicious of its flamboyance and whiff of decadence. Writing to a friend from France only a few years later, he would directly link it (and by implication its regulars, of whom Hulme was one) with decadence, arguing that 'the French poets . . . have given a nasty turn to English thought. It is all Café Royal poetry now.'[4]

The heart of the Café, where Rosenberg's introduction to both Hulme and Marsh would have taken place, was its ground-floor brasserie, known as the Domino Room and described memorably by Beerbohm as 'an exuberant vista of gilding and crimson velvet set amongst . . . opposing mirrors with fumes of tobacco ever rising to the painted and pagan ceilings'.[5] Walter Sickert's description of it as 'a sort of natural progression from the day-nursery of art school'[6] emphasizes its importance for artists, many of whom like Rosenberg and his group were current- or ex-Slade students. The Domino Room would be painted by at least two of Rosenberg's friends, Allinson and Nevinson.

Sonia, who also knew it, claimed that the Café Royal was 'too expensive' for frequent visits,[7] but Goldstein, hailing it as 'the mecca', remembered going there 'quite a lot' and making his sixpenny coffee and cake last all day.[8] Rosenberg was often with him, he recalled, hoping 'to meet literary personages to get their opinions on his work'. On the evening he met Marsh, however, it was his art that was to the fore, hardly surprising given the company.

Gertler had himself been introduced to Marsh shortly before by another painter, John Currie, who was also present, together with a fourth product of the Slade, 'Bobby' Roberts. (Less than a year later Currie, convinced that his mistress, Dolly Henry, was being unfaithful to him, would shoot her, then himself, in a tragic affair that electrified the London art world, causing Rosenberg to enquire anxiously after him from exile in South Africa.) It was natural, therefore, that Rosenberg, who was in his third year at the Slade by November 1913, should be introduced initially as a painter: Gertler, ever generous to his 'funny little' friend, was clearly hoping that Marsh would buy one of Rosenberg's pictures.

For Marsh, though remembered largely for his five *Georgian Poetry* anthologies, was also a connoisseur of graphic art. Conservative in his taste at the start, he had initially built up a fine collection of traditional English paintings, but in 1911 had become interested in modern art. His purchase of Duncan Grant's *Parrot Tulips* that year marked the beginning of a remarkable collection of contemporary British art, which by the end of 1913 included works by Gertler, Bomberg, Currie and Spencer. This startling change of direction was almost certainly a result of Roger Fry's first Post-Impressionist Exhibition of 1910, which had so disturbed Rosenberg's teachers at the Slade.

Marsh had known Fry at Cambridge and they remained good friends. Born into a completely different world from Rosenberg, the English upper middle class, Marsh had gone first as an Exhibitioner to Westminster School before going on as a Scholar to Trinity College, Cambridge. In both places he was recognized as an out-standing classicist, but at Cambridge and for the rest of his long life he moved equally between the worlds of art and literature as well as among high society. Entering the Colonial Office in 1896, by 1906 he had become Private Secretary to Winston Churchill only five years before Churchill's appointment as First Lord of the Admiralty. It was a post that would cause Marsh some difficulties during the First World War when many of his young male protégés would become pacifists.

Though his job as a top civil servant paid well, Marsh did not have unlimited funds, and he supported his young friends in a curious way. His mother's grandfather, Sir Spencer Perceval, had the distinction of being the only English prime minister to be murdered while in office, and the family was compensated with a government grant, one-sixth of which eventually came to Marsh. It was this 'murder money', as he called it, that financed his early patronage. Then, in August 1913, this income had been supplemented by a legacy from an aunt and Marsh resolved to buy even more pictures, despite Rupert Brooke's protest: 'I hate you lavishing all your mad aunt's money on these bloody artists.'[9] It was fortunate for Rosenberg that his meeting with Marsh took place only three months later, when he was clearly led to believe that he would be one of the 'bloody artists' so blessed.

Mumps in Marsh's teens had left him with (in his own words) a 'squeaking' voice. It had also, his biographer informs us, 'affected his physical constitution in a more serious way', a coy reference to impotence.[10] Hassall argued that it was this 'disability', rendering Marsh 'incapable of the act of love', that enabled him to 'cultivate a capacity for friendship which, untroubled by physical desire, could develop into a devotion characteristically feminine in its tenderness'.[11] It is a tactful explanation of Marsh's penchant for young men. (Cyril Connolly's witty paraphrase of this explanation would be that Marsh's 'prance was worse than his pounce'.)[12] Eighteen years older than Rosenberg, he was still unmarried when they met and treated his many protégés, all of them male, as surrogate sons, sometimes, as in Rupert Brooke's case, as idealized lovers. Gertler was also a great favourite, even though Marsh was unthinkingly snobbish and anti-Semitic in the manner of the day: 'Gertler is by birth an absolute little East End Jew' he had written blithely to Brooke just before meeting Rosenberg.[13] But his prejudices did not prevent him from helping true artistic merit where he detected it. In Gertler's case this would involve not just buying his pictures and introducing him to other potential customers but also making him a regular allowance, to enable Gertler to devote himself more single-mindedly to his art.

Rosenberg, lacking Gertler's more obvious assets, seems to have been less favoured by Marsh, as his 'poor little Isaac Rosenberg' remark indicates.[14] But it must be remembered that Rosenberg was less talented than Gertler in the area in which Marsh was most adventurous, art. When it came to literature, where Rosenberg was instinctively more experimental, Marsh was, ironically, fairly conservative, preferring the broad central ground occupied by such established poets as Robert Bridges, Lascelles Abercrombie, Gordon Bottomley, Walter de la Mare, John Drinkwater, James Elroy Flecker and John Masefield. The qualities looked for in poetry were to be 'intelligible', 'musical' and 'racy', by which he meant 'intensity of thought or feeling'.[15] To use the political terminology adopted by Robert Graves in his perceptive analysis of poetry of the Georgian era, Marsh was to the right of Pound, Aldington, Lewis and their acolytes but to the left of the 'old guard', still represented by poets like Austin Dobson, Henry Newbolt and William Watson. Graves's labelling of Rosenberg as 'a born revolutionary' emphasizes how wide the gap was between his and Marsh's expectations of poetry.

Described, not altogether unkindly, as one of 'the two great middlemen of the Georgian era',[16] Marsh would be responsible together with that other 'great middleman', Harold Monro, for raising the profile of that central ground and giving it a name in their five-volume *Georgian Poetry* anthology. Marsh had become involved with Monro indirectly through his great friendship with Rupert Brooke. When Brooke's *Poems* was published in 1911, Francis Meynell had suggested that Marsh review it for his friend Monro's *Poetry Review*, and the team that was to produce *Georgian Poetry* was born. It needed only a chance remark by Brooke to bring the anthology into being. Morro agreed to act as publisher and bookseller but it was Marsh who was to find the poets, make and arrange the selection and distribute payment.

To Modernists like Pound and to later generations generally the Georgians appeared and appear as a whole fairly traditional. But to some of their contemporaries they seemed quite revolutionary. William Watson, for instance, still clinging to the Tennysonian tradition in 1911, accused them of rejecting literary language for vulgar colloquialism, of being brutally 'realistic' in content, deliberately harsh in their rhythms and of rejecting traditional verse-forms. Nevertheless, the first number of *Georgian Poetry* in 1912 was an instant success, going into thirteen editions, and the four volumes that followed would keep Marsh very busy indeed over the next decade. It would also enable him to support young poets as well as artists, since he divided its not inconsiderable profits among the contributors. And when more established poets declined their royalties, he would scrupulously share them among his more impoverished bards.

The first volume of *Georgian Poetry* was only a year behind Marsh when he met Rosenberg, the second in active preparation, and there is little doubt that they discussed it. Marsh may even have asked for a contribution, since Rosenberg's first surviving letter to him makes it clear that he has sent Marsh some verse to which he has responded. Rosenberg's own response to Marsh's criticism sets the tone for the debate that will follow on what constitutes 'real' poetry. (Marsh had evidently written, like Binyon, 'with the paternal rod half raised in one hand and some sweets and chocolates in the other'.)[17]

> Thanks for your criticisms which of course I agree with. If a poem doesn't sound real it has missed its ends – but I think you can understand one's fondness for an idea or a line prompting one to show poems that one knows are otherwise poor.[18]

Apparently both grateful and docile, Rosenberg in this and all his subsequent letters to Marsh nevertheless defends his own point of view. It is a very different response from that of another young poet Marsh had taken under his wing only eight months earlier, Siegfried Sassoon. Flattered by the attention of the man christened 'the choragus of the new poets' by one of the most influential – and most reactionary – critics of the day, Edmund Gosse, Sassoon had gratefully accepted Marsh's advice 'to write either with one's eye on an object or with one's mind at grips with a more or less definite idea'.[19] And to begin with both Sassoon and Rosenberg probably benefited from this kind of sensible, if a little dull caution, which discouraged faults they were both guilty of, romantic fuzziness and facile emotionalism. Ultimately, however, Sassoon's reputation would suffer from his willingness to continue in the Marsh camp. Rosenberg's inability to do the same is a sign of how strongly his poetic genius demanded its own expression.

For the first seven months of Rosenberg's relationship with Marsh, however, his response was almost wholly positive. A trip to see a Yiddish play in Whitechapel with Marsh and Gertler goes unrecorded, though drama was more Rosenberg's area of expertise than Gertler's.[20] But his response to Marsh's subsequent gift of *Georgian Poetry 1911–1912* was almost effusive. The letter is worth quoting because it refers to at least one of the Georgian poets he later came to know partly through Marsh, a writer whose verse drama (represented in this anthology) either initiated or increased his interest in the genre, Gordon Bottomley. It also reflects Rosenberg's own aims in poetry by early 1914:

> Thanks very much for the book. I know so little of these men,[21] and from that little[,] I know how much I miss by not knowing more. I think the Queen's song of Flecker, delicious; and 'The end of the world' by Bottomley, very fine imagination and original. ... What strikes me about these men [is] they are very much alive, and have personal vision – and what is so essential can express themselves very simply. But writing about a poem is like singing about a song – or rather, as Donne says, fetching water to the sea, and in my case, very dirty water. You can talk about life, but you can only talk round literature; you will be talking about life, I think.[22]

Rosenberg was in particular need of Marsh's interest in the early months of 1914, when he faced a more than usually severe series of crises. His lungs had started troubling him again, necessitating yet another application to the Jewish Education Aid Society for money: the doctor had recommended that he spend time in the milder climate of the South Coast. On returning from this break he had been confronted by the vandalism of his Primrose Hill Studio, which he had lent to Redmond, forcing him to go to live with his family once more. And when he left the Slade at the end of March 1914 he had no prospect of supporting himself by painting yet was determined not to let his family finance him again. Life looked very bleak indeed.

His reasons for leaving the Slade a term short of the more usual three full years derived, on the surface, from money problems. Mrs Herbert Cohen had written rather impersonally to the JEAS in December 1913 that she 'did not wish to help this case for longer than one more term'[23] (i.e. by providing a living allowance) and, in the light of Professor Brown's recommendation the same month that Rosenberg be allowed only one more term, the Committee informed him that 'he must not expect further help after the end of the Easter Term'.[24] Brown's change of attitude from July 1912 suggests that Rosenberg's growing interest in poetry over art was beginning to show. While there are no known pictures from early 1914 there are certainly poems.

Yet his years at the Slade had not been wasted. In being taught to draw he had learnt 'to see more accurately',[25] to the benefit of his poetry which becomes increasingly visual. Tonks and his other teachers had also instilled in him the importance of form, and this too would help his poetry, though he would rarely achieve poetic form in predictable ways. His adventurousness in verse may have been another indirect result of his time at the Slade, where he had come into contact with a number of new artistic movements from abroad, some of which, like Vorticism, spilled over into poetry. While largely rejecting experimentalism in his graphic work – 'one is so cramped up here [i.e. in England] and one must either do cubism or leave the country,' he would complain by mid-1914[26] – his familiarity with these revolutionary movements may, as Deborah Maccoby argues, 'help to explain his "modernism" when compared with Owen and Sassoon, who were not artists'.[27] ('Art' she suggests 'is necessarily more open to innovative trends from abroad than is poetry, which is more traditional and inward-looking, because of its untranslatability, its difficulty in travelling.')[28] His rigorous training at the Slade had also convinced him, as he had told Mrs Herbert Cohen, that 'Art is not a plaything, it is blood and tears, it must grow up with one'.[29] And, above all, it had 'shown [him] possibilities'.[30] The 23-year-old who left the Slade at the end of March 1914 was not the same person who had crept timidly into it in October 1911. Both socially and creatively his horizons had been expanded.

Despite all that and despite a reprieve from the JEAS, which granted him one further month's living allowance for April, Rosenberg was feeling fairly pessimistic about his future by April 1914 and was particularly appreciative of Marsh's continued attentions. By mid-May Marsh had, over breakfast in his elegant set of rooms in Raymond Buildings, Gray's Inn, bought a painting from Rosenberg, *Sacred Love*, and, on the strength of this and other work he brought with him, invited him to contribute to an anthology of *Georgian Drawings* he was compiling which would contain fifty works by about twenty unknown artists. He had already decided to include Gertler, Currie, Stanley and Gilbert Spencer and the Nash brothers,

John and Paul, and Rosenberg was 'very pleased and proud' to be included in such talented company.[31]

Though *Georgian Drawings* never materialized as a book, the invitation to contribute and Marsh's purchase of his painting gave Rosenberg's confidence a much-needed boost, as would Marsh's later invitation to contribute to his 'Little Book', a private anthology of poems,[32] and his second purchase of a pencil and wash drawing 'Hark, Hark the Lark'.[33] He was also flattered to be invited to dinner at Marsh's club, followed by a viewing of his fine collection of pictures, and benefited from his practical help on a number of occasions. Marsh would respond immediately, for instance, to Rosenberg's request for money to have a second volume of poems printed in 1915, though Rosenberg would insist on giving him three nude studies in return ('quite good', Marsh judged).[34] He was especially helpful in dealing with officialdom, as the next few years would show.

Marsh's greatest gift to Rosenberg, however, lay ironically in the area in which they least agreed, poetry. From the very beginning to the very end (Rosenberg's last known letter from France would be to him), Marsh would respond, often by return of post, to the many poems, or drafts of poems, Rosenberg sent him, only the second person of any literary consequence to do so after Binyon. Marsh's interest appears initially to have stimulated a new spate of poems, for it is clear that he took Rosenberg's work seriously.

The fact that they differed widely in their views was not necessarily damaging to Rosenberg's verse, as has sometimes been suggested. Ian Parsons, for instance, may be right to argue that 'Marsh (for all his goodwill and generosity as a patron) was about the last person to appreciate the originality and force of Rosenberg's poetry, which he found obscure, difficult and lacking in form'; and that Rosenberg's work was 'far too elemental, too imaginative, and too occupied with the struggle to give expression to the intangible, to appeal to Marsh's civilized but limited taste'.[35] But he is forced to concede that it was from Marsh and other Georgians that Rosenberg 'received the encouragement he so anxiously sought'.[36] It was Marsh who would first show his work to Abercrombie and

Marsh who would be the only person to publish Rosenberg in book form during his lifetime. Even one of Marsh's greatest critics, Jon Silkin, who argues that 'we can have little regret for Marsh's dislike of Rosenberg's poems', acknowledges that it is 'unlikely that Marsh's acceptance could for long have diverted his powerful, original talent' and that Marsh's willingness to become involved 'on a work-to-work basis, rather than [with] the man as a whole' gave Rosenberg 'the independence he so evidently lacked with his former patrons'.[37]

These are grudging assessments, suggesting that Marsh's influence on Rosenberg was non-existent at best. But is this true? When William Watson accused the Georgians of despising craftsmanship, he was fastening on the one thing that bound these widely differing poets together. Craftsmanship was a quality Marsh insisted on. And Rosenberg's response to his criticism indicates that Marsh managed to convince him, too, of the need for more careful craftsmanship, as well as what Rosenberg had admired in *Georgian Poetry 1911–1912*, simplicity of expression. Marsh's further demand for 'intelligibility' would cause him more problems since, as he explored his own voice in the poems of 1914–15, he would attempt increasingly to convey several layers of meaning simultaneously. This could render his work incomprehensible, or at least obscure, and it did him no harm to be forced to make himself clearer.

In the case of 'Midsummer Frost', for instance, sent to Marsh towards the end of May 1914 and one of the most successful poems of this period, the first draft he submitted was confused and obscure in parts, lines 7 to 9 in particular, spoiling what was an otherwise striking opening:

> A July ghost, aghast at the strange winter,
> Wonders, at burning noon, (all summer seeming),
> How, like a sad thought buried in light words,
> Winter, an alien presence, is ambushed here.
> See, from the fire-fountained noon there creep
> Lazy yellow ardours towards pale evening,
> Dragging the sun across the shell of thought.
> A web threaded with fading fire.

Futile and fragile lure!
All July walks her floors that roof this ice,
My frozen heart the summer cannot reach,
Hidden as a root from air, or star from day.
A frozen pool whereon mirth dances
Where the shining boys would fish.[38]

While appearing to agree with Marsh ('You are quite right in the way you read [it]'), Rosenberg defends his poem with his usual tenacity, but his explanation, especially of the most obscure lines (7 to 9) is so convoluted as to prove Marsh's point. Nevertheless, it is a fascinating glimpse into his thought-processes:

I thought I could use the 'July ghost' to mean the Summer, and also an ambassador of the summer ... The shell of thought is man; you realise a shell has an opening. Across this opening, the ardours – the sense of heat forms a web – this signifies a sense of summer – the web again becomes another metaphor – a July ghost. But of course I mean it for summer right through ... [39]

Under Marsh's guidance he dropped the shell imagery, and the result is an opening which is decidedly more condensed and unified:[40]

A July ghost, aghast at the strange winter,
Wonders, at burning noon, (all summer seeming)
How, like a sad thought buried in light words,
Winter, an alien presence, is ambushed here.

See, from the fire-fountained noon, there creep
Lazy yellow ardours towards pale evening,
To thread dark and vain fire
Over my unsens'd heart.
Dead heart, no urgent summer can reach.
Hidden as a root from air or a star from day;
A frozen pool whereon mirth dances;
Where the shining boys would fish.[41]

It may have been in response to Marsh's expectations that Rosenberg sent him another more intelligible but no less compelling poem, 'Wedded' (II) in the spring of 1914. Inspired almost certainly by his eldest sister's marriage the previous August, the piece centres, like several of his earlier verses and pictures, on the Garden of Eden as a place both of innocence and of innocence lost. Written in a stanza form regular enough to please Marsh, the wavering feminine endings of its second, fourth and fifth lines nevertheless manage to convey a feeling of uncertainty as the lovers leave their initial innocence for Blake's world of 'experience':

> They leave their love-lorn haunts,
> Their sigh-warm floating Eden;
> And they are mute at once;
> Mortals, by God unheeden;
> By their past kisses chidden.
>
> But they have kist and known
> Clear things we dim by guesses;—
> Spirit to spirit grown:—
> Heaven, born in hand caresses:—
> Love, fall from sheltering tresses.
>
> And they are dumb and strange;
> Bared trees bowed from each other.
> Their last green interchange
> What lost dreams shall discover?
> Dead, strayed, to love-stranged lover.[42]

The last stanza, with its dramatic tree imagery driving home how estranged the lovers have become – 'bared trees bowed from each other' – anticipates one of Rosenberg's most successful drawings, 'The First Meeting of Adam and Eve', though there the lovers are powerfully drawn to each other, and suggests that the influence between his poetry and art was two-way.[43]

Parsons implies that Rosenberg would have fared better 'had his mentors been his fellow-combatants – Owen, Sassoon and Graves' rather than Marsh, among others.[44] It is a dubious proposition, given that both Sassoon and Graves themselves were protégés of Marsh during the war and that Owen was, to a large extent, a disciple of Sassoon. Graves would later turn away from Georgianism but he and Sassoon, at least, were firmly in the Georgian camp between 1914 and 1918, appearing (as Rosenberg himself would) in Marsh's third volume of *Georgian Poetry* in 1917. While Marsh's closeness to another First World War poet, Rupert Brooke, has been fully acknowledged, his promotion of many others – Robert Nichols and Wilfrid Gibson, for instance, as well as Sassoon and Graves – is often overlooked. His encouragement would be as important to them as to Rosenberg during those difficult years, and First World War poetry owes as much to Edward Marsh as to any other single person.

Not even Marsh, however, could save Rosenberg from the problems he faced by May 1914. The sale of one picture, though heartening, did not provide an income, and even had Marsh been prepared to do so, as in Gertler's case, Rosenberg was no longer certain of his vocation as a painter. Suddenly he announced, to Marsh among others, that he was leaving for South Africa.

Chapter 11

South Africa: 'I Have Lived in the Underworld Too Long'

June 1914–February 1915

So I've decided on Africa, the climate being very good, and I believe plenty to do. . . . I won't be quite lost in Africa. . . . I dislike London for the selfishness it instils into one, which is a reason for the peculiar feeling of isolation I believe most people have in London. I hardly know anybody whom I would regret leaving (except, of course, the natural ties of sentiment with one's own people); but whether it is that my nature distrusts people, or is intolerant, or whether my pride or my backwardness cools people, I have always been alone. Forgive this little excursion into the forbidden lands of egotism.

– IR to Winifreda Seaton, spring 1914[1]

South Africa was a turning-point in Rosenberg's life. Fresh from the Slade but freed from its daily grind, he produced more paintings and drawings in his eight months there than over the previous two years combined. He also wrote and delivered two authoritative lectures on art. Welcomed warmly into the local art community, he became friends with several of its leading lights and for the first time in his life enjoyed the prestige of being thought ahead of rather than behind current trends. Despite this close contact with Cape Town's art world, however, it was poetry that emerged finally as his chosen medium during his stay there. His release from the immediate need to earn a living, as well as from the Slade routine, his passionate relationship with a South African actress and his new and exotic surroundings all appear to have stimulated him to produce more verse than at any other period of his life. Furthermore, it was in Cape Town that he first heard news of the outbreak of war and wrote his first three poems on the subject.

Dislike of London was only one of several reasons Rosenberg gave for his decision to leave for South Africa in the early summer of 1914. With Marsh, for instance, he focused on the beneficial effect it might have on his art – 'I might . . . get ideas for real things'.[2]

With Mr Lesser of the Jewish Education Aid Society, to whom he applied for yet another grant to cover his fare, he emphasized his weak chest and the need to escape the city pollution. Knowing that Lesser would appreciate the point, since his society had granted Rosenberg money for models on at least one occasion during his Slade training, he also underlined how cheaply he would be able to find sitters for the 'interesting stuff' he intended to paint there: 'the Kaffirs would sit for practically nothing'.[3] An even more practical consideration, which he again stressed in his letter to Lesser, was that of having a 'relation' in South Africa with whom he could stay for at least a year until he was able to support himself from his painting.

The relation in question was his sister Minnie, who had met a young South African Jew, William ('Wolf') Horvitch, while he was visiting London.[4] They had married on 24 August 1913, an event witnessed by an unsmiling Rosenberg, and sailed for Cape Town a week later. Minnie's concern for Isaac did not lessen with distance, however, and when their mother wrote to tell her of his lung trouble in the winter of 1913–14 she begged him to come out to live with them. It was probably the deciding factor for Rosenberg, who had also considered emigrating to either America or Russia over the years. He had relatives in both places who would have supported him, but none of them as close or as loving as Minnie, one of whose treasured possessions in Cape Town was Isaac's schoolboy watercolour of Caxton and Edward IV.

Rosenberg presented his reasons for choosing South Africa in strictly practical terms, however, and Lesser, for one, was convinced, granting him the £12 for the fare without demur. Marsh, equally responsive, helped him with formalities at the Emigration Office and enquired anxiously about his lungs.[5] ('I have no tuberculosis as far as I know, but a weak chest' Rosenberg replied.)[6]

Rosenberg's decision to leave England, however he chose to present it, stemmed as much from restlessness and temperament as from practical considerations. Whenever he had found life difficult in the past, he had talked of going somewhere else: of America to Leftwich, of Russia to Binyon, of Africa, too, on a previous occasion to Miss Seaton. His inclination was to run away from difficulties rather than face them. Though this is understandable, given the number of formidable obstacles he faced throughout his life, it did not solve one of his main problems, which was how to earn enough to become independent of his family without returning to the drudgery of his earlier apprenticeship. Nor would his flight to South Africa fully resolve his other great dilemma, how to choose between art and literature. Whilst it was becoming increasingly clear to friends like Bomberg that his true vocation was that of a poet, he had failed to make any money at all from his verse, whereas there still seemed to him a possibility of earning a living by his art. He appears to have made at least two unsuccessful applications for the post of art teacher in early 1914,[7] but continued to hope that he might establish himself as a portrait-painter. The real question is why he decided to go all the way to South Africa to look for commissions.

The answer may lie in the lack of appreciation he detected in London. After Brown's dispiriting advice that it was time for him to leave the Slade, he had still hoped to be recognized elsewhere. And when Bomberg, who had been chosen to organize a separate Jewish section within a *Twentieth Century Art* exhibition at the Whitechapel Art Gallery, asked him to submit work (along with only ten other Jewish artists in England)[8] he may have believed a breakthrough was near. But judging from the two works that have been identified out of the five displayed – his 1911 portrait of his father and his illustration to Keats's *Isabella* (*The Murder of Lorenzo*)[9] – he stood no realistic chance of furthering his reputation in such a context. Yet it would constitute the largest public showing of his work during his lifetime. Whether the final choice was his or Bomberg's, it was ill-judged for an exhibition subtitled 'A Review of Modern Movements' and claiming to show 'the progress of art since the absorption of ... impressionist teaching'.

The decision to highlight Jewish art within the context of British Modernism was, as Rachel Dickson and Sarah MacDougall point out, 'groundbreaking'.[10] Unfortunately, it only threw into relief

Rosenberg's reluctance to venture much beyond the Pre-Raphaelites and Impressionists. Even the *Jewish Chronicle*'s review of the exhibition, written by someone who evidently knew and admired Rosenberg, regretted his choice of submissions in a brief dismissal: 'Knowing that Mr Rosenberg has done better work, we cannot praise his "Portrait of My Father", for the colouring is muddy and the characterisation weak. Much as we should have liked to speak favourably of his drawings, we are afraid the artist has given us little opportunity to do so.'[11]

Rosenberg's case was not helped by the fact that his portrait of his father was flanked by two of Gertler's most striking and experimental early works, *The Artist's Mother* (1913) and *Mother and Babe* (1913). In a section that was almost abrasively Modernist, including as it did work by Bomberg, Kramer, Meninsky, Epstein, Modigliani and Pissarro among others, Rosenberg's work suffered cruelly.[12] Though the *Jewish Chronicle* would criticize Bomberg's work even more fiercely than Rosenberg's, it was impossible to ignore the power of paintings such as his *Vision of Ezekiel*, *Jujitsu* or *In the Hold*. While Rosenberg would not have agreed completely with the reviewer's dismissal of Bomberg's exhibits as 'a waste of good pigment, canvas, and wall space',[13] his own assessment of his friend's work later that year suggests a lack of sympathy with Bomberg's growing interest in Cubism, Vorticism and Futurism: though conceding that it was 'undoubtedly interesting' he believed it had 'crude power of a too calculated violence – and is mechanical'.[14] This judgement comes as no surprise from the man who wrote (in the same essay on 'Art') that 'the only sensation [he had] ever got from a futurist picture [was] that of a house falling'.[15] But the future lay with Bomberg and his fellow-Modernists, not with Rosenberg.

By the time the *Jewish Chronicle* review of *Twentieth Century Art* was published on 15 May 1914, Rosenberg had already booked his passage to Cape Town, so its dismissiveness could not have influenced his decision to leave London. But there is little doubt that the lukewarm response accorded his art generally by early 1914 was one cause for his departure. His only reason for delay was the need to travel as cheaply as possible, which meant steerage, and there was no certainty as to when space would become available. He was simply told by the Union Castle Steamship office to pack his bags and be ready at short notice. Though it would be another fortnight before he caught the train from St Pancras to Tilbury, boarded his ship and physically left London, he had already detached himself from it mentally. While pleased to be invited in mid-May to view Marsh's art collection, since he was still hoping that Marsh would want to add another of his works to it, he appears to have turned his back on the London art scene. He seems to have completely ignored, for instance, the fierce battle raging between the Italian Futurist Marinetti and a rival group, the Vorticists, headed by Wyndham Lewis and Bomberg, which reached a crisis during Rosenberg's last few weeks in London. It is evident from his letters to Marsh that he was far too absorbed by thoughts of South Africa to care.

His excitement is understandable. When he did set out early in June, it was his first trip abroad.[16] It was also, apart from the brief crossing to the Isle of Wight in 1910, his first real sea journey. A distance of over 6,000 miles lasting more than a fortnight, it seems to have left him with an even stronger sense of belonging nowhere and everywhere. Though he had set out with the ostensible purpose of earning his living as a painter in Cape Town, he chose to express his feelings in verse, underlining his growing preference for poetry over art. He had spent his childhood near the docks both in Bristol and London and had written a poem about the sea for Bella Sidney Woolf's children's magazine, but the experience of sailing across the vast expanse of the Atlantic exposed him to quite different sensations, which he tried to pin down in three separate but related poems. Taken together they show how determinedly he worked at an idea, reusing imagery, sometimes whole lines, occasionally a complete stanza from one attempt in a second, often third version. 'Wistfully in Pallid Splendour', for instance, the most impressionistic of the three, makes no direct mention of the sea, yet manages to convey the sense of being suspended in time and space that a long voyage can bring. The supernatural and allegorical overtones of this little poem suggest the influence of Coleridge's 'Ancient Mariner', which he had perhaps been rereading in anticipation of his own sea journey:

Wistfully in pallid splendour
Drifts the lonely infinite,
A wan perfume vague and tender,
Dim with feet of fragile light.

Drifts so lightly thro' the spirit,
Breathes the torch of dreams astir
Till what promised lands lie near it
Wavering are betrayed to her.

Ghostly foam of unheard waters,
And the gleam of hidden skies,
Footsteps of Eve's whiter daughters
Tremble to our dreaming eyes.

O! sad wraith of joy lips parted,
Hearing not a word they say –
Even my dreams make broken-hearted
And their beauty falls away.[17]

In a second poem on the subject, written almost certainly just before or just after 'Wistfully in Pallid Splendour', Rosenberg repeats the third stanza, slightly revised, but relates his opening stanza more specifically to the sea and to his hopes of a fresh start in life:

Have we sailed and have we wandered
Still beyond, the hills are blue.
Have we spent and have we squandered,
What's before us still is new.[18]

And in a third version it is the imagery of drifting and pallor that is repeated to evoke the mysteriousness of a moonlit sea just before dawn:

Far Away
By what pale light or moon-pale shore
Drifts my soul in lonely flight?

Regions God had floated o'er
Ere He touched the world with light?

Not in Heaven and not in earth
Is this water, is this moon;
For there is no starry birth,
And no dawning and no noon.

Far away—O far away,
Mist-born—dewy vapours rise
From the dim gates of the day
Far below in earthly skies.[19]

The only break in Rosenberg's long 'drift' over the Atlantic was at the island of St Helena, where he sent a postcard to his mother. He also wrote to Marsh to thank him for a letter of introduction to Sir Herbert Stanley, a member of the South African government and (Marsh hoped) a potential sponsor. Uncharacteristically, Rosenberg confides that he is 'eagerly awaiting his arrival in Cape Town',[20] a hint that his complete change of circumstances was having its effect.

Rosenberg's first view of the city made a lasting impression on him. Spread out around the shores of Table Bay, Cape Town is dominated by Table Mountain, which towers over it at more than three and a half thousand feet, flanked by the scarcely less impressive Devil's Peak to the east and Lion's Head to the west, and this craggy scenery was to provide him with some memorable imagery in his poetry. 'Significance', for instance, written in Cape Town in an attempt to describe his struggle to create form out of seeming chaos, makes dramatic use of the city's rocky setting:

> ... Lean in high middle 'twixt two tapering points,
> Yet rocks and undulations control
> The agile brain the limber joints
> The sinews of the soul.
>
> Chaos that coincides, form that refutes all sway,
> Shapes to the eye quite other to the touch,

All twisted things continue to our clay
Like added limbs and hair dispreaded overmuch.[21]

Rosenberg arrived in the middle of Cape Town's winter – June can be a wet and miserable month – the sun was shining, the light and colour intensely bright after the greys of London. The effect was immediate, awakening a dormant sensuousness in poem after poem:

Summer's lips are aglow, afresh
For our old lips to kiss,
The tingling of the flesh
Makes life aware of this.[22]

The vibrant light and its effect on an already dramatic landscape, particularly as it arrived and departed at dawn and dusk, seems to have revived his interest in those two most mysterious and ambiguous periods of the day, since he wrote a number of poems centring on them in Cape Town.[23] 'The place is gorgeous – just for an artist' he reported to Marsh after his first 'fearfully busy week – seeing people and preparing for work'.[24]

Despite the very different climate and scenery, Rosenberg found himself staying in a district not unlike London's East End. Situated close to the docks (an area that has since been filled in, pushing the port further out into the bay), 'District Six', as it was called, attracted a similarly heterogeneous racial mix. Like the East End, too, it contained the greater part of the slums and the greater part of the very poor people of Cape Town. Its largest ethnic group was made up of Eastern European Jews escaping from pogroms, economic hardship and military service, the overwhelming majority of them, like Rosenberg's parents, from Lithuania.[25] Some 40,000 Jews had arrived in South Africa between 1881 and 1914, most of them disembarking at Cape Town, which was the first port of call, and gravitating naturally to the nearest residential area, District Six. By the time of Rosenberg's stay they constituted 60 per cent of its inhabitants. Kosher butchers, fishmongers, bakeries and greengrocers lined the streets in much the same way as they did in

Whitechapel. Most of the buildings dated from the end of the nineteenth or beginning of the twentieth century, many bearing 'The Star of David'. And there were at least nine synagogues.

Yet District Six occupied only about one square mile of the slope running down from Devil's Peak to the city's central business district in the lower portion of Cape Town. Rosenberg's sister and her husband lived with his parents in the higher part of the area at Hill House, 43 De Villiers Street, since demolished.[26] An area of small, mainly one-storey dwellings, it is unlikely that there was any more room in the Horvitches' house than in the one Rosenberg had just left in Stepney. And only a month after his arrival conditions would have become even more crowded and noisy when Minnie gave birth to her first child.[27] Rosenberg might genuinely believe that he had 'always been alone', but in the little house in De Villiers Street he was probably less alone physically than he had ever been. Minnie and Wolf were by no means the only Horvitch children living there, and Minnie was not his only close relative living in Cape Town. Both of his father's brothers, Peretz and Max Jacob, had moved there with their families by the beginning of the twentieth century and he was surrounded by cousins. Two of these – Sol, son of Peretz, and Janie, daughter of Max Jacob – though first cousins, had married the previous year in London. They returned to Cape Town to live, however, and were probably there during Rosenberg's visit. By 1914, Max Jacob had moved on again to Rhodesia and was dead, but his wife chose to remain in Cape Town with her youngest daughter Leila, opening a small shop in Wynberg, which Leila remembered Isaac visiting.[28]

Isaac's other uncle, Peretz, of whom he painted a striking portrait almost certainly in Cape Town,[29] served as an unofficial rabbi in the Constitution Street Synagogue, an ultra-orthodox establishment very near to De Villiers Street.[30] Isaac, no longer a practising Jew by 1914 despite his devoutness as a child, is unlikely to have attended services at the Constitution Street Synagogue. But he did mix freely with Cape Town's Jewish community, thanks partly to his brother-in-law. Wolf Horvitch had a secure but not highly paid job in the local post office at Caledon Square, his knowledge of both written and spoken Yiddish enabling him to help the more recent Eastern

European immigrant Jews ('Greeners') send money and letters home to the 'old country'. According to Rhona Dubow, whose father Mr Baskin arrived in Cape Town just after Rosenberg and rented a room in De Villiers Street, Wolf Horvitch was a popular figure in the local community, which greatly appreciated his help. Less than five feet in height, he was known affectionately in Yiddish as 'De klane Horvitch' (Little Horvitch).[31] A trusted member of the tight-knit Jewish community, he was in a position to introduce Rosenberg to many of its most influential members, some of them leading figures in Cape Town's cultural world.

In such a small city – it had fewer than 100,000 inhabitants in 1914, compared with London's four and a half million – the world of the arts was inevitably more circumscribed than in the English capital, and Rosenberg quickly began to feel its limitations. His first description of Cape Town to Marsh sets the tone:

> I am in an infernal city by the sea. This city has men in it – and these men have souls in them – or at least have the passages to souls. Though they are millions of years behind time they have yet reached the stage of evolution that knows ears and eyes. But these passages are dreadfully clogged up; gold dust, diamond dust, stocks and shares, and heaven knows what other flinty muck. Well, I've made up my mind to clear through all this rubbish.[32]

Condescending in the extreme, Rosenberg's reaction may yet have had some truth in it. But he makes no mention of the aspect of Cape Town that outraged the most enlightened of his contemporaries, its racial policy. The city contained an even broader social mix than London. There were the Dutch who had first colonized the Cape in the mid-seventeenth century, initially as a halfway station on their way to the East Indies. With them had come their East Indian servants and slaves, known as 'Cape Malays' and not to be confused with the native population of Bushmen and Hottentots, referred to as 'Kaffirs'. (Children of mixed race were known as 'Cape Coloureds'.) French Huguenots escaping religious persecution and British colonists had followed during the late seventeenth and eighteenth centuries. But by the beginning of the nineteenth century Cape

Town had passed solely into the possession of the British. The discovery of gold, diamonds and other precious minerals in the 1860s had created a great deal of wealth and had attracted, among others, a number of Jewish diamond merchants from Amsterdam before the main influx of Jewish immigrants from the 1880s onwards.

Rosenberg clearly believed that Cape Town had created a population obsessed with material gain, yet fails to point out what could not possibly have escaped his notice – that the wealth was confined almost exclusively to the white races. In the Union of 1910, the result of lengthy negotiations following the British defeat of the Dutch in the Boer War of 1899 to 1902, only a very small number of educated, property-owning black people were allowed to vote. And in 1913, the year before Rosenberg's arrival, the Land Act had deprived black Africans of their right to buy land outside their so-called 'reserves'. Olive Schreiner, the South African feminist, socialist and writer, complained to the English social reformer and sexual pioneer Edward Carpenter, after Parliament had voted in a Flogging Bill for black Africans: 'You don't know how bad things are in this land; we flog our niggers to death and wealth is the only possible end and aim in life ... there are money-making whites and down-trodden blacks and nothing in between ...'[33]

Rosenberg, who would meet a number of Schreiner's friends in Cape Town and the great lady herself on his return to London, might have been expected to share her indignation, especially given his own family's history of racial persecution. Such was his self-absorption, however, that he seems to have regarded all non-whites in Cape Town merely as a cheap source of models and to have reserved his scorn for the city's materialism. His criticism did not prevent him from enjoying this rare encounter with affluence, however. The explanation given by Minnie via her son Isaac was that Rosenberg 'obtained cultural satisfaction from mixing with the elite families', because they 'would of course have been interested in painting, poetry and the arts'.[34] The fact that they would also 'have been very divorced from the ordinary population of the Cape'[35] appears not to have worried Rosenberg at first, though it may eventually have influenced his decision to leave South Africa.

His acceptance into this world was rapid. Cape Town's cultural community being small, once he had presented Marsh's letter to Sir Herbert Stanley and the Horvitches had introduced him to other influential members of it, he found himself overwhelmed by invitations of hospitality and help. Minnie remembered that one of their first introductions had been to the man regarded by many as the leading figure in Cape Town's Jewish community, Morris Alexander. Thirty-six years old in 1914, Alexander had already had a varied and impressive career by the time Rosenberg met him. Educated at his own expense at the University of Cape Town, he had travelled to London for admittance to the Bar. His election in 1905 to South Africa's Legislative Assembly (based in Cape Town) was a sign of both his ability and popularity. (He would lead the Constitutional Democratic Party from 1921 to 1929.) But his most important achievement in his own eyes was his successful attempt to have Yiddish accepted as a European language in 1906. This had allowed thousands of Yiddish-speaking Jews previously excluded by a clause in South Africa's 1902 Immigration Act to enter the country, making Alexander something of a hero to the Eastern European immigrants. In a Jewish community sharply divided between assimilated Anglo-Jews, to which Alexander by birth and education naturally belonged, and the less privileged immigrants, he was one of the very few who straddled both camps. He would have been instinctively sympathetic to the self-made Rosenberg.

His wife Ruth would probably have been equally if not more responsive. Only two years older than Rosenberg, like him, her main interests were artistic and not confined to one discipline. Both literary and musical – she had a voice 'like a silver bell' according to Cape Town's leading rabbi, the Rev Bender – she wrote novels, articles, book and music reviews, as well as giving lectures on literature and her own song recitals. She was almost certainly the inspiration for a poem Rosenberg wrote during his stay, 'On a Lady Singing', the main motif of which anticipates his most beautiful war poem, 'Returning, We Hear the Larks':

> She bade us listen to the singing lark
> In tones far sweeter than its own.
> For fear that she should cease and leave us dark

We built the bird a feigned throne, –
Shrined in her gracious glory-giving ways
From sceptred hands of starred humility.
Praising herself the more in giving praise
To music less than she.[36]

Ruth had been brought up in England, at Cambridge, where her father, the Talmudic scholar Rabbi Solomon Schecter, taught. Arriving in Cape Town in 1908, the year after her marriage to Alexander, she had missed the intellectual stimulus of university life and by 1914 had formed a salon for writers, artists and poets, to which Rosenberg was invited. (Ruth still remembered him 'well' two decades later.)[37] A political activist like her husband, Ruth was more radical and was linked to a circle of highly independent, strong-minded feminists, which included Olive Schreiner, Emily Hob-house, Elizabeth ('Betty') Molteno and her 'partner' Alice Greene (the aunt of Graham Greene). Rosenberg may even have met Gandhi at Ruth's house, since the celebrated freedom-fighter (Ruth was proud to remember) was an honoured friend and stayed at the Alexanders' house on his last night in South Africa in August 1914. Gandhi had been in Cape Town since at least February 1914, when he wrote to tell his friend Kallenbach that he was a 'society' man now and that it was Ruth's friend Betty Molteno (whom Rosenberg would also get to know fairly well) who had been instrumental in introducing him to these circles. But Rosenberg appears to have been untouched by Ruth's radicalism, or that of her friends. It was her cultural contacts that attracted him, particularly the poets and artists among her group.

The most successful of these, the painter Edward Roworth, was known to Rosenberg slightly already through David Bomberg, though he may not have met Roworth personally until he arrived in Cape Town.[38] Roworth, of Dutch descent but English birth, had lent Bomberg his *Head* by Modigliani for the Jewish section of the Whitechapel Art Gallery Exhibition earlier in 1914. Bomberg claimed that Roworth was 'a good friend' to Rosenberg in South Africa and the latter certainly noted down Roworth's contact address in London as though intending to stay in touch.[39] Ten years older than Rosenberg, Roworth had been posted to South Africa with the Imperial Yeomanry during the Boer War and was so impressed by the country that he had returned to live there permanently in 1902. By 1908 he had established himself as a leading figure in Cape Town's art world, becoming President of the South African Society of Art that year. He would later be made Director of the South African National Art Gallery.

Trained, like Rosenberg, under Tonks at the Slade, Roworth's tastes in art extended no further than Impressionism and were already beginning to seem fairly conservative by 1914. His successor in the Michaelis Chair in Fine Art at Cape Town University, Professor Neville Dubow, dismissed him as 'a very mediocre painter, a kind of colonial version' of the fashionable Edwardian artist Alfred Munnings.[40] Kinder critics have described him as a painter in the style of the Dutch portraitist Frans Hals. His traditional technique was well suited to the time and place, however, and he was a major figure in the art world when he and Rosenberg met, something of a 'big fish in a little pond' according to the present director of the South African National Gallery, Haydn Proud.[41]

Roworth's later reputation would suffer enormously with Jews and Gentiles alike when, in reaction to what he termed the 'degenerate ballyhoo of modern art',[42] he supported Hitler's condemnation of 'Degenerate [i.e. Modernist] Art'. But in 1914 he was evidently not yet the martinet he later became, and was probably quite pleased to welcome a fellow ex-Slade student to his cultural backwater. He appears to have been friendly towards Rosenberg in a slightly condescending way. They were often seen together in Cape Town, an entertaining sight according to another of the Horvitches' friends, Morris Robinson, principal of Ashbey's Art Galleries and Auction House: 'It was most amusing to see Rosenberg and Roworth in the street. Rosenberg, small, thin and hat well over his ears and boots many sizes too big for him. Roworth, six feet six inches in height, broad-shouldered with a laugh that even cheered up Rosenberg.'[43] Rosenberg himself could see the humour in their physical differences, noting in the draft of a letter concerning his unfortunate tendency to quarrel with almost everyone he met: 'I suppose I haven't qu[arrelled] with Roworth because he never hears what I say he's so tall.'[44] The two also presented a sharp social contrast, the 'very English', 'very clubbable' Roworth[45] throwing into strong relief Rosenberg's pronounced Cockney accent, of which he seemed particularly conscious during his stay. Roworth's influence may account for a lack of further experiment in Rosenberg's pictures executed in Cape Town.

Technically, however, Rosenberg's South African pictures are up to the standard of his previous output, in some cases superior to it, though not all of his work has survived. His first undertaking, for instance, which was to paint 'two babies',[46] has either been lost or, as a friend in Cape Town maintained, was never completed, though it was a job he had started by the end of June. The commission had come through Marsh's letter of introduction to Sir Herbert Stanley, a predictably careful choice on Marsh's part. An assimilated Jew (the son of Sigismund Sonnethal, he had rapidly changed his name and become a devout Anglican), Stanley had graduated from Balliol College, Oxford, in 1891 and arrived in South Africa only four years before Rosenberg in 1910 as secretary to Viscount Gladstone, the Governor General. Though moving in very different circles from Rosenberg's family in District Six, the speed with which he found work for Rosenberg suggests that he empathized with him as an English-born Jew.[47]

The fee of £15 for this first commission, though not princely, seemed to Rosenberg very welcome, since it would help him pay his way until he established a regular source of income. Hoping for more commissions and some paying pupils, he was intending to get a room of his own, and not just for painting in. He also longed for somewhere to write the poetry that would not lie dormant. His sister and the Horvitches, as he explained to Marsh, though immensely kind, failed to 'understand the artist's [need for] seclusion to concentrate' and were always interrupting him.[48] Meantime he 'painted a Kaffir' (by which he means a black or coloured South African) and contented himself with 'pottering about'.[49]

Despite the impression created by this remark, Rosenberg must have been working hard at his painting, given the number of pictures he completed during his stay. Like Bomberg in Palestine nearly a decade later, he seems to have been inspired by the dazzling intensity of the light. No longer under pressure to produce work on demand, he practised the profession he hoped to adopt more freely, producing at least fifteen, possibly seventeen portraits. As well as between four and six self-portraits, he produced at least six other portraits in oils and five portrait-drawings during his stay. Puzzlingly, since many are of a high standard, he discarded most of these works, taking back with him to England only one, at most two, self-portraits, two other portraits in oils and a delicate pencil portrait of a female head, probably for sentimental reasons. Fortunately his family in Cape Town salvaged most of his rejects from the dustbin, allowing some assessment of his art during this period to be made.

Still unable to afford professional models, Rosenberg was obliged to confine his portraits in oils to himself, his family and three 'Cape Coloureds' (almost certainly servants or neighbours of the Horvitches in District Six). Most of these reflect the very different light in which they were painted. His portraits of Wolf Horvitch and Barnett Rosenberg – the latter painted from a photograph, as a memento for Minnie perhaps – are executed with a much lighter, brighter palette than his previous portraits and the 'Cape Coloureds' trio are equally vivid. His portrait of his sister, who had by the time he painted her given birth to her first child, is painted in warm colours; her downward glance, suggesting that she is gazing at her child, conveys a Madonna-like modesty and calm. (He was to choose a similar technique in his portrait of a heavily pregnant Sonia Cohen the following year, the Madonna allusion further reinforced by the added reference of her blue dress.) Minnie's son Isaac, who remembered many of these pictures hanging on the walls of his family home, found his mother's portrait 'full of composure'. He also recalled the force exerted by these pictures on him, particularly Rosenberg's self-portraits.

The overwhelming impression created by these self-portraits is an increased confidence, both technically and socially. The outstanding example of this, whether it was painted in South Africa or immediately on Rosenberg's return to England, is the self-portrait now in the National Portrait Gallery, where his technical skill and self-assurance are at their height.[50] Of the self-portraits known to have been executed in Cape Town, three out of the four suggest that the confidence could spill over into arrogance, which some of his behaviour there bears out. He himself described one of them as 'very gay and cocky',[51] a reference either to himself in his favourite green hat taken from the left, where he gazes more directly at the viewer than usual, or to his *Self-Portrait in a Red Tie*, where the tilt of the head suggests some disdain. A similarly defiant pose is adopted in his hitherto unknown self-portrait in a red tie and hat which may also have been painted in South Africa.[52]

Maurice de Sausmarez, who handled Rosenberg's art at the Leeds Exhibition in 1959, maintained that the works of the 1914–15 period have a quality that is 'intensely personal':

> The quality is not easy to characterize [he wrote in the Introduction to the Leeds Exhibition Catalogue], but it includes a simplification that moves towards compression of experience rather than towards the schematic, a design which is not arbitrarily imposed as in some of Stanley Spencer's work, but is distilled and inseparable from the content. The symbol always retains the sensuousness of the original experience and he mistrusts an art that uses 'symbols of symbols'.[53]

The omission of any landscapes from work carried out in one of the most dramatic city settings in the world is curious. Laurence Binyon thought he remembered seeing landscape as well as portrait studies among the paintings Rosenberg brought back from Cape Town, and Rosenberg himself tells Marsh of his intention to paint 'Kaffirs against characteristic landscapes'.[54] It is clear that he made at least one attempt at the genre, since he complained jokily to Marsh of trying to paint the sun, 'a very changeable creature . . . I can't come to any sort of understanding with this golden beast. He pretends to keep quiet for half an hour and just as I think, now I've got it, the damnid [*sic*] thing has frisked about.'[55] There may have been some landscapes among the bundle of paintings Rosenberg claimed to have lost overboard in Cape Town harbour on his return journey to England, but in the absence of any at all in the family's carefully preserved collection, it seems likely that he executed few if any there. This is particularly puzzling in view of the fact that his closest painter friend in South Africa, Roworth, was very keen on landscape painting.[56]

Rosenberg may have been deliberately limiting himself to work which he hoped would forward his career as a portrait-painter, but a more interesting possibility relates to his increasingly uneasy reaction to his surroundings. After his initial admiration for Cape Town and its setting, he had begun to feel that the city, and by extension himself, was 'walled in by the sharp upright mountain and the bay'.[57] While still describing the scenery as 'splendid stuff to paint', by late July 'the piled up mountains of Africa across the bay' had begun to strike him as 'lovely and *dangerous*' (my italics), making him think of 'savagery and earthquakes – the elemental lawlessness'.[58] When, another month later, bad weather returned, he appeared to revel in 'the wonderful storms and winds', but noted also the 'houses blown over – the very mountains shaken'.[59] It may have been this fiercer, more essential aspect of Africa that he felt unable to capture on canvas. Visits to such renowned beauty spots as Sea-Point, Camps Bay and Rondebosch appear to have gone unrecorded in paint, despite Roworth's example.

Chapter 12

'If You Are Fire': Marda Vanne and Poetry

June 1914–February 1915

If you are fire and I am fire,
Who blows the flame apart
So that desire eludes desire
Around one central heart?

A single root and separate bough,
And what blind hands between
That make our longing's mutual glow
As if it had not been.[1]

It was through Roworth that Rosenberg met another colourful local personality, Margueretha Van Hulsteyn, an actress who later became known on the London stage, playing opposite Gwen Ffrangcon-Davies, as 'Marda Vanne'. Four years younger than Rosenberg and equally small, she was nevertheless a striking figure, particularly in conservative Cape Town. At a time when hobble skirts and tea-tray hats were worn, with the wearer's face almost obscured by 'sausage' and 'kiss' curls, she would appear, as a close friend recollected:

in a black velvet princess garment, cut straight as a pencil, ermine trimmed, and reaching to her (then) unfashionably low heels. With her yellow hair bobbed and 'banged', and with her expression of natural innocence, and unnatural saintliness, she had the appearance . . . of an endearing pageboy in mediaeval history.[2]

Those who knew her well, however, saw through this saintly appearance to the 'suave little "enfant terrible"' beneath.[3] Renowned for her

Rosenberg's drawing of Marda Vanne, Cape Town, c. late 1914

daring and rebelliousness even among the bohemian circle in which she moved, she was known to her intimates as 'Scrappy'. And her intimates evidently came to include Rosenberg, who received at least one letter signed with this nickname.[4] She had already been married and divorced by the time Rosenberg met her, to a future prime minister of South Africa, Johannes Gerhardus Strijdom.

There was another softer, more sensitive side to Scrappy, however, which Rosenberg would have appreciated: she loved poetry. The same friend remembered a particularly poignant occasion, when 'little Margueretha Van Hulsteyn standing on the immense Cape Town Auditorium stage' recited 'in the pure ringing voice of a boy chorister the "Pioneers O Pioneers" of Whitman to a capacity audience of silent, homesick Boer prisoners of war, her own Dutch people'.[5]

There is no doubt that Rosenberg was attracted to Scrappy, or that she responded to his overtures. Morris Robinson, whose art gallery was a meeting-place for anyone with cultural aspirations, named her as the person most likely to have 'much information about

Rosenberg'.[6] He remembered the 'very nice drawing' Rosenberg did of her, a fine pencil portrait which accentuates her determined mouth and her defiance as well as her physical attractiveness. And it is clear that Rosenberg was taken by her daring, telling Sonia Cohen on his return to England about 'a fair-haired girl who had cut her hair short', a sign of great independence in 1914.[7]

Rosenberg also made a fair copy of one of his poems for Margueretha, 'If You Are Fire and I Am Fire' (quoted above), which reads very like a personal appeal or confession of passionate love. Written before he met her and included in Edward Marsh's 'Little Book' of poems, it evidently seemed to him an appropriate offering to her. Like the relationship itself, this is an enigmatic poem. While the sustained metaphor of fire and the references to 'a single root' and 'one central heart' suggest a sensual mingling, the startling paradox of 'blind hands' conveys separation and only a groping after contact. Parsons rightly singles this poem out for its 'simplicity and lyric grace',[8] qualities that begin to dominate Rosenberg's verse from 1914 onwards.

In view of the many passionate love poems Rosenberg wrote in South Africa – 'What If I Wear Your Beauty', 'I Have Lived in the Underworld Too Long', 'Sacred, Voluptuous Hollows Deep' and 'I Know You Golden' among others – and lines scribbled on her letter agreeing to meet him at her hotel in Muizenberg ('Heart is there hope', for example), it is impossible not to suspect an affair with Margueretha. Linked by imagery of fire, light and golden summer, all these poems point to a sensation of emerging from darkness into a new world not just of Africa but of physical fulfilment. 'I like an insect beautiful wings have gotten / Shed from you' the poet writes in 'What If I Wear Your Beauty', listing in sensuous language and explicit erotic detail the 'Sacred, voluptuous hollows deep' of the female body described in detail in a poem of that name:

> Warm, fleshly chambers of delights,
> Whose lamps are we, our days and nights.
> Where our thoughts nestle, our lithe limbs
> Frenzied exult till vision swims
> In fierce delicious agonies;

And the crushed life bruised through and through
Ebbs out, trophy no spirit slew,
While molten sweetest pains enmesh
The life sucked by entwining flesh.

O rosy radiance incarnate,
O glowing glory of heaven-dreamt flesh,
O seraph-barred transplendent gate
Of paradisal meadows fresh.[9]

Even without using poems like this for evidence, it is clear that there was something out of the ordinary in the relationship between Margueretha Van Hulsteyn and Rosenberg. When Wolf Horvitch went to ask her for her recollections of him only a few years later she was noticeably unforthcoming, saying that she had no memory of him at all, yet a close friend of hers, her fellow actress Gwen Ffrangcon-Davies, with whom she lived for many years, heard her speak of Rosenberg from time to time.[10] When Rosenberg's younger sister, Annie, wrote to invite her to several exhibitions of his work in the Thirties and Fifties, she acknowledged her relationship with him, though declined to attend the exhibitions.[11] Her letter to Rosenberg from the Alexandra Hotel, Muizenberg, written at the start of the relationship, is playful and slightly coquettish and makes it clear that he had already discussed his poetry with her and arranged to draw her:

> . . . Monday will do very well for me – I'll be in all the afternoon so just fetch me at the hotel. If my pen and pencil gave out and I had a sudden thought I'd remember it until I *had* something to write it with – my good thoughts are so rare you see.
> Yours in haste
> Scrappy v. H[ulsteyn]

The most likely explanation is that there was a brief affair that Margueretha afterwards regretted. Rosenberg's notes for his letter about his tendency to quarrel with almost everyone he met may well refer to her: 'If there must be a quarrel let's quarrel in a letter and get over it. / What should we quarrel about? I can't quarrel with anything you've said so I'll quarrel with what you have not said ..."[12] There was probably never much chance of a successful relationship between someone as contentious and insecure as Rosenberg and a girl who had earned the nickname 'Scrappy' at an early age. A significant number of Rosenberg's South African poems describe the loss of something wonderful which has momentarily lit up his life. It may not just have been his admiration for Elizabethan and Jacobean verse that caused him to write in one of his many verse fragments from South Africa about the fickleness of the love object, the play on 'fair' almost certainly a reference to Margueretha's blonde hair:

> Kiss me once more
> You have been fair
> And cruel and foul.
> You have been fair
> Kiss me once more.[13]

His most finished poem on the subject, 'At Sea-Point', suggests that he was more successful at conveying a sense of desolation than of fulfilment and that, whatever the truth about his relationship with Margueretha, the loss of her, or someone very like her, prompted him to verse that anticipates some of his most striking war poetry. The opening metaphor of the earth 'crumbl[ing] away', for instance, inspired by the physical layout of Sea-Point, a beauty spot near Cape Town, foreshadows the 'darkness crumbl[ing] away' in 'Break of Day in the Trenches' and the 'roots of the earth' in the earlier poem are echoed in the latter's 'bowels of the earth':

> At Sea-Point
> Let the earth crumble away,
> The heavens fade like a breath,
> The sea go up in a cloud,
> And its hills be given to death.
>
> For the roots of the earth are old,
> And the pillars of heaven are tired.

The hands that the sea enfold
Hath seen a new desired.

All things upon my sense
Are wasted spaces dull
Since one shape passed like a song
Let God all things annul.

A lie with its heart hidden
Is that cruel wall of air
That held her there unbidden,
Who comes not at my prayer.

Gone who yet never came.
There is the shining sea,
And the shining skies are the same,
But they lie—they lie to me.

For she stood with the sea below,
Between the sky and the sea,
She flew ere my soul was aware,
But left this thirst in me.[14]

There is little doubt that someone inspired Rosenberg to frenzied poetic activity in Cape Town and Margueretha is the most likely candidate. We know he met her early in his stay, since he had quickly discovered Ashbey's Art Galleries, one of her own haunts.[15] Morris Robinson, who ran the gallery and auction house with his brother Walter, remembered Rosenberg coming in 'practically every day' and confirmed that Scrappy 'knew him well'.[16]

The Robinsons were Jewish and had arrived from Ireland with their parents in 1904 or 1905, when Morris was fourteen or fifteen.[17] Though his father became a rabbi in the affluent Gardens area at the city's main synagogue, the family lived near the Horvitches in District Six, where Wolf Horvitch introduced Isaac to Morris. (Like Alexander, Robinson was one of a limited number of Jews who moved easily between these two very different worlds.) The same age as Rosenberg, he also shared his dual artistic interests, having attempted to write poetry in his teens and continuing to sketch throughout his life. Robinson's son gained the impression from both his father and his mother (herself of Lithuanian Jewish parentage) that Robinson and Rosenberg were 'kindred spirits',[18] and Robinson's own reference to their 'long chats' bears this out.[19]

Robinson's main focus was on art by 1914, by which time he was deeply involved with the local art community, and Rosenberg was introduced to him primarily as a painter. He admired 'several fine paintings [of Rosenberg], one particularly nice one of himself'; nevertheless, he remembered him afterwards as being more interested in verse:

> ... but he was always writing poetry. His pockets were always full of bits of paper. One day I got him a note book and he filled it in no time with verse. He tried to get people interested in his verses but nobody would take it up.[20]

Robinson could not have known at the time how important his gift of a large black notebook would be in preserving a great deal of what Rosenberg wrote in Cape Town, though the poet did not entirely give up his habit of jotting fragments down on scraps of paper.[21]

Robinson was no more successful than Rosenberg in promoting his poetry but had no difficulty in attracting interest in him as an artist. Fresh from the Slade and London, one of the world's most important cultural centres, Rosenberg may well have seemed the 'absolute boon to Cape Town's limited cultural world' that his nephew claimed he was.[22] Robinson was able quickly to arrange for him to give some lectures on art to the town's Drawing Club.[23] Two in number, these constitute the bulk of Rosenberg's writings on the subject of the plastic arts and give some valuable insights into his approach to it. Focused on the evolution of contemporary art, they show, in Steven Connor's words, 'only a cautious openness to modernism in art' and are 'positively blimpish about Marinetti's futurist antics'.[24] Roworth's influence may partly account for Rosenberg's dismissiveness of a number of other contemporary artists besides

Marinetti, though absence from such friends as Bomberg could also have encouraged him to speak his mind more freely.

In order to discuss new movements in contemporary art Rosenberg feels obliged in his first lecture to give his audience a rapid tour of the main tradition in art, which he identifies as beginning with the 'high culture' of the Egyptians,[25] then developing through the Greeks' 'more idealistic ... more effeminate conception of beauty' and the School of Giotto 'which might be called the naturalistic school', its chief exponents Botticelli and Mantegna.[26] This first lecture ends rather abruptly with Leonardo da Vinci, perhaps because Rosenberg has allowed himself a long digression on his favourite creative spirit, Blake, which leads to a further digression on the differences between poetry and painting. The audience may have found this rather unsettling – and there is evidence that they did – but any serious student of Rosenberg will welcome his revealing comments on his rival arts:

[Blake's 'The Song of the Morning Star'] is a vital composition because its content is an infinite idea expressed coherently in a definite texture. The spaces harmonise in unexpected ways, the forms are expressive and consistent, the gestures are rhythmical, but surprise us, as though one's own private thought, too secret even to reveal to ourselves, were suddenly shown to us from outside. It is a limitless idea, responsive to the emotion but ungraspable to the intellect. A poem contains in itself all it would convey, which is infinity. This is brought about through movement, the rapid succession of images and thoughts, as in nature itself. Painting is stationary, it only begins a procession of thought, it suggests. But you think outside the painting, not in it.[27]

Rosenberg's second, and concluding, lecture manages to arrive, again rather breathlessly, at his contemporaries, via Michelangelo, Velázquez, Rembrandt, Ingres, Degas and other French Impressionists on the one hand and English art, represented by Gainsborough, Blake (again!), Alfred Stevens, Rossetti, Turner and Constable on the other.

The first of these two lectures, delivered shortly after Rosenberg's arrival in Cape Town, was probably based on notes taken from Roger Fry's Art History lectures at the Slade. The second, however, presented more problems, as he informed Marsh. In deciding loftily to 'clear through all [the] rubbish' of what seemed to him a highly materialistic, reactionary society, he needed help:

> Now I'm going to give a series of lectures on modern art (I'm sending you the first, which I gave in great style. I was asked whether the futurist[s] exhibited at the Royal Academy). But I want to make the lectures interesting and intelligible by reproductions or slides. Now I wonder whether you have reproductions which you could lend me ... I want to talk about [Augustus] John, Cézanne, Van Gogh, [J.D.] Innes, the early Picasso (not the cubist one), [Stanley] Spencer, Gertler, [Henry] Lamb, Puvis de Chavannes, Degas. A book of reproductions of the P[ost] Impressionists would do.[28]

In the event the 'series' of lectures was boiled down to one, which he completed by 8 August and sent to Marsh, though fully aware of how preoccupied the Private Secretary of the First Lord of the Admiralty must be 'with bristling legions of war-scented documents' by then.[29]

However mystifying Rosenberg's provincial audience may have found his second lecture, there were at least two listeners who appreciated it, Agnes Cook and her daughter Madge. Madge, who had met Rosenberg at Ashbey's Galleries which she frequented with her close friend Margueretha, was herself a painter. A precocious child of enlightened, upper-middle-class parents, she had been trained at an early age by one of Cape Town's most respected artists, Crosland Robinson (no relation of Morris Robinson), and become a pupil at the Académie Julian in Paris at thirteen. By 1914 she was already established with her own studio and pupils. A year older than Rosenberg (1889–1972), she was also a great deal taller, accentuating her height with flowing Pre-Raphaelite clothes she designed and made herself.

Together with her cosmopolitan background and bohemian upbringing, Madge almost certainly intimidated Rosenberg and he would probably have been both surprised and flattered by her admiration of his work. As an art critic she believed he had 'a rare approach', as an artist 'a sense of aesthetic draughtsmanship, developed almost to the point of genius' and as a poet a 'flame'-like quality.[30] Rosenberg was grateful to her for the occasional loan of her studio, where his portrait of her friend Margueretha was probably executed, and insisted on drawing her too. 'I am ashamed to confess' she wrote later, that 'being young and vain I excused myself from accepting [the pencil portrait] because I (privately) did not think it flattering enough.'[31]

Madge's mother Agnes's response to Rosenberg was more mature. In her mid-fifties by 1914, she was the editor of *South African Women in Council* magazine. Of British birth – descended, she was proud to remember, from a Scottish earl – she and her husband had brought with them to South Africa when they arrived in 1894 cultural aspirations that they passed on to their two daughters. A pianist of professional standard, Agnes Cook was also very interested in art and literature, publishing books of poetry herself later on. Hungry for news of fresh developments in the wider art world and enormously hospitable – she and her husband ran a daily advertisement in the local paper inviting 'lonely foreigners' to their monthly At-Homes – it was not long before Rosenberg became a regular visitor to the family house in the coastal suburb of Camp's Bay and their apartment in central Cape Town.[32]

Agnes Cook remembered seeing 'a great deal' of the young painter-poet during his stay.[33] A 'truly marathon listener' according to her daughter,[34] she quickly won over the self-absorbed Rosenberg, who began to confide in her. 'So few people speak my language, Mrs Cook,' he told her 'wistfully'.[35] She herself was very admiring of Rosenberg's abilities both as a poet and a painter but believed that he was 'ahead of his time ... his outlook [too] unusual and progressive' for her fellow citizens, who knew 'hardly anything of modern art or poetry'.[36] Convinced that she was 'in the presence of genius', she feared that his 'subtleties and cleverness would go unappreciated'[37] and offered to publish both his 'Art' lectures and two of his poems in *South African Women in Council*. A rare appearance in print, Rosenberg could not resist mentioning it to Marsh, evidently buoyed by the recognition.

Three possible candidates for
Rosenberg's drawings of Madge
Cook, 1914 (*clockwise: whereabouts
unknown; Mrs Gerda Horvitch;
Jewish Museum, Cape Town*)

It was while Rosenberg was in Mrs Cook's editorial office discussing publication of the second of his 'Art' lectures,[38] that he met another admirer, her friend Betty Molteno. Miss Molteno had been 'delighted' with his two poems, 'Beauty' (II) and 'The Dead Heroes', included in *South African Women in Council*'s December issue[39] and invited him to stay with her in Rondebosch, a beautiful and exlusive suburb of Cape Town. In her sixtieth year when they met at the end of 1914, Betty was the eldest child of Sir John Molteno, the Cape's first prime minister after the Union Act of 1910, and sister to the speaker of the Legislative Assembly, based in Cape Town, moving in quite different circles from the Horvitches and their friends in District Six. Yet Rosenberg seems to have had more in common with her and her world than with his own family. After almost six months in South Africa he was feeling (in his own words) 'isolated and lost' when they met, but according to him she 'took some of the isolation away'.[40] Her love of poetry, which her partner Alice Greene shared, almost certainly explains this unexpected rapport between two such outwardly different people. Months after his stay with her he would still have vivid memories of 'Miss Green[e] reading [Flecker] so beautifully on New Year's Day'. And shortly after arriving back in England he would send her 'some poems I think you'll like'.

Yet she was as acutely conscious as the Alexanders were of the problems posed by racial discrimination and poverty in Cape Town, especially for black and coloured South Africans. Like her close friend Olive Schreiner, she devoted a great deal of her time and energy to fighting social inequalities, one reason perhaps why she wanted to help Rosenberg. She was also, according to one of her relatives, a 'radical feminist lesbian' and had been headmistress of the progressive Collegiate Girls' High School in Port Elizabeth. (One of her many enlightened moves had been to introduce the wearing of 'bloomers' for the girls to enable them to have gym lessons.) When she and Alice Greene, her deputy, left the school in 1900, it was partly because their concern for the Boers and their determination to achieve the vote for both coloured South Africans and women were beginning to seem more pressing. By the time Rosenberg came into contact with the circle of independent women

Self-portrait, 1910/11

People on the Seashore, 1910

The Road, 1911

Highgate, 1911

The Fountain, 1911

The Artist's Father, oils, 1911

Sacred Love, composition in oils for The Slade, 1912

The Murder of Lorenzo, composition in oils for The Slade, 1912

Head of a Woman 'Grey and Red', oils, 1912

Left: Self-portrait, oils, 1912

Below: Self-portrait, oils, 1914

in which Ruth Alexander also moved, Betty Molteno and Alice Greene were central players in it.

Like the two other leading figures in the group, Olive Schreiner and Emily Hobhouse, Miss Molteno had found the reactionary climate of Cape Town increasingly difficult and was based in London by 1914. But she was staying temporarily at Rondebosch with a younger brother in luxurious surroundings at Sandown House, Sandown Road.[41] Rosenberg's description of his visit there, whilst appreciative, suggests that his situation made him even more conscious than normal of his own lack of privilege.

I'm living like a toff here [he wrote to his family in England]. Early in the morning coffee is brought to me in bed. My shoes (my only pair) are polished so brightly that the world is pleasantly deceived as to the tragedy that polish covers. I don't know whether there are snakes or wild animals in my room, but in the morning when I get up and look at the soles of my shoes, every morning I see another hole. I shan't make your mouths water by describing my wonderful breakfasts – the unimaginable lunches – delicious teas, and colossal dinners. You would say all fibs. I won't tell of the wonderful flowers that look into my window and the magnificent park that surrounds my room. Of the mountains climbing right to the sheerest top until the town the sea and fields were like little picture postcards lying on the pavement to one looking from the top of the Monument.[42]

Despite such unaccustomed luxuries, Rosenberg's letter ends with his hope 'to be back in England' soon, on the surface a surprising decision. It was probably not so much his inability to buy himself new shoes which inspired it, as pride. He had already shown with both Mrs Cohen and Marsh how difficult he found it to accept patronage, and though Miss Molteno's was offered far more tactfully than Mrs Cohen's, he appears to have had no hesitation in rejecting her offer to rent a room for him in the adjoining suburb of Bishop's Court, where he could write and paint in peace.

However beautiful Rosenberg found his surroundings at Rondebosch there is no evidence that he tried to paint them. But it is

likely that the active birdlife of the peaceful suburb inspired at least
one poem:

> A bird trilling its gay heart out
> Made my idle heart a cage for it
> Just as the sunlight makes a cage
> Of the lampless world its song has lit. . . .[43]

The image of a cage is not accidental, I believe, linking back to his
sensation of being held prisoner by sexual passion but relating also
to his deprived circumstances in life, of which Rondebosch makes
him particularly aware.

Whatever Rosenberg's problems in accepting Miss Molteno's
help, he did take advantage of her offer to write a letter of introduction to Olive Schreiner, whom he would visit shortly after his
return to London. (He was to find her 'an extraordinary woman . . .
full of life' and was delighted by her praise of what he called his
'Kaffir pictures'.[44] 'If I'd done more I'd have given her one' he told
Marsh.)[45]

Rosenberg's visits to Betty Molteno, the Cooks and a number of
other friends in Cape Town suggest that he led a far more sociable
life there than in London, possibly because he was able to make a
fresh start. 'This coming away has changed me marvellously' he
wrote to Marsh a few months after his arrival, 'and makes me more
confident and mature.'[46] This renders his decision to leave even more
puzzling until the third sentence of his letter is noted: 'It's a fearful
nuisance, this war.'

Chapter 13

'On Receiving News of the War'

August 1914

By the time you get this [Rosenberg wrote to Marsh in the autumn of 1914] things will only have just begun I'm afraid; Europe will have just stepped into its bath of blood. I will be waiting with beautiful drying towels of painted canvas, and precious ointments to smear and heal the soul; and lovely music and poems. But I really hope to have a nice lot of pictures and poems by the time all is settled again; and Europe is repenting of her savageries.[1]

Rosenberg's letter to Marsh shows a detachment he is unlikely to have felt had he been in England at the outbreak of war. Place does matter in this respect. It is probably no coincidence that one of the earliest and fiercest critics of the conflict, Charles Hamilton Sorley, was in Germany among German friends when war was declared; or that the initially jingoistic Siegfried Sassoon was at home with his mother and her friend, whose sons were colonels on the Active Service List, in a deeply conservative, very English part of Kent; or that Rupert Brooke, staying with Marsh, an establishment figure, had been dining with the First Lord of the Admiralty, Winston Churchill, a few days previously. All three enlisted at once, though Sorley did so reluctantly. Of the major First World War poets only Wilfred Owen and Rosenberg did not do so, and Owen, like Rosenberg, was not in England at the time. In Rosenberg's case, there were also other factors at work.

Rosenberg is unlikely to have known much of the tensions building up in Europe in July after the assassination of the Austrian Archduke Ferdinand by a Serb patriot on 28 June 1914, since to begin with only the statesmen and diplomats were involved. While Churchill's closest confidant, Marsh, was inscribing 'WAR CLOUDS' in his diary on 24 July, Rosenberg was busy writing to him about his need for a book of reproductions of contemporary artists. And when, at the end of July, the whole of Europe waited to hear whether Russia would side with Serbia against Austria and Germany, thus precipitating a large-scale war, it is possible that he was still unaware of the crisis.

His second 'Art' lecture written at this time does, however, appear to predict an impending catastrophe and it may be that he knew of the threat but did not feel involved. Few Capetonians, at such a distance, had any idea of what lay ahead and reports of events in the far-off Balkans evoked only limited interest. Even when the possibility of war began to be discussed in earnest as the great powers started to mobilize at the end of July, most South Africans hoped that their country would not be involved, despite the bellicose tone of some of their newspapers. Many were still hoping to remain uninvolved when France came out on the side of Serbia and Russia on 3 August. But when on 4 August Britain was more or less forced to join in because of her informal alliance with France and Russia, together with Germany's invasion of neutral Belgium, the news would certainly have affected Britain's loyal colony in Cape Town. South Africa had no right of neutrality; its only choice was the extent of its participation. Military considerations soon dominated the life of the town, with sites like Table Mountain placed off-limits and censorship introduced. Rosenberg could not help but be fully aware that war was under way.

Yet he continued to feel detached from the whole business, as his letter to Marsh only four days after Britain's declaration of war shows: he is far more interested in the possible effect of his second 'Art' lecture than in Marsh's role in the crisis:

> I enclose the lecture. By the time it reaches you I expect the world will be in convulsions and you'll be in the thick of it. I know my poor innocent essay stands no chance by the side of the bristling legions of war-scented documents on your desk; but know that I despise war and hate war, and hope that the [German] Kaiser William will have his bottom smacked – a naughty aggressive schoolboy who will have *all* the plum pudding. Are we going to have Tennyson's 'Battle in the

air', and the nations deluging the nations with blood from the air? Now is the time to go on an exploring expedition to the North Pole; to come back and find settled order again.[2]

The Tennyson prophecy is from 'Locksley Hall',[3] which concludes with the narrator's resolve to defend his country. But, as his letter makes clear, Rosenberg had no desire to do that, and no intention of enlisting, quite the opposite; he wanted to get as far away from it all as possible. And he was not alone in his attitude. Many of his family's neighbours and friends in District Six were unwilling to volunteer, though the assimilated Jews in wealthier districts of Cape Town came forward enthusiastically. The more recent immigrants from Eastern Europe objected for several reasons. Some of them had suffered personally at the hands of the Russians where they came from and were not prepared to fight for an army which included them as allies. For others the main obstacle was financial: they would be unable on meagre army pay to continue sending money home to their families whom they wanted to join them. However valid these objections, they caused a great deal of anti-Semitism in Cape Town and divided its Jewish community, as happened in London too.

Rosenberg is, in any case, still more concerned on 8 August with the 'row' he hopes to 'kick up' with his lectures and with finding pupils.[4] And though he is forced to accept, two or three months later, that the war has 'killed all that',[5] he still seems to regard the conflict as no more than a passing nuisance. Perhaps, like many people, he thought it would be 'over by Christmas'.

But he does promise Marsh that he will produce some paintings and poems with which to 'smear and heal the soul', enclosing in the same letter one of his most original and powerful responses to the war, 'The Female God'.[6] This Female God, in various guises, will play an important role in his war poetry, her most striking appearance being in his own favourite, 'Daughters of War'. His conception of her is almost certainly affected by his relationship with Margueretha and the 'elemental lawlessness' he detects in his surroundings, both of which now become linked to the 'savageries' of war. A corresponding change of attitude towards the Deity takes place.

Rosenberg's early vision of a loving and beneficent God (evidenced in poems such as 'Night and Day') had already hardened by 1912 into the concept of a sterner Being capable of 'shunning' His creatures ('Spiritual Isolation'), or acting with fickleness towards them ('O'er the Celestial Pathways'). His sometimes tyrannical behaviour springs, the poet dares to suggest, from weakness not strength. Later still He is viewed as simply indifferent ('The Blind God'), His blindness towards His creatures' sufferings arousing in the 'tortured' poet a desire to 'cheat' Him ('Invisible Ancient Enemy of Mine'). But this Power is still conceived as male and in some way linked to the Jewish God of the Old Testament. It is in South Africa that the concept of a rival female deity first emerges, the poet's rebellion against the harsh male God he has vowed to cheat taking the form of a close, possibly sexual relationship with the 'Female God' he conjures up.

This blurring of the line between a physical, human love object and an idealized, mystical female had already started in some of Rosenberg's earlier love poems ('Lady, You Are My God'), but she had still not usurped the powerful male God. In the beautiful but savage, rather threatening scenery of South Africa, in thrall to a real-life, fickle woman, the Female God emerges as a true rival to the male. 'The idealised woman', as Deborah Maccoby writes, 'acquires a highly sinister aspect. She is still beautiful and still worshipped but she becomes all-engulfing, devouring, cruel'[7] like her male counterpart. Rosenberg's first poem on her portrays her as a Medusa-like figure, the emphasis, as in many of his earlier poems to his 'mistress', on her treacherous hair, and 'The Female God' works consistently on both the sacred and the sexual levels:

> We curl into your eyes.
> They drink our fires and have never drained.
> In the fierce forest of your hair
> Our desires beat blindly for their treasure.
>
> In your eyes' subtle pit
> Far down, glimmer our souls,
> And your hair like massive forest trees
> Shadows our pulses, overtired and dumb.

Like a candle lost in an electric glare
Our spirits tread your eyes' infinities.
In the wrecking waves of your tumultuous locks
Do you not hear the moaning of our pulses?

Queen! Goddess! animal!
In sleep do your dreams battle with our souls?
When your hair is spread like a lover on the pillow,
Do not our jealous pulses wake between?

You have dethroned the ancient God.
You have usurped his sabbaths, his common days,
Yea! every moment is delivered to you.
Our Temple! our Eternal! our one God!

Our souls have passed into your eyes,
Our days into your hair.
And you, our rose-deaf prison, are very pleased with the world.
Your world.[8]

Rosenberg's Female God, like Robert Graves's White Goddess –
the triple goddess who represents the ancient power of fright and
lust among other things – functions as both matriarchal deity and
poetic Muse but is also identified through the erotic description of
her with human sexuality. Graves's White Goddess is the better-
known, but Rosenberg's Female God pre-dates her by many years
and was almost certainly an influence on his admirer, Graves, adding
yet another strand to Graves's formidable list of mythological,
anthropological and archaeological sources. For Rosenberg had
access to a culture largely unknown to Graves, that of the Hasidic
Jewry of Eastern Europe.

The oral tradition of Hasidic Jewry, familiar to Rosenberg through
his parents, included many examples of supernatural female power,
especially in the movement called Kabbalah.[9] The teachings of Kabbalah emphasize, as Beth Ellen Roberts points out in her article on
'The Female God', 'emotion and feeling over rational and legalistic
thought, symbolism and image over abstract concepts of God, and

action over passive acceptance', words that apply closely to Rosenberg's own poetry.[10] Kabbalah, she continues, argues 'the multiple natures of God, masculine and feminine' and acknowledges 'an array of demons and beasts unknown in mainstream Judaism'.[11] Lilith, for example, who will appear in Rosenberg's plays *The Amulet* and *The Unicorn*, features in Jewish legend as 'a usurper of the power of the masculine God, as the seducer of men and as a killer of children', roughly equivalent to the English vampire.[12] There is also a second female figure, Shekinah, sometimes known as the Sabbath Bride, or Queen,[13] who represents the feminine side of God.

Lilith's attempts to usurp Shekinah and the other aspects of her legendary powers explain many of the puzzling references in 'The Female God', but there is more to the poem than that. A highly ambivalent figure, Rosenberg's female God also reflects his own ambivalence towards the sex. Physically weak yet exerting great power over men, as he witnessed in his parents' and his own relationships, women are seen as both salvation and damnation, both a safe haven and a dangerous lure. They can appear to him as they do in the words of another poem, '[l]ike some fair subtle poison':

> ... To lure my soul with the beauty of some enthralling sin.
> To starve my body to hunger for the mystic rapture there.
> O cruel; flesh and spirit your robe's soft stir sucks in,
> And your cold unseeing glances, and the fantasies of your hair. ....[14]

There is no doubt that in developing his notion of 'The Female God' in autumn 1914 Rosenberg was also beginning to explore the nature of war. It is the most interesting of his early poems on the subject and may even be his first. But it is an indirect approach and most critics start their discussion of his war poetry with his more overt handling of the subject, 'On Receiving News of the War: Cape Town':

> Snow is a strange white word.
> No ice or frost
> Have asked of bud or bird
> For Winter's cost.

Yet ice and frost and snow
From earth to sky
This Summer land doth know.
No man knows why.

In all men's hearts it is.
Some spirit old
Hath turned with malign kiss
Our lives to mould.

Red fangs have torn His face.
God's blood is shed.
He mourns from His lone place
His children dead.

O! ancient crimson curse!
Corrode, consume.
Give back this universe
Its pristine bloom.[15]

This first explicit war poem of Rosenberg's has naturally received a great deal of attention, attracting a number of interpretations. Beth Ellen Roberts, for instance, having discerned Lilith's presence not only in 'The Female God' but also in other late 1914 poems ('Her Fabled Mouth' is one), detects it here, arguing that 'the descent of the world into war must have appeared to Rosenberg as the waxing of Lilith's power'.[16] In this context the conjunction of 'kiss' with the idea of war in stanza three becomes logical, rather than 'unusual' as Jon Silkin finds it.[17] Lilith's power over the male God has been achieved through seduction and the 'ancient crimson curse' of the final stanza can be seen as a clear reference to Lilith, traditionally portrayed as red-haired, red-lipped and dressed in scarlet.

Rosenberg's work as a whole shows that he seldom writes out of a single ethos, however. He is as likely to be referring to the spilt blood of Christ in stanzas four and five, for example, as to Lilith. Leone Samson points out how firmly the poem is rooted in both the Old Testament and the New. She links its 'oppositional imagery' of blood and snow with a passage from Isaiah that would have been read out in synagogue in late July or early August: 'Be your sins like crimson, / They can turn snow-white; / Be they red as dyed wool, / They can become like fleece'.[18]

The main interest of the poem for me is biographical, showing how strongly Rosenberg's public attitude towards the war was affected by his initial reception of the news in South Africa. Its measured technique and formal rhetoric were possible only to someone as detached as he was in Cape Town in August 1914. This may, as Bernard Bergonzi and others have argued, have enabled him to see 'the catastrophic nature of war much more clearly than most of his contemporaries',[19] but it was a relatively easy attitude for him to adopt and the resulting poem, despite its arresting opening, is disappointing. Its most striking feature, as Deborah Maccoby notes, is its emphasis on 'the strange, weird quality of the War', brought out through the idea of snow suddenly appearing in the 'hot sunny lands of South Africa'.[20] It displays none of the hard-won tensions of his later verse, written after he had experienced the actuality of war. 'August 1914', for example, written two years after the date of its title, is clearly (as he writes to Mrs Cohen) 'red from the anvil',[21] forged in the conflagration he witnessed in France:

> What in our lives is burnt
> In the fire of this?
> The heart's dear granary?
> The much we shall miss?
>
> Three lives hath one life—
> Iron, honey, gold.
> The gold, the honey gone—
> Left is the hard and cold.
>
> Iron are our lives
> Molten right through our youth.
> A burnt space through ripe fields,
> A fair mouth's broken tooth.[22]

The striking, and contrasted, imagery of the 'heart's dear granary' and the smithy in which Mars, the God of War, is (as in 'Marching') forging men's destinies is combined in the final stanza to extraordinary effect as bullets tear both through 'ripe fields' and delicate human flesh. Another highly effective contrast is made between life before the fighting – 'The gold, the honey' – and the 'iron' after it starts – 'Left is the hard and cold'. Far less declamatory than 'On Receiving News of the War', every word is made to count in this densely packed poem written from direct experience. While the refining effects of fire in burning out the dross from the gold are not ignored, the last verse with its intensely tactile and visual image of steel tearing through human flesh suggests that by August 1916 Rosenberg would find the price too heavy a one to pay.

The two other poems written overtly on war in Cape Town are further evidence of how much Rosenberg's attitude towards it would change once he became directly involved. 'The Dead Heroes', almost certainly a response to the enormous Allied losses at the Battles of Mons, Marne and Ypres between late August and late October 1914 and chosen by Agnes Cook to accompany his first 'Art' lecture in the December issue of *South African Women in Council*, reads like occasional verse composed from a sense of duty, its language archaic, its tone impersonal and its content jingoistic:

> Flame out, you glorious skies,
> Welcome our brave,
> Kiss their exultant eyes;
> Give what they gave.
>
> Flash, mailèd seraphim,
> Your burning spears;
> New days to outflame their dim
> Heroic years. . . .[23]

In 'To Wilhelm II' that 'naughty aggressive schoolboy who will have *all* the plum pudding' is brought sternly to task in lines which Rosenberg himself described as 'doggerel',[24] and which struck his 1937 and 1979 editors as so unfinished that they placed them in the

'Fragments' section of his work. Again, it is in sharp contrast to the war poetry that will follow a year later:

> It is cruel Emperor
> The stars are too high
> For your reach Emperor,
> Far out they lie.
> It is cruel for you Emperor
> The sea has a stone,
> England—they call it England,
> That cannot shine in your crown. . . . [25]

Minnie claimed that 'when the 1914–1918 War broke out [Isaac] was determined to return to England and join the army',[26] and his first three 'war' poems appear to support her view. Yet the final sentence of his letter to Marsh of 8 August – 'Now is the time to go on an exploring expedition to the North Pole' – suggests that enlistment was not only far from his intention but that he would go to great lengths to avoid it. And his second letter on the subject to Marsh a few months later shows that he believed that pursuing his art would help counter the effects of war far more than fighting. His subsequent acceptance of Betty Molteno's invitation to stay with her was hardly the act of someone bent on enlisting.

Why then did Rosenberg decide to return to England in February 1915? Once it becomes clear that the family's explanation is unconvincing, his decision to leave the hospitable Horvitches, their welcoming, appreciative cultural circle and Cape Town's balmy climate becomes puzzling. But it is puzzling only if one relies solely on his family's version of his stay. There is another, more subversive account of events given by Morris Robinson, who saw Rosenberg almost daily during his visit. There is also Rosenberg's own retrospective comment on his true state of mind in Cape Town. Since these versions have remained buried until now, it is Rosenberg's family's interpretation which has been current.

Minnie's memoir, and her brother's letters for the most part, paint a picture of happiness, success and mutual appreciation against a backdrop of glorious weather and splendid scenery. While neither the weather, nor the breathtaking tableaux of mountains and sea, nor his hospitable reception are in question, their account of Rosenberg's own attitude and behaviour is seriously at variance with Robinson's more critical assessment. This cannot be dismissed as simply malicious or misguided, since it is confirmed by the testimony of the minister of Cape Town's Chief (Garden) Synagogue, the Rev A.P. Bender. When asked by Morley Dainow's journalist brother, David, in 1922 about Rosenberg's visit, Bender, a charitable man, nevertheless replied that he was 'a blooming nuisance who didn't know what he wanted. We're glad he's gone.'[27] Joseph Cohen, to whom Dainow repeated this in 1960, explains Bender's surprising remark by saying that 'there were those who would never let him forget he was an alien among his own people'.[28] Allowances must also be made for the fact that Bender, an assimilated Anglo-Jew with a Cambridge education, was not wholly sympathetic towards the more recent Eastern European immigrants of District Six. (There are still those in Cape Town today who describe him as a 'snob'.) But Dainow also went on to say, in a remark omitted by Cohen, that 'Others [presumably in the Jewish community] said [Rosenberg] was "meshugga" [crazy] and they were glad when he was gone.'[29] Some of his South African relatives, apart from the Horvitches, certainly gained the impression that he was 'a difficult personality' who was 'not ever satisfied with things'.[30]

These less idealized accounts of Rosenberg in Cape Town are invaluable because they help to provide a more convincing explanation for his sudden departure. While there was no pressure on him to support himself, his desire to do so is understandable: he did not want to live on the Horvitches indefinitely. But his explanation for his failure to find work, either as a portrait-painter or a teacher, is not entirely convincing in the light of Robinson's revelations. Rosenberg blamed his failure in this respect on the war, which (he wrote to Marsh) had 'killed all that'.[31] Robinson, however, remembered two specific occasions when Rosenberg had the possibility of a job, but was too insecure, too proud or too disaffected to seize the chance.[32] Robinson had managed to arrange an interview for him with the head of the local art school, but Rosenberg's reaction, which he related proudly to Robinson, makes it fairly clear why he failed to get work either in Cape Town or anywhere else:

> Rosenberg appeared before this teacher in the classroom with his hat on his head, but before he could say a word he was ordered to remove his hat. He resented the way in which he was asked and was told that if he did not remove his hat immediately he would be thrown out of the room. He told the master to go to a hot place and cleared out.[33]

Provoking as the situation may have been, a little swallowing of pride would probably have been more sensible.

Other evidence given by Robinson suggests that Rosenberg might not, in any case, have made a good teacher. Though he spent 'days' preparing the first lecture on art that Robinson arranged for him to give, his delivery of it appears to have been far from the success he described to Marsh ('I gave it in great style'):[34]

> Knowing his outlook on art [Robinson wrote] I feared for his reception and unfortunately his lecture lasted under an hour and although questions were not allowed, some members asked him if the Old Masters were also in the same category as the Victorian[s]. He got rather tied up with some of the questions and in a furious manner told the questioners to read more, and refused to answer.[35]

Rosenberg did not suffer fools gladly, as his reaction to Mrs Cohen's well-meant advice over *Joy* had shown. Bomberg, understandably hurt by his friend's dismissal of his work in his second 'Art' lecture as 'of too violent a nature', maintained that Rosenberg's main fault was 'intolerance'.[36] Often interpreted as arrogance by the outside world, it was not calculated to make him an ideal teacher.

That still left portrait-painting as an option, but even there his temperament seems to have prevented him from succeeding. Robinson, who urged him to complete his commission to paint Sir Herbert Stanley's friend's babies, 'as through this he would have gained more work', recalled that 'he always found some excuse for not attending [the sessions] and so the paintings remained unfinished'.[37] Robinson was relieved, therefore, when despite this dilatoriness,

Rosenberg got a commission to paint 'a very important business man' of Cape Town. But on enquiring when he intended to start, the painter replied, 'Never.' On being asked the reason, 'he told me that he did not like the looks of the man and said that he looked too prosperous.'[38]

It is a revealing anecdote, underlining Rosenberg's scorn for what he regarded as South Africa's philistinisim. 'Nobody' he had told Marsh 'had an ounce of interest in art.'[39] Robinson's wife Hettie, who did not marry him until 1919, but appears to have met Rosenberg during his stay, told their son Norman that Rosenberg left Cape Town because he was 'not happy – he didn't like the cultural life, found it too narrow'.[40] 'Think of me,' he had written to Marsh early on, 'a creature of the most exquisite civilization, planted in this barbarous land.' His efforts to 'clear through all [the] rubbish' with his lectures having failed, he grew increasingly nostalgic for the wider cultural life of London. An important motive for him going to Cape Town had been to escape London: now, ironically, one main reason for his decision to leave was nostalgia for London. 'Write me of Spencer, Lamb, Currie and the pack of them' he begged Marsh and, most urgently of all, 'Write me of poetry.'[41] While Cape Town had been ready to acknowledge him as a painter, he had found only a few people to appreciate his poetry. His growing dedication to poetry over art may have been the single most decisive factor in his resolution to return home.

There was also a social problem. While Minnie's house may have been rather humbler than he had expected, and noisier and more crowded after the arrival of her baby, he was at least in familiar circumstances in District Six. Surrounded by his uncles, aunts and cousins and their largely Jewish neighbours, he was not completely divorced from the life of Stepney and Whitechapel. But when he moved out, as he did quickly, into the more privileged social circles of Sir Herbert Stanley, Edward Roworth, the Cook family, the Alexanders and their friends and, finally, the luxurious surroundings of the Moltenos' Rondebosch house, he may have begun to feel out of place. It was as if he had been transplanted from the Whitechapel to the Bloomsbury Group in London. His letter to his family written during his stay with Betty Molteno certainly suggests that it made him more aware of his own deprivations. The world of 'the toffs', he implies in his slightly self-mocking description, can only involve 'fibs' and deceit for someone of his background. His reference to the 'tragedy that polish hides' may not be quite so flippant as it sounds. And this heightened awareness of his social shortcomings did nothing to increase his precarious confidence, as a fragment of verse written in South Africa shows:

> O cockney who ma[?]keth negatives
> You negative of negatives.[42]

Yet, ironically, it had been the seemingly so different Betty Molteno who had been the only person able to help, as he told her in his second letter to her from England in mid-1915, which underlines just how unhappy he had been in Cape Town:

> Your letter makes very vivid to me that strange time in my life (though everything in life is strange to me) when my mind was so full of dark thoughts and terrors and I seemed to myself to be an accidental flame God's heat had lit and He unknowing of it; a flame blown away from the furnace of its birth.[43]

Her letter to him which evoked this response had brought back 'very vividly the only time of all that time I wish to remember', that is his stay with her.[44]

It is an extraordinary letter, and far franker than any of his others, not just for its startling revelation of his true feelings in South Africa but also for its self-awareness, which suggests that he was slowly learning to deal with his own difficult personality:

> I dislike saying such things as I believe people ought to understand, but I am beginning to change my notions about these matters, for I find that by keeping silent, people not only not understand, they misunderstand, and I would dread to be thought unfeeling as much as I would to be thought overfeeling or sentimental.[45]

But what was it that had made Rosenberg most unhappy in South

Africa? His sustained imagery of fire in his letter to Betty Molteno suggests that it might have been his unsatisfactory relationship with Margueretha. Equally, the reference to 'dark thoughts and terror' implies something more threatening – the outbreak of war, perhaps, or the elemental lawlessness of South Africa itself. My own belief is that more important than all these factors, and underlying them all, was his insecurity at being cut off from all he knew – 'a flame blown away from the furnace of its birth'.[46] It was homesickness that drove him back, and he would probably have returned to England even earlier had he not wanted to avoid the worst of its winter.

It is in his poetry that this homesickness becomes clearest, expressing itself most strongly in what may have been his last poem written in South Africa, 'The Exile':

> A northern spray in an all human speech
> To this same torrid heart may somewhat reach,
> Although its root, its mother tree
> Is in the North.
> But O! to its cold heart, and fervid eyes,
> It sojourns in another's paradise,
> A loveliness its alien eyes might see
> Could its own roots go forth.
>
> O! dried-up waters of deep hungering love!
> Far, far, the springs that fed you from above,
> And brimmed the wells of happiness
> With new delight.
> Blinding ourselves to rob another's sun
> Only its scorching glory have we won,
> And left our own homes in bleak wintriness
> Moaning our sunward flight.
>
> Here, where the craggy mountains edge the skies,
> Whose profound spaces stare to our vain eyes;
> Where our thoughts hang, and theirs, who yearn
> To know our speech.
> O! what winged airs soothe the sharp mountains' brow?

From peak to peak with messages they go,
Withering our peering thoughts that crowd to learn
Words from that distant beach.[47]

Rosenberg's complete engagement with his subject here forms a telling contrast to his three earlier set pieces on war. The poem's tree imagery, with the emphasis once more on roots, also points to Rosenberg's true motive in returning home. Beautiful as Cape Town's 'craggy mountains' are, they are completely alien, leaving his thoughts (in two more of his recurrent images) 'hang[ing]', his inspiration 'dried up'. The poem, organized around contrasted metaphors of heat and cold, is riddled with allusions to the Icarus myth, in which Daedalus, the master-craftsman, makes wings for himself and his son, Icarus, who in his hubris flies too near the sun. Communication, the poet appears to be saying, while superficially possible in this southern land, has been cut off. The poet-craftsman of 'The Exile' must leave the sun and return to his northern roots.

Chapter 14

'No More Free Will Than a Tree': From Cape Town to Enlistment

March–October 1915

I've been a whole day in London and feel very happy, in spite of not being able to see London because of a very thick fog [Rosenberg wrote to Betty Molteno at the beginning of March 1915]. My voyage was pretty vile and I'm very glad it's over. The moment I got on board I was waylaid and seized and taken charge of by one of those busy servants of death who are known in life as colds and coughs. He stuck pretty tight to me and worried and annoyed me all through the voyage, but he wearied of me at last, or got frightened by the searchlights at Dover, for he left me there. I had no other company on board.[1]

Rosenberg had begun 1915 in the luxurious surroundings of summer Cape Town, but was to end it in 'revolting' army barracks at Bury St Edmunds. For the England to which he returned in early March that year was conspicuously different from the one he had left in June 1914. By the time his ship docked, England had already been at war for seven months and the need for fighting men had grown rather than diminished.

What would have struck Rosenberg immediately on landing, after the novelty of the searchlights at Dover, was the scarcity of young men in civilian clothes. Rodker recalled the scene by 1915: 'Practically all the men, certainly "the men" in the trenches, in camp ... Streets full of Khaki but the towns, the daily round, empty as it were.'[2] England's honouring of her treaty to defend Belgium against Germany had inspired many to volunteer even before war was declared on 4 August; Siegfried Sassoon was one of the first. And when Kitchener made his public appeal on 7 August for more men, they flooded into hastily opened recruiting offices at the rate of 1,500 a day. (The final number of volunteers would be a formidable 2.4 million.) Like Sassoon, many of the poets still remembered from the First World War volunteered at its outset, as I have noted. Julian Grenfell was already serving in Britain's small professional army, but Robert Graves, Rupert Brooke, Robert Nichols, Charles Hamilton Sorley, Richard Aldington and Ivor Gurney all accepted that it was their duty to defend their country, a belief instilled at the public schools most of them had attended.[3] The young Edmund Blunden left school early in 1915 to fight, and the older Edward Thomas had enlisted by Easter the same year. Brooke, whose war poetry epitomizes this initial patriotic fervour, expressed how the majority of them felt when he wrote in 'Peace' in 1914:

> Now, God be thanked who has matched us with His hour,
>   And caught our youth, and wakened us from sleeping,
> With hand made sure, clear eye, and sharpened power,
>   To turn, as swimmers into cleanness leaping,
> Glad from a world grown old and cold and weary,
>   Leave the sick hearts that honour could not move . . .

When Rosenberg eventually returned to England patriotic feelings still ran high, and he would be forced to consider his own attitude towards enlistment very seriously during the next seven months as the fighting intensified and spread. The battle of Mons in August 1914 had been followed closely by the first battles of the Marne and Ypres and Germany's alliance with Turkey, making it clear that the war would not be 'over by Christmas'. By January 1915, when Russia appealed to England for help against Turkey, over a million Belgian, French and British soldiers had been killed in France and Belgium. As the fighting spread over a still wider area a serious shortage of men became evident. In France a continuous line of trenches stretching from Switzerland to the English Channel swallowed up manpower as the two sides settled into a war of attrition. British and French troops were also needed to fight in the Gallipoli Peninsula, where the Russians were attempting to open the way to the Black Sea through the Dardanelles. In the Middle East British and Indian soldiers, having beaten off a Turkish attack on the Suez

Canal, were preparing to invade Palestine and yet another expeditionary force from India was advancing from the Gulf towards Baghdad. By April, only a month after Rosenberg's return, the second battle of Ypres had begun, and the end of the war seemed further away than ever as the two sides reached deadlock.

Instead of uniting the British government these troubles seem to have divided them, as Rosenberg may have been aware through Marsh. For it was Marsh's boss, Winston Churchill, who was at the centre of the problem: the ruling Liberal Party, under Herbert Asquith, was attracting increasing criticism for Churchill's handling of operations in the Dardanelles as First Lord of the Admiralty. When the Conservative Lord and First Sea Lord Admiral Fisher resigned in protest on 15 May 1915, Churchill was forced to accept a transfer to a lesser post, taking Marsh with him, and by 25 May Asquith was obliged to form a coalition government.

The British people themselves were more united, primarily by a growing hatred of the enemy. Anything German was frowned on, even their music. Someone with a German-sounding name like Rosenberg, or his friends Bomberg, Goldstein and Gertler, would almost certainly attract animosity. (Ironically, Jews were often linked together with Germans in the general hostility to foreigners.) Though Rosenberg makes no mention of any such treatment, it could have been a factor in his final decision to enlist. He may also have been presented with a white feather, to signify cowardice for not volunteering. Any able-bodied young man, even someone as evidently unfit for fighting as himself, was expected to be at the Front defending his country. Kitchener's accusing finger would have pointed down at him from large recruiting posters on every street corner.

Rosenberg was by no means the only East End Jew of military age not to have enlisted by mid-1915, however. Though recruitment had been exceptionally high among assimilated Anglo-Jews anxious to prove their loyalty to their adopted country, as in South Africa, it was noticeably lower among more recent immigrants, especially Russian Jews. And the Whitechapel/Stepney area, where Rosenberg had returned to live with his family in Dempsey Street, was the centre of the 100,000 strong Russian-Jewish community. Like their South African kinsmen most of these had suffered great hardship at

Lord Kitchener's iconic appeal (*Bridgeman Art Library*)

the hands of the Russians and many, as Rosenberg knew from his own father, had fled to England to escape conscription into the dreaded Russian army. Emanuel Litvinoff recalled vividly the 'racial memories' handed down to him and his contemporaries by their immigrant parents, 'stories of far lands we would never see with our own eyes, of wonder rabbis and terrible Cossacks spearing Jewish babies with their lances, of families cowering in cellars as mobs battered at doors shouting "kill the Jews and save Russia!".'⁴ Despite Russia's alliance with England against Germany, on the whole Russian Jews had no wish to fight with or alongside their oppressors. Though many of them were unnaturalized and technically 'aliens', they were defined as *'friendly* aliens', and therefore eligible to fight. But of the 25,000 men of military age in this group, few volunteered. Rosenberg, who *was* a British subject, nevertheless appears to have shared this reluctance. His parents went even further, making it clear to him from an early age that they did not agree with fighting in any context: 'My parents are Tolstoylians [*sic*] and object to my being in khaki', he would write later.[5] He was particularly conscious of his mother's dread of the army, which in Russia had treated Jewish soldiers barbarically.

Another factor that deterred him from enlisting and related to the Russian-Jewish problem was the attitude of his close friends. Most of them, though not all Russian, were opposed to the war. Gertler, whom Rosenberg contacted immediately on his return, thought it 'wretched, sordid Butchery' and became a conscientious objector.[6] Leftwich, Goldstein, Rodker and Winsten felt much the same, but while Gertler, Leftwich and Goldstein were exempted from fighting for technical reasons,[7] Rodker and Winsten were not and would be sent to prison once conscription was introduced in early 1916.[8] Rodker had been 'wild to join' when war broke out, but was prepared to serve only in a regiment of the Foreign Legion comprised mainly of Russians, Belgians and Italians, which seemed to him 'exactly right for the foreigner' he felt himself to be. When this regiment was disbanded after discipline broke down, he changed his mind, for reasons that undoubtedly influenced Rosenberg too:

> . . . I knew about war, and how inconclusive it always had been and most of my childhood I had seen Boer War veterans begging in the streets, and all through my boyhood and adolescence I had been Socialist then Anarchist, and always anti-capitalist and so anti-militarist, and knew it would be and was, a bloody mess . . .'[9]

According to Rodker most of his fellow members in the Stepney Young Socialist League became conscientious objectors and he maintained that his attitude mirrored that of many East End Jews who, like him, believed that: 'We personally had nothing to lose, so it was difficult to see what the country was fighting for.'[10] And it is clear that Rosenberg felt equally disaffected. When he did eventually enlist he would stress that he 'never joined the army from patriotic reasons',[11] and he would continue to share his parents' and friends' belief that 'nothing can justify war'.[12] Of his immediate circle only he and Bomberg would volunteer, and neither would do so out of loyalty to England.

Bomberg and Rosenberg had both started in 1915, however, determined to carry on with their own work, despite almost overwhelming odds. For added to the well-nigh hysterical rejection of all things German, there was a growing disapproval of the arts. To the mass of the population it seemed frivolous to carry on painting pictures or writing poems, especially if these were at all experimental, as Bomberg's art and Rosenberg's poetry were. At most the public could accept overtly patriotic work, such as Brooke's 1914 sonnet sequence, as a possible incentive to greater war efforts. Anything less obviously committed was felt to be irrelevant, even indulgent. As Sir Claude Phillips rather pompously put it in the *Daily Telegraph*: 'Less than ever do we feel inclined to look on with equanimity at these pranks, by which in piping times of peace, it was possible to be mildly interested – or at any rate amused.'[13] Another critic dismissed the work of two of Rosenberg's contemporaries at the Slade on similar grounds: 'This sort of art with its silly affectations and morbid extravagances has been killed by the war, and any attempt to revive it has happily no chance of success. People are in much too serious a mood nowadays to be amused by feebly vicious suggestions or by comic perversion of artistic principles.' Even Harold Monro, owner of the Poetry Bookshop, confessed to Marsh at the end of 1914 that everything except the war had 'sunk into silly insignificance': 'I am holding on somehow and must pull through of course, but "business" has absolutely stopped. From the day war was declared scarcely anyone has entered the shop.'[14]

For Rosenberg, feeling himself 'in the prime and vigour of his powers',[15] the situation was dire. Already conscious before leaving England of the obstacles he must overcome to succeed as either a painter or a poet, these now seemed to him almost insurmountable. Yet he refused to accept the inevitable, if anything increasing his efforts. It is clear from a number of his letters in 1915 that one of his main reasons for not enlisting, despite Ezra Pound's suggestion that it might resolve some of his problems, was that he still had work he needed to do. 'I think the world has been terribly damaged by certain poets (in fact any poet) being sacrificed in this stupid business' he wrote in what appears to be a draft reply to a letter from Pound.[16]

Rosenberg's pencil drawing of his father, 1915 (*Tullie House Museum and Art Gallery*)

'There is certainly a strong temptation to join when you are making no money.'

If he hoped to earn his living through portrait-painting, however, he went about it in the wrong way, choosing as his subjects four people he knew could not afford to pay him – his father, Sonia Cohen, Clara Birnberg and (possibly) himself. Starting immediately on his return on what would be among the greatest achievements of his painting career, he executed on 7 March the last in a series of finely drawn portraits of his father, always readily available in the winter. Less idealized than his 1913 drawing, this shows how skilful he has become at characterization by 1915. His father's quizzical eyebrows and penetrating yet rather distant gaze suggest someone whose thoughts are active but dwell on other than practical matters. His portrait of Sonia, painted either the same month or the next,[17] displays a similar sensitivity towards the sitter, as well as a powerful attraction to her. Eight or nine months pregnant, unmarried and recently turned out of the lodgings Rodker had found her when they separated early in the pregnancy, Sonia's melancholy is evident. But so too is an apparent acceptance of the situation, however resigned. This lends an air of serenity to the portrait which Rosenberg evidently hopes will remind his viewers of the old masters: 'I've done a lovely picture I'd like you to see' he wrote to Marsh in the spring of 1915. 'It's a girl who sat for Da Vinci, and hasn't changed a hair since, in a deep blue gown against a dull crimson ground. If you have time to see it I'd also like Gertler to be there if he can.'[18] Sonia's 'deep blue gown' forms a striking contrast to the 'dull crimson' background, which Sonia remembered Rosenberg choosing for himself from the stationer's shop (Strakers) beneath Rodker's flat, where she was temporarily staying. He was therefore able to choose the exact shade of paper he wanted to pin on a board as background.

His use of the same background for his next portrait, *Clara Birnberg*, dated 1917 by Ian Parsons but clearly executed in 1915, indicates that he painted it, too, in Rodker's Whitechapel room, especially when we learn from Sonia that Clara was one of her few female friends at this time. Clara, either engaged or married to Winsten by 1915, shares the same melancholy air but lacks the Madonna-like modesty of Sonia. This is not simply a matter of iconography – her dress is more green than blue – but her whole demeanour is different. It is a harsher less sensual portrait, revealing as much about Rosenberg's feelings for Sonia as about Clara's own character. It is also less finished and almost certainly the picture to which he refers in another letter to Marsh of spring 1915: 'I think you will like to see it, though if I'd had a little longer on it it would have been very fine indeed. But the model cleared off before I could absolutely finish.'[19] Unfinished though it may be, the portrait of Clara, with its strong, impressionistic brush-strokes, has power. While Rosenberg describes his painting of Sonia as 'a lovely picture' reminiscent of Leonardo da Vinci and was confident enough of it to want Gertler to see it, he has no hesitation in claiming that his portrait of Clara would, with slightly more work, have been 'very fine indeed'.

His self-portrait, however, whether painted in South Africa or London, is his 'finest' of all, the one chosen out of many by the National Portrait Gallery to represent him after his death. A summation of all his previous attempts to capture himself on canvas, it is superior both in terms of characterization and technique. The arrogant, defiant look, which Rosenberg admitted could seem 'cocky',[20] has been replaced by a cooler, more genuinely confident gaze at the world. The sideways glance of the eyes under the shadow of the hat-brim gives the whole an enigmatic, elusive air. More detailed than the previous self-portraits, the paint is placed more thickly on the canvas in small vertical strokes reminiscent of Van Gogh.[21] Exactly half the size of the Sonia and Clara portraits, nevertheless it is equally compelling despite its more subdued tones.

As if this were not enough to prove his powers, Rosenberg also produced two of his most interesting compositions during this period. (Though he had failed to submit anything in time for the New English Art Club Summer Show, he may have been hoping to have them accepted for the Winter one.)[22] Both, like *The Murder of Lorenzo* and another lost illustration to Keats's 'La Belle Dame Sans Merci', draw their inspiration from literature and are of particular relevance to the war poetry to come. The first, 'Hark, Hark, the Lark', a charcoal and monochrome wash traditionally attributed to 1912, partly because of its Cubist influence, must surely be the picture he described in a letter to Marsh that could only have been written after he met Marsh in late 1913:[23]

> I'm doing a nice little thing for Meredith's 'Lark Ascending':
>> Their faces raised
>> Puts on the light of children praised.
> Everybody is in a sort of delirious ecstasy, and all, feeling in the same way, express their feelings in different ways, according to their natures.[24]

His further reference, in a letter known to be written in 1915, to 'wanting to get the hands and feet a bit more explained'[25] in a picture he hopes to sell to Marsh, is added evidence that 'Hark, Hark, the Lark' was executed during this period, since the hands, and particularly the feet, are conspicuously lacking in detail. They also, despite his intentions, look more in pain than in 'delirious ecstasy'. Perhaps, like his soldiers in 'Returning, We Hear the Larks', who will be aware that 'Death could drop from the dark / As easily as

Rosenberg's charcoal and monochrome wash, 'Hark, Hark, the Lark'. ?1912/1915
(*University of South Carolina*)

song', Rosenberg is attempting to convey his sense of a potential
danger lurking in beauty.

His second composition, 'The First Meeting of Adam and Eve',
shows even stronger literary links, to Emile Verhaeren's 'Sovran
Rhythm', in which (Rosenberg wrote to Miss Seaton) 'the words
lose their interest as words and only a living and beautiful idea
remains'.[26] Verhaeren's subject, 'Eve meeting Adam', was given strong
visual expression by Rosenberg in a striking chalk drawing subsequently presented to one of his two great heroes among the Georgian poets, Gordon Bottomley: 'It is a drawing of Adam and Eve
when first they see each other and rush in frenzy to meet' Rosenberg
would explain to him.[27] A sensitive critic of both art and literature,
Bottomley would at once detect the same imagination at work behind
the painter and the poet in this powerfully erotic, skilfully composed

Rosenberg's chalk drawing, 'The First Meeting of Adam and Eve', c. 1915 (*Tullie House Museum and Art Gallery*)

drawing of a nude Adam almost grappling with the naked Eve towards whom his semi-erection helps spell out his sexual attraction. Bottomley, who admired the work greatly, told Harding that he always associated it with the poem Rosenberg had presented to Margueretha Van Hulsteyn at the height of his passion for her, 'If You Are Fire and I Am Fire', and also with 'the little poem [Rosenberg] redrafted in such an infinity of ways: "I mingle with your bones".'[28]

The latter, which was the first poem Rosenberg sent to Marsh for his opinion after returning to England, backs up Bottomley's sense of the link between his two methods of artistic expression. 'The One Lost', as Rosenberg would entitle his poem (in an apt reflection of his own state of mind by mid-1915), expresses in words what he attempted to convey in his picture of the two lovers irresistibly drawn to each other, yearning to be one flesh, yet almost fighting to remain separate:

> I mingle with your bones.
> You steal in subtle noose

This lighted dust Jehovah loans,
And now I lose.

What will the Lender say
When I shall not be found
Safe sheltered at the Judgement Day,
Being in you bound? . . .[29]

This, as Bottomley would later write to Rosenberg, 'has utterance of the really great, simple kind'.[30] Judging from the fact that Rosenberg sent a draft of this poem to Marsh so soon after returning to England,[31] it is probable that it (and behind it Verhaeren's verse) initially inspired 'The First Meeting of Adam and Eve'. But it is also likely that, as he worked on his drawing, his first concept of the poem was altered and influenced by his attempt to express the idea visually, making his final version of the poem more precisely realized.

Begun as a 'joke', Rosenberg included his first draft of 'The One Lost' in a letter to Marsh that reminds him of his promise to buy one of his pictures. He needed money for a specific cause, having returned to England with a plan to publish another collection of poems. Following Marsh's positive response to his 'little thing'[32] and his helpful advice on it, 'The One Lost' would be among the pieces from 1915 included in it.

When Marsh sent Rosenberg a cheque for £2 10s, the amount he needed to pay the printer, he had no guarantee of being repaid. But Rosenberg was determined to reciprocate. 'Hark, Hark, the Lark' and 'The First Meeting of Adam and Eve' may have been started with this in mind, but, if so, were evidently not completed in time. Instead he presented his patron with the three nude sketches previously mentioned.[33] Marsh also helped by reading the poems Rosenberg planned to include. 'For God's Sake! don't say they're obscure'[34] Rosenberg begged him, still smarting from Marsh's detailed criticism of 'Midsummer Frost' the previous year, though still evidently recognizing the value of his advice. Despite working long hours at the Admiralty before Churchill's departure from it, Marsh put in a lot of time on Rosenberg's poems according to his biographer, who also notes Rosenberg's appreciation. 'My technique in poetry is very clumsy, I know' he would write to a friend a few months later, almost certainly as a result of his many discussions with Marsh about his work at this time.[35]

By 'technique', he explained, he meant 'construction and command of form', always his greatest challenge.[36] It was, however, far more evident in the new poems he sent Marsh to read in spring 1915, together with some he had already seen, 'Midsummer Frost', 'Wedded' (II) and possibly a few of the South African poems. Together they decided to include 'Midsummer Frost', 'Wedded' (II), 'If You Are Fire . . .' and seven other fairly recent poems.[37] Rosenberg, wanting to make his collection representative of his development as a whole, also planned to include six poems from his previous volume, *Night and Day*,[38] and a few pieces he had written since returning from South Africa.

Of the latter, his favourite, he told Marsh, was 'God Made Blind', another poem where he struggles to define his ideas about God:

It were a proud God-guiling, to allure
And flatter, by some cheat of ill, our Fate
To hold back the perfect crookedness, its hate
Devised, and keep it poor,
And ignorant of our joy,—
Masqued in a giant wrong of cruel annoy,
That stands as some bleak hut to frost and night,
While hidden in bed is warmth and mad delight.

For all Love's heady valour and loved pain
Towers in our sinews that may not suppress
(Shut to God's eye) Love's springing eagerness,
And mind to advance his gain
Of gleeful secrecy
Through dolorous clay, which his eternity
Has pierced, in light that pushes out to meet
Eternity without us, heaven's heat.

And then, when Love's power hath increased so
That we must burst or grow to give it room,

And we can no more cheat our God with gloom,
We'll cheat Him with our joy.
For say! what can God do
To us, to Love, whom we have grown into?
Love! the poured rays of God's Eternity!
We are grown God—and shall His self-hate be?[39]

Rosenberg's explanation of his poem to Marsh suggests that he felt bitter about his own difficulties by mid-1915:

The idea in the poem ... I should think is very clear. That we can cheat our malignant fate who has devised a perfect evil for us, by pretending to have as much misery as we can bear, so that it withholds its greater evil, while under that guise of misery there is secret joy. Love – this joy – burns and grows within us trying to push out to that Eternity without us which is God's heart. Joy-love, grows in time too vast to be hidden from God under the guise of gloom. Then we find another way of cheating God. Now through the very joy itself. For by this time we have grown into love, which is the rays of that Eternity of which God is the sun. We have become God Himself. Can God hate and do wrong to Himself?[40]

Rosenberg's belief that his idea in 'God Made Blind' is 'very clear' serves only to highlight the complexity of his thought processes. Like Donne and many of the Elizabethan poets toying with 'conceits' and revelling in paradox, he plays in various ways with the concepts of God, Fate, Love, Joy and Deception, ideas which have dominated his verse from early 1914. From the title onwards the poem conjures up, in turn, a God who is Cupid, the blind God of Love, a malignant God of 'hate' and the narrator himself who, through his love, has become 'the poured rays of God's Eternity' and has therefore cheated his Fate of 'the perfect crookedness, its hate / Devised'. The narrator's rebellion against this cruel Male God is closely linked to the alternative 'Female God' who preoccupied Rosenberg in South Africa and also to the idea contained in 'The One Lost', where the poet escapes God's wrath through the sexual love hinted at throughout 'God Made Blind'[41] and spelled out in the final stanza of 'The One Lost':

> And I, lying so safe
> Within you, hearing all,
> To have cheated God, shall laugh,
> Freed by your thrall.[42]

Deborah Maccoby detects in 'God Made Blind' 'a characteristically Jewish conception of the flesh as penetrated and transformed by the spirit, so that the flesh itself becomes holy and consecrated',[43] yet Rosenberg's explanation to Marsh, in which 'cheating God' is central, hardly bears this out. His poem reads more like an attempt to come to terms with the 'perfect crookedness' he believed Fate had devised for him, about which he was feeling particularly resentful in 1915 as increasingly difficult circumstances hemmed him in.

Rosenberg changed his mind about his planned collection several times before deciding on its final form, the most significant alteration being that of the title from *The Poet* to *Youth*. He now wanted to make his poems more universal, applicable to human beings in general rather than to the poet in particular. Shelley's influence, so evident in *Night and Day*, is replaced by the Blake of *Songs of Innocence and Experience*, as Rosenberg's outlining of his scheme to Marsh indicates.

Its main difference from Blake's work is his plan to divide it into three rather than two parts. In the first, 'Faith and fear', 'the idealistic youth believes and aspires towards purity'; in the second, 'The cynic's lamp', 'the youth has become hardened by bitter experience and has no more vague aspirations, he is just sense'; in the third, 'Change and sunfire, the spiritualizing takes place. He has no more illusions, but life itself becomes transfigured through Imagination, that is real intimacy – love.'[44] In his anxiety to avoid weakness of form in his work, he appears to have tried extra hard to shape his collection. Later on he would regret the inclusion of the middle section ('The cynic's lamp'), removing it physically from at least four copies given to friends,[45] and thus bringing *Youth* even closer to Blake's *Songs of Innocence and Experience* in conception.

With Marsh's cheque assured, Rosenberg approached Narodiczky and 'Crazy' Cohen again, who offered to print approximately a hundred copies of an eighteen-page pamphlet, including a paper cover with a list of contents on the reverse, for his money. It is a sign of Rosenberg's progress towards acceptance as a poet that, unlike *Night and Day*, he was able to sell ten copies immediately. At 2s 6d each, this helped cover his costs, though his motive was not primarily mercenary: 'My notion in getting them printed is that I believe some of them are worth reading,' he wrote to Marsh, 'and that like money kept from circulating, they would be useless to myself and others, kept to myself. I lose nothing by printing and may even make a little money.'[46]

He now had something more mature than *Night and Day*, and apart from his untidy scribbles, to show to prospective editors and patrons. Besides his family and close friends like Gertler and Bomberg, the bulk of the copies given away were to influential literary figures such as Pound, who sent it on to the *Poetry* magazine in Chicago, though Harriet Monroe failed to have it reviewed. It is also highly probable that the poet Alice Meynell, a pillar of the literary establishment, was sent a copy, with a letter which shows that it was not Rosenberg's first approach to her:

> Dear Madaam [*sic*],
>   Mrs Siordet once showed you some poems of mine and drawings I did at the Slade. You liked the drawings very much and said the poems wanted more work. I think there are too few poems to ask you to forgive the intrusion on your time, and only hope you will not think there are too many that require forgiveness.
>   Yours sincerely
>   Isaac Rosenberg.[47]

Rosenberg's decision to submit his poems to, among others, a newly established magazine, *Colour*, on his return to England may have made him aware of the need for a respectable 'portfolio' in literature as well as art.[48]

Rosenberg's first opportunity to use *Youth* to show off his talents as a poet came shortly after its publication and in a rather unfortunate way. 'I'm glad you hit it off with the printer' Marsh had written to him on 12 April 1915. Will you come to breakfast on Thursday?'[49] When Rosenberg arrived at Marsh's Gray's Inn apartment on 15 April however, it was to be their last meeting for some time. Eight days later, on St George's Day, Marsh would suffer the greatest sorrow of his life when Rupert Brooke died on his way to fight in Gallipoli. Marsh felt that 'my whole plan of life ha[s] broken down',[50] and would spend the next few months trying to come to terms with his loss. The crisis was exacerbated by Fisher's resignation as First Sea Lord less than a month later, followed by what he called the 'awful catastrophe'[51] of Churchill's demotion (and his own with it) to the Duchy of Lancaster. 'My great sorrow has so completely absorbed all my power of feeling for the present that I really have nothing left over, even for the greatest masterpiece' Marsh confessed to Gertler on 26 May.[52]

By this time Rosenberg had thoroughly antagonized the normally patient Marsh by his self-absorbed attempts to interest him in one of his own 'masterpieces'. It was not so much the attempt to sell him a picture Marsh seems to have minded as Rosenberg's self-pitying reaction when Marsh sent him an understandably miserable explanation of his failure to respond. ('It is as if the sun had gone out' Marsh had written):[53]

I am very sorry to have had to disturb you at such a time with pictures. But when one's only choice is between horrible things you choose the least horrible. First I think of enlisting and trying to get my head blown off, then of getting some manual labour to do – anything – but it seems I'm not fit for anything. Then I took these things to you. You would forgive me if you knew how wretched I was. I am sorry I can give you no more comfort in your own trial but I am going through it too.[54]

According to Leftwich, to whom Rosenberg showed Marsh's letter, he was 'very angry that Marsh should be so concerned about someone whom he considered to be a very inferior poet'.[55] Marsh may have suspected Rosenberg's true feelings about Brooke since, despite Rosenberg's prompt apology for his 'weak and selfish letter',[56] the rift would take some time to heal. That it healed at all is a tribute to the extraordinary tolerance and sympathy shown by Marsh, with all the calls on his public life, to his demanding protégé.

Fortunately, by late April Gertler, still anxious to share his own good luck with his less fortunate friend, had introduced Rosenberg to another potential patron, Sydney Schiff,[57] and the 'poet' (for so he was described) could count on having *Youth* almost ready to show him. A connoisseur of both art and literature like Marsh and Binyon, but far wealthier than either, Schiff was already a generous patron to a number of struggling painters and writers including, among Rosenberg's friends, the poet Aaronson as well as Gertler. He had written one book under his own name, *Concessions* (1913), by the time he met Rosenberg and was attempting a second, which would be published as *War-Time Silhouettes* (1916) under the pen name Stephen Hudson. He would also establish himself as a translator, most famously for his completion of Scott Moncrieff's translation of *A la Recherche du Temps Perdu*, and would become a friend of Proust's, as well as of James Joyce, T.S. Eliot and Katherine Mansfield, among others. By 1915 he was a familiar face in London's literary and artistic circles, together with his second wife, Violet, the sister of the novelist Ada Leverson (Oscar Wilde's 'Sphinx').

While rightly known for his generosity, however, Schiff was also reputed to be rather too ready with his advice and would become a figure of fun to some of those he helped. 'He used to give a good deal of money to poor artists,' Aaronson explained, 'so they all despised him.'[58] His most notable protégé turned ingrate was Wyndham Lewis, who satirized him cruelly as 'Lionel Kein, Esq.' in *The Apes of God*.[59] Gilbert Cannan's 'Mr Tilney Tysoe' in *Mendel*, though described as 'a fool of a patron' who delighted in 'the Bohemianism of his young friends', is not quite so unkind a portrait.

Lewis's caricature of Schiff, as of Rodker, ridicules his Jewishness – signposted in *The Apes of God* by his name, his nasal voice, his 'black toffee-eyes' and yellowing complexion – but it was precisely Schiff's Jewishness that Rosenberg appears to have found most helpful. Unlike the ultra-English Marsh, Schiff understood the problems of anti-Semitism and Rosenberg would feel able, later, to write freely to him on the subject, when Schiff would try to remedy it. Yet

Schiff's Jewishness, unlike Mrs Cohen's, does not appear to have narrowed his horizons.

Lewis also portrays Schiff as a cultural snob, an urbane 'old club-man' (he was twenty-two years older than Rosenberg), hinting with his own particular brand of snobbishness that Schiff's money came from commerce. (His family were international stockbrokers.) Rosenberg, however, appreciated Schiff's wealth and had no hesitation in asking him for a loan or anything else he felt he needed.

What he did react to was Schiff's unfortunate tendency to lecture what Lewis describes as 'his bankrupt young artists'.[60] Whether or not he ever lectured Rosenberg 'on man's duty to his fellows ... with avuncular winds of wheezy emotion'[61] (as Lewis gleefully puts it), he certainly reminded him on several occasions that his lot could have been a great deal worse. His reaction to Rosenberg's frequent bouts of self-pity was more immediate and more robust than Marsh's and, ironically, elicited some memorable replies from Rosenberg.

Overall, however, the progress of Schiff and Rosenberg's relationship from April to October 1915 suggests that Schiff was not a satisfactory substitute for Marsh, which may have been a contributory factor in Rosenberg's eventual decision to enlist. Unlike Marsh, Schiff does not seem to have been able to sustain Rosenberg's belief in the importance of his creative work. Perhaps he lacked Marsh's authority: certainly there are no detailed discussions of any of Rosenberg's work to equal those Rosenberg wrote to Marsh. Nevertheless, Schiff did a great deal for Rosenberg, and the discovery of his letters to Schiff after his death in 1944 has added significant details to our knowledge of his life and attitude towards war from mid-1915 to late 1917.

After meeting Schiff, almost certainly in April at the Café Royal, Rosenberg replies to a letter Schiff has written, evidently suggesting that he would like to see his paintings. Though Rosenberg protests that 'buying pictures of me is the last thing in the world I expect people to do, in the best of times',[62] he clearly hopes Schiff will and invites him to Dempsey Street for a viewing. He also promises to send his poems when *Youth* arrives from the printers. Schiff's response must have been very positive, since Rosenberg replies immediately with his only remaining copy of his first volume, *Night and Day*, repeating his promise to send *Youth*. And when *Youth* materializes, Schiff is one of the first to buy it – not one but two copies at twice the asking price. Rosenberg's faith in him is shown by the fact that on 4 June, when sending *Youth*, he also encloses the first draft of a verse play he hopes to publish, 'Moses'.

Schiff has meantime been away on holiday, but Rosenberg's accompanying letter alerts him to a dramatic development in the war which has taken place on the last day of May, the advent of Zeppelin airships over London, especially the East End: 'We just missed being blown to pieces by a bomb,' he writes from Dempsey Street, 'a factory near by was burnt to pieces and some people killed.'[63]

It was an incident that brought the war, literally, to Rosenberg's doorstep. The sinking of the British passenger liner the *Lusitania* on 7 May 1915, which killed over 1,000 people, had already shocked the British public into a greater awareness of the severity of the situation. Even Rosenberg, still determined not to enlist, was moved to write another patriotic war poem:

> Chaos! that coincides with this militant purpose.
> Chaos! the heart of this earnest malignancy.
> Chaos! that helps, chaos that gives to shatter
> Mind-wrought, mind-unimagining energies
> For topless ill, of dynamite and iron.
> Soulless logic, inventive enginery.
> Now you have got the peace-faring Lusitania,
> Germany's gift—all earth they would give thee, Chaos.[64]

As this and other poems of mid-1915 show, Rosenberg's increasing awareness of the war emerges as an overwhelming impression of 'Chaos', of a world gone awry. In 'Significance' this is linked to a sense of fate closing in on the narrator and his urgent desire that his 'hands' should 'use all ere we lose'.[65] His situation, as a man of military age who does not for various reasons want to fight, almost certainly accounts for a striking poem of this period, 'Chagrin', in which the central image from the Old Testament of Absalom hanging by his hair from the branches of a tree[66] appears to reflect the poet's own helplessness at the hands of fate. This, in turn, is linked to the New Testament image of Christ hanging from the Cross, a hint of the sacrifice that may be required of the narrator:

> Caught still as Absalom,
> Surely the air hangs
> From the swayless cloud-boughs,
> Like hair of Absalom
> Caught and hanging still.
>
> From the imagined weight
> Of spaces in a sky
> Of mute chagrin, my thoughts
> Hang like branch-clung hair
> To trunks of silence swung,
> With the choked soul weighing down
> Into thick emptiness.
> Christ! end this hanging death,
> For endlessness hangs therefrom.[67]

Chaos returns in the third stanza when 'Invisibly – branches break / From invisible trees', but this time appears to relate to the poet's own creative processes, which make him feel superior even to Icarus in his journey to the sun (one of his own 'inspired "suntreaders"')[68] enormously powerful and, then, completely helpless:

> ... The cloud-woods where we rush,
> Our eyes holding so much,
> Which we must ride dim ages round
> Ere the hands (we dream) can touch.
> We ride, we ride, before the morning
> The secret roots of the sun to tread,
> And suddenly
> We are lifted of all we know
> And hang from implacable boughs.[69]

The poem ends where it began, with the narrator 'hang[ing] from implacable boughs', his thoughts of 'mute chagrin' dangling 'like branch-clung hair' in the 'thick emptiness' of his surroundings. The 'chaos' of war has also become the chaos preceding artistic creation. Rosenberg's ability to convey abstract concepts in intensely physical detail, so evident here, will become a marked feature of his war poetry.

It is no coincidence that Rosenberg started during this same fraught period to plan what would become his most sustained attempt to express his dread of what the war might do to him and his aspirations, his one-act drama *Moses*. Based on another Old Testament figure but set, even more pertinently, at the time of the Hebrews' imprisonment in Egypt, *Moses* (in Rosenberg's own words) 'symbolizes the fierce desire for virility, and original action in contrast to slavery of the most abject kind',[70] a very different response to the war from any other literature of the period. Instead of Brooke-ian notions of honour, sacrifice and duty, the emphasis will be on the potential loss of freedom involved in serving one's country, especially, as in Rosenberg's case, in the ranks.

The temporary coolness between Rosenberg and Marsh probably explains why it was Schiff to whom he sent his first draft of *Moses*, Schiff's interest in *Youth* encouraging him to believe that he had found a satisfactory substitute for Marsh. He wrote on 8 June:

> I am very glad you have taken the trouble to read my things and have found something you like in them – most people find them difficult and won't be bothered to read into them.[71]

He was even more pleased when Schiff suggested sending *Youth* to his friend Arthur Clutton-Brock, an art critic for *The Times* who also wrote on other subjects: 'I wonder whether Mr Clutton-Brock could get me some Art writing to do for any journals he is connected with?'[72] His next sentence, however, suggests that he was not at all hopeful of resolving his need to earn a living. Ironically, since it was mainly guilt at not being able to help support his mother (as all his younger siblings were) that made this need so urgent, it was his mother who made him hesitate to take what was beginning to seem the only way out:

I am thinking of enlisting if they will have me, though it is against all my principles of justice – though I would be doing the most criminal thing a man can do – I am so sure that my mother would not stand the shock that I don't know what to do.[73]

A month later, heartened by an encouraging letter from Clutton-Brock (but which he loses at once), he is still trying to find an alternative to enlisting, and the choice still appears to lie between earning money as a writer or a painter. (With the loss of so many men to the army, there were plenty of jobs to be had if he had been prepared to accept anything.) After a not-so-subtle attempt to interest Schiff in buying some of his pictures, he describes a visit to the New English Art Club's Summer Show, an occasion that almost certainly inspires him to submit three of his own works, a drawing (unspecified but just possibly 'Hark, Hark, the Lark'), 'The Family of Adam and Eve' (whereabouts unknown) and his *Head of a Woman: Grey and Red*, which had been shown once before. His choice of these may have been stimulated by 'a remarkable painting' by Gertler he admired at the Summer Show, which he argued 'put him easily next to [Augustus] John amongst our painters',[74] though he also believed that John's 'fine' head of Bernard Shaw made Gertler's portrait seem merely 'clever'. The painting, which veers towards Cubism or Vorticism, is almost certainly of Gertler's friend Dorothy Brett, but the 'horrible distortion' of her features (noted by the *Observer* critic) makes it impossible to say for sure.

More significantly, Rosenberg's response shows that he is still very much engaged with painting, though it will be virtually his last remark on the subject. By September he is writing to Schiff concerning two drawings he has sent him:

I had meant to do a composition but have not been able to in my present state of mind. I have decided not to think of painting – at least until I have achieved some kind of (no matter how small) independence, by doing what is called an honest trade – I am going to learn something and in a few months I may start earning a little. Painting was once an honest trade, now the painter is either a gentleman, or must subsist on patronage – anyway I won't let painting interfere with my peace of mind[.] If later on I haven't forgotten it I may yet do something. Forgive this private cry but even the enormity of what is going on all through Europe always seems less to an individual than his own struggle.[75]

Rosenberg's decision finally to abandon painting was prompted by more than a proud refusal to 'subsist on patronage', or disappointment at Clutton-Brock's failure to find him work. By September 1915 even someone as opposed to war as he was could no longer ignore 'the enormity of what [was] going on all through Europe' and even further afield. News of the death, on 5 June, of the young sculptor Gaudier-Brzeska, who had gone to fight for his country, France, had shocked the art world, including Rosenberg, though he had met him only once. ('He gave one a good impression. It is awful bad luck.')[76] Reports of Allied forces' failure to force their way through the Dardanelles to Russia and the high death toll there continued through the summer. In September an unsuccessful attempt to shatter the German front line and recover the mining districts round the French towns of Loos and Lens began, involving 500,000 Allied troops and resulting in 60,000 casualties.

By October, while the battle of Loos still rages, Rosenberg sends Schiff 'some small poems' he has managed to write in his 'awful state of mind'.[77] But like the drawings he sends as he announces his decision to give up painting, this appears to be a symbolic gesture, marking his farewell to writing poetry while he concentrates on learning an 'honest trade'. Desperate to avoid enlisting, he has taken the (to him) humiliating decision to ask Hentschel for his engraving job back. 'It is very mechanical work though my skill in drawing is of great use in it. It is process work – preparing blocks for the press – but it is very unhealthy having to be bending over strong acids all day – and though my chest is weak I shall have to forget all that' he tells Schiff with a mixture of self-pity and pride.[78] Methods have moved on in his absence of nearly five years, however, and Hentschel turns him away, advising him to go to night school for a refresher course of several months.[79]

Schiff readily lends the money for evening classes, which Rosenberg plans to repay with a drawing, and Rosenberg's future seems set. But Schiff had also, in sending the money, reminded Rosenberg that he was 'luckier than other victims',[80] and it may have been the further aggravation of having to justify himself that finally broke his resolve. He could equally well have decided that, without his creative life, nothing much mattered any more. For despite his robust response to Schiff about the 'nature of [his] upbringing' giving him genuine grounds for grievance, and in direct contradiction of his assurance that he has definitely decided against enlisting – 'Since more men means more war – besides the immorality of joining with no patriotic convictions'[81] – his next letter in late October 1915 is headed:

Priv[ate] I. Rosenberg,
Bat[talion] Bantam, Reg[iment] 12th Suffolks,
New Depot, Bury St Edmunds.

It was a resolution of sorts. He no longer had to worry about earning money; his mother would receive a separation allowance and half his pay; he would be clothed and fed and he would have to endure the daily disapproval of the civilian population no more.

Chapter 15

'Yea I a Soldier': 'This Rat Trap Affair'

October–December 1915

As to what you say about my being luckier than other victims [Rosenberg wrote to Schiff in October 1915] I can only say that one's individual situation is more real and important to oneself than the devastation of fates [?states] and empires especially when they do not vitally affect oneself. I can only give my personal and if you like selfish point of view that I[,] feeling myself in the prime and vigour of my powers (whatever they may be) have no more free will than a tree; seeing with helpless clear eyes the utter destruction of the railways and the avenues of approaches to outer communication cut off. Being by the nature of my upbringing, all my energies having been directed to one channel of activity, crippled from other activities and made helpless even to live. It is true I have not been killed or crippled, been a loser in the stocks, or had to forswear my fatherland, but I have not quite gone free and have a right to say something.[1]

When Rosenberg finally gave up the struggle to support himself and walked in to a recruiting office in late October 1915, his intention was to join the Royal Army Medical Corps. Though not a declared pacifist like Rodker and Winsten, he had been influenced by his parents' objection to war, admitting to Schiff that the idea of killing upset him. Being just under the regulation height of 5 feet 3 inches, however, his request was rejected. The equally short Stanley Spencer had managed to bypass the regulations to become an orderly in the RAMC in June that year, but Spencer's country upbringing may have given him a healthier appearance than his East End friend and it was probably Rosenberg's frail physique as much as his lack of height that prompted the rejection. The only option open to him was to join one of the so-called 'Bantam' battalions, formed after the initial flood of volunteers had died down and casualties risen, in a desperate attempt to remedy an acute shortage of men. By lowering the height required for infantrymen in Bantam battalions a new source was tapped, and by the time Rosenberg enlisted two exclusively Bantam divisions, each of over 20,000 men, had been created – the 35th and the 40th. One small unit in the 40th Division was the 12th Battalion of the Suffolk Regiment, to which Rosenberg and many other undersize Londoners were sent once the strictly territorial basis for recruiting had given way to more urgent needs. The Suffolk Regiment, founded in 1685, had previously taken pride in its regional character, enlisting its members mainly from Suffolk, Cambridgeshire and the Isle of Ely.[2] Some of its earliest wartime battalions had retained this territorial character. The 7th Battalion, for instance, which Sorley joined from his home in Cambridge, was made up, according to him, of 'sleepy Suffolk fellows with imperturbable good tempers and an intelligent interest rather than an active co-operation in their military duties'.[3] Sixty per cent of them were farm labourers, most of them fit and strong, unlike the 12th Battalion formed under more pressing conditions just over a year later. (By that time Sorley would be dead, killed by a sniper's bullet at Loos in the same month Rosenberg enlisted.)

To begin with the quality of Bantam recruits had been high. The idea of the Bantams had been inspired by a powerful, broad-chested coal miner, who had walked the entire 150 miles from his Durham home across the Pennines but been turned down by every recruiting station he entered because of his height, even after he had finally offered to fight every man in the office. Many of the earliest Bantams were sturdy coal miners or factory workers from the North, where the average height was lower overall. The Scots fared particularly well when they formed a Bantam Battalion of the famously pugnacious Highland Light Infantry, which was quickly christened the 'Devil Dwarfs'. But as 1915 passed and the need for replacements in France and Gallipoli became urgent, standards were lowered. And by the time the far from robust Rosenberg was allowed into the 12th Suffolks his fellow recruits, according to him, were 'a horrible rabble'.[4] 'Falstaff's scarecrows were nothing to these' he wrote to Marsh, with whom he was back in touch. 'Three out of every four have been scavengers the fourth is a ticket of leave'.[5] His reference to Shake-speare's ragged band of hopeless soldiers in *Henry IV*, refuse collectors and convicts released early from prison to serve in the army, would have revealed to Marsh Rosenberg's feeling that he had landed among the dregs of humanity. His battalion, he was convinced, was 'the most rascally affair in the world'.[6]

The whole experience of arriving at the Suffolks' regimental depot in Bury St Edmunds, being given an army number (22648) and assigned to C Company of the Bantam Battalion was clearly a great shock to Rosenberg. Though he had grown up in an area that Marsh would no doubt have dismissed as a 'slum', his family thought of themselves as respectable and self-sufficient and they had their pride. Rosenberg's early contact with the middle-class Amshewitzes, his years as an art student and his visit to Cape Town had all given him far greater expectations than many of his fellow recruits. His education, particularly after leaving Board School, and his artistic aspirations set him apart from them and this would cause problems for both sides at the start.

Naturally fastidious about food, having been brought up with fairly strict dietary laws, he found it especially repellent to have to 'eat out of a basin together with some horrible smelling scavenger who spits and sneezes into it'.[7] There was little enough food without having to share it, since the army was badly overstretched and rations for the men in short supply by late 1915. Sorley's introduction to the Suffolks a year earlier had been very different. Having automatically been given a commission because of his public school background, he wrote to a friend from an Officers' Training Camp in September 1914 that they were 'living . . . like princes': 'We sleep in beds under roofs. We have 5-course dinners . . . The comfort is regal.'[8] Rosenberg grew particularly resentful of the difference between the rations given to the men and those enjoyed by the officers, 'who have not got to eat our food'.[9] He believed that his initial troubles in the army were 'mostly caused by the unsufficient [*sic*] food; one felt inert and unable to do the difficult work wanted'.[10] His letters for the first four or five months are full of pleas for something to eat, preferably sweets or chocolates. He was unable to ask his mother to begin with, since he had enlisted without telling her, an indication of how sudden his decision had been. Even after she had learnt of it and recovered from the shock – 'it nearly killed [her]' he told Schiff[11] – he hesitated to tell her how poor conditions really were, especially the food.

It was not just food he lacked. Like many other recruits he arrived at the depot with nothing more than the clothes he wore, expecting to be issued immediately with a uniform and full kit. But he had to spend his first few weeks without them, reporting to Schiff at the end of October: 'I'm roughing it a bit, having come down without even a towel. I dry myself with my pocket handkerchief.'[12] Even after he had received his full kit his grievances continued. First it was his boots, which were so stiff and clumsy that he developed large blisters. Asking the long-suffering Schiff to send money for new ones, he complained: 'I should have been told to soften my boots and I would not have had this damned bother.'[13] While privates' boots were undoubtedly crude, botched affairs, as Sassoon came to realize when he had to inspect his men's feet, Captain Frank Waley, who would be one of Rosenberg's officers in France, insisted that all recruits 'were told to oil their boots and there was Dubbin for this'.[14] He believed that Rosenberg simply had not taken in the instructions. Still working on his projected poetic drama, *Moses*, if only in his mind for the moment, he would later attribute his absentmindedness as a soldier to it.

For he remained much more interested in art and literature than in everyday life. Though arriving without a towel, he had not forgotten to bring books with him, Donne's poems and Thomas Browne's *Religio Medici* (the latter chosen perhaps in the expectation of going into the medical corps). Some of his many requests to his faithful supporters Schiff, Marsh and Winifreda Seaton were for books, though they had to be small enough to fit into his only storage space, his pockets.

His first request for reading matter came from the depot's Military Hospital, where he found himself shortly after his arrival. 'Don't be alarmed at the [letter] heading,' he told Schiff, 'in running before the colonel I slipped on some mud and gravel and cut my both hands rather badly.'[15] As the predicted few days in hospital became a week, his thoughts turned to painting, conscious that the New English Art Club, which had accepted the three works he had submitted, would be holding its Winter Exhibition. At the same time he began to see the possibilities in his new surroundings: 'I might do something Sundays,' he wrote to Schiff, 'the landscape is quite good.'[16] Schiff took the hint and sent him the small box of watercolours, pencil and sketchbook specified. No pictures of the attractive Suffolk countryside round Bury St Edmunds have survived, but Rosenberg's return to painting was the first sign of a more positive response to army life. He also started to find 'hospital incidents' interesting and, bored by his slow convalescence, he enjoyed sketching his fellow invalids. Since he had invariably to present the results to his sitters, none of his efforts is included among his surviving works, though some of them may still lie forgotten in family attics.

He continued to be unhappy, however, reserving specific complaints for appropriate recipients. He consulted the civil servant Marsh, for example, about the bureaucratic muddle that prevented his mother receiving the money owed her by the army:

> I thought if I'd join there would be the separation allowance for my mother. At Whitehall it was fixed up that 16/6[d] would be given including the 3/6[d] a week deducted from my 7/-[shillings]. It's now between 2 and 3 months since I joined; my 3/6[d] is deducted right enough, but my mother hasn't received a farthing. The paymaster at barracks of course is no use ...[17]

Rosenberg's sense of being caught up in an impersonal system had made him suspect from the first that his mother was 'going to be swindled in this rat trap affair'.[18] He would probably not have been surprised when the allowance problem dragged on into 1916: by January of that year, though his mother was receiving half his pay she had still not been sent the separation allowance.

For Schiff, Rosenberg reserves an equally serious complaint, of anti-Semitism, a problem he believes his fellow Jew will understand. After describing how 'revolting' and 'unbearable' life is in the 12th Suffolks, he adds: 'Besides my being a Jew makes it bad amongst these wretches.'[19] He gives no specific examples, but does imply that some of his fellow soldiers have been aggressive and hostile when he tells Schiff that 'with cigarettes I could make myself more liked'.[20]

There is no proving or disproving his accusation. The dislike he detected could equally well have stemmed from his being so obviously different from the majority of his fellow privates. There were undoubtedly cases of anti-Semitism in the British army in both world wars, though less in the Second, when there was more sympathy for what Jews were suffering. The curator of the Jewish Military Museum in London, who served in the Second World War, argues that 'as in most other areas there were individual cases of anti-Semitism but it did not generally last. You were all in it together and you "got on with it"!'[21] Other people, including the Jewish chaplain who knew Rosenberg in France, Rev M. Adler, believed it was a problem.[22] The nearest I can come to an informed answer in Rosenberg's case is to quote two testimonies by soldiers who knew him.

The first soldier, Corporal Harry Stansfield, who served with Rosenberg in France, describing him as 'an untidy, polite but painfully reserved man', remembered one morning 'sitting on a step in the support trench trying to talk to him':

> He was always a shy sort of fella, very quiet and seemed to keep to himself. He was writing and paid little attention to me. I wanted to show friendship because I think he thought he was often shunned because he was Jewish. Believe me, we didn't think much about a person's background one way or the other. When you were in the trenches, all we wanted to know was if you were a reliable comrade or if you weren't. Religion or race had nothing to do with it.[23]

After hinting at possible paranoia ('I think he thought he was shunned because he was Jewish'), Stansfield added that another Jewish soldier in their company, Lieutenant Sternberg, was 'well-liked' by all the men because he was 'a very good and heroic officer'.[24]

That was at the Front. It may be that some form of anti-Semitism existed in the 12th Suffolks in England. Captain Waley, himself Jewish, thought it 'highly unlikely that there would have been discrimination against Rosenberg on entirely racial grounds'.[25] There probably was ill feeling towards him, he suggested, 'mostly on account of his careless way of dressing and unsoldierliness'. (Looking at a photograph of Rosenberg later, he thought 'he must have been polished up by [his sister] Annie. I never saw him looking so smart.')[26] It seemed to Waley that he might well have been called a 'dirty Jew', since he *was* 'dirty' in the military sense.[27]

Whatever the truth of the situation, Rosenberg felt personally victimized at Bury St Edmunds: his grievances, imaginary or not, seemed very real to him. Living as he did mainly in his imagination, where his Jewish hero, Moses, had more substance for him than his fellow soldiers, he began to identify even more closely with him as someone of unbounded potential caught up in a slavery he is determined to resist. All Rosenberg's pride and a little of his inclination towards self-pity emerge in a poem written between 1915 and 1916:

> Moses, from whose loins I sprung,
> Lit by a lamp in his blood
> Ten immutable rules, a moon
> For mutable lampless men.
>
> The blonde, the bronze, the ruddy,
> With the same heaving blood,
> Keep tide to the moon of Moses,
> Then why do they sneer at me?[28]

Rosenberg's racial pride is renewed among his mainly Gentile fellow soldiers who, he implies, are still governed by the commandments drawn up by Moses. His sense of difference from 'the blonde, the bronze, the ruddy' will emerge again in 'Break of Day in the Trenches', where he appears to identify more closely with the lowly rat than with the 'haughty athletes'. Schiff's response to Rosenberg's complaints of anti-Semitism was to offer to write to his colonel to see if, as Rosenberg requests, 'some kind of sense of difference could be established between myself and the others, not that my sensitiveness should not be played upon but only that unnecessary trouble shouldn't be started'.[29] It is probably not surprising that Rosenberg did not get on well with his fellow soldiers at first: his 'sense of difference' could have struck them as arrogance and his shyness as aloofness.

Whether it was Schiff's intervention or his own more positive side finally emerging, Rosenberg began to settle down and make friends. (By December he would refer to 'devour[ing]' some chocolates Marsh has sent 'with the help of some comrades'.)[30] The complaints, though they never entirely stop, decreased and his sense of humour reasserted itself. Writing to Marsh in early November he is able to admit:

> I suppose my troubles are really laughable, but they do irritate at the moment. Doing coal fatigues and cookhouse work with a torn hand and marching ten miles with a clean hole about an inch round in your heel and bullies swearing at you is not very natural. I think when my hands and feet get better I'll enjoy it.[31]

Oddly enough, once Rosenberg's feet and hands did recover, he rarely complained about the aspect of army life many recruits found most difficult, the rigorous regime in primitive conditions. He had written to Schiff from hospital before his training began in earnest: 'Any kind of work if one [can] only be doing something is what one wants now.'[32] Nevertheless, it is remarkable how well he adjusted to the harsh physical requirements. 'The kind of life does not bother me much' he told Schiff in early December. 'I sleep soundly on boards in the cold; the drills I find fairly interesting ...'[33]

Yet this was someone whose health had caused constant concern from childhood, whose weak lungs had sent him all the way to South Africa in search of a milder climate. Perhaps the strenuous physical exercise, combined with country air, had achieved what no amount of attention from doctors and his family could, an improvement in health. Though at first he had difficulty mastering his duties, by December they seemed to him 'not unpleasant'.[34]

It was an arduous routine. The day started, as early as 5 a.m., with washing, shaving, dressing and bed-making. From about 5.30 to 6.30 a.m. there was drill (on an empty stomach). After breakfast there were more physical exercises and more drilling until about 12.30, when 'dinner' would be served. Another three hours of drill, some musketry and field training, including the use of Lewis guns, rifles, hand-grenades and mortars, would follow. And from 7.30 to 10.30 p.m. there might be night training, often involving long route marches. In between there would be 'fatigues', which varied from helping in the cookhouse to washing up or carrying coal, as well as constant kit inspection.

Instead of weakening under these strenuous demands, Rosenberg grew stronger, until by May 1916 he would feel 'in splendid condition and ... ready for the rotten job' ahead.[35] He did so well that he was even recommended for promotion, to lance corporal, a position he carefully considered: 'The advantage is, though you have a more responsible position, you are less likely to be interfered with by the men, and you become an authority' he told Miss Seaton.[36] He does not give his reason for declining the stripe, though the implication is that he is reluctant to assume responsibility. But his refusal could have resulted from his association of 'authority' with the 'brutal militaristic bullying meanness' he found around him.

His greatest problem in the army, as in civilian life, was with those who had any kind of power over him. One of his first pro-nouncements on his new way of life – 'This militarism is terrorism to be sure'[37] – sets the tone for the next few months, during which he complained constantly of his superiors, especially to Schiff: 'We have pups for officers – at least one – who seems to dislike me – and you know his position gives him power to make me feel it without me being able to resist ...'[38] Remarks like this suggest that his reaction was as much against class and race as against bullying, particularly since his complaints about his 'little impudent pup [of] an officer' cease for the three months during which a Jewish subaltern replaces the Gentile one, but resume when he, in turn, is replaced by another Gentile. He tells Miss Seaton, after a particularly severe punishment: 'It's not worth detailing what happened and expressing how ridiculous, idiotic and meaningless the Army is, and its dreadful bullyisms, and what puny minds control it.'[39] However justifiable his treatment was in official terms, it would continue to strike Rosenberg as 'rotten and unjust'.[40]

'The Army is not a place for individualists' Colonel Maple tells Captain Dubin in Scott Turow's *Ordinary Heroes*. Rosenberg from his schooldays onwards had been too much of an individualist to accept authority easily. Yet in the army he was always contravening its laws and inviting punishment from 'authority'. According to

Captain Waley, he was 'completely hopeless' as a soldier, being incapable of the kind of discipline expected of him in an organization run on 'smartness and uniformity'.[41] It was considered very important, Waley stressed, for officers and 'other ranks' alike, to have neat hair and a close shave: 'all belts, buttons and boots must be highly polished and strict discipline maintained in all respects'.[42] Rosenberg, he recalled was 'never smart'; his buttons were 'often not done up correctly let alone polished' and he was equally 'unmilitary in his performance of duty'. Hence his punishments.

Yet, as I have noted, his attitude towards army service gradually improved. For his creative side, never long submerged, enabled him to see possibilities even in the undeniable hardships he was suffering. 'One might succumb[,] be destroyed' he acknowledged to Schiff during his first month, '– but one might also (and the chances are even greater for it) be renewed, made larger, healthier.'[43] The offer of promotion and his gradual recognition as 'a poet and an artist'[44] also boosted his confidence.

One important turning-point was in November, when he received a letter from the man he thought England's 'best living poet', Lascelles Abercrombie.

> A good many of your poems strike me as experimental and not quite certain of themselves [Abercrombie wrote in early December 1915]. But on the other hand I always find a vivid and original impulse; and what I like most in your songs is your ability to make the concealed poetic power in words come flashing out. Some of your phrases are remarkable; no one who writes poetry [could] help envying some of them.[45]

Marsh, who knew of Rosenberg's admiration for one of his own favourite Georgians, had sent Abercrombie some of Rosenberg's verse in spring 1915. The death of Brooke had intervened and he had not followed it up. It was not until warmer relations had been re-established between him and Rosenberg in the autumn that he wrote to remind Abercrombie about Rosenberg – 'I went all hot with shame, to think how I'd clean forgot him' Abercrombie replied[46] – prompting Abercrombie's letter to Rosenberg. His perceptive response to the younger man's verse, less cautious than that of the conscientious Marsh, who felt it his responsibility, like a stern school-master, to correct rather than encourage, 'bucked' Rosenberg greatly.[47] 'I have asked him to sit for me' he told Marsh, '– a poet to paint a poet.'[48]

He had started reading Abercrombie as early as 1911 and admitted to Marsh that a passage from his own 'Night and Day' (reprinted as the 'Song of Immortality' in *Youth*) was 'absolutely Abercrombie's idea in the "Hymn to Love"'.[49] By April 1914 he had read at least two of Abercrombie's verse plays[50] and also knew his 'Olympians', which he urged Miss Seaton to read. But by October 1916 he would still write that 'The poem I like best of modern times' was his 'Hymn to Love', which was 'more weighty in thought, alive in passion and of a more intense imagination' than any he knew.[51] Abercrombie seemed to him 'the first poet in the world', 'miles and miles above everybody', 'a mighty poet and brother to Browning'.[52]

Rosenberg's first attempt to emulate Abercrombie in 'Night and Day' suggests that it was what he identified as his 'weighty ... thought' and 'intense imagination' that had initially attracted him to a poet otherwise so different from him. Abercrombie's 'Hymn' became Rosenberg's 'Song' and Abercrombie's conceit of mortal man being, literally, an 'expression' of God is echoed in Rosenberg's 'Mortals ... spoken of God's mouth'. There were other similarities, but by late 1915 Rosenberg was probably also struck by another side to 'Hymn to Love', the dangers which, it implies, lurk in life. Phrases such as 'hazardous are the stars', 'the lives travelling dark fears' or 'down the blind speed of a fatal world we fly' would have seemed to him even more applicable to his own situation in 1915 than in 1911.

Ian Parsons has argued that Rosenberg was 'not so fortunate' in having Marsh as his patron and not 'much more fortunate in the literary luminaries – Laurence Binyon, Lascelles Abercrombie and Gordon Bottomley – to whom Marsh showed his work',[53] the impli-cation being that these poets were too academic, too reactionary for the 'revolutionary' Rosenberg. Yet this seems to me precisely the kind of influence to benefit a poet whose creative impulse was too vigorous to be squashed but whose insecure sense of form and carelessness could benefit from their more craftsmanlike approach.

Moreover, it was Abercrombie's, and later Bottomley's, encouragement, I believe, which kept him writing poetry in almost impossible circumstances. To receive a letter of praise from one of his two main models for verse drama just as he was contemplating resuming work on his own first effort in the genre, *Moses*, was the best possible encouragement at the time, and much needed.[54]

The odds against Rosenberg were enormous. As a private he had less time, and more physical labour, than an officer. He also had fewer leaves, the period when the officer-poets wrote most of their war poems. (The first leave he requested, after being excused duties for forty-eight hours following inoculations, was turned down, though he was desperate to see how his mother was coping, and during the whole of his twenty-two months in France he would be granted only a single break of ten days.) His lack of privacy in army barracks made it almost impossible to concentrate and he warned Schiff early on 'not [to] expect any continuity or even coherence' from his writing.[55] Repeating a similar warning to Marsh, he described another serious problem, which throws light on the nature of his war poetry once he begins to write it in earnest: 'There is always behind or through my object some pressing sense of foreign matter, immediate and not personal which hinders and disjoints what would otherwise have coherence and perhaps weight.'[56] At the same time, it was precisely this 'pressing sense of foreign matter' and disjointedness that enables him to convey the reality of war so strongly in his verse. He had from the outset an acute awareness of the disruption and chaos looming, and not just for the ordinary soldier. The time was out of joint for almost everyone, and his ability to convey this sense of dislocation is one of his greatest gifts as a poet.

It was partly through chance that he had first turned to creative work in the army, when he found himself in hospital with time and materials to paint. But he was already beginning to believe in himself 'more as a poet than a painter', convinced that he got 'more depth' into his writing,[57] and at the first opportunity he returned to poetry. Donne's verse had not been enough to make him 'feel for poetry much' in his 'wretched surroundings'.[58] It was his own 'utmost distress of mind', he told Abercrombie, that sent him back to it, though the same mental state also made it hard for him to write.[59]

His first real chance to write came during his four days' leave at Christmas. Shortly before it he tells Schiff that, having 'hardly given poetry or painting a thought' since he enlisted, he feels as if he were 'casting [his] coat ... like a snake or a butterfly'.[60] It would still be a poet who emerged from the chrysalis, but one with wholly new experiences behind him. By the time his leave expires he has written his first army poem, 'Marching':

> Marching – as Seen from the Left File
> My eyes catch ruddy necks
> Sturdily pressed back,—
> All a red brick moving glint.
> Like flaming pendulums, hands
> Swing across the khaki—
> Mustard-coloured khaki—
> To the automatic feet.
>
> We husband the ancient glory
> In these bared necks and hands.
> Not broke is the forge of Mars;
> But a subtler brain beats iron
> To shoe the hoofs of death,
> (Who paws dynamic air now).
> Blind fingers loose an iron cloud
> To rain immortal darkness
> On strong eyes.[61]

Rodker, whom Rosenberg met during his leave, believed 'Marching' to be a great work and sent it, on his behalf, to Harriet Monroe's *Poetry* magazine in Chicago. Rosenberg, who owned at least two copies of this prestigious magazine – mainly, I believe, because they contained poems by Pound[62] – must have been greatly encouraged by this first response. Rodker's admiration was based partly on its 'ultra-modern' subject-matter,[63] underlining how instinctively Rosenberg gravitated towards Modernist practice. By *Georgian Poetry* standards it would have seemed odd to find soldiers' strenuous daily activity 'poetic', which may explain Marsh's negative reaction when Rosenberg sent 'Marching' to him in late December 1915. (Another reason may, as Joseph Cohen has suggested, relate to the fact that in the letter that accompanied his poem, Rosenberg wrote to the highly patriotic Marsh: 'I never joined the army from patriotic reasons. Nothing can justify war.')[64] Yet it is evident that, however punishing Rosenberg had found marching at first, and however routine it had become to him after a few months in the army, he also saw beauty in the sight of a solid wall of men – 'all a red brick moving glint' – swinging along in a uniform khaki formation with machine-like coordination.

Bomberg, like Rosenberg, would eventually reject the Vorticists' worship of the machine, but he was still influenced by them at this time and it may have been one of Bomberg's paintings, such as *War Scene*, that Rosenberg is partially envisaging here.[65] Even Gertler, when he came reluctantly to depict the war he loathed, would do so through a machine metaphor, *The Merry-Go-Round*.[66] The emphasis on colour and shape in the first stanza of 'Marching' suggests strongly that Rosenberg's initial response had been that of a visual artist but that, lacking the time and materials to paint the scene, he had tried to capture it in words later.

It may have been this need to channel his dual creative energies into one medium that gave him, he believed, 'more depth' as a poet from December 1915 onwards. The intensely concrete first stanza of 'Marching' leads on to a more abstract, metaphorical second, where the humble modern soldier is dignified with an 'ancient glory' by the poet, who uses the phrase to introduce the central paradox of the piece, the contrast between the living, vulnerable human beings, with all their potential, and the destructive, inhuman nature of the war in which they are involved, made worse in the twentieth century by its devastating machines. This last point is emphasized in another contrast set up between the ancient forge of Mars, where the Roman god of war 'beats iron / To shoe the hoofs of Death' and modern warfare, controlled by a 'subtler brain', a more impersonal ('blind') force, loosing 'an iron cloud' of shrapnel, shells and bullets from the sky. (Aeroplanes have replaced horses.) The soldiers, made 'immortal' by the 'rain' of ammunition, are also deprived of their sight as they are overwhelmed by the 'darkness' of death.

In struggling to paraphrase 'Marching' the full complexity of Rosenberg's concentrated language comes through. Through it he is able not just to convey the similarities and differences between ancient and modern warfare and its positive as well as negative aspects, but also to make his reader visualize the actual (the marching soldiers), the mythological (the forge of Mars) and the abstract (War and Death) simultaneously. Though he feared that Marsh would find the few lines he added 'vague',[67] there is a great deal of concrete detail in the original poem, even down to the wet winter weather he was himself experiencing, pinning this exploration of the nature of war firmly to earth.

Marsh appears to have still found the poem 'vague'. Whereas Rodker thought the phrase 'To paw dynamic air', with its suggestion of a contained, explosive force, 'very fine',[68] Marsh would almost certainly have found it obscure. Rosenberg's frequently mixed metaphors ('Blind fingers loose an iron cloud', for instance) offended his sense of style. 'Marching' is, in its own way, as difficult and ambiguous as a poem he had earlier criticized, 'Midsummer Frost'.

Marsh may also have been uneasy about the metrical irregularity of the poem. Written in free verse, each line is adapted metrically to its content. The rhythm of the marching men, for example, is caught in the repeated stress patterns of lines 5 to 6:

> Swing across the khaki—
> Mustard-coloured khaki . . .

While line 7 stresses the machine-like aspect of the activity:

> To the automatic feet.

And when emphasis is called for the stress pattern changes again:

> Not broke is the forge of Mars.

It is significant that Rosenberg sent 'Marching' to Abercrombie as well as to Marsh. Abercrombie's metrical experiments in 'Hymn to

Love' were not its primary appeal for Rosenberg, I believe, when he first tried to imitate it in 1911, but five years later they chimed in with his own Modernist desire to fit, as Pound advised, 'metre to mood'.

In this respect 'Marching' differs from the kind of war poetry being written by almost all the other First World War poets. Rosenberg's treatment of war is also quite different from most of his fellow war poets. Neither satiric like Sassoon, nor grieving like Owen, the closest writer to him is another painter-poet, David Jones, equally open to both the visual and experimental, and who also relies heavily on mythology in his work. But it is not only a matter of technique, nor is it just because (like Jones's) it is written from the viewpoint of a private rather than an officer that Rosenberg's poetry is so different. It is also being written by a Jew with centuries of persecution behind him, who often identifies with the persecuted rather than the persecutor, but who looks at everything from his own odd angle of vision.

Chapter 16

Moses: a Farewell to England

December 1915–May 1916

Rosenberg thought 'Marching' one of his 'strongest' poems to date and was encouraged to take up *Moses* again. He was urged on by 'Crazy' Cohen, one of the few friends he saw during his Christmas leave, partly because his mother was so overjoyed at his homecoming she would hardly let him out of her sight. (He had still not dared to tell her that he had signed on for 'General' rather than 'Home' service and was likely to be posted overseas.) Bomberg, who had enlisted in the Royal Engineers a month after Rosenberg joined the Suffolks, was not on leave. He also failed to see Marsh, who was busier than ever, having recently brought out with Harold Monro's encouragement and help the second volume of *Georgian Poetry (1913–1915)*.[2] Apart from Rodker, not yet forced into hiding by the conscription that would be introduced a month later, Rosenberg saw only Sonia, Schiff and Cohen.

His meeting with the printer, still full of literary schemes despite the failure of their magazine collaboration in July, indicates that he was already planning to have *Moses* published. But Cohen was to contribute more than just the printing. Under his ingenious suggestions the plot of the verse play, so far consisting only of 'scraps' jotted down around a sketchy outline, took shape. Rosenberg thought Cohen 'superb' and his ideas for a plot 'quite an original thing', as he would tell a bemused Marsh:

There is a famine in Egypt caused by the superabundance of slaves who eat up all the food meant for the masters. To prevent this, all the back molars of the slaves are drawn, so they eat less. The plot works round this.[3]

Rosenberg conceded that his plot was 'droll', a word he would use again several times, to striking effect, only six months later in one of his greatest poems, 'Break of Day in the Trenches'. (The idea of something half-comic, half-serious obviously appealed to him.) But Marsh, predictably, found the plot outlandish. His classical grounding rebelled at Rosenberg's complete disregard for Aristotle's dictum that a thing should be probable as well as possible. But to Rosenberg his unlikely plot allowed him to express his outrage at the near-starvation he had suffered in the army. It also enabled him to explore the indignities of being, as he felt himself to be, a slave in a repressive system ('The doctor here ... is a ridiculous bullying brute' he had written to Schiff a few weeks before his Christmas leave, 'and I have marked him for special treatment when I come to write about the army')[4] and despised for being Jewish, he believed.

Besides helping with the plot, Cohen had almost certainly agreed to print *Moses*, together with a few poems, as a booklet similar to the two he had previously produced on Narodiczky's press. It was probably the need to pay for this, as well as continued concern about money for his mother, that prompted Rosenberg to offer Schiff one of his paintings for 5 guineas when he met him on leave in late December.

It would be some time before Rosenberg had a chance to work on *Moses* in earnest, though he continued to jot down 'little scraps'. He arrived back at Bury St Edmunds after Christmas to find the 12th Suffolks in the process of drastic change. By the end of 1915 the failures of Vimy Ridge and Loos had shown that the problem of breaking the German front line was still unsolved and Rosenberg's Bantam Division, the 40th, was urgently needed in France. In its current state it was still not fit for fighting, however. Despite a pruning which had begun in September 1915, it had become clear that many of the recruits in the 12th Suffolks were substandard and further action was needed. A draft of relatively fit men from the Battalion, including Rosenberg, was therefore transferred to bring another equally unsatisfactory unit, the 12th South Lancashires, up to strength.[5] By 5 January 1916 he found himself in A Company of the 12th South Lancashires at Blackdown Camp, Farnborough (where, most unusually, he was given a new army number, 24520).

It is proof of Rosenberg's increased fitness and perhaps also of his improved morale at finding himself at the top rather than the bottom of the pile, that he does not complain about his transfer and the strenuous training introduced by the Battalion's Commanding Officer, Lt. Col. Ritchie, in preparation for the Front. He does, however, complain about almost everything else. Food, or rather lack of it, continues to head the list, together with the desperate nature of his fellow soldiers. He writes to Marsh at the beginning of January 1916:

> We get very little food, you know, and sometimes none, so if one has only 6d. (and often for unaccountable reasons it is not even that) you can imagine what it is like. If I had got into a decent reg that might not have mattered, but amongst the most unspeakably filthy wretches, it is pretty suicidal.[6]

He hardly needs to add, as he does, that he is 'not in a very happy mood'. He has had to sleep on a damp floor on arrival and is suffering from a bad cold. He has also been put on coal-fatigue, 'a most inhuman job'.[7]

Life seemed to him very bleak indeed in Alma Barracks at Blackdown Camp and his self-pity was probably justified. His account of near-starvation, for instance, was evidently not an exaggeration. Those who were not fortunate enough, like him, to have food and money sent by family and friends threatened mutiny daily. One regiment near to the 12th South Lancashires did eventually 'break out' and, according to Rosenberg, 'some men got bayoneted'.[8] News of the introduction of conscription also depressed him, since he believed that it would give hope to the enemy 'to have brought England to that step'.[9] (Perhaps he also feared that it would produce an even less satisfactory intake of soldiers.) So desperate was he about conditions for the ordinary soldier that, despite his scorn for authority and fear of responsibility, he asked Marsh about the possibility of getting a commission. Given his general unsoldierliness, he was unlikely to have succeeded had he pursued the idea, but it is intriguing to think how it might have affected his poetry, particularly his main project in early 1916, *Moses*, which focuses on oppression and power.

Rosenberg was resilient, however, and by the end of January he was finding life 'pretty tolerable': 'except for the headachy moments I get it's not so bad down here' he informed Marsh.[10] Strange as it may sound, it could have been the news that his battalion would be 'going out' in the middle of February that cheered him up. Sorley, a year earlier and in far less punishing conditions, had nevertheless decided that even France would be preferable to 'complete stagnation among a mass of straps and sleeping-bags and water-bottles'.[11]

The most important explanation for Rosenberg's more positive mood, however, was his change of officer already mentioned, from a 'bullying pup' of an English public school man to a Jewish second-in-command who knew of him 'from his people'.[12] His recognition of Rosenberg 'as a poet and an artist' not only ensured that there was less bullying all round, but also that Rosenberg was inspired to return to verse. By 11 March he had completed a poem called 'Sleep', which added at least one more 'scrap' to *Moses*, and finished his second army poem, 'Spring 1916'. Both pieces reflect how intensely he was living in his imagination as he went about his everyday duties.

'Sleep', though not overtly a war poem, indicates that the war was reinforcing Rosenberg's belief in a malicious God – in this case 'gods'. He thought the poem important enough to pursue it through a number of drafts, printing one of the first as a separate poem in his *Moses* collection and incorporating four lines from a later one into his play, *Moses*,[13] lines that suggest how difficult he was finding it to express himself in such alien conditions:

> Upon my lips, like a cloud
> To burst on the peaks of light,
> Sit cowled lost impossible things
> To tie my hands at the noon's height.[14]

A reference to Keats in one draft strengthens the impression that 'Sleep' is influenced by 'Hyperion', where a dreamer/narrator views the fallen Titans in all their majesty. Rosenberg's gods are so huge that they have their 'elbows in the dawn, and wrists / Bright with the afternoon'.[15] Their attitude towards mortals is vindictive ('What though the cunning gods outwit us here / In daytime and in playtime'), but can be sidestepped ('Surely they feel the gyves we lay on them / In our sleep'). Addressing the 'subtle gods' directly next, he asks: 'Do you not shake when a mortal slides / Into your own unvexed peace?' In dreams and in our imagination, he appears to argue, we can 'cheat' the gods, just as the narrator of 'God Made Blind' had vowed to do. And when we are dead ('our bodies flat and straight') we can 'cheat' them of their ultimate power, the ability to punish us in life. (An earlier draft had read 'And you are chained, fooled gods! / And cannot wreak your hate.')[16]

The theme of a malignant power punishing the weak and innocent is repeated in 'Spring 1916', where a season traditionally depicted as the youngest and most hopeful of the year is viewed as something very different. As in Eliot's *The Waste Land*, where April becomes the 'cruellest month' because of the false hopes of renewed life it brings, Rosenberg's spring is seen as deceitful, even sinister, by 1916. The season (which Rosenberg was experiencing himself as he wrote his poem) is personified as a woman transformed from her previous youthful gaiety into a 'ruined Queen', pregnant, through the seductions of the evil war god, with Death:

Spring 1916

Slow, rigid, is this masquerade
That passes as through a difficult air;
Heavily—heavily passes.
What has she fed on? Who her table laid
Through the three seasons? What forbidden fare
Ruined her as a mortal lass is?

I played with her two years ago,
Who might be now her own sister in stone,
So altered from her May mien,
When round the pink a necklace of warm snow
Laughed to her throat where my mouth's touch had gone.

How is this, ruined Queen?

Who lured her vivid beauty so
To be that strained chill thing that moves
So ghastly midst her young brood
Of pregnant shoots that she for men did grow?
Where are the strong men who made these their loves?
Spring! God pity your mood.[7]

The imagery here is deliberately stark, almost certainly reflecting Rosenberg's own shock at finding the formerly gay young Sonia heavily pregnant but without Rodker on his return from South Africa. ('I played with her two years ago, who might be now her own sister in stone.') Hardy's Tess, about whom he had written, makes it likely that he also had her in mind, as well as Eve, tasting of 'forbidden fare' in the Garden of Eden. All the joyfulness and playfulness of a pre-war spring beauty has given way to a 'slow, rigid' masked Queen who 'passes as through a difficult air; / Heavily— heavily passes', the awkward movement of the pregnant woman mimicked by the unexpected adjective 'difficult' and the repeated 'heavily', which slow up the verse.

The allusions to war that permeate the poem from the dated title onwards – 'this masquerade', 'forbidden fare', 'that strained chill thing', 'ghastly' – are all the more effective for being oblique. And the contrast between the normal expectation of the new life perpetuated in spring and the reality of what 'Spring 1916' is likely to bring forth – the death of many of spring's 'young brood / Of pregnant shoots that she for men did grow' – is particularly poignant. The other strong contrast, between the young girl of two years previously with her 'May mien', her 'vivid beauty' and delicate pink neck, and the 'strained chill thing that moves / So ghastly' by 1916, brings a fittingly ominous end to the poem.

The changes of mood, from the sombre opening to the happier events of two years previously back to the tragic present, are conveyed through a skilfully varied metre, which is nevertheless contained and shaped within a strict rhyme scheme. Gordon Bottomley especially admired Rosenberg's inventive and 'expressive' choice of the word 'difficult' in conjunction with 'air' and the use of 'pink' to allude to but not specify a young girl's neck, for 'its simplicity and audacity ... [which] shewed the poet's instinct to be creative with his language as well as with his thought'.[18] Rosenberg himself was so pleased with 'Spring 1916' that he sent it to Abercrombie, together with 'Marching', and tried unsuccessfully to get both poems published.

Not long after completing 'Spring 1916' Rosenberg was transferred yet again, bringing him even nearer to the threat of death hinted at in his poem. With the prospect of France now imminent and the 12th South Lancashires still nowhere near fighting standard, the authorities had ordered another more stringent 'weeding out'.[19] From a total of more than a thousand men just over two hundred survived the cull, Rosenberg once again retained. 'I am in another regiment now,' he wrote to Winifreda Seaton some time in late March or April from the 11th (Service) Battalion, the King's Own Royal (Lancaster) Regiment, 'as the old one was smashed up on account of most of the men being unfit.'[20] (There may be some pride at his own survival here.) Still in the same camp and again in A Company he was given yet another army number (22311), one that would survive his final transfer in 1918.

Conditions with the 11th King's Own were an improvement on the 12th Suffolks and the 12th South Lancashires. The army was beginning to take its Bantam Battalions more seriously and to provide them with adequate food, accommodation and training. The Regiment itself was formed mainly from tough moorland men. When it announced the 'urgent formation' of the 11th Battalion, it had made no mention of the word 'Bantam', merely specifying a required height of between 5 feet and 5 feet 2 inches, a chest expansion of 33 inches and an age between nineteen and forty. Their poster had promised that 'You and your friends will be kept together and trained at Lancaster as far as possible'.[21] The response was heartening and, as the area had not previously been 'combed' for Bantam recruits, the standard higher than in the 12th Suffolks or 12th South Lancs. The Battalion, welcomed by the regular soldiers at the depot, worked hard at its training and won the Regimental Prize for general smartness at its 'passing out' parade eight weeks later. They would prove to be such brave fighters in France that on one occasion, replacing a hardy non-Bantam battalion, the 14th Argyle and Sutherland Highlanders, they found an unsigned poem from the Scots, beginning:

> There's a regiment of Bantams, in a place I mustn't name
> Who for cussedness and courage stand alone,
> You'd pass them by in Blighty with a look of mild surprise
> You'd calculate the column was awantin' p'raps in size,
> By glory on the other side you'd hand 'em out the prize.
>
> – King's Own[22]

The dilution of the original battalion with the remnants of other Lancastrians, Londoners and East Anglians created some problems. Though the food, Rosenberg could finally report, was 'much better', conditions were still 'unsettling'.[23] In thanking Miss Seaton for the homemade biscuits and cakes she continued to send, he claimed that 'Every other person' in his new battalion was 'a thief'. The harsh punishments given to those who mislaid equipment were enough to turn almost anyone to robbery, as Rosenberg admitted: 'in the end[,] you become [a thief] yourself, when you see all your most essential belongings go, which you must replace somehow.'[24]

He had a great deal to distract him by March 1916, however, and there are no further references to the subject. With embarkation within the next few months now a certainty, training was intensified and expanded. His hope of an Easter leave, to celebrate Passover with his family, was dashed by the need to be trained in 'ball-firing', a decision he knew meant that the 40th Division was 'ready for the front'.[25] He had been aware since October 1915 that he was likely to be sent out in the spring, but these increased preparations made it seem more real, and with it the strong possibility of his own death. The first rumour of a move towards the end of 1915 had caused him to write to Marsh:

> All of this must seem to you like a blur on the window, or hearing sounds without listening while you are thinking. One blur more and I'll leave you a clean window – I think we're shifting to Shoreham in a week.[26]

By late December he had written again, in response to another rumour of a spring move: 'I think this is a decent photo of me and if anything were to happen that would be as far as I got.'[27] 'Marching', 'Sleep' and 'Spring 1916' all deal with death in various ways, and his current work, *Moses*, was to end with the distinct possibility that the protagonist would die.

It seemed more important than ever, therefore, to finish his verse play and have it published before leaving England. He had 'got into trouble' on his first day with the 11th King's Own, he told Miss Seaton, because he had been 'working on "Moses" – in my mind, I mean – it was through my absentmindedness while full of that that I forgot certain orders, and am now undergoing a rotten and unjust punishment'.[28] But the working of his 'curious' plot into the fragments already written could not be carried out in army barracks, and it was not until he was granted six days' embarkation leave during the third week of May that he was able, at last, to slot it all together.

Rosenberg spent virtually the whole of his embarkation leave wrestling with *Moses*. After a short journey from Frimley, near Aldershot, to Waterloo, he had arrived home on or about 19 May 1916 determined to get his play, and some poems, ready for publication. Faced with the uncertainties of when exactly he would be leaving England, where he would be going and, most pressingly of all, whether he would survive the ordeal, his belief in himself as a poet sustained him. Cohen, still full of ideas and suggestions, was his constant companion as they prepared this his third pamphlet, *Moses*, for the press.

Since Rosenberg had not yet dared tell his mother he was going overseas, she was not quite so possessive on this occasion, leaving him, theoretically, freer to visit friends. But he was so bound up in his book that he saw very few friends and arrived late for an appointment with Marsh at Gray's Inn because of business with Cohen. By the end of his six days' leave *Moses* was safely with the printer, who hoped to have it off the press by the time Rosenberg left England.

Cohen now operated from his tenement flat in Ocean Street, Stepney Green, though he still had access to Narodiczky's machines, and *Moses* appeared under his own imprint, The Paragon Printing

Works. There was no time for Rosenberg to check the proofs himself but Annie, who had taken over from Minnie in her encouragement of her brother's genius, checked them for him. From this time onwards, until her own death in 1961, she would devote herself to promoting his work, acting as his agent, secretary, sales staff and post office, among other things. *Moses*, written in Rosenberg's scrawling hand on pages torn from an old diary, could not have been easy to decipher, and it is a tribute to his sister's devotion that she typed it all out so determinedly. It is an even greater tribute to Cohen's idealism that he was prepared to produce *Moses* for nothing. Both he and Rosenberg hoped, rather unrealistically, to pay for it by selling some hardback copies at 4s 6d each. Most of the copies, however, were covered in bright yellow card covers and sold for a shilling each, though many were given away by the author.[29]

From Rosenberg's first reference in his letter to Schiff of 4 June 1915 to 'a sketch for a play' to finished copies of it, accompanied by nine of his favourite poems,[30] was a period of just under a year. But judging from the amount of manuscript material *Moses* generated,[31] and given that Rosenberg was not able to work on it at all for his first few months in the army, it seems likely that he had started work on it earlier, possibly in Cape Town. (The contrast between Pharaoh's privileged Egyptian court and the browbeaten Hebrew slaves may reflect some of Rosenberg's own sense of difference between the white and black population there, or between the easy life of Cape Town and his East End home.)

None of the manuscripts is dated but it seems fairly certain that the 'sketch' Rosenberg sent to Schiff in June 1915 consisted of a single scene of just under 150 lines in mainly blank verse. Of its four characters only Moses is named. The scene opens with a conversation between two Hebrew slaves as to which side Moses – born to a Hebrew slave but brought up by an Egyptian princess – will choose. His subsequent intervention in the beating of one of the slaves by their Egyptian taskmaster signals his decision to return to his 'roots'. Renewing his vow to lead his people out of slavery, he murders the taskmaster as a first, necessary step.

One of the central concerns of the final text is already addressed here – the need to choose between two cultures – but it is not difficult to see why Rosenberg felt it necessary to expand on this and other similar early versions. Essentially undramatic, they lack both psychological and narrative complexity. His great admiration for Shakespeare had almost certainly encouraged him to turn to verse drama in the first instance, and there are signs of his influence throughout the early drafts of *Moses* – the rhythms of the blank verse in which they are written, for example, the portrayal of Moses as a cross between Hamlet, Othello and Macbeth, the portrayal of the Egyptian taskmaster as a reverse Shylock ('You stole my daughter' he tells Moses, who is having an affair with her). And a more recent appreciation of Milton's great blank verse epic *Paradise Lost* had almost certainly encouraged Rosenberg's decision to attempt his own epic. His early reverence for the Romantics, who had attempted to revive verse drama after the dominance of prose Restoration comedy in the eighteenth century, may also have influenced his choice. (He thought Beatrice's speech on death in Shelley's *The Cenci*, for instance, 'most wonderful'.)[32] And he had followed late nineteenth- and early twentieth-century efforts to revive verse drama in an age dominated by the prose plays of Ibsen and Shaw, admiring playwrights such as Stephen Phillips,[33] Lascelles Abercrombie and, possibly, Yeats.

Even the most recent of these poetic plays, however, are in blank verse, and skilful though Rosenberg has become at the form by 1915, it leaves him too little scope to express his own particular vision and genius, more suited to freer verse-forms. By early 1916, therefore, he has made sweeping changes. He has introduced his 'curious little plot', which centres on Pharaoh's cruel edict ordering the Hebrew slaves' teeth to be extracted, and has added a second scene.[34] His cast now includes not only the slave-master Abinoah's daughter (and Moses's mistress), Koelue, but also her new lover, the Egyptian Prince Imra, who arrives to arrest Moses at the end of the play. Rosenberg also develops the character of his two slaves, enabling him to differentiate and explore various Jewish types. The completed text is over three times the length of his first draft and includes a number of fine passages of both blank and free verse.

It is Rosenberg's free verse, however, that shows him at his best, as even the fairly traditional Marsh acknowledged when he chose

Moses's passionate free-verse speech to his mistress for inclusion in *Georgian Poetry 1916–1917*. Working dramatically, this shows us Moses at the very moment of his decision to sacrifice Koelue's 'red lips of flesh' for 'the huge kiss of power' and to return to his 'roots', where she becomes insignificant ('small at the roots, like grass'):

> Ah! Koelue!
> Had you embalmed your beauty, so
> It could not backward go,
> Or change in any way,
> What were the use, if on my eyes
> The embalming spices were not laid
> To keep us fixed,
> Two amorous sculptures passioned endlessly?
> What were the use, if my sight grew,
> And its far branches were cloud-hung,
> You, small at the roots, like grass,
> While the new lips my spirit would kiss
> Were not red lips of flesh.
> But the huge kiss of power.
> Where yesterday soft hair thro' my fingers fell
> A shaggy mane would entwine,
> And no slim form work fire to my thighs.
> But human Life's inarticulate mass
> Throb the pulse of a thing
> Whose mountain flanks awry
> Beg my mastery—mine!
> Ah! I will ride the dizzy beast of the world
> My road—my way.[35]

Rosenberg's alterations to his early drafts are all additions to the biblical story from which the play originates, where Moses simply murders an Egyptian who is beating a Hebrew slave, then buries him in the sand.[36] Rosenberg evidently believed, like his great mentor Blake, that he must fashion his own mythology 'or be enslav'd by another man's'.[37] By introducing an Egyptian mistress for Moses and making her the daughter of the slaves' overseer he adds further psychological interest to the plot, since by killing Abinoah Moses must automatically forfeit his daughter, Koelue. And the invention of Pharaoh's odd edict, while forcing Moses to choose where his loyalties lie, also allows Rosenberg, as I have suggested, to vent his feelings about his own near-starvation in the army. Most important of all, his additions to the original story enable him to explore his protagonist and his conflicts in more depth.

For, as the title implies, it is Moses who stands at the centre of this play and it is here that Rosenberg's interpretation differs most significantly from the Old Testament. Despite Rosenberg's apology to Zangwill when he sent him his play ('I have not worked him out in quite the way I wished'),[38] Moses emerges powerfully from the page. His weaknesses, particularly his susceptibility to women, fill him out in a way the Bible does not. Rosenberg creates a complex, at times puzzling figure, whose large physical appetites and attraction towards worldly things are balanced by an acute spiritual and political conscience, yet who remains believable to the end.

There is no doubt that part of Moses's plausibility stems from Rosenberg's close identification with him, especially in his attraction to women, his protest against an oppressive regime and his reaction to Abinoah's crude anti-Semitism ('Dirt-draggled mongrels, circumcised slaves / You puddle with your lousy gibberish / The holy air' ...).[39] Joseph Cohen has argued that Moses is 'simply an extension of the poet Rosenberg'[40] and there are striking similarities – Moses's great articulateness, interrupted at times by a stammer ('halt speech'), his 'roughness' (after he chooses to return to his Jewish roots) and his disguise as a 'minstrel', the ancient equivalent of a poet, in which he sings several lyrics. He resembles his creator too in his attitude towards God. Cohen sees the play itself as Rosenberg's 'culminating poem on the theme of his rejection of God',[41] pointing to a passage taken from a separate poem, 'God', also included in *Moses*:

> ... Ye who best God awhile,—O, hear, your wealth
> Is but His cunning to make death more hard.
> Your iron sinews take more pain in breaking.
> And he has made the market for your beauty
> Too poor to buy although you die to sell.[42]

And Rosenberg makes it quite clear, in a speech Bottomley thought particularly fine, that his hero, like himself was 'sick of priests and forms'.[43]

But tempting as it is to see Moses simply as Rosenberg 'in the winter of 1915–16, fulfilling himself as a poet in a quickened, over-energized moment in history, corresponding mythically to its parallel moment in Ancient Egypt',[44] there are striking differences between this Moses and his creator. His huge physical stature, his great sexual prowess and his privileged social position all distinguish him sharply from Rosenberg. Moses may be, as Martin Taylor believed, 'Rosen-berg writ large', his creator having given him the things he was most conscious of lacking.[45] It would be equally wrong to interpret Moses as straightforward wish-fulfilment, however. He is a leader of his people who will play a vital historical role Rosenberg never envisioned for himself.

At least one reader seems to have been converted from his view of Moses as a tyrant and 'bloody-minded charlatan' by reading Rosenberg's play: Robert Graves, in the army himself by the time *Moses* was published, wrote in 1925:

> Perhaps it was Isaac Rosenberg's magnificent play Moses that first converted me to a more generous view. Rosenberg brings out well the strange power that Moses must have had over the people in the later days of captivity, the sense of heroic strength that he inspired. [A quotation by the young Hebrew 'Yesterday as I lay nigh dead with toil', ending 'Am I not larger grown!' follows here.] We may expect that among oppressed or enslaved peoples ... Moses will continue to be regarded as the type of heroic deliverer rather than as a narrow-minded, unpitying upholder of Law and Order ... Isaac Rosenberg, a race-proud Whitechapel Jew whose ambition was in continual conflict with circumstances, was a natural champion of Moses the deliverer ... [46]

Graves's reading of *Moses* as a socialist plea on behalf of an oppressed minority is shared by a number of critics.[47] And his view of Moses as, above all, the 'heroic deliverer' of his people is echoed by others, who give *Moses* a specifically Zionist interpretation.[48] For such critics it marks a return to the Jewish and overtly Zionist themes of Rosenberg's early poems 'Ode to David's Harp' and 'Zion', and they lay particular stress on his frequent reference to 'roots' in the play.

To read *Moses* in this way, however, is to ignore Rosenberg's own shifting views on Moses. His 1913 words 'Moses must die to live in Christ',[49] for example, do not suggest a committed Zionist, an interpretation which in any case limits the play in a way I believe Rosenberg never intended. Martin Taylor, who edited the manuscripts of *Moses* for a facsimile edition and was therefore more familiar with it than most, saw it as a parable, quoting Samuel Hynes's definition of 'parable' as something:

> ... functional – that is message-bearing, clarifying, instructive – but ... not didactic. Rather it is an escape from didacticism; like a myth, it renders the feeling of human issues, not an interpretation of them. It is non-realistic, because it takes its form from its content, and not from an idea of fidelity to the observed world.[50]

Rosenberg, Taylor suggested, was ahead of his time, and much nearer to the verse dramatists of the 1930s who were, in Auden's words, 'not concerned with telling people what to do, but with extending our knowledge of good and evil, perhaps making the necessity for action more urgent and its nature more clear, but only leading us to a point where it is possible for us to make a rational and moral choice'.[51] Though not overtly about the First World War, *Moses* can be and was surely meant to be applied to that war in its exploration of the nature of violence, oppression and power. As such, it is one of the few epic poems to come out of that conflict which, as Bernard Bergonzi has shown, was dominated by a lyric verse unable in many cases to bear the weight of its tragic content.[52] When Rosenberg told Marsh in late 1916 that 'the Homer [i.e. epic poet] for this war has yet to be found', he was almost certainly hoping to fulfil that role,[53] since he argued in the same letter that Whitman's epic poem of the American Civil War, *Drum Taps*, got 'very near the mark' and Whitman was his ideal in war poetry. ('"Drum Taps" stands unique in my mind' he told Leftwich.)[54]

Not everyone appreciated Rosenberg's epic effort. Marsh, as usual, was his sternest critic. Despite Rosenberg's plea that he should 'make allowances' for *Moses* since he had to write it in a 'very scrappy manner', Marsh thought its plot 'quite ridiculously bad' and that he must 'pay a little attention to form and tradition'.[55] 'I hope you mix plenty of powder with your jam' he warned Bottomley, with reference to Bottomley's glowing praise of *Moses* to its author. 'I do want him to renounce the lawless and grotesque manner in which he normally writes.'[56] Binyon, whose measured approach was by now beginning to amuse as well as impress Rosenberg, observed that the poetry in *Moses* came out 'in clotted gushes and spasms'.[57] Even Bottomley, whose praise of the play made Rosenberg very proud indeed, admitted later to Binyon that it was a 'pity Rosenberg had not more sense of shape'.[58] Like another admirer of *Moses*, and fellow Georgian, R.C. Trevelyan, to whom Rosenberg sent a copy at Rodker's suggestion, Bottomley found the work in places 'inchoate' and 'maimed'.

Such criticisms were not surprising, coming as they did from Marsh and his friends. While Rosenberg's work in *Moses* is less 'clotted' and less 'inchoate' than in previous works, it comes nowhere near the smoothness and finish of Georgian poetry as a whole. Nor could it, since its very roughness was needed, both to express Moses's own character and to reflect the abrupt and violent decisions he makes during the course of the play. Like Rosenberg talking to Leftwich and his friends in Whitechapel, he seems both highly articulate and almost incoherent as he struggles to express his inner conflicts. His rebellious reaction to Pharaoh's savage decree, for example, bursts out in short, staccato lines that betray his excited, disturbed state. The violence of his decision is mirrored in the imagery of frenetic madmen, tornadoes, exploding brains and powerful weapons, which contrasts with the broken vessels and uprooted trees of a 'dead universe', representing the inertia Moses vows to overcome:

> MOSES. Fine! Fine!
> See in my brain
> What madmen have rushed through,
> And like a tornado

Torn up the tight roots
Of some dead universe.
The old clay is broken
For a power to soak in and knit
It all into tougher tissues
To hold life,
Pricking my nerves till the brain might crack,
It boils to my finger-tips,
Till my hands ache to grip
The hammer—the lone hammer
That breaks lives into a road
Through which my genius drives.[59]

The overall effect is one of barely contained frenzy about to burst its banks like a swollen river. If the links between the various metaphors are not always easy to make, they are all intentional and all essential to the final effect. Whereas Marsh implied that Rosenberg's work suffered from carelessness, it often displayed the opposite quality in its densely packed and closely worked-out sets of images. 'Rosenberg is always thinking' Charles Sisson wrote, '– a painful process – and it is always towards clarity that he is striving. What he had to say was important enough for him to want, desperately, to make it clear.'[60]

Even Marsh found *Moses* 'really magnificent in parts' and believed that the speech beginning 'Ah! Koelue!' was 'absolutely one of the finest things ever written'.[61] Bottomley was less grudging, arguing that, while Rosenberg had 'paid the customary allegiance to Pound-isme, Unanisme and the rest', he had done so 'with an energy and vividness which distinguishe[d] him from the others'.[62] Dennis Silk also emphasized the 'active and dynamic quality' of Rosenberg's thinking in *Moses*, which he believed to be 'Jewish, or rather Hebraic' in its quality, as distinguished from the 'static, peaceful, moderate and harmonious' type of thought he attributed to the 'Greek mode', passed down in the classical training of Marsh and most of his friends.[63] Sisson, pointing out that Moses's murder of Abinoah in the second scene 'evokes a world of violence and agony supposed, by Englishmen before 1914' to have been 'superseded', argued that

Gordon Bottomley by Sir William
Rothenstein, c. 1923 (*BACS*)

Rosenberg 'carried in him the unerased memory of former times which are also the future', while the world of writers like Rupert Brooke was 'merely Georgian, or Edwardian'.[64] One of Rosenberg's greatest achievements in *Moses*, he claimed, was that 'the experience he sought to represent was not merely a reportage of his personal life but an apprehension of the complexity of a wide universe', for which drama was 'a natural medium'.[65]

Sisson's piece appeared over half a century after the play's publication but, fortunately for Rosenberg, the most comprehensive appreciation of it was written at the time and sent to him by the man who was beginning to replace Abercrombie as his 'great God of poetry',[66] Gordon Bottomley. It seemed especially valuable coming from someone who, like Trevelyan but unlike Marsh, had himself attempted verse plays and knew the problems involved:

[*Moses*] is a prodigious advance ... It is not only that it has so much the sureness of direction of which I have just been speaking, but it has the large fine movement, the ample sweep which is the first requisite of great poetry, and which has lately dropped out of sight in the hands of exquisite lyricists who try to make us believe there is great virtue in being short of breath. Such speeches as '[Ah! Koelue!]

305

/ Had you embalmed your beauty' and 'I am sick of priests and forms'
... are the very top of poetry, and no one ever did better; but I value
still more the instinct for large organisation which holds the whole
together.[67]

Rosenberg, Bottomley emphasized to a sceptical Marsh, was 'a poet
de longue haleine' (lit. 'of long breath').[68]

Rosenberg's response to Bottomley – 'I had to read your letter
many times before I could convince myself you were not "pulling my
leg"' – reveals how used he had become to adverse criticism and how
demoralizing he found it:

> People are always telling me my work is promising – incom-
> prehensible, but promising, and all that sort of thing, and my meek-
> ness subsides before the patronizing knowingness.[69]

The conviction of being understood, for once, seems to have made
Rosenberg less guarded with Bottomley than he was with someone
like Marsh and encouraged him to define his aims in poetry, as well
as to acknowledge his faults:

> Simple *poetry* – that is where an interesting complexity of thought is
> kept in tone and right value to the dominating idea so that it is
> understandable and still ungraspable. I know it is beyond my reach
> just now, except, perhaps, in bits. I am always afraid of being empty.
> ... I think what you say about getting beauty by phrasing of passages
> rather than the placing of individual words very fine and very true.[70]

'Understandable and still ungraspable': the words might stand above
the gateway to Rosenberg's poetry from *Moses* onwards.[71]

Rosenberg would not read Bottomley's praise of *Moses* until early
July, when the older, invalid poet was finally well enough to respond
to the copy Rosenberg sent him via Trevelyan shortly after publication. But his confidence in himself as a poet had increased since
joining the army. Even after having both 'Marching' and 'Spring
1916' returned from several literary magazines and realizing that his

public was 'still in the womb', he believed in his new work, especially his play. His increased fitness also added to his confidence and his response to the prospect of France was correspondingly positive. Ready for the 'rotten job' ahead of him, he spent his last few days in England sending off copies of *Moses*, which had finally arrived from Cohen in late May, his last letter accompanying one to Abercrombie.

On Thursday 25 May King George V came to inspect the 40th Division before it left for the Front and expressed himself (in the words of the Division's historian) 'most eulogistically regarding the turnout and bearing of the men'.[72] The Commander-in-Chief, according to the 11th King's Own chronicler, 'was good enough to inform the Divisional Commander that he considered the Parade "was quite the best witnessed on Laffans Plain since the outbreak of the War"'.[73]

Rosenberg's account, to Marsh, was more humorous and possibly nearer the truth:

> The King inspected us Thursday. I believe it's the first Bantam Brigade been inspected. He must have waited for us to stand up a good while. At a distance we look like soldiers sitting down, you know, legs so short.[74]

Three days later on 28 May an advance party of senior officers left Blackdown Camp in Surrey for France to join the 1 Corps of the First Army near Lillers. A full division, made up of approximately 20,000 men, 6,000 horses, 64 guns and over 1,000 vehicles, could not be transported overseas all at once, and the operation lasted approximately one week, the bulk of the division shipped from Southampton to Le Havre between 29 May and 5 June. The 11th King's Own were scheduled to leave on the evening of 2 June, though Rosenberg still appeared uncertain of their destination ('whether it's France or the Coloured Countries I couldn't say' he wrote to Schiff).[75] The men turned in their gear, then waited, perhaps the most trying time of all. Having passed his final medical, Rosenberg now knew for certain what he had still not dared to tell his family, that he would be in France within the week. On the next to last day of his wait he finally let Annie know his fate, and she hurried to her brother's camp the following day, still hoping to avert the situation:

> It was bleak [she remembered]. I didn't see a soul except Isaac coming towards me from the other side of the high fence. Talking to him through the wire I said, 'But Isaac you're not fit.' He said, 'I've been examined and passed.' I asked him to let me go and see the medical officer. He wouldn't let me do it. I asked him how much money he had, and he replied 'One Shilling'. I didn't know whether he needed anything, but had ten shillings with me, which I gave him. I wasn't with him more than an hour. I stood there begging him not to go. He said goodbye and disappeared into the distance. I just stood at the fence feeling as if someone had given me a good hiding.[76]

Annie's artless account brings out the sense of isolation that always seemed to surround Rosenberg. Despite his evident efforts to make friends, he was still essentially alone in a universe of his own creation. The other men occupied themselves by adding to their regimental songs to keep their spirits up, which they would sing self-mockingly (to the tune of 'The Church's One Foundation') as they marched on board their troopship[77] at Southampton:

> We are the Bantam sodgers,
> The short arse companee
> We have no height, we cannot fight.
> What bloody good are we?
> And when we get to Berlin, the Kaiser he will say
> Hoch, Hoch, mein Gott, what a bloody fine lot
>   is the Bantam companee![78]

Rosenberg's head, meantime, was full of a very different kind of verse. As he thought of what lay ahead and the reasons for it, he wrote 'a prophecy of the fall of empire' which Frank Kermode and John Hollander rightly claim 'ranks perhaps highest among Rosenberg's visionary fragments':[79]

> A worm fed on the heart of Corinth,
> Babylon and Rome.

Not Paris raped tall Helen,
But this incestuous worm
Who lured her vivid beauty
To his amorphous sleep.
England! famous as Helen
Is thy betrothal sung.
To him the shadowless,
More amorous than Solomon.[80]

A variation on the theme of 'Spring 1916', in which the central image is the seduction of the 'ruined' Queen by the war god, Rosenberg now portrays this seduction in wider historical and mythological terms, linking England's fall to that of other more ancient civilizations. The English 'Queen' of 'Spring 1916' has become Helen of Troy, for whom another war was fought. 'This incestuous worm', with its appropriately phallic overtones, creates connections both to Satan, the Serpent in the Garden of Eden, and to the worms that will invade the many corpses of those who will die in the coming conflict.

Similarly, while his fellow soldiers' accounts of the crossing concentrated on its length (eight hours), the lack of food or light and the general seasickness, Rosenberg's instinct was to turn it into a work of art. If he did sketch himself on the deck of the overcrowded ship, as a reference in one of his letters suggests, his drawing has not survived, but his poem on the subject has. Its portrayal of the awkward, huddled bodies of the soldiers anticipates his vision of the unnatural, grotesque nature of war which would emerge even more intensely at the Front in poems like 'Louse Hunting' and 'Dead Man's Dump':

The Troop Ship
Grotesque and queerly huddled
Contortionists to twist
The sleepy soul to a sleep,
We lie all sorts of ways
But cannot sleep.
The wet wind is so cold,

And the lurching men so careless,
That, should you drop to a doze,
Wind's fumble or men's feet
Is on your face.[81]

Written either during the crossing, or shortly after arrival at Le
Havre, the poem might almost have been a description of a night
in the trenches, towards which the entire 40th Division was now
proceeding.

Chapter 17

In the Trenches

June–August 1916

From France
The spirit drank the Café lights;
All the hot life that glittered there,
And heard men say to women gay,
'Life is just so in France'.

The spirit dreams of Café lights,
And golden faces and soft tones,
And hears men groan to broken men,
'This is not Life in France'.

Heaped stones and a charred signboard shows
With grass between and dead folk under,
And some birds sing, while the spirit takes wing.
And this is life in France.[1]

When the 11th King's Own Royal Lancasters arrived at Le Havre in the early hours of 3 June 1916, most of them had never seen France before. Rosenberg was no exception, yet he felt more familiar with it than most. Introduced to French literature in his teens by his half-Japanese friend Mitchell, and encouraged later by Rodker's passionate interest in it, he had read fairly widely among its poets and novelists. He had also become well acquainted with French artists, especially during his time at the Slade, when he had heard Bomberg and others describe their visits to Paris. Their often lurid accounts and his own familiarity with writers like Stendhal, Balzac, Flaubert, Baudelaire and Verlaine had led him to imagine a country centred on café life and love affairs. His impression of a 'hot life' of decadence could not have contrasted more sharply with the reality he encountered when he arrived there halfway through one of the bloodiest wars in history.

As the last two lines of 'From France' imply, however, Rosenberg's response was not entirely negative; he could still envisage room for the 'spirit' to 'take wing' there. This may have been partly related to the fact that the 11th King's Own arrived in the finest weather seen in Northern France that year. Leaden skies had given way to brilliant blue ones and, as Rosenberg noted, in an inversion of one of his favourite Keats poems, 'La Belle Dame Sans Merci', 'some birds' were still singing. According to one of his fellow Bantams, 'Larks and other songbirds were everywhere',[2] a detail Rosenberg would expand on later in one of his most successful war poems. Le Havre, too, smelling fresh and clean in the morning air, seemed welcoming to the troops. And as they marched off the ship along its wide avenues, past old but well-tended houses, the inhabitants, who had greeted the first Bantam contingents with derisive cries of 'Hey piccininy! Piccininy – soldat!', were now friendly and admiring, noting how 'solides' these small British soldiers were.[3]

This gentle introduction to France continued, with the troops allowed, after depositing their equipment in a camp overlooking the bay, to wander about the town. Apart from the noticeable lack of young men in civilian clothes and some alarming reports on the battle of Jutland in the English papers, they could almost have been on holiday in a pleasant seaside town.

The next morning, seated on a train heading north-east for Lillers, however, the reality of war became more apparent to the 11th King's Own as they travelled towards the Front. The 40th Division had been summoned to France for support in one of the most ambitious – and costly – battles of the war, the Somme. Since Rosenberg's own entry into the army in October 1915 the Allies had suffered two significant defeats on the Western Front. British losses at Loos of over 43,000 in autumn 1915 had been followed in early 1916 by the even greater massacre of Verdun, when French dead and wounded amounted to 315,000 or more. The need for a counter-attack seemed urgent and the battle of the Somme was the Anglo-French attempt to break through the German lines by means of a massive infantry assault. In deference to the French, who were desperate to relieve pressure on Verdun, the date of the planned offensive was brought forward to 1 July 1916. Since nearly three-quarters of the thirty-eight divisions already in France were to be committed to this, another nineteen divisions were brought out to replace them in the line, the 40th being one of them. So that when Rosenberg and his fellow soldiers of the 11th King's Own arrived in France as part of 120th Brigade, they were destined for the Somme area but not for the main British battle front between Hébuterne and Maricourt.

For Rosenberg the real unpleasantness of war started, characteristically enough, with blisters on his feet, probably on the march from Lillers to billets at Lières and Lesbesses. True to form, he had lost all his socks (among other things) in the departure from England: 'so I've been in trouble, particularly with bad heels' he told Miss Seaton; 'you can't have the slightest conception of what such an apparently trivial thing means.'[4] A week in billets did not mean a week's rest, but seven days of intensive training as the 11th King's Own prepared for their first tour of the trenches, and his feet suffered. He had still not told his mother he was in France, but was now driven to write to her for more socks, and his sister remembered her packing the parcel 'without anger but profoundly saddened, her tears falling on the clothing as she bundled it up'.[5]

Rosenberg himself was missing his family, his mother in particular, and one of his earliest poems in France may have been written as the full impact of the separation set in:

> Wan, fragile faces of joy!
> Pitiful mouths that strive
> To light with smiles the place
> We dream we walk alive.
>
> To you I stretch my hands;
> Hands shut in pitiless trance
> In a land of ruin and woe,
> The desolate land of France.

Dear faces, startled and shaken
Out of wild dust and sounds,
You yearn to me, lure and sadden
My heart with futile bounds.[6]

The title given to this poem in earlier editions was 'Home-Thoughts from France',[7] but despite its echo of Browning's 'Home Thoughts from Abroad' with its yearning for the English countryside ('Oh, to be in England, / Now that April's there ...'), echoed by Rosenberg's own words to Marsh ('I wish I were in England'),[8] it is evident here and throughout his war poetry that the pastoral has very little appeal for him. Unlike Owen, Sassoon, Sorley or Edward Thomas, for example, who identify closely with the English countryside in their verse, Rosenberg's thoughts turn more to people than to nature, partly for reasons that emerge in a letter written to Miss Seaton after over a year in France:

> Most of the French country I have seen has been devastated by war, torn up – even the woods look ghastly with their shell-shattered trees; our only recollections of warm and comfortable feelings are the rare times amongst human villages ... [9]

It may have been his sense of the importance of people, his family in particular, that prompted Rosenberg to write another poem, started shortly after arriving in France, but not finished until autumn 1917, 'In War'. Though the incident, as he would tell Bottomley, 'happened to one of our chaps, poor fellow',[10] not himself, there is little doubt that his active imagination had envisaged a situation in which *he* might be the soldier in a burying party discovering that the corpse is his own brother. 'In War' would be a rare lapse into melodrama by one of the First World War's subtlest and most indirect poets, but redeemed by its opening verses which could stand as a moving elegy to all the dead:

Fret the nonchalant noon
With your spleen
Or your gay brow,

For the motion of your spirit
Ever moves with these.

When day shall be too quiet,
Deaf to you
And your dumb smile,
Untuned air shall lap the stillness
In the old space for your voice—

The voice that once could mirror
Remote depths
Of moving being,
Stirred by responsive voices near,
Suddenly stilled for ever.[11]

These opening stanzas of 'In War' may also have been written in response to Rosenberg's first experience of death in the trenches, where the 11th King's Own were sent after a week in billets. From ten miles west of Béthune they were moved forward to Béthune itself for what their historian euphemistically called 'practical training in warfare'.[12] This occurred on 12 June when the 11th King's Own was attached to the 44th Brigade of the 15th Division, which was in the line at Hulluch, near Loos, an area still hotly fought over. Rosenberg's A Company was attached to the 9th Battalion, Black Watch, and his platoon (the third) attached to one of its companies. After two days each platoon garrisoned a part of the trench system, being responsible both for Defence and Work.

Before entering the trenches steel helmets, made mandatory the same month, were issued and Rosenberg's self-portrait in a steel helmet, executed in black chalk and gouache on ordinary brown wrapping paper, probably dates from this time.[13] A striking design, in which the oval of what Bottomley called 'that fine medieval helmet'[14] is echoed in the almond-shaped oriental-looking eyes and contrasted with the elongated lines of nose and face. It is, as Bottomley noted, 'interesting and sensitive and vivid',[15] depicting its subject as a romantic, remote but powerful figure, which suggests that even Rosenberg saw something glamorous about the war before

Self-portrait, in black chalk and gouache on brown wrapping paper, 1916
(*Private Collection*)

he actually experienced it. (The effect would have been quite different
if he had chosen to portray himself in, for instance, the clumsy gas
helmets also issued.) If so, this impression does not appear to have
survived his first tour of trenches.

Trench systems varied in different parts of the line, depending
largely on whether they were constructed in clay or chalk (as was the
case in Rosenberg's Lens/Loos area). At the beginning of the war
troops on the Western Front had simply dug ditches in which to
shelter from enemy fire, but by June 1916, when Rosenberg first
experienced them, trench systems were more sophisticated. Much
wider and deeper passageways were constructed, usually in several,
roughly parallel, lines, so that if a section of the front line were taken,
reinforcements could be moved up from the rear, via communication
trenches. Each line was zig-zagged irregularly to prevent the enemy
from firing straight along it, as well as to reduce the impact of bombs.
Sandbags added further protection against enemy fire, as well as
support for the unstable trench walls.

In front of the first line tangled masses of barbed wire were laid to impede enemy penetration, and narrow passages, or 'saps', ran out to observation posts in the neutral area between the two forces, aptly named 'no-man's-land' and almost invariably pitted with deep craters left by exploding shells from both sides. This scene of desolation would later inspire one of Rosenberg's most powerful war poems, 'Dead Man's Dump', but when he first arrived in France it was the trenches themselves that most concerned him.

One feature that dwelled on his mind were the dugouts excavated in the trench walls to provide room for shelter, sleep and even, in the case of officers, a little cooking. Those fortunate enough to sleep in a reasonable dugout were grateful for the wooden bunks they contained, though they were no wider than two feet and covered in chicken-wire. But dugouts, like trenches, varied greatly, some so crowded and rat-infested that it was virtually impossible to sleep. (Lack of sleep was one of the most demoralizing aspects of trench life, the soldiers' nocturnal regime allowing very little opportunity to rest.) 'Of course if you're lucky and get a decent dugout' Rosenberg reported to Trevelyan after a short time in the trenches 'you sleep quite easily – when you get the chance, otherwise you must sleep standing up, or sitting down, which latter is my case now.'[16] His sketch of himself in a dugout (the second he had attempted, apparently, after losing his first effort) shows him crammed into a small recess with a tin of marmalade and an unexpectedly friendly-looking rat at his feet, in that 'grotesque and queerly huddled' position unwittingly anticipated in 'The Troop Ship'.

Mud was another chief feature of the trenches. Most trenches were paved with 'duck-boards' to walk on and avoid slipping, their earth walls 'revetted', that is lined with wood, to prevent further crumbling, and were bearable in dry weather. But Rosenberg was unfortunate and it rained hard during his first tour of trenches in mid-June. '[W]e've had vile weather, and I've been wet through for four days and nights' he wrote to Miss Seaton once his battalion was back in billets at Sailly-la-Bourse.[17] After a further complaint about sore feet, he added: 'We've had shells bursting two yards off, bullets whizzing all over the show, but all you are aware of is the agony of your heels ...'

Self-portrait sketch from the trenches, c. 1916 (*Imperial War Museum*)

Three days of so-called 'rest' followed, during which in reality the soldiers were kept hard at work though in less danger. The food was very little better than in the trenches, consisting mainly of Fray Bentos corned (i.e. 'bully') beef and biscuits so hard and dry they were known as 'dog biscuits', washed down at breakfast, lunch and supper with 'what they called' tea.[18] Maconochie's tinned stew was a very occasional treat. Curiously enough, Rosenberg's complaints about food did not continue in France, which suggests how very bad it had been in England. During their second tour of trenches in the same sector from 19 to 23 June, each company was kept intact and made fully responsible for an area of defence. That, however, was the sum total of training in trench warfare the 11th King's Own received before being declared ready for the line. During it two men had been killed and twenty-three wounded, two of whom subsequently died.

It was a relatively benign introduction to the trenches, but one that had an immediate impact on Rosenberg, acting as a catalyst for the series of extraordinary poems which followed. Starting with 'Break of Day in the Trenches', these represent the fusion of his years of poetic apprentice work and achievement before the war with first-hand experience of conditions at the Front. Sassoon, commenting on the 'poignant and nostalgic quality' this first trench poem had for him, explained: 'Sensuous front-line existence is there, hateful and repellent, unforgettable and inescapable.'[19] Rosenberg's unique, intensely graphic and unusual angle of vision has the added interest of belonging to a private rather than an officer like most of the war poets. And it is evident from this first poem to emerge from his personal contact with the trenches that his view as an ordinary soldier will be very different from that of officer-poets like Owen, Sassoon or Brooke. It will also be quite distinct from that of the only other privates to come near his achievements, Ivor Gurney and David Jones.

'Break of Day in the Trenches', almost certainly completed during July 1916, like many of his best poems was worked on in successive versions and subject to a number of significant changes even after it was sent to Harriet Monroe's *Poetry* magazine and published there in December.[20] Rosenberg's first version, 'In the Trenches' is a relatively straightforward narrative in regular, rhymed stanzas, highlighting the more obvious features of trench life, the scarlet poppies that grew in the chalky ground in defiance of the churned-up earth along the parapets and their association with spilt blood, the white dust that covered everything in hot weather and the shells that fell continually, dealing an apparently random death to the trenches' occupants:

> I snatched two poppies
> From the parapet's edge,
> Two bright red poppies
> That winked on the ledge.
> Behind my ear
> I stuck one through,

One blood red poppy
I gave to you.

The sandbags narrowed
And screwed out our jest,
And tore the poppy
You had on your breast . . .
Down—a shell—O! Christ.
I am choked . . . safe . . . dust blind—I
See trench floor poppies
Strewn. Smashed you lie.[21]

Rosenberg himself described 'In the Trenches' as 'a bit com-monplace' when he sent it to Sonia Cohen,[22] and it is true that it gives no new insights into life at the Front. There is also more than a hint of melodrama in its sudden, breathless ending which, as Bottomley pointed out on receiving a copy, 'falls away a little'.[23] But as Rosenberg explained to Marsh shortly after writing the poem:

You know the conditions I have always worked under, and particularly with this last lot of poems. You know how earnestly one must wait on ideas, (you cannot coax real ones to you) and let as it were, a skin grow naturally round and through them. If you are not free, you can only, when the ideas come hot, seize them with the skin in tatters raw, crude, in some parts beautiful in others monstrous. Why print it then? Because those rare parts must not be lost. I work more and more as I write into more depth and lucidity, I am sure.[24]

'In the Trenches' represents the 'raw, crude' version of what was quickly transformed into 'Break of Day in the Trenches'. With the vivid contrast between the red poppies and white dust firmly in place and already linked to notions of mortality, Rosenberg proceeds to add another familiar feature of trench life, the rat. At the same time he projects a more fully realized setting, which now includes the stretch of no-man's-land between the opposing lines, technically neutral ground which he will put to symbolic use in his completed poem. In setting the scene more specifically at dawn, a period of ambiguity and half-light, Rosenberg is able to signal a wider, less obvious range of emotions and themes. His opening lines indicate that he will be dealing with an experience common to all front-line soldiers, sentry duty at dawn, but that he will handle his subject in an original way:

> The darkness crumbles away.
> It is the same old Druid Time as ever.[25]

The idea of 'darkness crumbl[ing] away', like the erosion of the coastline in 'At Sea-Point' or the trench walls themselves, emphasizes the gradualness of the returning light and leads to a second, equally startling image of Time as a priest at an ancient religious rite, which is puzzling only until we discover Rosenberg's original explanation to Marsh that he wanted to convey 'the sanctity of dawn'.[26]

The central, simple 'action' of the piece then takes place:

> Only a live thing leaps my hand,
> A queer sardonic rat,
> As I pull the parapet's poppy
> To stick behind my ear.

A meditation on the nature of war follows as the narrator wittily addresses the only living creature near him, the rat, in a conceit very like Donne's poem about another pest, 'The Flea', where the narrator also plays with the arbitrariness of man-made boundaries:

> Droll rat, they would shoot you if they knew
> Your cosmopolitan sympathies.
> Now you have touched this English hand
> You will do the same to a German
> Soon, no doubt, if it be your pleasure
> To cross the sleeping green between.
> It seems you inwardly grin as you pass[27]
> Strong eyes, fine limbs, haughty athletes,
> Less chanced than you for life,
> Bonds to the whims of murder,

> Sprawled in the bowels of the earth,
> The torn fields of France.

Stripped of its usual front-line connotations of hated scavenger, Rosenberg's rat becomes a symbol of neutrality, free to cross national boundaries and in doing so to point up the absurdity of war. While the soldiers on each side of no-man's-land sit in holes dug in the ground, waiting to kill or be killed, the rat moves both safely and easily in a world turned upside down, appearing to mock Man's futile aspirations. The word 'droll', which Rosenberg has already used unexpectedly in conjunction with a rat,[28] indicates that the mockery is gentle rather than fierce, stemming from detachment rather than outright hostility. It is, the reader is led to suspect, Rosenberg's own point of view. Since the narrator is clearly not one of the 'haughty athletes', or the mysterious 'They' who make all the decisions, he becomes identified with the rat, an interpretation that Rosenberg's own lowly position as a private, possibly also as a working-class Jew in a hierarchical and class-conscious army, appears to support.[29]

Yet it is also clear from the last eight lines of 'Break of Day in the Trenches' that the narrator himself is as trapped in the situation as his fellow soldiers, his only freedom being that of debating the situation with his alter ego, the rat:

> What do you see in our eyes
> At the shrieking iron and flame
> Hurl'd through still heavens?
> What quaver—what heart aghast?
> Poppies whose roots are in man's veins
> Drop and are ever dropping,
> But mine in my ear is safe—
> Just a little white with the dust.

The strong echoes of Blake's 'The Tyger' with its hammer-like repetitions ('And what shoulder and what art / ... What dread hand and what dread feet? / What the hammer? What the chain? / In what furnace was thy brain? / What the anvil? What dread grasp') reinforce the sense of the contained power and violence stacked against the narrator. His final return to the poppy, however, a symbol not only of spilt blood and, through its opiate qualities, oblivion, but also of a natural order of things to which Man too belongs, implies acceptance of, or at least resignation to the situation.

Despite debts to Blake, Donne and others, 'Break of Day in the Trenches' could only have been written by Rosenberg. Its language and metre are as subtle and varied as its themes and emotions. Yet the overall effect, as Rosenberg himself claimed, is 'surely as simple as ordinary talk'.[30] The rhythms of the free verse change to mimic, now the narrator 'pull[ing]' (with insistent alliteration reminiscent of the explosive sounds around him) 'the parapet's poppy', now the agile rat, a 'live thing leap[ing]' his hand, now the hammering of anticipated shells in the repeated questions 'What quaver—what heart aghast?' and, finally, the quiet resignation of the narrator's acceptance that, in the words of the Bible Rosenberg knew so well, 'dust we are and to dust we shall return'. The circularity of Man's passage from dust to dust is reflected in the circularity of the form, the poem ending with the speaker's poppy still safely (if precariously) behind his ear. Paul Fussell, among others, has found 'Break of Day in the Trenches' superior even to 'Dead Man's Dump', and therefore 'the greatest poem of the [First World] War' in its 'loose but accurate emotional cadences' and 'gently ironic idiom'.[31]

Rosenberg's eagerness to seize any chance to write poetry in the army had already got him into trouble in England and would do so again in France. But no amount of punishment could destroy his belief in its importance, especially in a period of great violence and destruction. 'If poetry at this time is no use it certainly won't be at any other' he told Marsh as he struggled to complete 'Break of Day in the Trenches'.[32] His 120th Brigade had gone into Divisional Reserve behind the line near the mining town of Bruay, south-west of Béthune, and the 11th King's Own were billeted in the nearby village of Petits Sains, remaining there from 25 June to 10 July. Their official purpose was to rest and continue training, but for Rosenberg it was a chance to write. He was already planning 'a sequence of dramatic war poems', he told Bottomley by 23 July, and considered 'Break of Day in the Trenches' worthy to join 'Marching', 'The

Troop Ship' and 'Fret the Nonchalant Noon' in this embryonic collection.

His luck and relative leisure continued into August, since he was temporarily relieved of trench duty, as a delighted Annie reported to Trevelyan on 9 July: 'My brother has been transferred . . . to a Salvage Office and his letters are therefore much brighter and seems [*sic*] to be written in a better Spirit.'[33] Writing to Bottomley, only his second letter to him, but second in under a fortnight, Rosenberg explains a little more clearly what was involved:

> For the last week or two I've been in a quieter but more interesting job than trenches. I've got to rummage behind the lines among shattered houses and ruins for salvage. We come across all kinds of grim and funny odds and ends. . . . More material for poem. I don't know how long this job will last but its fairly safe anyway[,] except for Stray shells which don't count. I do trust you are not worried by ill health and are happy.[34]

(His temporary job as a kind of superior 'scavenger' may help to explain further his close identification with the rat in the poem he was currently revising.) So that while the rest of his battalion moved into the line for the first time as a unit, taking over a dangerous section of the Maroc Front in the Lens area, Rosenberg was able to think about 'more material' for his verse. He remained in the Salvage Office during the 11th King's Own's second and longer tour of duty in the Calonne sector, which is when he wrote to tell Bottomley of his good fortune on 23 July. 'I am thankful and relieved to know that you are all right so far,' Bottomley replied on 8 August, 'and I hope we shall go on and take enough villages to keep you at your present occupation for some time to come.'[35]

When Bottomley's good wishes arrived Rosenberg was still in the Salvage Office, having been left behind yet again when his battalion moved into the Loos area on 4 August. But grateful as he was for this third reprieve, he was anxious that his friends should realize that life was not exactly idyllic even out of the Front Line:

> We are kept pretty busy now [he wrote to Marsh on 17 August] . . .

We had an exciting time today, and though this is behind the firing line and right out of the trenches there were quite a good many sent to heaven and the hospital. I carried one myself in a handcart to the hospital, (which often is the antechamber to heaven).[36]

Rosenberg's letter to Bottomley on the same subject, written a few days earlier, is even more revealing, since it details a curious habit he had developed for providing himself with the reading material he so sorely missed, as well as helping to explain the many echoes from the Bible in his war poetry:

A friend sent me the Georgian book a few weeks ago, but it is so awkward out here to have books in cloth that I must send it back again. In fact at any time I prefer cheap bound books I can spoil by reading anywhere. I often find bibles in dead mens clothes and I tear the parts out I want and carry them about with me. I am pretty fagged just now, having just got back from a wild goose chase up the trenches after some stuff. Yesterday we had a lively time carrying chaps to the hospital in a handcart; its a toss up whether you're going to be the carried or the carrier.[37]

In such circumstances even poetry sometimes failed him, his efforts resulting only, as he told a sympathetic Schiff, in 'abortions'.[38] One such miscarriage was 'Pozières', which even Rosenberg admitted was 'a patriotic gush[,] a jingo spasm':[39]

Glory! glory! glory!
British women! in your wombs you plotted
This monstrous girth of glory, this marvellous glory.
Not for mere love-delights Time meant the profound hour
When an English man was planned. .... [40]

'Our armies deserve better than I can hymn them,'[41] Rosenberg told Bottomley, revealing the patriotic purpose of his poem. It was written in mid-August, several weeks before the battle for Pozières Ridge on the Somme ended in murderous defeat on 3 September, with 23,000 men expended in the effort to gain, after six weeks, a tiny piece of land just over a mile deep. But the poem would have been just as inappropriate if the battle had ended in success, since the whole enterprise was undertaken by the Anzac Corps and it was Australian and New Zealand mothers whose 'wombs', if any, should have been praised.

The real motive for writing 'Pozières', however, seems to have been a misguided attempt to produce the kind of conventional war poem Rosenberg thought might be published in a literary magazine. Schiff's failure to place one of his earlier poems with the editor of the *Nation*, H.W. Massingham,[42] may have been the prompt for this, since it was to Massingham that Rosenberg now sent 'Pozières', in the belief that he would 'like it better than the other'.[43] It was yet another instance of Rosenberg's unawareness, since the *Nation*, unlike *The [Saturday] Westminster Gazette*, was one of the few English magazines to take a more critical attitude towards the war in 1916, Massingham being partly responsible for Sassoon's very public protest against it a year later.[44] A further irony was Rosenberg's decision to send his 'jingo spasm' to Rodker, presumably because he hoped his friend might help place it for publication, as he had 'Marching'. But no one was less likely to appreciate his 'patriotic gush' than Rodker, now in hiding, as a conscientious objector, from the police, even though he might have agreed with Rosenberg's rationalization that 'a poet must put it on a bit thick' at times.[45]

The most surprising aspect of the whole affair, however, is Bottomley's praise for a poem that, like 'The Dead Heroes' (written from similar motives), is clichéd, melodramatic and lifeless: 'I like it very well,' he wrote to Rosenberg on 7 September 1916, 'and it is in the right key for the event. ... Lines 2 to 5 [quoted above] seem to me very good indeed, something like first-rate.'[46] One can only assume that he was trying to encourage Rosenberg to continue writing in difficult circumstances and that his qualification – 'I fancy, though, it is still too near to the event to have settled down into its final form; it has the qualities of a new and well-invented interjection – an interjection long enough to leave me breathless' – was nearer to his real opinion of the poem. Whatever the truth, it gave Rosenberg the confidence to submit a slightly amended 'Pozières' with a design for the 40th Division's 1917 Christmas card. But

Rosenberg performed so badly when he tried to conform to what he thought was expected, that even the army rejected it.

However poorly one of his poems turned out during his unexpected respite from the trenches, it did give him time for letter-writing, and he made several enquiries about his closest friends. Bomberg, who had been transferred from the Royal Engineers to the King's Royal Rifles, had arrived in France the same month as Rosenberg, who now wrote anxiously to their mutual friend Schiff: 'I do hope nothing will happen to him out here, more than ever.'[47] 'I *must* write to him' he vowed.[48] He was even more anxious about Rodker's situation and, unable to contact a man on the run, appealed to Sonia:

I have been anxious to hear from you about Rodker. ... Write me any news – anything. I seem to have been in France, ages. I wish Rodker were with me, the infernal lingo is a tragedy with me and he'd help me out. If I was taciturn in England I am 10 times so here; our struggle to express ourselves is a fearful joke. However, our wants are simple, our cash is scarce, and our time is precious, so French would perhaps be superfluous. I'd hardly believe French manners are so different to ours ... [49]

Rosenberg's concern was not just for his old East End friends. He was also so worried about a fellow soldier in his unit that he consulted Marsh about his problems. This change from the almost complete self-absorption of his former life, together with his extraordinary determination to create poetry out of the hardships he was now encountering, suggests that the effect of army life, especially in France, was by no means all negative.

Chapter 18

'The Desolate Land of France'

August 1916–April 1917

Winter has found its way into the trenches at last, but I will assure you, and leave to your imagination, the transport of delight with which we welcomed its coming [Rosenberg wrote to Binyon in autumn 1916]. Winter is not the least of the horrors of war. I am determined that this war, with all its powers for devastation, shall not master my poeting; that is, if I am lucky enough to come through all right. I will not leave a corner of my consciousness covered up, but saturate myself with the strange and extraordinary new conditions of this life, and it will all refine itself into poetry later on.[1]

By the second half of August 1916, as fighting continued in the Calonne sector held by the 40th Division, Rosenberg was back in the line: 'We are still salving France and our peregrinations find us in the trenches about twice a week' he told Bottomley just before 29 August; 'we hope it won't be long before we'll be salving the German Trenches.'[2] In spite of the almost jocular tone, he found himself in far more danger than before. By the end of the month, when the 11th King's Own went into Brigade Reserve after two consecutive tours of trench duty, his battalion alone had had fifteen killed and forty-nine wounded, compared with no deaths and twenty-two wounded the previous month. And, as the Divisional historian rather insouciantly records, things began to get even 'more breezy' in early September.[3]

Rosenberg's enquiries about the possibility of being transferred to the Camouflage Section of the Royal Engineers under the painter Solomon J. Solomon – 'I know him a bit' he told Marsh[4] – may have been a direct response to the situation. Nothing came of his enquiry, however, and things continued to deteriorate. After another spell in

Brigade Reserve at the beginning of September, he was sent with his battalion to the Maroc Sector of the Line. Despite several minor operations against the Germans during July and August, the trenches had been bearable. Even in September and October with the increased fighting on both sides they were still fairly dry, 'winter conditions' having not yet set in, according to the Divisional historian.[5] But Rosenberg, who spent the greater part of these two months in the line, began to find conditions challenging:

> It has been wet and mucky in the trenches for some time, [he wrote to Bottomley as early as mid-September] and the cold weather helping, we are teased by the elements as well as by the German fireworks, I don't think I've been dry yet these last few days.[6]

By the beginning of November, when the 40th, which had been relieved by the 24th Division on 20 October, was on a long march south, bad weather arrived in earnest and Rosenberg's health and spirits suffered even more. 'Weather extremely cold' his Battalion Diary records on 11 November, as the 120th Brigade proceeded to Hébuterne near Beaumont Hamel on the dreaded Somme. By 12 November Rosenberg was telling a sympathetic Bottomley, who also suffered from weak lungs: 'We are getting well into November now and have already had it bitter cold in the trenches and warm again and wet. . . . I hate the cold.'[7] He was still trying to write,[8] but there was 'little time' as he fancifully put it 'for Pegasus to ride in or to watch him riding'.[9] During his ten days in the trenches at Hébuterne he and his battalion experienced rain, storms and even snow. It was in these unpropitious circumstances that Rosenberg celebrated his twenty-sixth birthday on 25 November 1916.

The 11th King's Own was still marching south by the beginning of December: 'We are in a rougher shop than before,' Rosenberg reported, 'and the weather is about as bad as it can be but my Pegasus, though it may kick at times, will not stampede or lose or leave me.'[10] By now he was feeling 'pretty crotchety'. 'When will this plague be over?' he asked Binyon, 'everybody and everything seems tumbling to pieces.'[11]

Heavy rain continued during the 40th's three weeks' training near

Abbeville in early December, and by the time it was ordered to relieve the 33rd Division on the Somme on the 19th, the trenches had become a living nightmare. As the historian of the 40th Division, not given to exaggeration, records:

> Now began three months in the most God-forsaken and miserable area in France, bar, possibly, the salient of Ypres. The whole countryside was a churned-up, yeasty mass of mud, as a result of the vile weather and of the battle [i.e. of the Somme] which even yet had not petered out. The weather was awful. Constant rain was varied by spells of intensely cold weather and some very heavy snowfalls. Mud and dirt were everywhere. The French had been in occupation of the Line, and, however gallant our allies may have been, their notions on sanitation were mediaeval. Billets in the back area were camps of dirty, wet and decrepit huts. Seen at that period of the year the countryside was bleak, mournful, uninviting and miserable; roads cut up; villages badly knocked about, and everywhere 'signs of the advance of large bodies of troops' ... So much for the back area, Bray to Corlu.[12]

The writer then goes on to give an even more horrific account of the trenches.

Rosenberg, however, whose life was such an extreme mixture of good and bad luck, had by this time been withdrawn from the line again, just as the 11th King's Own returned to it on 31 December.[13] This was almost certainly as a result of his letter to Marsh earlier in the month complaining of feeling 'run down and weakened'.[14] ('I fancy it was a touch of the flue [*sic*]' he wrote to Bottomley.)[15] Marsh also received a letter from Annie, whom Rosenberg had asked to write too,[16] and contacted a friend in the War Office, A.J. Creedy. Though Creedy replied on 8 January 1917 that he could not interfere in such matters, since Rosenberg was under the jurisdiction of General Headquarters, not the War Office, he had almost certainly already 'had a word' in the right quarters. (Undoubtedly at some point Rosenberg's Commanding Officer, Colonel Ritchie, was contacted about him, as I shall show.) By the time Marsh, following Creedy's advice, wrote 'privately, unofficially and without invoking the power of his connections'[17] to Rosenberg's Adjutant, Captain O.G. Normoy, in mid-January, emphasizing the poet's 'budding genius' as instructed, Rosenberg had already been transferred to the 40th Division's Works Battalion.

'It is a sort of navvy Batt[alion] to repair the roads' Rosenberg explained to Bottomley.[18] Less grateful than might be expected for this reprieve, he added: 'Naturally we are in less danger than before, but we are practically always under fire of some sort.'[19] Part of the reason for his discontent was that the intense cold and biting winds, which he so hated, continued throughout January, affecting him as he reminded the long-suffering Marsh, more than most:

> . . . though this work does not entail half the hardships of the trenches the winter and the conditions naturally tells [*sic*] on me, having once suffered from weak lungs, as you know. I have been in the trenches most of the 8 months I've been here, and the continual damp and exposure is whispering to my old friend consumption, and he may hear the words they say in time.[20]

Anxious to be right away from the Front, Rosenberg is evidently still not fully appreciative of what he later begins to recognize as his 'luck' and asks if Marsh can find him a job as 'a draughtsman at home; or something else in my own line, or perhaps on munitions'. It may have been as a result of this second letter that he was moved again.

It is not clear when his transfer to Captain Frank Waley's Trench Mortar Battery took place. Waley could not remember the precise date, but he did recall that it was Colonel Ritchie who initiated it, probably believing that Rosenberg might be happier serving under a fellow Jew. Ritchie certainly felt that he would 'stand a better chance in a small unit, where uniformity was not so essential'.[21] Ritchie knew Waley's family, having served as a subaltern under Waley's uncle in the Boer War. He had commanded the 12th South Lancs until it was broken up, when he was given charge of the 11th King's Own, so was fairly familiar with Rosenberg. Since he and Waley were friends and in the same division it was quite natural that he should think of Waley when searching round for a suitable officer for Rosenberg. (It is quite unthinkable that so much fuss would have been made about Rosenberg without Marsh's initial intervention.)

Waley clearly remembered the Colonel ringing him up and asking if he could look after a 'completely hopeless' soldier called Rosenberg. He promised to try to find a place for him, though with eight guns to man he did not want any 'duds', and finally took him on as assistant battery cook until something 'more suitable' could be found.

Rosenberg seemed quite 'happy' in this position, peeling potatoes most of the time and getting 'comfortably dirty' over the cookhouse fire. His uniform was almost black, Waley recalled, and he found him a 'miserable-looking fellow, normal above the waist but short in the legs'. He regarded Rosenberg as a 'bit of a harmless freak', whilst sympathizing with his inability to conform. Rosenberg responded to his sympathy by showing him his poems, which were usually scribbled on scraps of paper or the backs of used envelopes. Waley, who expected poetry to have a regular metre and rhyme, found the verses extraordinary – 'they meant nothing to me' – and he 'chucked them away'. One only he remembered – 'something to do with a rat' he said – probably because it was so dissimilar to conventional war poetry, being experimental in technique and not specifically patriotic in content. ('Perhaps if he had given me "From France" or "The Immortals",' Waley wrote later, 'I would have kept them.')[22] Rosenberg never showed him any of his sketches, so he did not realize that he was an artist too. 'If I had known,' he said, 'I could have lent him paints.' By an odd coincidence, of which he learnt much later, Waley's brother-in-law, Hubert Waley (brother of Arthur, the sinologist), had been at the Slade at the same time as Rosenberg. The last Waley saw of his 'eccentric' private was when he was transferred to a Pioneer Battalion.

Waley, far from resisting the transfer back to a Works Battalion, had probably encouraged it. He was almost certainly referring to himself when he admitted that 'units always tried to get rid of their unsatisfactory soldiers and the units to which these were sent often found means of returning the man'.[23] But as he also pointed out, that did 'not mean that Rosenberg was a bad man, a bad poet or anything' except that 'he was not the type . . . who could make a soldier or even look like one'.[24] He was quite capable, for example, of forgetting to wear his gasmask, a serious offence by 1917, almost certainly because his mind was on poetry not war and not (as he claimed) because his memory, 'always weak', had deteriorated in France.[25] The punishment – seven days' pack drill, which he did between 'going up the line and sleep' – was heavy and exhausted him, further unfitting him for his duties. If he was understandably annoyed, so were his frustrated officers.

Rosenberg's various transfers would keep him out of the fighting until the end of May 1917, when he would be attached to the Royal Engineers, still remaining mainly behind the lines. Though January was 'in purely military terms ... uneventful' according to the Divisional historian,[26] every day out of the trenches was one less risk to run, a blessing not yet properly recognized by Rosenberg. In February and March, as the Germans carried out their strategic withdrawal to the Hindenburg Line and the 11th King's Own, with other units of the 40th Division, pursued them in even worse weather, he was still not fully appreciative of being exempt from their increasingly dangerous operations, writing mournfully to Marsh after his second medical in February:

> ... it appears I'm quite fit. What I feel like just now – I wish I were Tristram Shandy for a few minutes so as to describe this 'cadaverous bale of goods consigned to Pluto'. This winter is a teaser for me; and being so long without a proper rest I feel as if I need one to recuperate and be put to rights again. However, I suppose we'll stick it, if we don't there are still some good poets left who might write me a decent epitaph.[27]

By April, when there was a more realistic possibility of better weather arriving, the tone of his letters grows less despairing. His battalion had been withdrawn with the rest of the 40th Division to work on the infrastructure of the area, systematically laid waste by the Germans as they retreated, to slow down the Allies' advance. While noting the devastation – 'as far as houses or signs of ordinary human living is concerned, we might as well be in the Sahara Desert'[28] – Rosenberg nevertheless adopts a more positive attitude: 'However, we've been in no danger – that is, from shell-fire – for a good long while, though so very close to most terrible fighting.'

But as the Divisional historian, commenting on work behind the lines, warns: 'If the reader now thinks that he is going to accompany the 40th Division to a land of milk and honey he may as well slough off the misunderstanding herewith.' Rosenberg's duties were punishing, involving, among other things, helping to build or repair roads, railways and bridges, delivering barbed wire and metal stakes to the front line under cover of dark and, when the need arose, as it frequently did, taking the wounded to hospital or bringing in and burying the dead. Friends and families tried to keep his spirits up with letters and parcels from England, but as Bottomley acknowledged: 'I am afraid that what your new occupation has lost in danger it has gained in general unpleasantness.'[29] Rosenberg had spent ten months in France without a break. His hope of leave for Christmas, not a very realistic one for a private, had not materialized and he and his fellow soldiers had spent Christmas Day being strafed by the Germans, even if they had been served Christmas dinner (two days earlier) by their officers. It was a far cry from the fraternization between the enemy troops of Christmas 1914.

What is remarkable about Rosenberg's time in France is that, despite all these hardships and his many complaints about them, he never lost sight of his vocation as a poet. When the mud was at its worst and daily life a nightmare of floundering through it, he was appropriating this and other equally unpleasant experiences into his work. He had been planning a second verse play along the lines of *Moses*, encouraged by Bottomley, who thought he should take on another Jewish theme. After considering a Jewish play with Judas Maccabeus for hero (in which, rather extraordinarily, he had planned to 'bring about a meeting between Christ and Judas'),[30] then abandoning it in the second half of 1916, he began to sketch out his ideas for one called *Adam and Lilith*. He was still working on his 'most gorgeous play, *Adam and Lilith*', which followed Jewish legend in making the two man and wife, in August 1916,[31] and continued to develop the idea intermittently throughout the winter of 1916–17. Now retitled *The Amulet*, a first draft was sent to his sister for typing in May 1917.[32]

Though this version too, like *Adam and Lilith*, would eventually be abandoned, certain features would survive, most strikingly the curious incident in which one of the three main characters, Saul, who now replaces Adam as Lilith's husband, gets stuck in his mule-cart in deep mud, a scene Rosenberg had undoubtedly experienced many times on the Western Front:

> ... The slime clung
> And licked and clawed and chewed the clogged dragging wheels
> Till they sunk nigh to the axle. Saul sodden and vexed
> Like fury smote the mules' mouths, pulling but sweat
> From his drowned hair and theirs, while the thunder knocked
> And all the air yawned water, falling water,
> And the light cart was water, like a wrecked raft,
> And all seemed like a forest under the ocean.[33]

Later in the play when Lilith, drawn to the naked Nubian who has rescued Saul from the mud, tells him 'I think there is more sorrow in the world / Than man can bear . . .',[34] she is surely expressing Rosenberg's own feelings in France. The Nubian's resounding reply is likewise almost certainly autobiographical: 'None can exceed their limit, lady, / You either bear or break.'[35]

Besides this attempt at a second verse play in France, Rosenberg had also written a poem with a Jewish theme, 'The Destruction of Jerusalem by the Babylonian Hordes', and completed a first draft of 'Daughters of War' in the final months of 1916. But his most effective use of his trench experience this winter occurs in an unlikely place for poetry – with lice. His 'sequence of dramatic war poems', as he had told Bottomley in July 1916, was to contain 'amusing' as well as 'serious' material.[36] He also intended to make the series 'a startler', the poems in it 'pysological' (*sic*) and 'individual',[37] which may account for his unusual choice of subject-matter.

According to Bomberg, whose first letter from the Front requested 'malted milk tablets' and 'delousing powder', the prevalence of lice was 'the worst thing to put up with in the trenches'.[38] Most men arrived in France lice-free and might remain so for a time in fine weather. (Rosenberg's first request for delousing powder is not made until he has been in France at least six weeks in the summer of 1916.)[39] But when the cold weather arrived, and with it the need to wear more layers, there were very few ordinary soldiers who were not troubled by this invasive pest. Baths at Divisional Headquarters were meant to free the men of it, when they handed in their lousy clothing and received a fumigated set in return. But baths were rare and, in any case, though the lice had been destroyed by fumigation, the eggs had not and quickly hatched out with the warmth of soldiers' bodies. Few remedies proved effective, though men covered themselves in Harrison's Pomade, the best-known of the delousing powders, or tried to burn the eggs out of their seams with a cigarette or candle, a dangerous procedure that sometimes set their clothes on fire.

As early as August 1916, Rosenberg is complaining of 'the rotten weather in the trenches, mucky and souzing and cold'.[40] By the autumn, writing to tell Laurence Binyon how 'far, very far' away Binyon's daily haunt, the British Museum, seems to him, he adds: 'situated as I am Siberia is no further and certainly no colder.'[41] Yet given the choice between the increased lice associated with warmer clothing, or being cold, he does not hesitate.

> I have gone less warmly clad during the winter than through the summer [he writes to Bottomley], because of the increased liveliness on my clothes. I've been stung to what we call 'dumping' a great part of my clothing, as I thought it wisest to go cold than lousy.[42]

It was clearly a subject on which he felt strongly. But his decision to write a poem about it was unusual at a time when even the most disillusioned of the war poets hesitated to highlight such undignified aspects of trench life. In any case, it was not a subject likely to concern officer-poets quite so much, since (for various reasons) they suffered less from lice. Rosenberg's two poems on the theme, 'The Immortals' and 'Louse Hunting', were written from a private's viewpoint and give another side to the war. It is a perspective that from the time of his arrival in France and with the exception of his unfortunate experiment, 'Pozières', rejects what he calls the 'begloried sonnets' of Rupert Brooke.[43] Like the elevated war songs of other patriotic young men, they reminded him too much of 'flag days'.[44] He preferred the more difficult but no less concerned realism of

Whitman in *Drum Taps*, or Wilfrid Gibson's 'low plane' approach in *Battle*.[45] He had been sent Gibson's collection of war poems in the winter of 1916 and found it 'in one way . . . the best thing the war has turned out'.[46] 'Most who have written as poets have been very unreal' he tells Marsh with reference to war poetry, 'and it is for this reason, their naturalness, I think Gibson's so fine.'[47]

Rosenberg is not Gibson, however, and in his hands the 'natural' rapidly takes on surrealistic overtones. Realistic descriptions of familiar army scenes are raised, as poems like 'Marching' or 'Break of Day in the Trenches' show, to a symbolic level of great intensity equal to that of such classic Modernist texts as *The Waste Land*.

Ironically, it was an apparently staunch supporter of the old traditions, Bottomley, who encouraged Rosenberg to write on more unconventional themes, as well as being indirectly responsible for his very untraditional handling of such subjects as louse hunting. Rosenberg had first conceived the idea of a poem of this kind in July 1916, shortly after completing 'Break of Day in the Trenches', but on another common trench pest, fleas, rather than lice:

> I thought your Flea Hunt was a great subject [Bottomley had responded on 8 August]; you must cherish it and carry it through. If I were you I should not tell too many poets about it, or certainly one of them will not be able to keep his hands off it. I myself find it difficult to resist it.
>
> But what a subject for a painter too; an absolutely untouched chance for a painter of nudes. Goya or Daumier would have made the real thing of it.[48]

Though Rosenberg replies that he thinks Bottomley should write such a poem, since he is not planning to compose any more verse 'till we've settled down again',[49] he responds enthusiastically to Bottomley's painter references, agreeing that 'it is a thing Goya would go mad on'.[50] Just as his comments on 'In the Trenches' had helped Rosenberg to transform it from the 'commonplace' to the extraordinary, so Bottomley's response to the younger poet's plan to write 'an amusing little thing called the louse-hunt'[51] helped transform 'The Immortals' to 'Louse Hunting'.

Too exhausted and demoralized to write such a poem during the harsh winter of 1916–17, Rosenberg evidently brooded on Bottomley's remarks. By 5 January 1917 he is thinking about 'The Louse Hunt', but by 8 February has still not produced the piece. Inspired, however, by those two great artists of the grotesque, Goya and Daumier, he has executed a drawing on the subject. Shortly after that he appears to have made his first attempt at the poem:

The Immortals

I killed them but they would not die.
Yea! all the day and all the night
For them I could not rest or sleep,
Nor guard from them nor hide in flight.

Then in my agony I turned
And made my hands red in their gore.
In vain – for faster than I slew
They rose more cruel than before.

I killed and killed with slaughter mad;
I killed till all my strength was gone.
And still they rose to torture me
For Devils only die in fun.

I used to think the devil hid
In women's smiles and wine's carouse.
I called him Satan, Balzebub.
But now I call him, dirty louse.[52]

It was Bottomley's response to the drawing rather than to his poem, however, which appears to have encouraged Rosenberg to produce his more original handling of the subject in 'Louse Hunting'. While admiring his 'Rear Elevation of a Flea-Hunt' sketch, Bottomley had felt it was 'a *static* Flea Hunt' (my italics):

> . . . I should like to see what you would make of the active Flea-Hunt which you first described [he wrote on 19 March 1917], with the men

338

jumping over candles and singeing the fleas. That would yield quite a different kind of composition, all moving and flowing lines, like a Witches' Sabbath of long slim bodies as if Botticelli had gone mad and designed a naked ballet for the Russian dancers.[53]

Heartened by Bottomley's interest and further inspired by the vision of the hunt as a Witches' Sabbath or Botticelli gone mad, Rosenberg returned to the subject and produced an almost exact poetic equivalent of Bottomley's letter, together with his earlier references to Goya and Daumier. But, as Bottomley pointed out, it had been Rosenberg's own idea originally, 'all summarized in your letter of last summer', which had read:

Last night we had a funny hunt for fleas. All stripped by candlelight some Scots dancing over the candle & burning the fleas, & the funniest, drollest and dirtiest scenes of conversation ever immagined [sic]. Burns 'Jolly Beggars' is nothing to it. I have heaps of material. I feel all your advice and am very grateful for it. If you knew how much I have destroyed because I felt it would be completely unintelligable [sic] to most, you would anyway praise my prudence.[54]

The result is an intensely visual recreation of, in Bottomley's appreciative words, 'a night scene in which Rosenberg took part . . . a barn full of naked soldiers – Scottish and others – singing, swearing, and laughing, in mad antics as they pursued the chase':[55]

Louse Hunting

Nudes—stark aglisten
Yelling in lurid glee. Grinning faces of fiends
And raging limbs
Whirl over the floor one fire,
For a shirt verminously busy
Yon soldier tore from his throat
With oaths
Godhead might shrink at, but not the lice.
And soon the shirt was aflare
Over the candle he'd lit while we lay.

Then we all sprung up and stript
To hunt the vermin brood.
Soon like a demons' pantomime
The place was raging.
See the silhouettes agape,
See the gibbering shadows
Mixed with the battled arms on the wall.
See gargantuan hooked fingers
Dug in supreme flesh
To smutch the supreme littleness.
See the merry limbs in hot Highland fling
Because some wizard vermin
Charmed from the quiet this revel
When our ears were half lulled
By the dark music
Blown from Sleep's trumpet.[56]

The visual origins of this poem are far more evident here than in 'The Immortals'. The naked bodies of the soldiers 'stark aglisten' in the flames, their 'Grinning faces' and contorted limbs, their silhouettes and 'shadows / Mixed with the battled arms on the wall' and their 'gargantuan hooked fingers' digging into their own flesh for lice bring the scene to life in a manner worthy of Goya's blackest visions. The reader does not need to know, as the ex-Slade student Rosenberg probably did, that Daumier, dubbed the 'Michelangelo of caricaturists', was imprisoned for his lampoon of the French king as Gargantua, to appreciate the grotesque enlargement of the men's 'gargantuan hooked fingers'. Rosenberg's verse is at its best when, as here, his artistic vision is subsumed into his poetic one.

'Louse Hunting' also offers what visual art does not always give, a sense of frenzied movement, being as 'dynamic' (to use Bottomley's distinction) as 'The Immortals' is 'static'.[57] Its staccato rhythms and uneven, often abruptly short lines, so different from the ordered quatrains of 'The Immortals', evoke a powerful sensation of the soldiers' frantic efforts to rid themselves of the pest. Organized, like 'Break of Day in the Trenches', round one simple, central action, as

The Artist's Sister, Minnie Horvitch, oils, 1914

Above:
The Artist's
Father, oils,
1914

Left:
The Artist's
Brother-in-law,
'Wolf' Horvitch,
oils, 1914

Right:
Self-portrait (in green hat looking left), oils, 1914

Below:
Self-portrait (without hat, rounded shirt collar), oils, 1914

Cape Coloured Woman,
oils, 1914

Cape Coloured Man, oils,
1914

Cape Coloured Girl, oils, 1914

Portrait of Clara Birnberg, oils, 1915

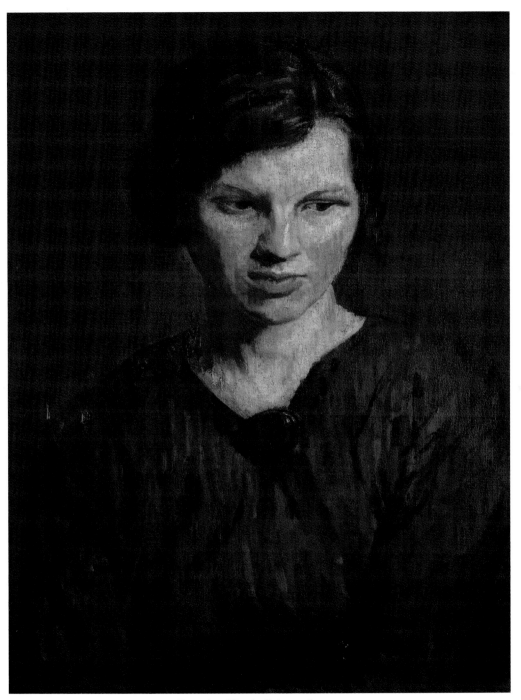

Portrait of Sonia Cohen, oils, 1915

Self-portrait (hand in lapel), oils, ?1914

the half-asleep soldiers leap up to join in the hunt, the poem recreates their wild activity. The 'raging limbs', the 'verminously busy' shirt one of them 'tore from his throat', the energy with which his fellow soldiers 'sprung up' to join the hunt, all reflected in exaggerated form by the shadows cast by the flames on the wall, create a scene of chaos and carnage.

This effect is reinforced by the sound of their 'yelling' and the imagery, which conjures up Satanic rituals and other supernatural practices, adding to the weirdness of the occasion. Rosenberg's allusion to Burns's 'Jolly Beggars' and Bottomley's to a Witches' Sabbath seems to have reminded Rosenberg of Burns's 'Tam O'Shanter', where the witches in wild pursuit of Tam perform similar 'hot highland flings'.[58] (Burns's own poem 'To a Louse' suggests another link between the two poets.) The densely packed language, in which one impression merges into another – 'raging limbs' and 'one fire', for instance, already preparing us for the actual conflagration that follows ('shirt . . . aflare') – reflects on the one hand the disordered mingling of the soldiers' bodies, on the other the 'moving and flowing lines' of the scene envisioned by Bottomley.

Rosenberg's use of the mock heroic technique is particularly effective. The mock heroic is generally used to reduce a subject to absurdity, Don Quixote tilting at windmills, for example. While Rosenberg achieves this, rendering the soldiers' grand 'battle' with the 'supreme littleness' of the lice ridiculous, he also manages, inversely, to relate the absurdity and hopelessness of *this* battle to the bigger battle in which the men are involved. The implacability of the lice becomes that of the real enemy, the Germans. In this context the literal nakedness of the louse hunters becomes a metaphor for their vulnerability in battle. And the final reference to sleep, from which (in a circular movement that shapes the poem) they have been aroused and to which they will presumably return, can be read as a euphemistic reference to the 'big sleep', death, that awaits most of them. The camaraderie of the lice-hunting soldiers, as the isolated activity of the first-person narrator in 'The Immortals' is replaced by the 'we' of 'Louse Hunting', becomes another parallel with the experience of men under fire.

Rosenberg told Bottomley in his letter of early April 1917

concerning lice: 'I think I could give some bloodcurdling touches if I wished to tell all I see, of dead buried men blown out of their graves, and more, but I will spare you all this.'[59] His more indirect approach, however, is no less powerful a comment on the war.

Chapter 19

'Returning, We Hear the Larks' and 'Dead Man's Dump'

May–June 1917

We have learnt out here to be a bit callous [Rosenberg wrote to Bottomley at the end of May 1917] and have worn the edge off our teeth with much grinding, but the 'spring of tears' remains.[1]

Rosenberg's complaints about the coldness of the weather and the state of his feet had continued to the end of April 1917. The increased 'excitement' in the trenches to which he referred that month was not yet involving him directly, but he still felt 'hardly equal to what is required',[2] which by 1917 was a great deal. Nineteen sixteen had ended in a sense of defeat for the Allies: the Somme offensive had failed, Russian morale was at a low ebb, Romania had been overrun and, at sea, Jutland had been at best a negative encounter. Nineteen seventeen was to be the Year of Victory, with an aggressive Allied spring offensive planned at Arras for April, when every soldier would be needed. Rosenberg had already witnessed one result of this plan in early spring when the Germans, alerted to Allied intentions, began their withdrawal to the Hindenburg Line in an attempt to deal with their inferior numbers. He now learnt of other developments; as the battle of Arras opened on 9 April with an attack by the British Third Army to the east of Arras (not very far from his own battalion) and by the Canadian Corps, with one brigade of the 5th Division, on Vimy Ridge. Though both engagements were successful, the battle overall, which dragged on until 16 May, was another costly failure on both sides, with 150,000 British and 100,000 German casualties. It was his experiences at Arras, among other things, that led Sassoon to make his public anti-war protest a few months later.

And it was at Arras that another Great War poet, Edward Thomas, was killed.

Though the 11th King's Own, situated with the rest of the 40th Division somewhere between St Quentin and Arras, was 'clear of the main offensive', as their historian reports, it was 'far from being in a backwater'.[3] After spending the first three weeks of April helping restore communications in the area abandoned by the retreating Germans, on 20 April the 40th entered the Hindenburg Line at Gouzeaucourt, near Cambrai. The following day the 11th King's Own took the village of Beaucamp after fierce skirmishing with heavy losses. They and their fellow battalions in the 40th Division continued to be involved in the intense fighting along the Hindenburg Line into May, though the effect on Rosenberg in the Divisional Works Battalion was still not dramatic.

By this time, as his letter to Marsh of 8 May indicates, the weather had improved greatly and so, too, had his spirits:

> We are camping in the woods now and are living great. My feet are almost healed now and my list of complaints has dwindled down to almost invisibility.[4]

Whereas the 'harsh and unlovely times' of the first four months of 1917 had made his 'flighty Muse abscond and elope with luckier rivals', with the renewal of 'summer and sweeter times' and the continuation of his relatively undemanding job, he felt able, as he had hoped, 'to hunt and chase her' once again.[5]

He made immediate use of the experiences he had accumulated, but had lacked the energy to write about, during the harsher weather. Significantly his choice now turns from the neutral rat and the lowly louse to more elevated, or less ridiculous creatures, larks, reflecting his own greater involvement in the war. One of the most regular of his activities by May was a journey up to the line at night with various supplies for what he called 'the poor fellows' there.[6] Less dangerous than actually being in the trenches, it was nevertheless far from safe. But there were consolations, the song of the larks at dawn, as he returned exhausted to camp, being one of them. The beauty of

Self-portrait sketch in full profile, July 1917 (*Imperial War Museum*)

their song is a recurring theme in Romantic verse, and Rosenberg's familiarity with the best-known example, Shelley's 'To a Skylark', emerges at numerous points in his own poem on the subject. The lark is also, like the poppy, a familiar symbol of life at the Front. But while Rosenberg's title, 'Returning, We Hear the Larks', promises a similarly Romantic handling of the theme, the poem itself, from its grimly realistic opening lines onwards, quickly undercuts such expectations:

> Sombre the night is.
> And though we have our lives, we know
> What sinister threat lurks there.
>
> Dragging these anguished limbs, we only know
> This poison-blasted track opens on our camp—
> On a little safe sleep.[7]

By introducing the larks' song in such an obviously dangerous context, Rosenberg is already departing from Shelley's association of it with natural beauty and the nature of poetic inspiration. While Rosenberg recognizes the beauty of the unseen larks' song, the abstract rapture of Shelley's ode, as Steven Connor notes, 'is suddenly made actual and concrete, in the almost physical sense given of the song raining beneficently down on the exposed skin of the upturned faces':[8]

> But hark! joy—joy—strange joy.
> Lo! heights of night ringing with unseen larks.
> Music showering our upturned list'ning faces.

Though Rosenberg has taken his imagery directly from Shelley (line 35 of 'To a Skylark' reads 'From thy presence showers a rain of melody'), his opening stanza has already alerted the reader to the possibility of something more ominous descending from the sky. The larks' song may drop as benignly as Portia's 'gentle rain from heaven', but the sky is equally likely to 'rain' bullets or shells. And the concluding stanza makes a clear link between beauty and danger. It also extends this chain of association to the war itself, through its two striking, final similes of a blind man and a beautiful woman:

> Death could drop from the dark
> As easily as song—
> But song only dropped,
> Like a blind man's dreams on the sand
> By dangerous tides,
> Like a girl's dark hair for she dreams no ruin lies there,
> Or her kisses where a serpent hides.

The blind man, like the soldiers, cannot actually *see* the danger he is in; the soldiers, by association, are equally powerless and in just as much danger as he is. The point is reinforced through another of Rosenberg's recurring images, the seductive, ultimately destructive power of 'a girl's dark hair ... Or her kisses where a serpent hides'. Her unawareness, like the blind man's, will not save her, or her victims either, from the danger – victims who, by the end of the poem, have become identified with the soldiers. Her role harks back to 'The Female God' and forward to 'Daughters of War'. Shelley himself describes his lark's song as 'Keen as are the arrows / Of that silver sphere' (line 21) and compares the lark to 'a high-born maiden / In a palace-tower, / Soothing her love-laden / Soul in secret hour' (lines 41 to 44), images that Rosenberg echoes: but Shelley nowhere suggests in 'To a Skylark' a link between beauty and danger. By doing so in the context of war Rosenberg makes the subject his own, despite its borrowings.

He himself is his own greatest influence. His charcoal drawing 'Hark, Hark the Lark', for instance, based (as I have shown) on lines from Meredith's 'The Lark Ascending' –

> And every face to watch him raised
> Puts on the light of children praised . . .

– depicts apprehension as well as joy in the faces of the six nude figures listening to the bird's song, and this graphic rendering of the scene undoubtedly contributed to the visual impact of 'Returning, We Hear the Larks'. (He had, for instance, already imagined their 'upturned list'ning faces'.) The nakedness of the men and women in the drawing suggests their vulnerability, and while the soldiers in 'Returning, We Hear the Larks' are not literally naked (as they are in 'Louse Hunting'), they are just as exposed to the potential danger in the sky. His Slade competition entry, *Joy*, too, almost certainly inspired some of the other visual details of the poem. Since the picture itself is lost, this cannot now be proved, but the influence of the piece written in conjunction with it can, reading in part like a prose equivalent of the verse. 'Joy – joy – the birds sing, joy –' Rosenberg had written in its last sentence, 'the rivers, joy – the happy leaves, for the fear of Time haunts not, and the hands of fate are afar.'[9] The 'hands of fate' may be 'afar' in this earlier piece but, significantly, the writer is already conscious of them.

Unusually, in the case of his most successful war poems, there are no extant comments either by Rosenberg or his friends on 'Returning, We Hear the Larks'. Even the dutiful Marsh is silent on the subject. We know that Rosenberg sent it to Rodker in about May 1917, presumably with a letter now lost, but he may not have sent it to Marsh at all, possibly anticipating criticism of its technique. Unlike Rodker, a great admirer of Modernist verse, Marsh could not have been expected to appreciate the irregularity of the poem, particularly in its brilliantly changing rhythms. In the first two stanzas Rosenberg bombards the reader with line after line of strong beats and abrupt rhythms that convey the heaviness of the soldiers' spirits, as well as their boots, an impression reinforced by a series of threatening adjectives – 'sombre', 'sinister', 'anguished', 'poison-blasted'. Only with the promise of 'a little safe sleep' in the sixth line does the tone – and the metre – change, the third stanza being much lighter in its rhythms to reflect the delight felt by the soldiers at the sound of the larks' song. But as the imagery of the blind man and beautiful girl in the final stanza goes on to hint, there is a deep, underlying irony in the situation which makes the lyric technique seem a deliberate mockery. The extreme compression of this imagery, through which the subject-matter is indirectly but nat-urally developed, allows Rosenberg to arrive at a mastery of form unsurpassed in his poetry. 'Returning, We Hear the Larks' is a perfect illustration of his own concept of 'Simple *poetry* – that is where an interesting complexity of thought is kept in tone and right value to the dominating idea so that it is understandable and still ungraspable'.[10]

The fine weather that seems to have given Rosenberg the energy to write 'Returning, We Hear the Larks' continued throughout May, and by the end of the month he had produced a second poem, yet another draft of a third and done some more work on his play *The Amulet*. There was no lack of material for someone naturally interested in the weird and unusual. 'You complain in your letters that there is little to write about' he had told Marsh after four months in France

> my complaint is rather the other way. I have too much to write about, but for obvious reasons my much must be reduced to less than your little. My exaggerated way of feeling things when I begin to write about them might not quite have healthy consequences.[11]

Sending Marsh some passages from *The Amulet* he warns him: 'Don't think from this I've time to write. ... It is only when we get a bit of rest and the others might be gambling or squabbling I add a line or two, and continue this way.'[12] Since the 40th Division were still fighting in the Hindenburg Line, he was kept busy servicing it in their Works Battalion. But towards the end of the month he was transferred to the Royal Engineers, a move that led to the writing of a second great war poem, 'Dead Man's Dump', as he reported to Bottomley:

> I am now with the Royal Engineers and we go wiring up the line at night. We took a village and the REs did all the wiring and some digging in front of it. I wrote a poem about some dead Germans lying in a sunken road where we dumped our wire. ... We go out at night and sleep in the day in these woods behind the line. It is that I've had a little more time in the day to myself and am with a small loading party by ourselves that I've been able to write ... lately.[13]

Rosenberg's wiring job involved carrying barbed wire and metal stakes up to the line in 'limber'-carts, to repair any damage done to the tangled coils of barbed wire designed to protect the Allies from the enemy. One particularly unpleasant aspect of the job, he told Marsh, was 'running over dead bodies lying about'.[14] Though he clearly loathed the dangerous, macabre journey to no-man's-land, always undertaken at night, his poem on the subject, 'Dead Man's Dump', shows that the desolate scene had a powerful effect on his imagination both as an artist and a poet:

> The plunging limbers over the shattered track
> Racketed with their rusty freight,
> Stuck out like many crowns of thorns,
> And the rusty stakes like sceptres old
> To stay the flood of brutish men
> Upon our brothers dear.
>
> The wheels lurched over sprawled dead

But pained them not, though their bones crunched,
Their shut mouths made no moan,
They lie there huddled, friend and foeman,
Man born of man, and born of woman,
And shells go crying over them
From night till night and now.[15]

The painter has combined with the poet here to give an arresting portrayal of this sinister night scene. The intense visualization of the limber-carts and their 'rusty freight' is complemented by the harsh sounds they make, the jagged, jerky rhythms reflecting their jolting progress over corpses and the underlying theme of sudden, brutal death. And the artist's vision of 'crowns of thorns' and 'sceptres old' is seized on by the poet to point, metaphorically, to a crucifixion of latter-day Christs, the soldiers, which lends a dignity and nobility to their apparently meaningless deaths. Likewise, the picture conjured up of King Canute seated on the seashore, trying in vain to turn back the tide, allows the poet to suggest how ineffectual the barbed wire is likely to be in keeping back the enemy. The dead are shown lying 'sprawled' and 'huddled' side by side, regardless of which *side* they are on, silent in death, with only the shells to 'cry' for them. The following eleven stanzas are equally evocative both visually and aurally.

It is a memorable opening and one typical of Rosenberg in its graphic detail. What is not typical is his choice of subject. It is the first – and only – work in which he gives a direct description of the carnage he was witnessing. It may have been the fear he expressed to Marsh of what might happen if he allowed his 'exaggerated way of feeling things' free rein which had made his earlier treatment of war more indirect, since when he does allow his imagination to approach the subject more directly in 'Dead Man's Dump' the effect is almost overwhelming. From its shockingly colloquial title onwards, the poem presents an uncompromising view of the reality of war, that 'sensuous front-line existence … hateful and repellent, unforgettable and inescapable' which Sassoon had recognized in Rosenberg's work. Rosenberg had vowed the previous year 'not [to] leave a corner of [his] consciousness covered up' but to 'saturate' himself with 'the strange and extraordinary new conditions' of life in France, and 'Dead Man's

Dump' is one of the most dramatic results of that vow. Imaginatively it is more wide-ranging than any of his other poems and presents a more varied set of emotions, the narrative viewpoint shifting constantly throughout. The driver's point of view gives way quickly to that of the more detached narrator who questions, in a section Bottomley admired enormously – 'this kind of [astonishing and entrancing] quality' he told Rosenberg, 'is your high[est]-watermark yet'[16] – the philosophical implications of death:

> Earth has waited for them
> All the time of their growth
> Fretting for their decay:
> Now she has them at last!
> In the strength of their strength
> Suspended—stopped and held.
>
> What fierce imaginings their dark souls lit
> Earth! have they gone into you?
> Somewhere they must have gone,
> And flung on your hard back
> Is their soul's sack,
> Emptied of God-ancestralled essences.
> Who hurled them out? Who hurled?
>
> None saw their spirits' shadow shake the grass,
> Or stood aside for the half-used life to pass
> Out of those doomed nostrils and the doomed mouth,
> When the swift iron burning bee
> Drained the wild honey of their youth. (ll. 14–31)[17]

The Female God has become merged with Mother Earth and taken the soldiers to herself, a theory Rosenberg will develop more fully in his last great war poem, 'Daughters of War'. A number of critics have seen similarities to Owen's technique in 'Dead Man's Dump', and the stanza beginning 'None saw their spirits' shadow shake the grass' is certainly nearer to his lyrical technique and more regular verse forms. But the passage as a whole shows how *unlike*

Owen Rosenberg is. As Charles Tomlinson observed, pinpointing as he did so the quality which above all marks Rosenberg out, 'Owen doesn't have this sense of the numinous, of "God-ancestralled essences".'[18] Commenting on the 'half-used life', 'joined' later on in the piece 'to the great sunk silences', Tomlinson concludes:

> Yet we have the sense at the back of the poem – and this is where Rosenberg is least like Owen – that the waste was not merely that of human life but the waste of death. Rosenberg seems to be implying that, had there been possible among those half-used lives the open readiness for the music of destiny, the half-used life could have achieved a heightened spiritual power, an intensity which would have been beyond pity because having no need for it. This was a conception which an essentially humanistic poet like Wilfred Owen never entertained ... [19]

As the stanza on the 'half-used life' shows, Rosenberg's feeling is more of self-identification and empathy than of Owen's 'pity'. He had already used the iron and honey metaphor in 'August 1914', when he had written, almost certainly with himself in mind:

> Three lives hath one life—
> Iron, honey, gold.
> The gold, the honey gone—
> Left is the hard and cold.[20]

Writing in the spring of 1916 before he had seen active service, he could nevertheless prophesy, with some apprehension, no doubt, in the final lines of 'August 1914', that young men like himself would become only:

> A burnt space through ripe fields,
> A fair mouth's broken tooth.

From questioning Earth ('Have they gone into you?') and imagining the thoughts of the dying soldiers, the poet now turns back to those who have, so far, survived:

> What of us, who flung on the shrieking pyre,
> Walk, our usual thoughts untouched,
> Our lucky limbs as on ichor fed,
> Immortal seeming ever?
> Perhaps when the flames beat loud on us,
> A fear may choke in our veins
> And the startled blood may stop. (ll. 32–8).[21]

But however philosophical the poet becomes he constantly reminds us of the unrelenting nature of the scene –

> The air is loud with death,
> The dark air spurts with fire
> The explosions ceaseless are. (ll. 39–41)

– and the viewpoint never remains the same for long. From a brief return to the dead and dying –

> Timelessly now, some minutes past,
> These dead strode time with vigorous life,
> Till the shrapnel called 'an end!'
> But not to all. In bleeding pangs
> Some borne on stretchers dreamed of home,
> Dear things, war-blotted from their hearts. (ll. 42–7)

– the view shifts to the horror of a stretcher-bearer (a job Rosenberg had often carried out) and his companions:

> A man's brains splattered on
> A stretcher-bearer's face;
> His shook shoulders slipped their load,
> But when they bent to look again
> The drowning soul was sunk too deep
> For human tenderness.
>
> They left this dead with the older dead,
> Stretched at the cross roads. (ll. 48–55)

It is a grotesque tour of the battlefield in which our 'guide' halts every now and then to give a close-up of the scene:

> Burnt black by strange decay
> Their sinister faces lie
> The lid over each eye,
> The grass and coloured clay
> More motion have than they,
> Joined to the great sunk silences. (ll. 56–61)

Rosenberg's most extraordinary 'imagining', however, is to project himself next into the mind and supine body of one of war's many victims at the very moment of his dying, then swiftly back in stark contrast to the drivers of the limber-carts as they start on their return journey and bring the 'tour – and the poem – to a close:

> Here is one not long dead;
> His dark hearing caught our far wheels,
> And the choked soul stretched weak hands
> To reach the living word the far wheels said,
> The blood-dazed intelligence beating for light,
> Crying through the suspense of the far torturing wheels
> Swift for the end to break,
> Or the wheels to break,
> Cried as the tide of the world broke over his sight.
>
> Will they come? Will they ever come?
> Even as the mixed hoofs of the mules,
> The quivering-bellied mules,
> And the rushing wheels all mixed
> With his tortured upturned sight,
> So we crashed round the bend,
> We heard his weak scream,
> We heard his very last sound,
> And our wheels grazed his dead face. (ll. 62–79)

The angle of vision, particularly in these last two stanzas, is highly unusual – the dying soldier gazing up at the hoofs and bellies of the approaching mules – and something Rosenberg, the painter-poet, can do exceptionally well. The 'normal' view of things has been, literally, distorted. Consciously or not, Rosenberg has, in a technique reminiscent of Post-Impressionism, rejected straightforward representation in favour of a selection of the most significant aspects of the scene. 'Dead Man's Dump' achieves in words what Stanley Spencer's Burghclere war murals achieve in paint.

Equally impressive is Rosenberg's control of his material. The constantly shifting viewpoint, disrupted further by philosophical questionings, could so easily have resulted in confusion for the reader, that 'obscurity' of which even his kindest critics accused him. Yet by employing, as in 'Returning, We Hear the Larks', the relatively simple device of a journey, he has managed to shape his material without straitjacketing it. Unlike 'Returning, We Hear the Larks', however, the journey here is towards the Front as well as away from it, allowing him to explore a fuller range of sights and emotions and bringing it nearer to the circular movement of 'Louse Hunting' and 'Break of Day in the Trenches'.

Rosenberg's maturity as a poet also shows itself in his technical control of language, which enables him to emphasize his points through such devices as alliteration – 'their shut mouths made no moan' *sounds* so final; internal rhyme – 'the   track / Racketed …' *sounds* so jolting; and unanswerable rhetorical questions about the nature of death. And though it is possible to detect echoes of literary borrowings – the Bible, Blake, Francis Thompson and Wilfrid Gibson, among others[22] – none of these models is allowed to dominate and the poem remains uniquely Rosenberg's.

Even the imagery seems, if possible, more condensed and powerful than previously. The 'crowns of thorns' of the first stanza, for instance, is echoed in another crucifixion metaphor in stanza ten ('Stretched at the cross roads') and the King Canute allusion in stanza one is reinforced by the reference to the 'floods of brutish men' in the same stanza and the 'tide of the world' in the next to last one. The image of being broken on the wheel (of fate?) is repeated, both literally and metaphorically, throughout. And behind it all a contrast is built up in the piece between the 'young' soldiers and the 'old men' who sent them to war. (Deborah Maccoby sees this as starting with the reference to the 'young rebel', Christ, and the 'old King Canute'.)[23] Rosenberg called one of his earlier attempts at the subject 'The Young Dead', but when he refers in this, the final version to leaving 'this dead with the older dead' he is almost certainly being ironic, since this only draws attention to the fact that they are mostly all 'young', or at least that none of the dead is going to grow any 'older'. The other implied contrast in 'Dead Man's Dump', between light and dark, is equally significant. Though it is 'dark' when the limber-carts visit the line, as we know, and the 'dark air spurts with fire', the soldiers' 'blood-dazed intelligence' at the moment of dying is 'beating for light'.

Unsurprisingly, Marsh found Rosenberg's technique disturbing, in particular his combining of rhymed with unrhymed verse, but he must have said something positive as well, since Rosenberg (after admitting 'Regular rhythms I do not like much') replied by 27 May that he 'liked' his criticism of 'Dead Man's Dump'.[24] In this same letter Rosenberg refers to 'a much finer poem' he was in the process of refining. Started the previous October, it was his most ambitious work to date and would not be completed for at least another month and a half, though Marsh would be invited to read some of the seven or eight surviving typescript drafts on the way.[25]

Part of the delay was due to shortage of time. His unofficial attachment to the Royal Engineers was formalized by the end of May, when he wrote to Bottomley about his transfer. At the beginning of June he wrote to tell his mother of his change of address to 'c/o 229th Field Company, Royal Engineers', and as the 40th Division's activity in the Hindenburg Line continued, so did his nightly trips to the Front with barbed wire. 'The British offensive centre of gravity', as Liddell Hart wrote, 'had been transferred northwards after the failure of Arras – to open brilliantly at Messines on 7 June and to fade out still more miserably [than Arras] in the swamps of Passchendaele in October.'[26] Though the 40th Division's historian talks of its 'quiet' summer further south, he emphasizes the fact that 'quiet' in a world war is a distinctly relative term:

The quiet enjoyed by the Division in that gorgeous June of 1917 was not exactly the quiet experienced lying in a punt in a shady backwater on the Thames; nor the ease felt on a sunny afternoon in watching Surrey v. Middlesex at the Oval.[27]

Rosenberg had neither punted on the Thames nor watched county cricket at the Oval, but he would probably have agreed entirely with the Divisional historian's conclusion that 'what quiet generally amounted to on the Western Front during the Great War was simply this: you knew any given morning that it was "odds on" your turning in that night unwounded and alive', and that 'that means a great deal in war'.[28]

Rosenberg's Brigade, the 120th, had started June in Brigade Reserve, then become part of the Divisional Reserve at Sokel-le-Grand until 19th, when it had entered the line for nine days, in the Villers-Plouich Sector, ending the month again in Brigade Reserve. But the men were kept busy whether in or out of the front line, the Royal Engineers being no exception. When the 120th were preparing to attack, for instance, the Sappers were responsible for 'consolidation', preparing and delivering dumps of tools and wiring materials to the trenches.[29] Their other jobs this summer included general trench work, digging wells and constructing and repairing billets and Brigade Headquarters, all quite demanding work for someone as slight as Rosenberg. On 27 June, at the end of his brigade's nine-day stint at Villers-Plouich, he is complaining to Marsh that he is 'fearfully rushed'.[30] He was still trying to complete 'Daughters of War' but 'saw no hope of doing the play [i.e. *The Amulet*]' on which he had also hoped to work 'while out here'.[31] His main problem was a novel one and points to the depth of his imaginative involvement in his work: 'I have a way, when I write,' he explained to Marsh, 'to try to put myself in the situation and I make gestures and grimaces.'[32]

By July the war diary of the 40th grows less enthusiastic in its entries, as their historian notes, 'particularly after logging the fact that on the 13th, divisional headquarters were shelled for three quarters of an hour during the morning by an 8-inch high velocity gun'.[33] The 11th King's Own were still going in and out of the line at Villers-Plouich and by the end of the month the Divisional diary describes the German artillery as 'rather active', a typical understatement contradicted by its account in the previous sentence of a heavy trench mortar at nearby Gonnelieu being 'destroyed by a bombardment of 5.9's which registered ten direct hits'.[34] Again it is no surprise to find Rosenberg telling Bottomley on 20 July, the day before his battalion returns to the line at Villers-Plouich for the second time that month, that he was 'more busy now' than ever.[35] '[T]hings are so tumultuous and disturbing' he explained to Schiff, who was feeling neglected, 'that unless one has everything handy . . . one cannot write letters.'[36]

Writing poetry in such conditions became increasingly difficult, 'but I generally manage to knock something up if my brain means to' he told Bottomley on 20 July.[37] Despite his complaints he recognized how fortunate he was. Writing to congratulate Marsh on getting back his old job as Private Secretary to Churchill, now Minister of Munitions, he says he can 'imagine how busy you will be kept', the implication being that he is equally 'busy' himself.[38] But the letter ends on a positive note, showing none of the self-pity of earlier years: 'though of course my work pretty much leaves my brain alone especially as I have a decent job now and am not rushed and worked as I was in the trenches.' There is an intriguing reference in a letter to Schiff the same month about 'jot[ting] down some ideas now and then' but not sending them because they are 'actual transcripts of the battlefield' and he knows Schiff 'won[']t like that'.[39] It is not clear which notes Rosenberg is referring to. He may be thinking of fragments like the one beginning 'Yea I a soldier, say I have not suffered at all / If this is suffering',[40] which he would eventually incorporate into *The Unicorn*. But it is also quite possible that these jottings have been lost, confirming his own 'great fear' that he might lose what he had written – which, as he told Bottomley this same July, 'can happen here so easily'.[41]

Fortunately 'Daughters of War', which he eventually managed to finish in late summer, has survived. Since he considered this his 'best poem and most complete, most epic',[42] it allows us to assess his aims and attitude more closely than any other of his war poems.

Chapter 20

'Daughters of War' and a Last Leave-Taking
July–September 1917

I don't suppose my poems will ever be *poetry* right and proper until I shall be able to settle down and whip myself into more expression [Rosenberg wrote to Bottomley in July 1917]. As it is, my not being able to get poetry out of my head and heart causes me sufficient trouble out here. Not that it interferes with the actual practical work; but with forms and things I continually forget, and authority looks at [things?] from a different angle and perspective. This even may (or may not) interfere with my chances of an early leave (the earliest was late enough) but will never break the ardour of my poetry.[1]

Rosenberg's epic ambitions, hinted at earlier in his claim that 'The Homer for this war has yet to be found', are immediately apparent from the title of 'Daughters of War' onwards. An echo possibly of Emerson's 'Daughters of Time',[2] in it Rosenberg signals his intention of creating his own mythology. Somewhere between the male war god of Classical legend and Odin's messenger maidens of Norse sagas, the Valkyries, the warlike 'Daughters' fulfil a role similar to their Scandinavian equivalents, whose special function is to kill the heroes selected by the gods for death in battle and conduct them to Valhalla. Rosenberg's warrior maidens, who also owe some of their attributes to the Amazons and to his own Female God, do not actually kill those destined to die in battle, but wait, even more sinisterly, to possess them in death, just as the Earth in 'Dead Man's Dump' 'waited' for the soldiers, 'fretting for their decay'.

'Daughters of War' is a challenging poem, and Rosenberg's own explanation of it to a puzzled Marsh its best introduction:

The first part, the picture of the Daughters dancing and calling to the spirits of the slain before their last cries have ceased among the boughs of the tree of life, I must still work on. . . . the description of the voice of the Daughter I have not made clear, I see; I have tried to suggest the wonderful sound of her voice, spiritual and voluptuous at the same time. The end is an attempt to imagine the severance of all human relationship and the fading away of human love.[3]

Marsh's continuing problems with the poem produce, a month later, Rosenberg's clearest statement of all on his aims in his war poetry:

I have changed and rechanged ['Daughters of War'] and thought hard over that poem and striven to get that sense of inexorableness the human (or inhuman) side of this war has. It even penetrates behind human life[,] for the 'Amazon' who speaks in the second part of the poem is imagined to be without her lover yet, while all her sisters have theirs, the released spirits of the slain earth men; her lover yet remains to be released.[4]

Reading the poem in the light of these words, it is difficult not to wonder whether that sole surviving 'earth man' was Rosenberg himself and the poem partly a premonition, or at least apprehension, of his own death.

Though Rosenberg had started 'Daughters of War' in the autumn of 1916 – 'my poem came when I was brooding over Judas Maccabeus' he told Bottomley[5] – he had not sent Marsh a draft until June 1917, almost certainly because he anticipated his bewilderment, despite his careful explanation. He was also anxious to make the poem as perfect as possible by the time Marsh saw it, since he was hoping that the editor of *Georgian Poetry* would include it in his 1916–17 volume with the speech from *Moses*: 'It is at least as good as my Koelue speech, and there is more of it.'[6]

He had no such hesitation in showing 'Daughters of War' to Bottomley, however. 'This poem is the real thing,' Bottomley responded to the first draft on 21 December 1916, 'and contains real poetry in an intensity which is not granted many people to reach.'[7] Comparing its 'mysterious, inscrutable texture' with the work of such differing masters as Milton, Whitman, Whistler, Titian, early Rossetti, Stravinsky and Mozart, he argued that 'the formation of the texture causes a feeling of music in the mind',[8] a music which his references to both Stravinsky and Mozart suggest will contain harsh discords as well as pure melody. Though he was 'not quite sure that [he] quite underst[oo]d every phrase of it', even after Rosenberg's numerous revisions, he believed 'its music and its movement [to be] of the grandest kind' he told the gratified poet six months, and many drafts, later.[9]

Bottomley's approach to the poem is a helpful way into its history and its complexities. He had initially found its opening 'not sure-footed ... not certain of its direction', citing as an example 'the grand and impressive image of the tree-root' which seemed to him 'only half dug out', a remark that evidently caused Rosenberg to add a parenthetical explanation of his 'root' metaphor in later drafts:

> Space beats the ruddy freedom of their limbs—
> Their naked dances with man's spirit naked
> By the root side of the tree of life
> (The underside of things
> And shut from earth's profoundest eyes).
>
> I saw in prophetic gleams
> These mighty daughters in their dances
> Beckon each soul aghast from its crimson corpse
> To mix in their glittering dances.
> I heard the mighty daughters' giant sighs
> In sleepless passion for the sons of valour,
> And envy of the days of flesh
> Barring their love with mortal boughs across—
> The mortal boughs—the mortal tree of life,
> The old bark burnt with iron wars
> They blow to a live flame
> To char the young green days
> And reach the occult soul;—they have no softer lure—
> No softer lure than the savage ways of death.[10]

The visionary narrator and the monolithic figures are again reminiscent of Keats's *Fall of Hyperion*, but Rosenberg's own voice is immediately heard, conjuring up a scene of visual intensity equal and in many ways similar to the naked, capering Gargantuan nudes of 'Louse Hunting', though the Daughters are performing more of a seduction-cum-war-dance than a 'hot Highland fling'. Bottomley, who instantly fastened on the pictorial quality of 'Daughters of War', was probably thinking of the great colourist Titian's use of reds and greens in his early work and Rossetti's sumptuous visions of womanhood when he compared the poem's texture to that of these two artists among others. Rosenberg's view of his Daughters as 'spiritual and voluptuous at the same time'[11] certainly brings Rossetti to mind. Bottomley may also have been thinking of Michelangelo's 'huge titanic limbs and volcanic energy of motion' (Rosenberg's own words in 'Art')[12] and remembering the statuesque female nudes of his lost picture, *Joy*. There are links, too, with his 'Female God' – 'Queen! Goddess! animal!' – in the 'sleepless passion' of these Immortals for mortal men, as well as echoes of his earlier love poetry in his use of imagery of imprisonment and fire to convey sexual subjugation.

'Daughters of War' is about more than the 'sexual fantasies' Joseph Cohen sees in it, however.[13] As Bottomley notes, 'when the poem finds its pace it steadies itself', so that the appreciative reader feels with him, in the middle section, as if Rosenberg 'were the man who invented the Valkyries and the Amazons for the first time',[14] as the dead men wonder at the Daughters' strength and all-consuming power:

> We were satisfied of our Lords the moon and the sun
> To take our wage of sleep and bread and warmth—
> These maidens came—these strong everliving Amazons,
> And in an easy might their wrists
> Of night's sway and moon's sway the sceptres brake,
> Clouding the wild—the soft lustres of our eyes.[15]

> Clouding the wild lustres, the clinging tender lights;
> Driving the darkness into the flame of day,
> With the Amazonian wind of them

Over our corroding faces
That must be broken—broken for evermore
So the soul can leap out
Into their huge embraces.
Tho' there are human faces
Best sculptures of Deity,
And sinews lusted after
By the Archangels tall,
Even these must leap to the love-heat of these maidens
From the flame of terrene days,
Leaving grey ashes to the wind—to the wind. (ll. 20–39)

The point of view is a shifting one, as in 'Dead Man's Dump', moving from the narrator to the dead soldiers, though it will not remain there. The contrast between the vulnerable young men, longing only for mundane daily comforts of 'sleep and bread and warmth', and their unearthly lovers throws powerfully into relief the gulf between life and death which they are about to cross. These 'strong everliving Amazons' will destroy earthly time ('Of night's sway and noon's sway the sceptres brake') and earthly love ('the flame of terrene days'), so that the men's souls 'can leap out / Into their huge embraces', leaving their bodies as 'grey ashes to the wind'. So Rosenberg's epic intentions unfold, less clearly than Milton's in *Paradise Lost* or Whitman's in *Drum Taps* but no less daringly, as Bottomley's comparison of him to these two poets suggests.

'Daughters of War' is 'at its best', Bottomley claims, 'at the end, where it is simple as well as complex'.[16] Here, as Rosenberg had explained to Marsh, 'the "Amazon" who speaks is imagined to be without her lover yet, while all her sisters have theirs':

One (whose great lifted face,
Where wisdom's strength and beauty's strength
And the thewed strength of large beasts
Moved and merged, gloomed and lit)
Was speaking, surely, as the earth-men's earth fell away;
Whose new hearing drunk the sound
Where pictures lutes and mountains mixed

With the loosed spirit of a thought,
Essenced to language, thus—

'My sisters force their males
From the doomed earth, from the doomed glee
And hankering of hearts.
Frail hands gleam up through the human quagmire,
    and lips of ash
Seem to wail, as in sad faded paintings
Far sunken and strange.
My sisters have their males
Clean of the dust of old days
That clings about those white hands,
And yearns in those voices sad.
But these shall not see them,
Or think of them in any days or years,
They are my sisters' lovers in other days and years.'
    (ll. 39–61)

It was probably this section of more muted colours and half-lit, shadowy figures that prompted Bottomley's comparison with Whistler. But there are sudden, chilling, reminders that it is a battle-field not a drawing-room Rosenberg is depicting, as 'frail hands gleam up through the human quagmire and lips of ash / Seem to wail', a scene he had no doubt witnessed. The ambiguity of this description – it could, in the context, also refer to the yearning hands and distraught faces of the women left behind mourning for their 'earth-men' – and the poet's possible sympathy for these women indicates an ambivalence in his attitude towards war. His Amazons, who represent the awful powers at work in war, are from one view-point splendid figures of strength and purity, but from another destructive, Lilith-like vampires devouring men for their own selfish ends. This duality seems to be the nearest he can get to expressing his mixed feelings about the experience he was being forced to undergo in France. His occasional thoughts of suicide in civilian life suggest that death had occasionally had a certain attraction for him which may have increased at the Front. In 'Daughters of War' he not only attempts (in his words to Marsh) 'to imagine the severance of all human relationships and the fading away of human love', but also appears to be trying to come to terms with his own possible death. The conclusion, which is an unsettling one with no sense of closure, may have been deliberately open-ended: the 'end' for him had not yet come.

Nearly twenty years after first reading it Bottomley still believed 'Daughters of War' to be 'a finer war poem than anyone else achieved' in that conflict.[17] It was, he argued, Rosenberg's big achievement, his masterpiece, reaching up to a symbolism as great as Blake's from the still realistic level of 'Dead Man's Dump'.[18] F.R. Leavis also argued that it was one of the truly great English poems, though he placed Rosenberg with Keats and Hopkins rather than Blake.[19]

Marsh, unfortunately, did not agree with such large claims and continued to find 'Daughters of War' obscure. His decision not to include it in his third Georgian Poetry anthology deeply disappointed and puzzled his protégé. Unlike Bottomley, he was not ready for the difficulties and apparent discordances of a 'music' Bottomley had compared with Stravinsky as well as Mozart. Bottomley's attempt to explain Marsh's decision marks him out as Rosenberg's most sympathetic, perceptive and, despite his disclaimer, helpful critic. It also helps to explain why Rosenberg's poetry has never become 'popular' as Brooke's, Owen's and Sassoon's has:

I understand very well your wishing that 'Daughters of War' could go in too [he wrote on 7 August 1917]. It is your most remarkable poem for vision and originality and texture of language, and to me it gives the most certain promise of a fine future ...

Yet I understand equally why Mr Marsh demurs: I am probably a very bad and misleading guide for you, for I am always ready to meet a poet halfway when he says things I like in a way that I like; and I have only myself to please: but the public which Mr Marsh, as editor, has to consider will not meet you halfway, but will require you to go all the way ...

If I were asked I could not deny that I thought 'Daughters of War' obscure; I could not, in fact, always explain to anybody what it means.

But the feeling is so right, and the salient points are firm enough to enable me to leap from one to the next. .... [20]

Bottomley's belief in him was one of Rosenberg's greatest consolations at the Front, next to poetry itself. While the more worldly Marsh's involvement with the war increased – 'I fancy poetry is not much bothering you or anybody just now' Rosenberg had written to Marsh at the end of May just before he joined Churchill at the Ministry of Munitions – Bottomley's world, like Rosenberg's, continued to revolve almost solely round poetry. 'I've heard of the air raids' Rosenberg wrote to Marsh four days after Germany's first use of deadly Gotha bombers to replace Zeppelins in air strikes on London, 'and I always feel most anxious about my people. Yet out here, though often a troublesome consolation, poetry is a great one to me.'[21] Bottomley's intelligent, sympathetic response to any verse he did manage to produce under almost impossible circumstances kept him going, and he was encouraged and stimulated by the poems Bottomley sent him by himself and others. His 'Atlantis', for example, which came to Rosenberg as 'the news of a great victory might come'[22] in May 1917, not only strengthened Rosenberg's belief in the importance of poetry, but also influenced his 'Daughters of War', however slightly.[23]

'I wish I could get back and read your plays,' Rosenberg wrote to Bottomley in late July 1917, 'and if my luck still continues, I shall. Leaves have commenced with us but it may be a good while before I get mine.'[24] One problem the 11th King's Own faced was men overstaying their leave: each time they did so, leave for their fellow soldiers was stopped. Rosenberg noted: 'Leaves are so chancy',[25] but his luck did hold and by mid-September he was on his way home to London.[26]

Apart from helping with a raid on enemy trenches in the Gonnelieu sector, his unit had had a relatively quiet August. The first half of September was a little busier. The 229th Field Company of the Royal Engineers moved to the Gouzeaucourt sector, where it helped excavate a new line in front of Villers-Plouich and began preparations for winter accommodation. And when Rosenberg set off on 14 September on his two-day journey to England, he missed the 229th's busiest night that month as parties of sappers helped an infantry company carry out raids on enemy trenches either side of the Cambrai Road, some of them using Bangalore torpedoes to destroy wire and some mobile charges to blow in dugouts. One officer and two privates were wounded, making the timing of Rosenberg's leave seem even more fortunate.

Reporting first to Brigade Headquarters Rosenberg was given a railway warrant and sent on to the Corps Reinforcement Camp for any outstanding pay to be settled. He also had to report for a bath and a clean set of clothes, and somehow to obtain a chit stating, probably erroneously, that he was free from lice and scabies. Only then could he catch his train to his 'port of embarkation', in his case probably Le Havre, when his ten days' leave officially began. It was a tortuous process, made all the more frustrating by his longing for home. He had started to miss his family almost immediately on arrival in France nearly sixteen months previously, and this yearning intensified over the period, especially once the German bomber raids started at the end of May. He also wanted to see his old friends and to meet two of his new ones, Bottomley and Trevelyan, for the first time. Most ambitiously of all he hoped to use the time to complete his play, by now rechristened *The Unicorn*.

Like many soldiers returning home after prolonged absence abroad, however, Rosenberg found that the reality could not live up to what he had fondly imagined in France. Most soldiers found the gulf between civilian perceptions of the war and their own experience of it unbridgeable, which may explain Rosenberg's own sense of bewilderment. 'I am afraid I can do no writing or reading' he wrote resignedly to Bottomley on 21 September, halfway through his leave.

> I feel so restless and un-anchored. We have lived in such an elemental way so long, things here don't look quite right to me somehow; or it may be the consciousness of my so limited time here for freedom – so little time to do so many things bewilders me.[27]

A big disappointment was not seeing Bottomley, who had been away from home when Rosenberg's letter arrived with news of his leave.

But as he told the older poet, the 'greatest thing' of his leave after seeing his mother was getting Bottomley's letter of explanation:

> I wish I could have seen you, but now I must go on and hope that things will turn out well, and some happy day will give me the chance of meeting you.[28]

That day would never arrive, but it is interesting to see how optimistic Rosenberg could be in the most unpromising circumstances. ('I live in an immense trust that things will turn out well' he had written to Bottomley from the Front two months before.)[29]

Another disappointment was not meeting Trevelyan, also away when news of Rosenberg's leave arrived, the consolation this time being not so much Trevelyan's letter of explanation but the play he enclosed with it, an 'Operatic fable' with the curious title of *The Pterodamozels*, self-published by Trevelyan in 1916. Rosenberg's response to this anti-war tract, in which the Kaiser and the kings of the relevant countries are court-martialled, suggests that his own attitude towards the war was hardening:

> The play is gorgeous, one of the chiefest pleasures of my leave days; and for this I thank you indeed. The ideas are exactly what we all think out there – and the court-martial of the Kaiser and kings etc might have been copied from one of ours. The fun and the seriousness is splendidly managed together and I only wish the thing had the power of its purpose – I suppose it will be in the end through such literature that we will get satisfaction in the end – just as the French Revolution was the culmination of Revolutionary Literature.[30]

He clearly approved wholeheartedly of the main character, Percival's, decision to escape to 'Circe's Island' and his response when asked by his companion, Gigadibs, why not return to Europe:

> PERCIVAL: Home to Hell, you mean.
> What! Back to twentieth-century barbarism,
> Tribunals, churches, trenches, patriotism,
> Daily-Mail government and the Servile State,

Wars of attrition, everything we most hate!
No thank you. No, I've crossed my Rubicon.[31]

Writing to Bottomley five months later, Rosenberg would seem even more convinced of 'how deeply true' Trevelyan's farce was: 'He has the sentiments of most of us out here.'[32]

In an equally revealing letter to Trevelyan about his play, written shortly after he returned to France, Rosenberg described in outline how he had spent his leave:

Your play was all I read at home – I read it in bed – the rest of my time I spent very restlessly – going from one place to another and seeing and talking to as many people as I could.[33]

This uncharacteristic gregariousness had started, according to one of his oldest friends, Joseph Leftwich, even before he reached home.

I was walking along the [Mile End] road when I heard someone running behind me [Leftwich wrote] ... it was Rosenberg in uniform. He had been on a bus going home from the station to see his mother and he had caught sight of me and had jumped off. He looked well and fit. He still looked small and weak, but army life had improved him physically. He was more boisterously happy than I had ever known him before, and he was noisily indignant because he had heard that some people had been saying that he hated the army and wanted to wangle his way out. It was not true, he clamoured. He liked the life and the boys, and he had to fight. He wasn't going to let these people go about spreading rumours that he was funking it.[34]

Leftwich's report suggests that, however critical Rosenberg was becoming of the war, it had made him more outgoing and altogether more confident, a view reinforced by two poems undoubtedly inspired by his return to England as a hardened soldier, 'Girl to Soldier on Leave' and 'Soldier: Twentieth Century'. In both the soldier is referred to as a latter-day offshoot of that ancient race of mighty gods, the Titans, becoming a 'Titan lover' for the girl:

Girl to Soldier on Leave
I love you—Titan lover,
My own storm-days' Titan.
Greater than the son of Zeus.
I know who I would choose.

Titan—my splendid rebel—
The old Prometheus
Wanes like a ghost before your power—
His pangs were joys to yours.

Pallid days arid and wan
Tied your soul fast.
Babel cities' smoky tops
Pressed upon your growth

Weary gyves. What were you,
But a word in the brain's ways,
Or the sleep of Circe's swine.
One gyve holds you yet.—

It held you hiddenly on the Somme
Tied from my heart at home.
O must it loosen now?—I wish
You were bound with the old old gyves.

Love! you love me—your eyes
Have looked through death at mine.
You have tempted a grave too much,
I let you—I repine.[35]

The reference to Prometheus, the Titan who stole fire from Zeus for mankind and was punished with (to quote another poem by Rosenberg) 'unthinkable torture', shows how influential Trevelyan's play had been, since one of its main characters symbolically carries this name as he struggles to defend mankind against the 'tyrants' who have started the war. Rosenberg's allusion to 'Circe's swine' also links his poem to *The Pterodamozels*, suggesting that his 'girl' is part of a conspiracy to encourage young men to go to war.

Yet the 'soldier', apparently in response to the 'girl', also compares himself to great warriors of the past:

Soldier: Twentieth Century
I love you, great new Titan!
Am I not you?
Napoleon and Caesar
Out of you grew.

Out of unthinkable torture,
Eyes kissed by death,
Won back to the world again,
Lost and won in a breath,

Cruel men are made immortal.
Out of your pain born.
They have stolen the sun's power
With their feet on your shoulders worn.

Let them shrink from your girth,
That has outgrown the pallid days,
When you slept like Circe's swine,
Or a word in the brain's ways.[36]

If, as seems likely, this poem reflects Rosenberg's own mood during his leave, it suggests (as Leftwich's account also does) an ambivalence in his attitude towards being a soldier. Despite the sufferings, his life in France appears to have made his previous existence seem 'pallid' (to quote the 'girl') and unexciting ('when you slept like Circe's swine'). As Sorley had written of his time in the army, and despite his consistent criticism of the war, 'But this has freed the spirit, glory be.'[37] At some level Rosenberg may have felt sorry for those young men left behind in England, though he was anxious to see a number of them.

Leftwich, whose Dutch nationality exempted him from military service, was one of the few close friends Rosenberg did manage to see. Bomberg was still in France, Rodker in a penal settlement for Conscientious Objectors, and Winsten also in prison for refusing to fight. He may have seen Sonia, since he refers to learning of Rodker's fate through 'friends of his', and he definitely saw Marsh, just back on 18 September from a trip to the Front with Churchill. But Schiff was also away when Rosenberg called at his house, sending a pound for him to spend as compensation.

It was probably in the hope of seeing *someone* he knew that Rosenberg visited the Slade, Bolt Court School of Art and the Café Royal, where he finally bumped into a friend, Lazarus Aaronson. Aaronson was sitting at a table near the door with Jacob ('Jack') Isaacs, a future Professor of English Literature at Queen Mary College, University of London, and also on leave.[38] Aaronson remembered Rosenberg coming in 'suddenly' in a 'bowler hat [and] a large brown suit' (both borrowed for the occasion from the family wardrobe), looking like 'a bookie's runner'.[39] Like Rosenberg, both Aaronson and Isaacs were aspiring poets, and Isaacs showed Rosenberg his most recent efforts. Rosenberg, in turn, showed them a typescript of 'Dead Man's Dump' and discussed his plans for *The Unicorn*. He was carrying some copies of his previous publications, presumably in the hope of meeting someone influential, or at least interested, and proudly presented Isaacs with *Moses* and *Youth* (signed 'From the Youth') and Aaronson, who may already have possessed *Youth*, with *Moses*.[40] The meeting was brief, since Rosenberg said he had an appointment but it evidently made an impression on him: 'I know Isaacs, who I like – but his poetry didn't appear to me much good' he would write to Leftwich a few months later.[41] Then, in an afterthought which underlined his distracted state of mind during his leave, 'but then, when he showed it to me I was on leave and poetry was quite out of my line then'. He did no work on his play and wrote no other verse, though he may have drafted 'Girl to Soldier on Leave' and 'Soldier: Twentieth Century'.

Rosenberg had been deprived of reading material at the Front for months on end, yet faced with a plentiful supply of it he read little apart from Trevelyan's play. He attended the theatre once, possibly with fellow Tommies, possibly with his youngest brother, now also in the army but home on leave. Having 'nearly got turned out for giving expression to our feelings about it', however, 'we have been to no more [plays]', he told Bottomley.[42] He just missed the publication of *Georgian Poetry 1916–1917*, which appeared at the end of September shortly after he was obliged to return to France.

Before he did so his family were able to organize studio photographs of him with Elkon. Several were taken in army uniform, but in at least one he is again wearing the family suit and hat. Elkon, nine years younger, is the taller, more dashing of the two, and looks protective of his older, shyer-looking brother, his arm round him in the photograph where they are both standing, and resting proprietorially on his shoulder in the other two.

It was not long after this, probably on 28 September 1917, since he had missed, deliberately or otherwise, 'about three days' trains',[43] that Rosenberg said goodbye to his family and friends, the last time they would ever see him.

Chapter 21

'When Will We Go On With the Things That Endure?'

October–December 1917

But God's unthinkable imagination
Invents new tortures for nature
Whose wisdom falters here.
No used experience can break, make aware
The imminent unknowable.
Sudden destruction
Till the stricken soul wails in anguish
Torn here and there.[1]

Rosenberg had arrived in England looking 'fit and well', according to Leftwich, and ten days of being pampered by his mother could only have strengthened him further. Yet less than a fortnight after getting back to France he contracted a 'flu severe enough to put him in hospital and keep him there for over two months. This apparent misfortune, brought on by the return of colder, wetter weather, turned out to be, as he recognized, another example of how 'lucky'[2] he had been in France thus far, since it was during this period that his Division fought its worst engagement of the war, the battle of Cambrai. He was still attached to the Royal Engineers when he entered the hospital on about 10 October,[3] but had almost certainly been transferred back to his battalion by the time the battle started, since the 11th King's Own had been assigned one of the toughest areas of attack, Bourlon Wood, and needed every soldier possible.

Having been relieved in mid-October after six months in the line near Cambrai, the 40th Division had returned to the Front on 16

November, a few days before the infamous battle of Cambrai began. It was a move planned for a number of reasons. Towards the end of 1917, the so-called Year of Victory, the Allies seemed no nearer success than at its hopeful beginning. To the east, Russia, in the throes of revolution, had not only collapsed but defected, there was a virtual stalemate in Macedonia, and Romania was cut off from the Allies. This had allowed Germany to continue transferring troops from the Eastern Front, worsening an already grave situation on the Western Front. In the south the Italians had been defeated by the Germans, while in the north the British and French had been forced to abandon their attack on Flanders, mainly because of persistently bad weather.

Despite the mud, however, the third battle of Ypres had not been entirely unsuccessful. Apart from shaking German morale, it had compelled the enemy to transfer large forces to Flanders from other sectors of the line, relieving pressure on a badly demoralized French army. Haig, still in command despite enormous losses both at Arras and Ypres, planned to exploit this partial success by delivering a sudden blow at another sector of the Front but one where – with the mud of Flanders still fresh in his mind, no doubt – it would be dry enough to use the newly developed tanks for the first time in significant numbers. By choosing the sector opposite Cambrai he hoped to break the Hindenburg Line at a strategic point.

The breakthrough was, in fact, achieved in the first two days of the operation, which opened on 20 November, leaving the British in possession of the whole of the Flesquières Ridge and the ground up to Bourlon Wood. When the plans were formulated the 40th Division was allotted the task of capturing Bourlon Wood, a key position. Rosenberg's A Company of the 11th King's Own, according to the Divisional report, carried out 'exceptionally brilliant work' there[4] and ten non-commissioned officers and men in the battalion were awarded the Military Medal for their gallantry. But A Company alone lost 50 per cent of those who went into action. Rosenberg was indeed 'lucky' not to have been there. While he celebrated his twenty-seventh birthday on 25 November from the safety of his hospital bed, his battalion was being massacred at Bourlon Wood. (He would probably have fared no better had he stayed with the

Royal Engineers, who were amongst the last to retire from the Wood amid heavy fighting.) The 11th King's Own casualties this month were nine times higher than in the month Rosenberg had returned from England.[5] Overall casualties in the 40th Division amounted to a massive 3,363, with another 700 or 800 men taken prisoner.[6]

Rosenberg could hardly have failed to be conscious of the battle of Cambrai and its dire consequences, since casualties from it started flooding into his hospital in late November, during the last two or three weeks of his stay. So that it was no doubt with a full appreciation of his good fortune that he wrote in his letter to Leftwich on 8 December: 'I got out of this late stunt by being here.'[7] His brother Dave, now in the army like Elkon, had not been quite so fortunate. His tank unit had been in the surprise attack at Cambrai, where he was wounded in the leg. Like Isaac he was now in hospital, as too was their 'wilder' brother Elkon, serving with the South African Heavy Artillery.[8] Having all three sons safely in hospital allowed an anxious Mrs Rosenberg at least a short respite from her constant anxiety.

Rosenberg was doubly lucky in being well enough to read and write. He thanked Trevelyan quite early in his stay for another of his recent publications, a translation of the Roman philosopher-poet Lucretius, which Trevelyan had sent via Annie. It is not difficult to understand why *Lucretius on Death*, as Trevelyan called his selection from Book III of the poet's *De rerum natura*, should have appealed to Rosenberg in a hospital ward on the Western Front, though it is surprising at first to find him preferring the Roman's views to Shakespeare's on the same subject. In *De rerum natura*, an examination of the Epicurean philosophy in six books of verse hexameters, Lucretius attempts to deal with his contemporaries' superstition, their anxieties about death in particular, to which he devotes the greater part of Book III. Arguing that popular religion and the terrors introduced by it have no foundation, Lucretius insists that the soul dies with death. Since Man alone in Nature has free will, he argues, he must reject the foolish fear of death. 'It is a noble poem . . .' Rosenberg wrote appreciatively to Trevelyan shortly after reading it in late October. 'Hamlet's enquiring nature so mixed with theology, superstition, penetration, may be more human and general – But Lucretius as a mood, definite, is fine, proud philosophy. ... I got deep pleasure from it.'[9]

These remarks are proof, if nothing else, of Rosenberg's understandable preoccupation with death in France. It may have been with this in mind that he had chosen to take back with him from England another of Shakespeare's tragedies, *Macbeth*, though the additional choice of his comedies makes it more likely that he was simply taking the plays he had not yet read. He was certainly conscious of Shakespeare's apparent belief in an afterlife, reflected so memorably in Hamlet's speech 'To be or not to be', since his letter to Trevelyan ends:

And that old hawker of immortality how glad one feels, he is not a witness of these terrible times – he would only have been flung into this terrible distruction [*sic*], like the rest of us. Anyway we all hope it'll all end well.[10]

Rosenberg's selection of reading matter on his return to France had had to be very careful, given conditions at the Front, which makes his choice of a book by H.G. Wells highly significant. Not an avid fan of the popular novelist, he must have had a particular reason for reading him in such circumstances. Wells's most recent book, *Mr Britling Sees It Through* (1916), had revealed his growing criticism of a war he had initially approved in *The War That Will Endure* (1914). Rosenberg's responsiveness to Trevelyan's anti-war play a few months earlier suggests that he would have agreed with Wells's analysis of the situation by late 1917:

Everywhere cunning, everywhere small feuds and hatreds, distrusts, dishonesties, timidities, feebleness of purpose, dwarfish imaginations, swarm over the great and simple issues ... It is a war now like any other of the mobbing, many aimed cataclysms that have shattered empires and devastated the world; it is a war without point, a war that has lost its soul, it has become mere incoherent fighting and destruction, a demonstration in vast and tragic forms of the stupidity and ineffectiveness of our species.[11]

Sassoon, who had read *Mr Britling Sees It Through* almost a year earlier than Rosenberg, had been strongly influenced by it, as his poetry of 1917 shows. But it was not until both he and Rosenberg were in hospital escaping some of the worst of the fighting – Sassoon at Craiglockhart Hospital for Nervous Diseases for his public protest against the war – that Rosenberg had the chance to study Sassoon's poetry, which may have strengthened his own hardening attitude towards the war. Marsh's *Georgian Poetry 1916–1917*, which Rosenberg finally read in December, included eight poems by Sassoon, as well as Rosenberg's speech from *Moses*. Rather surprisingly, since Marsh was still a staunch supporter of the war, two of the Sassoon selection were forceful anti-war satires, 'They' and 'In the Pink'. On first reading 'They', a bitter attack on the complacency and inadequacy of the Church which ends with the Bishop's platitudinous response to the horrific injuries of ordinary soldiers, 'The ways of God are strange', Marsh had exclaimed: 'It's *too* horrible.' But as Rosenberg realized on reading it himself in France, 'Sassoon has power.'[12]

Sassoon's recognition of Rosenberg's genius would come a great deal later, in 1937, when he was flattered to be asked to write a foreword to Bottomley and Harding's *Complete Works*. He might not have been quite so pleased if he had known that he was the publisher's third choice, after both Eliot and Yeats had declined. Eliot, a director at Faber & Faber, had pleaded a conflict of interest, and Yeats, whose dismissal of war poetry is now well known, had refused because he found Rosenberg's verse 'all windy rhetoric'.[13] Sassoon had no reservations about Rosenberg's poetry, 'admir[ing] it greatly', despite his profound dislike of most Modernist verse. It was perhaps because it was so different from his own more traditional work that he found it 'not at all easy to write about', however, and in the event his piece would be more or less composed for him by Harding, who supplied among many other things Sassoon's often quoted phrase describing Rosenberg as 'a fruitful fusion between English and Hebrew culture'.[14]

Sassoon had got to know Marsh the same year as Rosenberg, but never met the younger poet, though he had just moved into Raymond Buildings, Gray's Inn, when Rosenberg breakfasted there with Marsh on 8 May 1914 before leaving for South Africa. On paper they shared a great deal: their Jewish blood, their dual interest in art and literature, their enlistment in the army and their need to write war poetry. Whereas Sassoon saw the war and its conduct in terms of a dishonest or cowardly establishment, however, Rosenberg had a more transcendental vision of it as the product of 'an ambitious and unscrupulous will'.[15] There was also a wide gulf between them in terms of class and education, which may explain why the highly class-conscious Marsh never introduced his equally snobbish neighbour to Rosenberg. And their very different approach to poetic technique almost certainly accounts for Sassoon's apparent lack of interest in Rosenberg's work while he was alive.

One thing Sassoon would have identified with in Rosenberg, however, was the fierce determination of the committed artist. Just as Sassoon, encouraged and helped by an admiring Owen, used his stay at Craiglockhart in late 1917 to write poetry – at the same time, incidentally, helping Owen to perfect one of his greatest works, 'Anthem for Doomed Youth' – so Rosenberg put his time at the 51st General Hospital to creative use.

In his first letter home from hospital, to reassure his ever-anxious family after more than a week's silence, he asked for watercolours. 'He wants to do a little painting,' his sister reported to Trevelyan in mid-October, 'a thing he hasn't had the chance to do for months.'[16] His fellow patients again provided captive models for him but, as at Bury St Edmunds, he was obliged either to give any portraits he completed to the sitters, or to abandon them on leaving hospital, and none is known to have survived.

His poetry is a different matter. 'I can only hope for hospital or the end of the war if I want to write' he would tell his fellow poet Rodker a few months after leaving it.[17] He wrote at least two new poems during his stay, 'Girl to Soldier on Leave' and 'Soldier: Twentieth Century', and, after hearing of an incident in which a fellow soldier in a burial party discovered that the corpse was his own brother, completed 'In War': 'it's sad enough I know,' he told Bottomley, 'but one can hardly write a war poem and be anything else.'[18] The equally 'sad' – and equally melodramatic – 'The Dying Soldier' may have been written at the same time.[19]

Though he described his war poems as 'absurd' in comparison

with Whitman's, he was feeling positive enough to persist with his idea of a small collection of them – 'as I think mine may give some new aspects to people at home' he wrote to Leftwich in his December letter – 'and then one never knows whether you'll get a tap on the head or not; and if that happens – all you have written is lost, unless you have secured them by printing.'

Despite the jokey euphemism, death was very much on his mind in a hospital filled with the heavy casualties of Bourlon Wood. In his determination to leave something worthy behind him he started work again on his play *The Unicorn*, into which he planned to put 'all my innermost experiences'.[20] He had been working on it since the summer and managed to add 'some bits' to it in hospital.[21] But he had been planning it in one form or another, as already indicated, since completing *Moses* in May 1916. Bottomley, whose own love of myth and legend had led him to explore ancient Britain in his verse play *King Lear's Wife*, for example, believed that (as Eliot was to imply in 1953) Rosenberg's Jewish heritage gave him access to 'a whole host of . . . gorgeous subjects which are your birthright'.[22] Only a month after the publication of *Moses* he had started directing Rosenberg towards that 'great field still almost untouched in the Old Testament stories', arguing that 'the right way of handling them has scarcely been found yet in English poetry'.[23]

It was undoubtedly in response to Bottomley's suggestion that Rosenberg continued with his plans to write something on a Jewish theme. His play on the great Jewish warrior Judas Maccabeus had not materialized and *Adam and Lilith* had also been abandoned, though the name 'Lilith' for the female character had been retained for his third attempt, *The Amulet*, a story of his own invention which freed him from the need for biblical or historical knowledge. Though Lilith's name is kept, she is no longer a figure from myth or legend but, together with her husband, Saul, an ordinary person into whose world an extraordinary force has burst. The setting, with its reference to pomegranates, figs and sherbet, is still vaguely biblical, but no attempt is made at 'truth of period', about which Rosenberg could not decide whether it was 'a good quality or a negative one'.[24]

The story opens with Saul sleeping off his exhaustion after being stuck in what sounds very like the mud of the Western Front, as I have suggested. The episode already quoted, where he is rescued by a large black stranger (echoes of South Africa, perhaps), known simply and generically as 'Nubian', not only allows Rosenberg to draw the parallels with the Great War that he aimed at, but also provides what there is of the plot: Lilith, whose husband has lost interest in her sexually, is magnetized by the powerful Nubian, whose jade amulet possesses magical qualities that may restore Saul's love for her. The play ends abruptly with her child, Amak, destroying the scrolls contained in the amulet (and with them its power) and the Nubian expressing his own attraction to Lilith, in words that hint at Rosenberg's own sexual starvation on the Western Front:

> What is this ecstasy in form,
> This lightning
> That found the lightning in my blood,
> Searing my spirit's lips?
> Aghast and naked
> I am flung in the abyss of days
> And the void is filled with rushing sound
> From pent eternities.
> I am strewn as the cypher is strewn.
> A woman—a soft woman![25]

The Amulet, too, was abandoned, however, perhaps because the closest parallels with its plot, which centres on sexual infatuation and frustration, were not with the war but with Rosenberg's personal life. Knowing of Rodker's lack of sexual interest in Sonia after she became pregnant, he may have hoped (like the Nubian) to restore the love of his two closest friends. At the same time he was almost certainly still attracted to Sonia himself, like the Nubian to Lilith, and possibly still hoping that she might return his love.

His final attempt at the play, The Unicorn, bears out this biographical interpretation, whilst also strengthening the plot. For the child has now disappeared from the cast list, just as Sonia's daughter had when she was sent to a children's home at the age of one. Saul and Lilith still feature, but 'Nubian' has been replaced by another huge black figure, also possessed of supernatural powers, Tel, and the Nubian's magical amulet by another feature from myth and fairy tale, a unicorn. 'I believe I have a good idea at bottom,' Rosenberg wrote to Marsh at the end of May 1917:

> It's a kind of 'Rape of the Sabine Women' idea. Some strange race of wanderers have settled in some wild place and are perishing out for lack of women. The prince of these explores some country near where the women are most fair. But the natives will not hear of foreign marriages and he plots another rape of the Sabines, but he is trapped in the act.[26]

Rosenberg had at one stage thought of having the story of the decaying race told in a myth read by Lilith, but wisely decided against it: his final choice has far greater immediacy. The plot now starts, more dramatically, in the middle of the action, with Saul being rescued from the mud by Tel, and its already strong sexual overtones are strengthened by the replacement of the jade amulet with the equally magical but more phallic symbol of the unicorn, its importance highlighted by being made the title of the play.

The unicorn is a highly ambiguous creature, reflecting perhaps Rosenberg's own ambivalence about war and 'all the devastating forces let loose by an ambitious and unscrupulous will'. Like Tel, there is something magnificent yet terrifying about this weird, white, one-horned creature, which serves as a symbol of both sexuality and sterility. In one version of the play Tel calls the unicorn, which serves his sexual needs in the absence of women, 'my eyes' love', adding: 'But you are barren.'[27] And Saul asks, in terror: 'Is the beast the figure of man's mateless soul / The dread and want of woman?' While the unicorn's whiteness suggests purity, its participation in the capture and rape of women implies supreme evil. It is, above all, a super-natural force disrupting, like the war (an equally sterile entity), the lives of ordinary people, as Rosenberg explained to Marsh in June 1917:

> The most difficult part I shrink from; I think even Shakespeare might: – the first time Tel, the chief of the decaying race, sees a woman (who is Lilith, Saul's wife), and he is called upon to talk. Saul

and Lilith are ordinary folk into whose ordinary lives the Unicorn bursts. It is to be a play of terror – terror or of hidden things and the fear of the supernatural.[28]

Unfortunately there is no record of Marsh's reaction when he read of Rosenberg's curious new addition and his implied comparison of himself with Shakespeare; having found the relatively restrained plot of *Moses* 'outlandish', he would certainly have had problems with *The Unicorn*, especially in its final form which Rosenberg had arrived at by late July. Rosenberg has now worked out the end of his curious plot, as he tells Bottomley. After Tel's rescue of Saul, the action will focus on Lilith, who is 'in great consternation, having seen the Unicorn and knowing the legend of this race of men':

> Afterwards a host of blacks on horses, like centaurs and buffaloes, come rushing up, the Unicorn in front. On every horse is clasped a woman. Lilith faints, Saul stabs himself, the Chief places Lilith on the Unicorn, and they all race away.[29]

Even Bottomley, 'always ready to meet a poet halfway', was puzzled. 'Who is Saul?' he asked. 'What is his relationship to the decaying race? Why has he a woman when they have none? Who are the blacks? Are they the same as the decaying race? Why does Saul kill himself?'[30]

It was probably an attempt to resolve these obscurities that kept Rosenberg busy on his play in hospital in late 1917. If so, it made little difference to the plot, which remains among the most bizarre of First World War works, though based just as firmly on a first-hand experience of war as the best of them are. But as students of Shakespeare know, particularly those who read his comedies (as Rosenberg was doing), plots do not have to be probable to be effective.

They do, however, have to work dramatically and allow the writer to explore important themes, and this is exactly what Rosenberg's parable achieves. Thematically it is richer than almost any other work of the period, partly because it is not overtly about war and is set in the context of wider questions that preoccupied Rosenberg throughout his writing life. Many of its themes have clear parallels with life on the Western Front while remaining universally applicable. The plot itself, however far-fetched, underlines, for instance, the destruction of a civilization, already briefly explored by Rosenberg the previous autumn in 'The Destruction of Jerusalem by the Babylonian Hordes' and encapsulated in the rape metaphor.

Another parallel theme is that of suffering and hardship endured, as by the troops in France. It is significant that the passage which expresses this most powerfully – Saul's reaction to the threat posed by Tel and his ravaging men (quoted at the head of this chapter) – was prefaced in one fragment with the words 'Yea I a soldier, say I have not suffered at all before / If this is suffering / A mother watching her son die, a soldier / With thews used, blasphemies . . .'[31]

The longing and needs of a race of womenless men, who satisfy their sexual cravings as best they can, are also highly reminiscent of soldiers in war, though few if any First World War poets apart from Rosenberg explored the theme:

> Behind impassable places
> Whose air was never warmed by a woman's lips,
> Bestial man-shapes ride dark impulses
> Through roots in the bleak blood, then hide
> In shuddering light from their self-loathing.
> They fade in arid light—
> Beings unnatured by their cravings, for they know
> Obliteration's spectre. They are few.
> They wail their souls for continuity,
> And bow their heads and knock their breasts before
> The many mummies whose wail in dust is more
> Than these who cry, their brothers who loiter yet.
> Great beasts' and small beasts' eyes have place
> As eyes of women to their hopeless eyes
> That hunt in bleakness for the dread might
> The incarnate female soul of generation.[32]

Any doubts that the play's themes relate to Rosenberg's experiences in France vanish when we learn that he had at one stage intended 'to open [it] with [T]he [T]ower of [Sk]ulls', a poem probably drafted, possibly completed during his hospital stay.[33] Spoken by an 'ancient hermaphrodite', its opening stanzas could be a description of a French battlefield in 1917 viewed by a horrified Rosenberg:

> These layers of piled-up skulls,
> These layers of gleaming horror—stark horror!
> Ah me! Through my thin hands they touch my eyes.
>
> Everywhere, everywhere is a pregnant birth,
> And here in death's land is a pregnant birth.
> Your own crying is less mortal
> Than the amazing soul in your body.[34]

The bleakness of the hermaphrodite's vision here, together with Tel's despair and his pronounced awareness of his own and his race's sterility without women to carry it on, enables Rosenberg to explore themes that reach beyond the war itself to more universal situations. In particular he examines the role of women, as 'the incarnate female soul of generation', and their power for both good and evil. Though these are themes he has explored before, in this context they are given more coherence in the enigmatic person of Lilith. Both an ordinary woman and a figure whose name links her to the female demon of Jewish folklore, she is as ambiguous as Tel and the Unicorn, reflecting her dual role as both the creator and destroyer of men. The description of her beauty, borrowed in part perhaps from Rossetti's poem of that name, the healing power of the music she plays to calm Tel and the link between the two underline the strength of Rosenberg's lifelong belief in beauty and art:

> LILITH: Beauty is music's secret soul
> Creeping about man's senses.
> He cannot hold it or know it ever,
> But yearns and yearns to hold it once. (ll. 147–150)[35]

Phrases, often whole lines are repeated from earlier explorations of similar themes, adding new layers of meaning to Rosenberg's heroic attempt to symbolize the war in terms of his own vision of it. Lilith's face, for example, 'flashes' upon Tel's consciousness 'Like heights of night ringing with unseen larks / Or blindness dim with dreams' (ii. 176–7), ambiguous words to express the double-sidedness of beauty and only slightly adapted from 'Returning, We Hear the Larks', where the joy of the soldiers in the beautiful birdsong could so easily have been terror at shells dropping from the sky.

Rosenberg regarded the version of *The Unicorn* that has come down to us as a 'sketch' only and was planning, among other things, to extend its one act to four.[36] But as Denys Harding, who edited it (with some difficulty) for the 1937 *Complete Works*, observed, *The Unicorn* and the many fragments that surround it are 'fascinating for their glimpses of creative writing in progress and for the astonishingly high quality of work done in seemingly impossible circumstances'.[37] For all its incompleteness, this last great work is a distillation of all Rosenberg's experience both as a man and as a poet.

Chapter 22

'Through These Pale Cold Days'

January–1 April 1918

What is happening to me now is more tragic than the 'passion play' [Rosenberg wrote to Marsh in January 1918]. Christ never endured what I endure. It is breaking me completely.[1]

'Wherever he was it wasn't the right place'[2] one of Rosenberg's relatives recalled of his visit to South Africa, a charge that held true in general.[3] But for understandable reasons he was grateful to be in hospital between October and December 1917. Once back in the line with the 11th King's Own at the beginning of January 1918 he felt quite differently, and for equally comprehensible reasons. 'I am back in the trenches which are terrible now' he wrote to Marsh towards the end of the month. 'We spend most of our time pulling each other out of the mud. I am not fit at all now and am more in the way than any use.'[4] His claim, in the same letter, to be suffering more than Christ on the Cross (which was censored) shows just how desperate he felt. Having managed, despite occasional lapses, to remain optimistic throughout his twenty months in France, he now finally felt destroyed both in body and mind.

The weather had been almost as bad as his first winter in France, with a snow blizzard concluding his first tour of trenches in the La Fontaine region near Bullecourt from 6 to 8 January, to be followed by thick mud as a thaw, then heavy rain set in. Only a grimly realistic description by Balzac, Rosenberg told the francophile Rodker, 'could give you the huge and terrible sensation of sinking in the mud'.[5]

A great deal has been written about the demoralizing effect of mud on soldiers at the Western Front, the most graphic perhaps the observation of a French soldier in March 1917: 'men die of mud, as they die from bullets, but more horribly. Mud is where men sink and – what is worse – where their soul sinks.'[6] This process in Rosenberg's case was fairly rapid once it started. He had managed to 'keep cheerful . . . in the face of the most horrible things' until the second half of 1917, a result he believed of being kept busy and having 'no time to brood'.[7] But that had been written while he still felt able to compose the occasional verse. Now, at the beginning of 1918, he began to lose his creative energy and with it his optimism.

His despair, however rationally he explained it, appears slightly puzzling at first sight. By comparison with other areas of the Western Front at the beginning of 1918, his circumstances were relatively mild, certainly no worse than other periods he had experienced in the trenches. He had spent January in the normal trench routine: four days in the front line, four in support and four in reserve; a bath and change of clothes when available, musketry practice and a few battalion parades. The 11th King's Own saw very little fighting beyond the usual daily bombardment on both sides and an occasional raid, with only four wounded recorded by the Battalion diary for the whole month. Then from early February to mid-March he was first in reserve then 'resting' behind the lines.

By this stage in the war, however, it was not 'rest' in any real sense of the word, and Rosenberg appears to have found this period, if anything, more demoralizing than his month in the trenches. It certainly does not seem to have given him the opportunity to recuperate physically or emotionally, as the term suggests. His routine now included just as much manual work, but without the adrenalin-rush of front-line action. Carrying heavy loads of supplies up to the line, clearing roads, preparing defences and moving ammunition were just some of the tasks involved. (Many soldiers claimed that they were worked more during this 'rest' than when they manned the firing line.) Despite Rosenberg's complaint about his physical condition to Marsh in January, by February it was not that which concerned him most. Like Richard Aldington's Winterbourne in *Death of a Hero*, he began to feel that the effect of 'long hours of manual labour under strict discipline must inevitably degrade a man's intelligence', and to find himself 'less and less able to enjoy subtleties of beauty and anything intellectually abstruse'.[8]

Rosenberg's own depression emerges starkly in a series of letters written during this so-called 'rest' period. 'You must know by now what a rest behind the lines means' he wrote to his faithful correspondent Miss Seaton in mid-February:

> I can call the evenings – that is, from tea to lights out – my own; but there is no chance whatever for seclusion or any hope of writing poetry now. Sometimes I give way and am appalled at the devastation this life seems to have made in my nature. It seems to have blunted me. I seem to be powerless to compel my will to any direction, and all I do is without energy and interest.[9]

Nine days later he was telling Rodker that 'after a day's dull stupefying labour – I feel stupefied' and asking him, with no real hope of a satisfactory answer, 'When will we go on with the things that endure?'[10] And in his most despairing letter of all he confesses to Bottomley at this time:

> since I left the hospital all the poetry has gone quite out of me. I seem even to forget words, and I believe if I met anybody with ideas I'd be dumb. No drug could be more stupefying than our work (to me anyway), and this goes on like that old torture of water trickling, drop by drop unendingly, on one's helplessness.[11]

It was in one such tortured state of mind that he had made his first attempt to get a transfer to the recently formed Jewish Battalion.[12] Destined for the hot, dry lands of the Middle East and manned mainly by Russian Jews, the Judeans, as they were otherwise known, seemed a natural choice for someone who not only believed that he was discriminated against as a Jew in the army, but also feared, above most things, the wet, cold winters of Northern France. Inspired partly by the Zion Mule Corps of the 1915 Gallipoli Campaign, which had been made up of Jewish refugees only too ready to fight the Turks, and commanded by the Russian-Jewish Zionist Vladimir Jabotinsky, the Jewish Battalion had encountered stiff resistance to its formation. Both the English and the assimilated Jews wanted integration not separation. But by November 1917, after Russia's withdrawal from the war had removed the last obstacle to enlisting for many Jews, it was in active formation. (Officially designated the 38th, 39th and 40th Battalions of the Royal Fusiliers, it would be known unofficially as the '999th Kosher Kitchen-ers' or 'Sheenies'.)

By the end of February 1918, when Rosenberg was planning his second application to join it, the Jewish Battalion would be on its way to Palestine, as would the half-Jewish Sassoon, who encountered it in a transit camp at Taranto. While for him the journey would be a reminder of his father's roots, for most members of the Battalion it was an affirmation of their Jewishness, possibly their Zionism. Whether this was true of Rosenberg is impossible to say, since he may simply have wanted to escape the trenches of the Western Front. But he followed the Judeans' movements with interest and planned to write 'a battle song' for them. If by doing so he hoped to ingratiate himself with them, however, he was disappointed, his application (if it ever reached them)[13] apparently ignored.

Rosenberg followed the Battalion's movements hopefully throughout the early months of 1918 – 'I think they are now in Mesopotamia' he wrote to Bottomley in March.[14] Several of his friends were with it, the sculptor Jacob Epstein among them, but he was to be disappointed. His family were even more so, since they had pressed him to apply in the first place, believing rightly that Palestine was a less dangerous theatre of war and that a transfer there would increase his chances of survival. Instead, and despite Marsh's usual efforts on his behalf,[15] Rosenberg not only remained in France but was transferred to a unit that saw some of the worst fighting of early 1918.

At first it seemed as if Rosenberg's transfer from the 11th King's Own on 7 February 1918 might do him good, since it brought him his prolonged 'rest' behind the lines. The most prestigious of the Regiment's battalions, and one of the first units to travel to France at the outbreak of war, it was very different from the Bantams. It had seen action at Le Cateau and proved itself an effective fighting machine, though at a great cost. The merger had been ordered by the Army Council which, owing to a severe shortage of men, had been forced to reduce the number of battalions in a division from twelve to nine. The 11th King's Own, already heavily depleted by its losses at Bourlon Wood, was chosen for disbandment because it came from a district where it was impossible to 'comb out' more men.[16]

So on 7 February, about a month after rejoining his battalion in the 40th Division, Rosenberg found himself travelling north to Bernaville to join a new unit, the 1st King's Own, and a quite different division, the 4th. The move away from the few friends he had made in the 11th King's Own clearly upset him. 'Things happen so suddenly here' he complained to Rodker after three or four weeks with his new battalion, 'that really nothing is unexpected . . .'[17] This unsettling change counteracted any potential benefits of a month behind the lines. And as February drew to its end, talk of a great German offensive made it even more difficult to concentrate on 'the things that endure'. His thoughts were now mainly on the coming battle and his own possible end. 'I believe our interlude is nearly over, and we may go up the line any moment now . . .' he told Bottomley in the first week of March. 'If only this war were over our eyes would not be on death so much: it seems to underlie even our underthoughts.'[18]

The poem Rosenberg included in this letter, 'The Burning of the Temple', the only work apart from a little sketching that he had managed to produce during his 'rest', supports his claim that his thoughts were constantly on death. They were also, as his application to the Judeans indicates, increasingly on Jewishness, as his own identity was threatened with extinction. The anti-Semitism he had detected on joining the army had started the process, making him not only more conscious of his Jewishness but prouder of it, as his response in 'The Jew' shows. This may have been one reason he had tried to follow Bottomley's advice and concentrated on Jewish material in his subsequent dramatic efforts. His early Zionism, sub-merged throughout his adult life, had resurfaced in poems such as 'The Destruction of Jerusalem by the Babylonian Hordes', written in autumn 1916, and now, in February 1918, in 'The Burning of the Temple'. His consciousness of his racial heritage emerges in his description of the carnage he is witnessing in France in terms of the vanished glory of the Jewish nation in its days of greatness under King Solomon, whose magnificent temple had been burnt down four hundred years later by the marauding Babylonians. The flames of the burning temple become the ferocious artillery fire of France,

as the poet appeals to Solomon, the wisest of men, to explain to him
the destruction he is seeing:

> Fierce wrath of Solomon
> Where sleepest thou? O see
> The fabric which thou won
> Earth and ocean to give thee—
> O look at the red skies.

> Or hath the sun plunged down?
> What is this molten gold——
> These thundering fires blown
> Through heaven—where the smoke rolled[19]

In the poem's closing lines, however, it is a prescience of his own
imminent demise that dominates, though still expressed through the
story of King Solomon's 'end' as his great legacy is destroyed:

> Again the great king dies.

> His dreams go out in smoke,
> His days he let not pass
> And sculptured here are broke
> Are charred as the burnt grass
> Gone as his mouth's last sighs.

Rosenberg, along with the rest of his division, had been aware of
the Germans' plan for a great spring offensive for several weeks
when he sent 'The Burning of the Temple' to Bottomley at the
beginning of March 1918. His (4th) division had been in reserve
since the end of February, though prepared to be called back to
the line at a moment's notice. His former Captain, Frank Waley,
who claimed that he could have helped Rosenberg to transfer to
the Jewish Battalion if he had asked him earlier – Waley had been
approached to serve in it himself – implied that Rosenberg's
unsuccessful application had been due to precisely this crisis:

'obviously no one would have been allowed to leave France just before the Boche attack.'[20]

Though the first half of March was unexpectedly sunny and warm, Rosenberg's pessimism persisted: 'but I dread the wet weather, which is keeping off while we are out, and, I fear, saving itself up for us' he wrote to Winifreda Seaton on 8 March,[21] then added, revealing how constantly his thoughts were on death: 'We will become like mummies – look warm and lifelike, but a touch and we crumble to pieces.' The anticipated attack was widely discussed and predicted to take place on 13 March, with the 1st King's Own moved south from Bernaville to a position a few miles east of Arras on 11 March in anticipation. Apart from a preliminary series of bombardments between Ypres and St Quentin, however, the full attack did not start until almost a week after expected. Many of the soldiers played off rounds in football competitions while they waited, but Rosenberg spent the interval writing to family and friends and almost certainly planning if not writing his last poem, 'Through These Pale Cold Days'.

All these activities were brought to an abrupt end for the 1st King's Own on 19 March, when they were moved into the line at the Greenland Hill sector near Arras. Two days later, further south on the Somme, heavy firing from the enemy's big guns and the shelling of all back areas alerted the Allies that the great German offensive of spring 1918 had begun.

General Erich von Ludendorff had launched this massive attack in the hope of winning the war with one decisive battle. The British army's shortage of trained men by January 1918 and the further weakening of its right flank to help the French were two good reasons for its selection as the main target. The defection of Russia in the autumn of 1917 and its signing of the Brest-Litovsk Treaty on 3 March 1918 had enabled the Germans to transfer yet more troops from the East to the Western Front, as Rosenberg was well aware. Conscious of his mother's natural anxiety about their Jewish relatives still living in Russia, and hoping that 'our Russian cousins are happy now', he tried to reassure her: 'Trotsky, I imagine, will look after the interests of his co-religionists.'[22] He rightly regarded Russia as 'an amputated limb' to the Allies' cause,[23] but wrongly thought of

Self-portrait sketch from the trenches, c. 1917 (*Imperial War Museum*)

America, who had entered the war in mid-1917 but were still training troops for it, as 'the cork substitute'.[24] The Germans, more wisely, saw the Americans as an enormous potential threat and wanted to strike before they restored the balance of power in the Allies' favour.

The Germans' main attack, directed against the British Fifth and Third Armies on the Arras–St Quentin front, helped by a thick early-morning mist on its opening day, had a successful start and moved quickly northwards. As a result by 23 March Rosenberg's 1st King's Own, part of the Third Army, found itself in the front line. Though Rosenberg, writing afterwards from reserve, told his brother Dave that his battalion had been 'very busy lately', he made no mention of the actual fighting. Yet it had been severe enough to deplete Rosenberg's 8th Platoon of B Company so badly that, by the time he communicated with Dave again a few days later, he had been transferred to the 6th Platoon of the same company, presumably to make up numbers.[25] His four days in reserve from 24 to 28 March were well earned but hardly restful, since the Germans had broken through the front line on 26th to capture ground they had not held since 1914. They were driven back the same afternoon but Rosenberg and his fellow soldiers in the 1st King's Own were ordered to 'Stand-To' – in full equipment, prepared for battle – at 4.30 every morning. Yet it was during these four hectic days that Rosenberg wrote or completed one of his most effective poems, 'Through These Pale Cold Days':

> Through these pale cold days
> What dark faces burn
> Out of three thousand years,
> And their wild eyes yearn,
>
> While underneath their brows
> Like waifs their spirits grope
> For the pools of Hebron again—
> For Lebanon's summer slope.
>
> They leave these blond still days
> In dust behind their tread
> They see with living eyes
> How long they have been dead.[26]

Sent with an apology to Marsh on 28 March: 'I've seen no poetry for ages now so you mustn't be too critical – my vocabulary small enough before is impoverished and bare'[27] – this poem is all the more effective for its uncharacteristic 'bareness', conveyed through its simple ballad form.

A number of critics have concentrated on a Zionist reading of the piece.[28] We know that Rosenberg had intended to write 'a battle song for the Judaens [*sic*]' and though he could 'think of nothing strong and powerful enough' in the little time available to him,[29] this last poem appears to be partly an attempt at it. The first two stanzas in particular could be read as a rallying cry for the Jewish Battalion returning to its soldiers' homeland. The 'dark' foreign faces of the Jews contrasted by implication with the 'blond' native English (as in his earlier poem 'The Jew'), the references to Hebron, one of the holy cities of Israel situated in the Judean hills near Jerusalem, 'Lebanon' well known to the Hebrews and their poets, and the three thousand years of their history since the great days of Solomon all point to a Zionist interpretation, where the 'waifs', or exiled Jews, yearn to return to their homeland.

It could also be read more literally, however, as Rosenberg's longing to exchange the extreme danger he was facing in the cold, wet trenches of France for the warmer, drier, less threatening Middle East, where he knew the Jewish Battalion was now stationed. The third stanza certainly suggests that his thoughts were directed towards his own danger and sufferings in the trenches, though he uses his race's survival of a long history of persecution as a way into it. The echo of 'dust' from 'Break of Day in the Trenches', where its presence on the poppy becomes an ominous reminder of mortality, and the poem's last line with its suggestion that the soldiers in the trenches are living dead at best, existing on borrowed time, is inescapable. Read in this way the fate of the Jews becomes a metaphor for all those under threat of extinction. The third word of the poem, 'pale', with its echo from Keats's 'La Belle Dame Sans Merci' (where the warrior from another age, 'palely loitering', sees 'Pale kings, and princes too, / Pale warriors, death-pale were they all'), supports such an interpretation.[30]

There is little doubt that 'Through These Pale Cold Days' is, among other things, a premonition of Rosenberg's own death, serving unintentionally as a moving epitaph. It was a foreboding shared not just by his anxious family, who expected each day to hear news of his death, but also by someone to whom he had grown unexpectedly close during his time in France, Gordon Bottomley. Bottomley would tell Binyon shortly after Rosenberg died that he and his wife had 'felt a change in him' in his last two or three letters and had had a 'presentiment', as with another soldier-poet friend, Edward Thomas, the previous year, 'He is going to die.'[31]

*

Rosenberg's end was still four days away when he sent 'Through These Pale Cold Days' to Marsh on 28 March 1918. At 3 a.m. that same day the Germans renewed their attack with an advance so rapid that Rosenberg, still technically in the reserve trenches, found himself in the new front line. He remained in this exposed position for a further three days, during which time many more of his fellow soldiers in the battalion were killed. When the 1st King's Own was finally ordered to retreat it looked as though Rosenberg might be one of the few to survive. Whether he volunteered for extra duty at the last moment, as a Jewish soldier from his battalion told his family later, is not known. If he did, it was for the first and last time, for he never reached reserves, having been killed by a German raiding party at dawn on 1 April 1918.

Rosenberg's end was marked by a certain pathos, for in his letter to Marsh four days before his death, as he returned to the trenches for the last time he had written: 'It's really my being lucky enough to bag an inch of candle that incites me to this pitch of punctual epistolary. I must measure my letter by the light.'[32] By the time Marsh received the letter on 2 April, Rosenberg's own light had gone out.

His remains lay unrecovered in no-man's-land for almost a fortnight, and it was not until 16 April that the news of his death reached London. His family's grief was overwhelming. 'The light has vanished from our house' his sister Annie wrote in an unconscious echo of his own words.[33] Friends wrote to sympathize. 'For me it will be one of the cruellest things which this cruel war has done' Trevelyan told Annie: 'None of the younger writers ... were his equals in imaginative power, and the imaginative use of words ... The war could crush his body, but could not crush what was best and most human in him.'[34] But the last, defiant words must be Rosenberg's, discovered among his belongings after he died:

How small a thing is art. A little pain; disappointment, and any man feels a depth – a boundlessness of emotion, inarticulate thoughts no poet has ever succeeded in imag[in]ing.

Death does not conquer me, I conquer death, I am the master.[35]

Abbreviations

AR	Anna Rosenberg
AW	Annie Wynick (née Rosenberg)
Berg	Berg Collection, New York Public Library
BL	British Library
BR	Barnett Rosenberg
Bristol	University Library, University of Bristol
Chicago	Regenstein Library, University of Chicago
CW	*The Collected Works of Isaac Rosenberg*, Chatto & Windus, 1979
CWHB	*The Collected Works of Isaac Rosenberg*, Chatto & Windus, 1937
CZA	The Central Zionist Archive, Jerusalem
DB	David Bomberg
DH	Denys Harding
DM	Deborah Maccoby *(God Made Blind*, Symposium Press, 2000)
EM	Edward Marsh
GB	Gordon Bottomley
IP	Ian Parsons
IR	Isaac Rosenberg
IRFP	Isaac Rosenberg Family Papers
IWM	Imperial War Museum
JC	Joseph Cohen
JEAS	Jewish Education Aid Society
JK	Jacob Kramer
JL	Joseph Leftwich
JLD	Joseph Leftwich diary for 1911
JR	John Rodker

JT	Joseph Cohen, *Journey to the Trenches*
KORL	King's Own Royal Lancasters
LA	Lascelles Abercrombie
LB	Laurence Binyon
LEC	Leeds University Rosenberg Exhibition Catalogue, 1959
LMA	London Metropolitan Archives
MG	Morris Goldstein
MGe	Mark Gertler
MH	Minnie Horvitch (née Rosenberg)
MHC	Mrs Herbert Cohen
Poems (1922)	*Poems* by Isaac Rosenberg, Heinemann, 1922
PHH	*Poetry Out of My Head and Heart*, Enitharmon Press, 2007
PPIR	*The Poems and Plays of Isaac Rosenberg*, Oxford UP, 2004
RCT	R.C. Trevelyan
Rem.	'Reminiscences of Isaac Rosenberg by his sister Mrs M. Horvitch', IRFP
RL	Ruth Löwy
SC	Sonia Cohen
SCM	Sonia Cohen Memoirs
SS	Sydney Schiff
SW	Stephen Winsten
Tate Archives	The Hyman Kreitman Research Centre, Tate Britain
Tower Hamlets	Tower Hamlets' Local History Collection, Bancroft Road Library, Bethnal Green
UP	University Press
USC	Joseph M. Bruccoli Great War Collection, Thomas Cooper Library, University of South Carolina in Columbia
WAG	Whitechapel Art Gallery
WS	Winifreda Seaton

Notes

INTRODUCTION

1 *The Poems and Plays of Isaac Rosenberg* PPIR, ed. Vivien Noakes, p. 141.

2 *Poems by Isaac Rosenberg* (*Poems* (1922)), Selected and Edited by Gordon Bottomley, with an introductory memoir by Laurence Binyon, p. 1.

3 *God Made Blind: Isaac Rosenberg: His Life and Poetry* (DM), Deborah Maccoby, Symposium Press, 2000, p. 51. The phrase 'policeman in poetry' was coined by D.H. Lawrence.

4 Marsh, *A Number of People*, p. 320.

5 Undated letter from Ezra Pound to Harriet Monroe stamped 20 September 1915, Special Collections Research Center, University of Chicago Library. Freely translated, I take 'ma che!' to mean 'But then, what do you expect?'

6 See, for example, DM, pp. 226–7.

7 Foreword to *The Collected Works of Isaac Rosenberg* [*CW*], ed. Ian Parsons, Chatto & Windus, 1984, p. ix.

8 ibid.

9 Quoted by James Wood in *The Broken Estate: Essays on Literature & Belief*, Pimlico, 2000, p. 139.

10 *Spectator*, 9 July 1937, in a review of Harding and Bottomley's *Collected Works of Isaac Rosenberg* [*CWHB*].

11 'Romance at the Baillie Galleries: the work of J.H. Amschewitz and the late H. Ospovat', *CW*, p. 287.

12 ibid. For a discussion of the concept of a 'Jewish' Art, see Tickner, pp. 285–6.

13 IR to WS, *CW*, pp. 180–1.

14 Frank Emanuel to Laurence Binyon, 28 April 1921, PHH, p. 126.

15 *CW*, p. 227.

16 Joseph Cohen's notes on an interview with David Dainow, University of South Carolina, Columbia. Prof. Cohen has very generously allowed me to use his notes of interviews with Rosenberg's friends (hereafter USC) in 1960.

17 *PPIR*, pp. 134–6.

18 *PPIR*, pp. 123–4.

19 *PPIR*, p. 139.

20 Related to the author by Frank Auerbach.

21 Silkin, p. 260.

22 Joseph Leftwich's diary (JLD) entry for 2 January 1911, Tower Hamlets Libraries, London.

23 Joseph Cohen's notes for his interview with Lazarus Aaronson, 28 January 1960, USC.

24 ibid.

25 ibid.

26 IR to RL, ?March 1912, *CW*, p. 186.

27 Letter from DB to JL, 8 April 1957, Tate Archives.

28 IR to SS, November 1915, *CW*, pp. 221–2.

29 IR to GB, February 1917, *CW*, p. 253.

30 *The Zionist Record*, 23 July 1935.

31 ibid.

32 ibid.

33 I prefer Ian Parsons's version of line 7 of this extract: 'It seems you inwardly grin as you pass', a reading also chosen by Denys Harding for *CWHB*, on the grounds that 'there is some uncertainty about what [IR] finally wanted there' (DH to IP, 31 January 1966, Bristol).

34 *PPIR*, p. 128.

35 ibid.

36 Quoted in Silkin, p. 259.

37 *CW*, p. 266.

38 *PPIR*, p. 133.

39 Compare the welter of images in the opening lines of 'Dead Man's Dump'.

40 Quoted by Joseph Cohen in *Journey to the Trenches; the Life of Isaac Rosenberg (JT)*, Robson Books, 1975, p. 182.

41 'Emerson', *CW*, p. 288.

42 Leavis, pp. 57–8. Owen is the war poet with whom Rosenberg has most often been compared over the years by, among others, Edith Sitwell, C. Day-Lewis, Jon Silkin, John Johnston, Charles Tomlinson and Deborah Maccoby.

43 JL to DH, 28 June 1937, Bristol.

44 See Collecott, 'Isaac Rosenberg (1890–1918)'; Searle, 'Spanning Two Languages'.

45 GB to DH, 22 August 1937, Bristol.

46 F. R. Leavis, 'The Recognition of Isaac Rosenberg', *Scrutiny*, vol. VI, September 1937.

47 ibid.

48 Silkin, p. 275.

49 These were Joseph Cohen's *Journey to the Trenches* (see note 40), Jean Liddiard's *Isaac Rosenberg: the Half-Used Life*, and Jean Moorcroft Wilson's, *Isaac Rosenberg: Poet and Painter*.

50 DM (see note 3).

51 Letter of October 1915, *CW*, p. 218.

52 IR to EM, 4 August 1916, *CW*, p. 239.

53 ibid.

54 *The Harper American Literature*, 2nd compact edition, HarperCollins, 1996, p. 1254.

55 Autumn 1916, *CW*, p. 248.

56 Graves, pp. 24–5.

57 Tomlinson, p. 4.

58 See, for instance, the recent study *Tommies* by Richard Holmes.

59 Samson, 'Isaac Rosenberg: Selected War Poems'.

60 See note 1.

61 Martin Lloyd, 'Poets and Patriotism – Three Experiences of the Great War'.

62 Loan 103/77, Dept. of Western Manuscripts, BL.

63 *CW*, p. 289.

CHAPTER I

1 This is a literal translation by Professor Chimen Abramsky from the Hebrew of IR's father, Barnett Rosenberg, which Martin Lloyd has kindly allowed me to reproduce. The original is in the Central Zionist Archives in Jerusalem.

2 The whereabouts of IR's grave were still unknown by the end of 1919, but an unverified report in the early 1920s claimed that his remains were buried at a point north of Fampoux and east of Arras. On 17 December 1926, however, as JC established, this report was discounted. IR's family were told by the War Graves Commission that the unmarked grave had been located at another point not far from Fampoux, where several of the soldiers killed in the same skirmish had been identified, though not IR. Nevertheless his name appeared on the original burial list with those whose remains had been identified. And when these bodies were re-interred nearby in the Balleuil Road East Cemetery, IR was allotted the twelfth headstone in Row D, plot 5, which bore also the Star of David and the simple inscription cited here.

3 IR clearly retained his understanding of Yiddish, since he arranged to see a Yiddish play in Whitechapel with Mark Gertler and Edward Marsh in November 1913.

4 Brodetsky, p. 30.

5 Devinsk had been known as Dünaberg until 1893.

6 As Lloyd P. Gartner explains, the Pale of Settlement covered parts of Poland and Western Russia: 'Within those territories they were kept off the land, excluded from the larger cities, and finally driven off a wide swath of border areas.' Gartner, p. 22.

7 Harry Freedman (father's name 'Fuhrman') wrote to IR's niece, Lydia Kellman, from Boston on 30.3.1992 to say that his mother, a cousin of Barnett (or 'Dovber') Rosenberg, and his brother Peretz emigrated to Leeds in the 1880s and lived there with 'Dovber and Peretz Rosenberg, who had settled there in 1886'. (IRFP)

8 Both of BR's younger daughters, Annie Wynick and Rachel Lyons, maintained

that their father chose peddling so that he could observe the Jewish Sabbath, and Deborah Maccoby speculates that he chose the trade as a way of 'evading responsibility'. DM, p. 75.

9 The Jewish population of Bristol by 1901 was 328,945.

10 IR's birth certificate identifies his father as 'Barnard' Rosenberg, a name he had adopted on arrival in England, but he was known as 'Barnett' to family and friends. He gives his trade as 'Licensed Hawker' and signs his name with an 'X', showing that he had not yet learnt to write English. IR's mother is given as 'Annie', though she is called 'Hannah' on other birth certificates and was known as 'Chasa' or 'Anna' to family and friends.

11 Various dates have been given for Minnie's birth, but the nearest is likely to be the one given by her father in his Hebrew poem on the subject (now at the Central Zionist Archives, Jerusalem): 'My Daughter Tsivia Malkah … called in England Minna born on Purim in the year 1882 or in 1883'.

12 *JT*, p. 13. Another interesting First World War poet, Charles Hamilton Sorley, was also one of twins, a fact that he believed gave him an insight into a different point of view from his own.

13 Mrs Rachel Lyons, in an interview with the author in 1973.

14 Rachel Lyons told me that the amount varied between five shillings and seven shillings and sixpence, only a quarter to a third of the amount of one pound ten shillings cited as the 'poverty line' in 1897 by Charles Booth.

15 Joe Rose in an interview with JC on 25.6.1960, notes now in USC. I am grateful to Dr Cohen for allowing me to make use of his material in this book.

16 'Isaac Rosenberg, the Anglo-Jewish Poet' by Dora Sowden, an article in *Jewish Affairs*, vol. 7, no. 12, December 1952, p. 22, for which the author interviewed Annie Wynick (née Rosenberg).

17 *JT*, pp. 108 & 110.

18 See the Joseph Leftwich Papers, CZA.

19 David Dainow in an interview with JC in March 1960. JC has noted the importance of trees in IR's art, especially in poetry and also the possible influence of the tree-goddess myth. See *JT*, n. 38.

20 ibid., p. 13.

21 See Searle, p. 38.

22 Rachel ('Ray') Lyons, the third Rosenberg daughter, told me in 1973 that Annie was the favourite girl and that her mother was 'not very nice' to Minnie.

23 Interview with the author 1973.

24 JC's father's translation of the autobiographical fragment left by Barnett Rosenberg, IRFP.

25 Joseph Leftwich Diary for 1911 at Tower Hamlets Library, entry for 24.1.1911. 'His mother does not look very artistic, but neither does [Isaac].'

26 Interview with the author in 1973.

27 ibid.

28 When Joseph Rose married after the First World War he told JC in his 1960 interview that 'Isaac's mother gave us a flat in [her house]'. Rose's name had been originally 'Rosenberg', though his family was not related to Isaac's.

29 Letter from IR's niece, Sheila Lynn, to his nephew, Isaac Horvitch, 22.1.1980, IRFP.

30 *JT*, p. 9.

31 BR's autobiographical fragment, IRFP.

32 Interview with JC (see note 15).

33 Searle, p. 38.

34 AW's Memoir in *Art and Letters*, London, Summer 1919.

35 IR to EM, late December 1915, *CW*, p. 227.

36 Sowden, p. 22.

37 Zangwill, p. 61.

38 *Poems* (1922), pp. 3 & 6.

39 *JT*, pp. 10 & 20.

40 *Leftwich at 85: a Collective Evaluation*, ed. S.J. Goldsmith, pub. by the Federation of Jewish Relief Organizations, the Association of Jewish Writers and Journalists and the World Jewish Congress Yiddish Committee, London, January 1978, p. 7.

41 BR's fragment begins with his birth in 1860 as 'Dovber' (or 'Berl') Rosenberg, into a fairly well-placed family of landowners, rabbis and scholars. The third of four sons of Hezek Rosenberg by his second marriage, he had two stepsisters by his father's first marriage. He tells of his childhood in the country at Shtat, a village near Vilna in Lithuania, and his growing love of the countryside. His student days training for the rabbinate follow, and his increasingly desperate efforts to escape conscription into the Russian army. It is while hiding in Devinsk that he meets and marries Anna Davidov. Forced to flee again, he takes his wife and their baby daughter to Moscow, where Anna's brother lives, and adopts the unlikely trade of butcher. Whether he then fled again, alone, into the Russian interior, as he claims, is less certain, but he and Anna are clearly separated for some time, since no more children follow until 1890, yet from 1890 to 1899 they would be born at regular intervals of approximately two years. Their next meeting appears to be in Bristol, where Anna has tracked her husband, now called Barnard, or Barnett, down. The birth of Isaac quickly follows.

42 DM, pp. 7ff.

43 Ray Lyons in interview with author, 1973.

44 Strictly speaking it is a fourth festival, Hanukkah, which most nearly approximates to Christmas, though its religious importance is less than that of Pesach, Yom Kippur and Rosh Hashanah.

45 Rem., p. 1.

46 IR to RL, ?Oct. 1916, *CW*, p. 247.

47 IR to BR, letter received 11.8.1917, *CW*, p. 261.

48 *CW*, p. 270.

49 Letter from Morley Dainow to BR, 6.10.1905, formerly in the possession of AW.

50 Rem., p. 1.

51 Cf. AW's words to Dora Sowden in Sowden, p. 23: 'On the pavements of Bristol he would draw quite passable pictures with chalk.'

52 IR to RL, Oct.–Nov. 1916, *CW*, p. 247.

53 IR to AR, 7 June 1917, *CW*, p. 256.

54 IR to AR, *CW*, p. 264.

55 Quoted in Gartner, p. 24.

56 'What was uppermost in our hearts in making the move to London was the free Jewish school system that our boy needed to enter badly.' BR's autobiographical fragment was translated from the Hebrew by Louis A. Cohen and rendered into English by his son Joseph, IRFP.

CHAPTER 2

1 *CW*, p. 181.

2 The following account is based on BR's autobiographical fragment, IRFP.

3 Brodetsky, pp. 24–5.

4 Cable Street was built in the late eighteenth century, though only a few of its Georgian houses now remain. Photographs at the London Metropolitan Archives suggest that the Rosenbergs' lodgings at the western end consisted of humbler two-storey artisans' dwellings, with shopfronts at ground level and attics above.

5 Gartner, p. 146.

6 Rocker, p. 5. Martin Gilbert, in his map of the East End of London in 1900 (*Jewish History Atlas*, p. 75), shows that about 50 to 74 per cent of the population in Cable Street were Jewish, but that immediately to the south the percentage was as low as 5 per cent.

7 Interview with the author, 1973.

8 *JT*, p. 18.

9 *PPIR*, p. 12.

10 Bernard Winehouse (in *Notes and Queries*, vol. 23, no. 1, January 1976, pp. 16–17) writes that the poem was published in a booklet accompanying a Palestine Bazaar held in London on 13 May 1912, below the reproduction of IR's sketch 'The Wharf', 'in which three brutalized faces appear against a background of cranes and warehouses'. Frank Emanuel had a copy of the booklet, as did GB, but Vivien Noakes failed to trace a copy, see *PPIR*, p. 304.

11 Booth, p. 86.

12 Quoted by Gerry Black in *JFS: the History of the Jews' Free School since 1732*, Tymsder Publishing, 1998, p. 121.

13 These and the following quotations on the subject are taken from BR's autobiographical fragment, IRFP.

14 Cork, p. 8.

15 Gartner, p. 226.

16 JL to DH, 18.6.1937, Bristol.

17 ibid.

18 W.B. Yeats, *Autobiographies*, Macmillan, London, 1955, p. 166.

19 St Paul's Church of England School was founded officially in 1870 on the site of a derelict Danish chapel, initially for the children of seamen. Planned, opened and managed by the East End social reformer the Rev. Dan Greatorex, the school was originally divided into Infants, Boys and Girls departments. But in 1896 the Boys and Girls departments were combined into the Mixed School, which Isaac attended. Annie and Rachel Rosenberg were registered in the Infants on 6 June 1898, almost certainly at the same time as Isaac. Rev. Greatorex had retired in 1897 and George Stevens was headmaster during Isaac's time there. St Paul's still flourishes as a primary school on the same site, surrounded now by high-rise blocks.

20 St Paul's School Logbook, LMA.

21 Litvinoff, p. 28.

22 Rocker, pp. 57-8.

23 The Leftwich Papers, CZA.

24 Walker, *East London*, Whitechapel section.

25 ibid.

26 Zangwill, p. 7.

27 Brodetsky, p. 32.

28 For further details on Samuel Montagu see pp. 85 & 124 of Gerry Black's *Jewish London*.

29 A report by Beatrice Webb (in her maiden name of 'Potter') in Charles Booth's *London*. pp. 204-5.

30 *PPIR*, pp. 7-8.

31 Brodetsky, p. 31.

32 *PPIR*, p. 8.

33 Joseph Leftwich, who came to England from Germany, said that he spent the first year of his English school life, at the age of seven, totally confused, since he could not understand English. IR probably felt similarly at St Paul's at the start.

34 IR to SC, *c.* June/July 1916 from France, *CW*, p. 245.

35 *CW*, p. 182.

36 JC interview with Sidney Scott, 29.6.1960, USC.

37 JC interview with David Dainow, March 1960, USC.

38 IR to GB, postmarked 11 July 1917, *PHH*, p. 95.

39 JC interview with Joe Rose, USC.

40 Rem., p. 1.

41 Interview with the author, 1973.

42 Married to Rev Asher Amshewitz, who died in 1903 and had previously been a tutor at the Montefiore College in Ramsgate before moving to Highgate. The family spelt their name Am*she*witz (*not* Am*sche*witz) according to one son, Ivor Amshewitz, who wrote to the *Jewish Monthly* on the subject in August 1950. The Amshewitzes were neighbours of the Lunzers, who had offered to help Anna when Minnie had needed an eye operation. The Lunzers also helped the second Rosenberg girl, Annie, to find work when she left school.

43 *The Zionist Record* (South Africa), 23 July 1937, in a review of *CWHB*.

44 Amshewitz's portrait of IR is often dated 1911, because of a reference in JL's 1911 diary, but his wife, Sarah Briana Amshewitz, dated it 1909 in her account of his work.

45 IR, 'Romance at the Baillie Galleries: the Works of J.H. Amschewitz and the late H. Ospovat', Summer 1912, *CW*, p. 286.

46 *The Zionist Record*, 23 July 1937.

47 *JT*, p. 26.

48 *The Zionist Record*, 23 July 1937.

49 Some of the facts that follow in relation to MG come from his interview with JC, 12.6.1960, USC.

50 *JT*, p. 19.

51 JC suggests that as a non-Jew, Ush-

erwood did not have to 'reconcile the drawing of figures with the second commandment, which prohibits the creation of graven images' (ibid.).

CHAPTER 3

1 *CW*, pp. 180–1.
2 Litvinoff, p. 92.
3 ibid.
4 Rem., p. 1.
5 Ivor Amshewitz in a letter to the *Jewish Monthly*, August 1950.
6 Rem., p. 1.
7 Among other Jewish charities there were the Jewish Temporary Shelter, the Jewish Benevolent Society, the Jewish Education Aid Society, the Israelite Marriage Portion Society, the Burial Society of the Federation of Synagogues, and the Soup Kitchen in Fashion Street, which Joseph Leftwich remembered visiting frequently as a child, and which he believed Rosenberg also knew.
8 The firm of Carl Hentschel went out of business in the 1940s and no records of it appear to have survived. There is a suggestion that IR worked for a second process-engraver in about 1909, a Mr Lascelles of Shoe Lane, but he was still working for Hentschel by the end of 1910, according to the minutes of the Jewish Education Aid Society at the Parkes Library, University of Southampton.
9 The premium at this time would have been between fifteen and twenty pounds, an impossible sum of money for the Rosenbergs to find.
10 *The Slade: A Collection of Drawings and Some Pictures done by past and present students of the London Slade School of Art*, London, 1907.
11 *Poems* (1922), p. 2.
12 ibid., p. 5. The last phrase was taken from a letter to Binyon by the artist Frank Emanuel, who knew Rosenberg during his apprentice years.
13 *CW*, pp. 297–8.
14 Translated literally, 'Hard and bitter is the Life'.

15 'In Art's Lone Paths I Wander Deep', *PPIR*, p. 4.
16 *PPIR*, p. 10.
17 *PPIR*, p. 12.
18 'Fleet Street', *PPIR*, p. 20.
19 This was sponsored by the Royal Society for the Prevention of Cruelty to Animals. Since IR's essay has not survived it is not known what he chose as his subject.
20 See Bella Sidney Woolf's children's page for the 7 September 1906 number. The subject of her literary competition that month was 'The Sea', with book prizes for first and second place. Though IR did not win he 'received a certificate equivalent to third place' (*JT*, p. 30), with Bella Sidney Woolf commenting: 'I. Rosenberg's was original but rather vague in parts.'
21 I have been unable to establish the accuracy or otherwise of this story, which in any case has various versions. Minnie said that the book fetched £40, while Annie claimed it eventually sold for £100.
22 Rem., p. 1.
23 Minnie's daughter, Sheila Lynn (née Horvitch), wrote to her brother Isaac Horvitch on 22 January 1980 remembering anecdotes told her by her mother, of 'Mom taking all the younger Rosenberg children from Stepney [?] to the West End theatres which she loved. They walked because they didn't have the bus fare, stood in the "Gods", and managed to save a penny which Mom would use to take them to a Lyons tea house, where they would share one cup of tea.' IRFP.
24 Toynbee Hall was named after the social philosopher and reformer Arnold Toynbee (1852–81), a young academic who believed passionately in the value of adult education for the working class. After his early death, possibly brought on by overwork, his friends the Barnetts had carried on his mission. In encouraging its staff to live as well as work in the area, in a 'collegiate atmosphere', Toynbee Hall was the first settlement of its kind. It became a model throughout the world.

25 Letter to Laurence Binyon, 18 December 1920, *PHH*, p. 131.

26 Morley Dainow's father, Rev. Israel Dainow, was known as the 'little magid'. His 'inability to make a living' (Morley's brother, David, told Joseph Cohen in his interview in 1960) meant that his wife (Morley's mother) had to run a drapery shop. David, who became a well-known Anglo-South African journalist and eventually wrote a humorous satire, *Our Shadcam* (1954), claimed to have known IR 'very well indeed' as a boy, talking to him and taking walks with him regularly. He also knew IR's sisters and visited the Rosenbergs' home. Morley Dainow would see IR twice only after leaving the Whitechapel Library, once at Bolt Court Art School in 1909 and once in 1913 when IR was already at the Slade. Morley Dainow served in the First World War but was still alive in November 1934, when he wrote to Denys Harding concerning his copy of 'Ode to David's Harp'.

27 I am grateful to Cyril Dainow and Rita Gold for this information.

28 Letter formerly in possession of Chatto & Windus.

29 IR implies that he, like his contemporaries, 'believes in Blake' but only 'tolerates' Tennyson (Prose Fragment VI, *CW*, p. 301), and he does not appear to have been influenced as much by Tennyson as by other nineteenth-century poets, probably preferring his great rival Browning, whom we know IR admired. Yet he is full of praise for Tennyson's 'Crossing the Bar' and shows signs of knowing 'Locksley Hall' well. When war breaks out in 1914, IR writes to EM: 'Are we going to have Tennyson's "Battle in the air"?' (*CW*, p. 205)

30 IR to WS, 1911, *CW*, p. 181.

31 *PPIR*, p. 3.

32 See 1 Sam. 16:14–19, 23, and 2 Sam. 6:5.

33 I am indebted to JC for this information.

34 *PPIR*, p. 3.

35 IR to WS, 1911, *CW*, p. 181.

36 ibid.

37 *PPIR*, p. 5.

38 Letter formerly in the possession of AW.

39 *JT*, p. 30.

40 JC, who first discovered this poem among the papers lent to him by AW, reads 'long' for 'lone' in the first line (*JT*, p. 201).

41 Collecott, p. 275. The IR quotation is from 'Day', ll. 67–9.

42 IR to MHC, ?Dec. 1912, *CW*, p. 186.

43 Entry for 24 January 1911, JLD.

44 For this and the following quotations from Amshewitz see *The Zionist Record*, 23 July 1937.

45 Letter of 17 June 1912 to Mr Spielmann, copy in IRFP.

46 This is hinted at but not specified in a report of a lecture given by Amshewitz in 1936 in South Africa, where he had emigrated in 1916 (see *Zionist Record*, 27 November 1936).

47 Frank Lewis Emanuel (1865–1948), brother of the artist Charles Emanuel, was a painter in both oils and watercolour, illustrator, printer and art critic, who wrote one book, *The Artist* (1903). He exhibited widely in Paris and Britain between 1885 and 1939 and his *Kensington Interior* is at the Tate. He taught etching at the Central School of Arts and Crafts from 1918 to 1930.

48 Letter dated 28 April 1921, *PHH*, p. 127.

49 ibid.

50 ibid.

51 ibid. This drawing was in the collection of JC and reproduced by him (*JT*, opp. p. 48). Frank Emanuel's brother Charles came across the drawing, together with Rosenberg's poem with a slight pencil portrait on its reverse, when sorting through Emanuel's papers after his death and presented them to AW. Emanuel also had a copy of IR's 'docker drawing' in a Zionist magazine, *A Piece of Mosaic*, though this has been lost.

52 GB to DH, 24 November 1935, Bristol.

53 The Leftwich Papers, CZA.

54 ibid.

55 GB to DH, 24 November 1935, Bristol.

56 Letter to LB, 28 April 1921, *PHH*, p. 128.

57 DB to JL, 8 April 1957, Tate Archives. DB, who had read Zangwill's reply to IR, said that Zangwill thought that 'In the Workshop' showed 'the greatest promise' of the early poems. After IR's death Zangwill, who had got to know JL by then, wrote to him defensively: 'I wonder now that Rosenberg was not brought more to my attention, though I fancy my brother Mark once showed me a little printed volume by which I was very much struck' (letter to JL, 18 July 1922, Leftwich Papers, CZA). In fact IR had written to Zangwill twice after his first letter, on the last occasion enclosing his privately printed *Moses*, but had received no direct reply.

58 Enclosed by IR in a letter presumably to WS, n.d., *CW*, p. 187.

59 IR to WS (?), n.d. *CW*, p. 187.

60 Little else is known about Winifreda Seaton, though AW attempted to find out more in 1959 when the Leeds Exhibition of IR's work took place. AW wrote to Miss Seaton's brother's firm of chartered accountants, 'Sayers, Seaton and Butterworth' of 62 Brook Street, London, W1, but was told by them that Christopher Seaton was dead and that his wife could find no material relating to IR among the family papers. She thought that Miss Seaton had died 'over 25 years ago', i.e. in the early 1930s (IRFP).

61 Letter to WS, autumn 1917, *CW*, pp. 264–5.

62 IR to WS, 1912 or earlier, *CW*, p. 183.

63 Letter of Dec.–Jan. 1912–13, *CW*, p. 198.

64 GB to DH, 5 December 1935, Bristol: 'There was a Miss Seaton, who fancied she was IR's Egeria at an art school ...' In classical myth Egeria is the goddess of fountains and childbirth.

65 Letter of 1911, *CW*, p. 181.

66 WS to LB, 18 November 1919, *PHH*, p. 129.

67 Letter of 1911, *CW*, p. 182.

68 Letter of late 1911–early 1912, *CW*, p. 191.

69 Letter of 1912 or earlier, *CW*, p. 183.

70 GB to DH, 5 December 1935, Bristol.

71 WS to LB, 18 November 1919, *PHH*, p. 129.

72 Letter of 1911, *CW*, p. 183.

73 WS to LB, 18 November 1919, *PHH*, p. 129.

74 Michael Sherbrooke's parents were originally called Czevzik. His father became a rabbi in the East End.

75 'To Michael Sherbrooke On Hearing His Recitation of "The Raven"', 1912, *PPIR*, p. 45.

76 'Romance at the Baillie Galleries', *CW*, p. 287.

77 *PPIR*, p. 13.

CHAPTER 4

1 IR to MHC, ?October 1912, *CW*, p. 180.

2 J.H. Amshewitz attended Birkbeck College from 1898 to 1900.

3 Bolt Court School, founded in 1893, was originally called the Guild and Technical School and situated at the headquarters of the Society of Lithographic Artists, Designers and Writers, and Copperplate and Wood Engravers (later known as SLADE) in Clerkenwell Road. When the space grew inadequate, it was relocated in 1895 to 6 Bolt Court, off Fleet Street, and renamed the Bolt Court Technical School. It was subsequently renamed again, the London County Council School of Photo-Engraving and Lithography and merged after the Second World War with the London College of Printing, which now forms part of the University of the Arts on the South Bank.

4 Paul Nash (1889–1946) went to Bolt Court School for the sake of economy, he claimed, between 1907 and 1909. When he won a prize there, it had been awarded by William Rothenstein, who invited Nash to visit him and encouraged him to go to the Slade. Nash saved a year's fees himself and attended between 1910 and 1911, the year before IR entered the Slade.

5 Hammond was considered expert enough to be entrusted with designing the title page of Bolt Court School's 1907–8 Report.

6 This is inscribed 'This drawing of Isaac Rosenberg was made by H.C. Hammond at Bolt Court Art School in 1914' and is now at the Berg. IR had presumably presented it to EM before leaving for South Africa in May or June 1914. EM has also attached to the bottom left-hand corner a small photograph of IR in army uniform, doubtless one of several IR sent him later from France.

7 DB to JL, 8 April 1957, Tate Archives.

8 ibid.

9 Nash, p. 75.

10 Birkbeck College, founded as the London Mechanics' Institution in 1823, changed its name to Birkbeck Literary and Scientific Institution in 1886, to Birkbeck Institute in 1891, and finally became Birkbeck College in 1906, the year before IR joined it. Its first permanent building was in Chancery Lane, its second in Fetter Lane from 1885 to 1951, when it finally settled in Malet Street.

11 'Sacred, Voluptuous Hollows Deep', *PPIR*, p. 90.

12 Alice M. Wright, who owned these, informed GB and DH of them in a letter of 3 November 1935 (Bristol) and sent the originals at their request. These are almost certainly the drawings reproduced by IP in *CW*, opp. p. 32.

13 'Henry Dixon. Artist. Oil. 1910' was shown at the Whitechapel Art Gallery 1937 exhibition of IR's work and was then in the sitter's possession. Its present whereabouts are unknown. Henry Dixon may have been the son of 'Messrs Henry Dixon and Sons', a firm that provided negatives for the Bolt Court School's Annual Report in the early twentieth century.

14 I discovered a copy of this pencil self-portrait by chance while researching IR material in Cape Town. It was reproduced in Sotheby's Catalogue of English Literature, 15 December 1982, but all attempts to trace the original have so far failed.

15 This 1910 *Self-Portrait* is now at the Tate Britain.

16 The pattern of Rosenberg's awards suggests that he started in 1907 with the 'General Course', which taught 'Drawing of a general character in outline and light and shade. The general principles of perspective, relief, breadth, effect, etc.'; then moved on the same academic year to 'Figure – Course I: Drawing heads, hands, feet from the cast – Study of anatomy – Full-length figures from the antique, animals, etc.'; and, finally, to 'Figure – Course II: Drawing and painting the figure from the living model, both draped and nude – Application of figure studies to pictorial or decorative composition in colour, or in black and white'.

17 *The Zionist Record*, 23 July 1937.

18 DB to JL, 8 April 1957, Tate Archives.

19 Details taken from *The Young Stalin* by Simon Sebag Montefiore, Weidenfeld & Nicolson, 2007.

20 DB to JL, 8 April 1957, Tate Archives.

21 Related to JC by AW (*JT*, p. 24).

22 DB to JL, 8 April 1957, Tate Archives.

23 ibid.

24 IR wrote 'Mitchell' on several of his manuscript poems, including 'Even now your eyes are mixed in mine' (*PPIR*, p. 326).

25 IR refers to at least three other students as friends at Birkbeck: (Dora) Cook, (Henry) Dixon and (Arthur) Boss.

26 Rem., p. 2.

27 The sketches appeared in *CW* (1979). The poems IR sent Alice Wright were 'We Are Sad With a Vague Sweet Sorrow', 'Spring', 'O'er the Celestial Pathways Deep', 'The Poet' (I) and 'Peace', all copied out in his hand and sent in 1912, after he had left Birkbeck College. Alice has also copied out, very beautifully, the sonnet to J.H. Amshewitz (IRFP, photocopy).

28 Alice Wright to GB and DH, 3 November 1935, Bristol. Miss Wright lived at 4 Tudor Mansions, Chetwynd Road, London NW5.

29 My italics. IR to Alice Wright, post-marked 10 August 1912, *CW*, p. 188. Miss Wright fortunately kept the envelopes in which some of IR's letters arrived, since he rarely dated them.

30 I was shown a copy by IR's sister, Ray Lyons, of one of the few books owned by IR left in the family, *William Blake, the Poems, with Specimens of the Prose Writings*, ed. by Joseph Skipsey, London, 1885. This has pencil notes for a poem on the front endpaper and is inscribed 'With all good wishes from L. and A. Wright, 13.X.1912'.

31 *PPIR*, p. 7.

32 IR wrote to GB (postmarked 15 August 1916), *PHH*, p. 81, in a phrase he erased: 'But Swinburne is gorgeous.' The prose piece occurs in IR's lecture on 'Art', part II, *CW*, p. 296.

33 There are powerful echoes of Keats's 'Ode on a Grecian Urn' and 'La Belle Dame Sans Merci' and Shelley's 'The Triumph of Life' in 'A Ballad of Time, Life and Memory'.

34 *PPIR*, p.11.

35 IR to LB, 1912, *PHH*, p. 63.

36 IR to GB, postmarked 22 October 1917, *PHH*, p. 118.

37 'The Slade and Modern Culture', *CW*, p. 301.

38 *PPIR*, p. 8.

39 *PPIR*, pp. 9–10.

40 *JT*, p. 48.

41 Annetta Raphael is also reputed to have become friends with Jacob Epstein after his arrival in London in 1905, to have gone to Spain and then to Italy, where she married and went to live in Naples.

42 Several of IR's friends suggested that his first full physical experience of sex was with one of the artists' models he met at the Slade between 1911 and 1914. There was talk of a model called Perry, 'who was around [Isaac] a lot' according to Sonia Cohen when interviewed by JC in 1960.

43 *PPIR*, p. 10.

44 'Shorter Fragments of Prose, VI', *CW*, p. 301.

45 *PPIR*, p. 10.

46 Letter of 1911, *CW*, p. 181.

47 DB dates his first meeting with IR earlier in 1905 or 1906, but this does not tally with his other facts.

48 Letter to Mr Ward, 10 October 1957 (Tower Hamlets).

49 DB was born 5 December 1890 in Bir-mingham, the fifth child of a Polish immi-grant leather-worker and his wife. His family moved to Whitechapel only a year or two earlier than IR's in 1895–6.

50 Taken from the unpublished memoir of Sonia Cohen (SCM), part of which her daughter, Joan Rodker, has kindly allowed me to see.

51 DB to JL, 8 April 1957, Tate Archives.

52 See *Poems and Drawings from the First World War* by David Bomberg, Gillian Jason Gallery, London, 1992.

53 Cork, p. 10.

54 ibid., p. 53.

55 ibid., p. 22.

56 SCM, p. 4.

57 ibid.

58 ibid.

59 Cork, p. 31. The remark was made by the painter Jacob Kramer's sister, Sarah, who would eventually marry DB's friend William Roberts.

60 Professor Frederick Brown, in advising the Jewish Education Aid Society in 1913 that he and his fellow teachers thought 'it would be best if this student did not return to the Slade', emphasized that they thought DB 'undoubtedly possessed of considerable artistic gifts' and that 'when he ha[d] learnt a little more modesty and humility' among other things, 'he [might] well become a noteworthy artist'. Ernest Lesser report to the JEAS, dated 9 May 1913. JEAS minutes, Parkes Library, Uni-versity of Southampton.

61 JC's interview notes with David Dainow, 1960, USC.

62 SCM, p. 2.

63 William C. Lipke, *David Bomberg: A Critical Study of His Life and Work*, London, 1967, p. 37.

64 There is a very early landscape in the

Marsh papers at the Berg, probably preserved by EM more as a curiosity than for its merit, of which it has very little.

65 Collecott, p. 77.

66 DB to JL, 8 April 1957, Tate Archives.

67 JC has accepted AW's memory of DB and IR holidaying together on the Isle of Wight in 1913 and they may well have made a second trip together then, but the 1910 visit definitely took place, as IR's painting *Shanklin. Oils. 1910*, exhibited at WAG in 1937 but subsequently either lost or retitled, shows.

68 *CW*, plates II and III. The view in *People on a Seashore* has some resemblance to a lettercard sent by BR to his daughter Minnie and family, and may include Culver Cliffs near Sandown (IRFP).

69 For an excellent account of Mark Gertler's life and work, see Sarah MacDougall, *Mark Gertler*.

70 Nash, p. 90.

71 John Woodeson, *Mark Gertler*, London, 1972, p. 111.

72 MGe's wife, Marjorie, wrote to AW after MGe's death, 'I know what a great regard he had for your brother' (IRFP).

73 Liddiard, p. 41.

74 Letter of 1912, *CW*, p. 186.

75 Mark Wayner followed Mark Gertler to the Slade with a grant from the JEAS (1909–10), but the grant was stopped when the JEAS discovered his unsatisfactory attendance record. Wayner, who was even poorer than Gertler, had been giving part of his grant to his parents, but this stopped in 1910, so Wayner was not at the Slade at the same time as IR.

76 Collecott, p. 273.

77 Minutes of JEAS for 16 December 1908, Parkes Library, University of Southampton. No initial for 'Rosenberg' is given in the minutes but it seems likely that it *was* Isaac, who may have been encouraged to apply after winning several prizes at Birkbeck College that year.

78 ibid., 9 November 1910.

79 ibid., 18 January 1911.

CHAPTER 5

1 *CW*, p. 302.

2 The Pre-Raphaelites were so named because they shared an ideological belief that art had taken a wrong turn since the advent of Raphael and his 'grand style' and needed to return to the standards prevailing before Raphael.

3 Quentin Bell, *Bloomsbury*, Omega edition, 1974, pp. 12–13.

4 Litvinoff, p. 9.

5 Juliet Stein writing in *The Times*, 8 May 1914.

6 JLD, entry for 24 January 1911.

7 Undated piece by JL in CZA, possibly written in 1937 in preparation for the exhibition at the WAG of IR's work.

8 JLD, 2 January 1911.

9 ibid.

10 ibid.

11 Lazarus Aaronson in an interview with JC, 28 January 1960, USC.

12 JLD, 4 February 1911.

13 ibid.

14 *CW*, p. 274.

15 *CW*, p. 198.

16 See Lawson, p. 19. Lawson quotes from David Feldman's *Englishmen and Jews: Social Relations and Political Culture 1840–1914*, Yale UP, 1994.

17 JLD, 19 September 1911.

18 Interview with JL in Searle, p. 41.

19 ibid.

20 JLD, 12 March 1911.

21 Leftwich, pp. xii–xiv.

22 ibid., pp. xiii–xiv.

23 JLD, 12 February 1911.

24 ibid.

25 This may be the *Self-Portrait* of 1910 now in the Tate.

26 JLD, 24 January 1911.

27 ibid., 2 March 1911.

28 JL himself accepted this. See Goldsmith, p. 4.

29 JLD, 5 February 1911.

30 I am grateful to Martin Lloyd for allowing me to use material from his MA thesis for the University of Southampton,

'Poets and Patriotism – Three Experiences of the Great War'.

31 IR's portrait of Clara Birnberg is dated 1917 in *CW* but it was almost certainly painted in mid-1915 after IR returned from Cape Town. His ten days' leave in September 1917 was spent mostly in visiting friends or lying in bed reading.

32 Stephen Winsten's review of *Poems* (1922), reprinted in *School*, November 1933.

33 ibid.

34 'Isaac Rosenberg' (1937), CZA.

35 JLD, 5 February 1911.

36 This is now in the possession of JR's daughter, Joan Rodker.

37 Joan Rodker, interview with the author, 8 June 2004.

38 At his Ovid Press JR published T.S. Eliot's *Ara Vos Prec*, Ezra Pound's *Hugh Selwyn Mauberley*, the drawings of Wyndham Lewis (he was included unfavourably in Lewis's *The Apes of God*), and the second and third printings of James Joyce's *Ulysses*.

39 Quoted by JR's friend, Professor Jack Isaacs in his obituary of JR, *The Times*, 11 October 1955.

40 Anne Willett in an interview with the author, 2 February 2004.

41 'A note' to JR's *Collected Poems 1912–1925*, The Hours Press, Paris, 1930.

42 i.e. in 'Chagrin', *PPIR*, pp. 103–4. See Jon Silkin's chapter on IR in *Out of Battle*.

43 IR, writing to JR from France (after May 1916), refers to receiving 'a box of Turkish [cigarettes? delight?] from Miss Pulley', a lady who ran a Peasant Pottery Shop on the same premises as the Poetry Bookshop, *CW*, p. 251.

44 *CW*, p. 268.

45 JLD, 12 February 1911. In 1912, JR would start to write a macabre poem, 'Webster'. This was never published but it contains an interesting reference to the Jewish mythical figure Lilith, which prefigures IR's use of Lilith in his later poetic dramas.

46 Undated letter, stamped '20 September 1915' by the *Poetry* office staff, Special Collections Research Center, Regenstein Library, University of Chicago. Since Pound also wrote to Harriet Monroe on 28 June 1915: 'Don't bother about Rosenberg, send the stuff back to him direct unless it amuses you', his undated letter probably precedes this one.

47 It was JR's recommendation of IR's poetry to R.C. Trevelyan in 1916 that first drew Bottomley's attention to it. Rodker had, in any case, been ready to edit the poems himself when AW approached him about it after her brother's death.

48 Mrs Löwy, who would help send IR to the Slade in October 1911, celebrated her silver wedding anniversary in December 1911.

49 So called in 'Rudolph', *CW*, p. 277.

50 Prose fragment VI, *CW*, p. 301.

51 *The Jewish Chronicle*, Supplement no. 167, February 1936, p. i.

52 *PPIR*, p. 13.

53 JLD, 3 June 1911. JL records the group's belief that the insistent rhythms, alliteration and onomatopoeia of 'In the Heart of the Forest' derived from Longfellow's 'Hiawatha' but also notes that IR vehemently denied having read it (JLD, 4 February 1911).

54 Letter of 1911 *CW*, p. 181.

55 ibid.

56 *PPIR*, p. 25.

57 *PPIR*, p. 24.

58 *CW*, p. 9.

59 *PPIR*, p. 15. Shakespeare's influence is also evident in other sonnets written shortly after 'My Days', such as 'The Present' and the first stanza, a sonnet in itself, of 'Love To Be'. IR may have studied Shakespeare at Toynbee Hall, which ran two annual courses devoted specifically to his work, as well as a course on Elizabethan Literature and two other courses on English Literature. There was also a 'Toynbee Hall Shakespearean Society', though I have not been able to establish if IR was a member. It was IR's enthusiasm for Shakespeare that started JL on a self-constructed study of his work.

60 When JR got to know Pound, *c.* 1912,

he would certainly have been introduced by him to Yeats, who was living in London, and a friend of Pound's, at that time.
61 *PPIR*, p. 99.

CHAPTER 6

1 *CW*, p. 276.
2 Prose fragment VI, *CW*, p. 301.
3 Interview with JC, 1960, USC.
4 ibid.
5 See *Self-Portrait. 1912, Self-Portrait in a Pink Tie. 1914, Self-Portrait in a Felt Hat. 1914* and *Self-Portrait. South Africa. 1914* for proof of IR's predilection for pink ties.
6 See *Self-Portrait. 1910.*
7 SCM, p. 2.
8 ibid.
9 *PPIR*, pp. 21–2.
10 Interview with SC, 1960.
11 ibid.
12 ibid.
13 ibid.
14 SCM.
15 Interview with JC.
16 ibid.
17 *PPIR*, p. 40.
18 *PPIR*, p. 27. Sonia, thinking back on the poems IR presented to her, referred to this poem mistakenly, I believe, as 'If You Are Fire and I Am Fire'. Since this was not written until 1914 she is almost certainly thinking of 'Heart's First Word' (I), in which the tenth line reads 'Whereby the lips and heart are fire'.
19 *PPIR*, pp. 31–2.
20 *PPIR*, p. 23.
21 Aaronson was introduced to IR by JR, whom he knew from school. Interview with JC, 28 January 1960.
22 ibid.
23 GB to DH, 22 August 1937, Bristol.
24 ibid.
25 Photocopy of letter to the *Jewish Monthly* (undated), Leftwich Papers, CZA.
26 'Judaism and Poetry', *Jewish Review*, autumn 1932, p. 39. Roditi gives 'chiasmus, that most perfect of parallelisms' as one

manifestation of this in IR's poetry, which, he argues, reflects 'the dualistic and dialectical rhythm of Jewish consciousness', pp. 48–9.
27 Silkin, p. 249.
28 IR to Israel Zangwill, 1910?, *CW*, p. 180.
29 Collecott, p. 271.
30 *PPIR*, p. 96. As Diana Collecott points out, 'the energetic cluster "troubled throng" should, of course, be followed by the singular verb "breaks", and this is just the kind of pedantic detail which would lead to criticisms of "blindness" or "carelessness"; but the plurality of words is the dominant idea here, leading into that vivid metaphor of smothered fire which would, if fanned, break *out* and *through* in many places.' (Collecott, p. 271)
31 Searle, p. 30.
32 Joseph Leftwich, *The Golden Peacock*, Robert Anscombe, 1939, p. 29.
33 JLD, 16 July 1911.
34 Apart from IR's *Self-Portrait* in oils, JL refers to one of Rodker (now lost) and a third, of a neighbourhood acquaintance and another aspiring writer, Lionel Woolf (also lost): 'IR painted a portrait of Lionel Woolf not long ago. Quite a good portrait.' (JLD, 15 September 1911)
35 I have been unable to trace any evidence that IR did so.
36 Since IR joined Hentschel's at the beginning of 1905, he had, technically, finished his apprenticeship, or was very close to doing so in January 1911, which may have made him less anxious to please and contributed to his dismissal.
37 Minutes of JEAS, 22 February 1911, Parkes Library, University of Southampton.
38 ibid.
39 See JLD, 17 March 1911, where IR tells JL that, in following Amshewitz's advice, he has spoilt his self-portrait.
40 JEAS minutes, 26 April 1911.
41 JLD, 9 March 1911.
42 Lily Delissa Joseph (1863–1940) trained at the South Kensington School of Art. Some of her best-known works are *The*

Family Group, Roofs, High Holborn (now at Tate Britain), *The Dome, The National Gallery, Interior, National Gallery, Trafalgar Square.* She had exhibited at the WAG in *Jewish Art and Antiquities*, 7 November–16 December 1906.

43 Exodus 20:4. *Catalogue of a Loan Exhibition of Paintings by Solomon J. Solomon and Lily Delissa Joseph (brother and sister)*, 6–26 May 1946, Ben Uri Gallery.

44 JLD, 17 March 1911.

45 See *Highgate*.

46 Cf. Mrs Joseph's picture of the London Port Authority.

47 JLD, 1 May 1911.

48 Sending GB a photograph of himself in September 1917 in civilian clothes, taken with his younger brother Elkon, who is in army uniform, IR observes: 'The suit and the hat is the family suit and hat and fits us all, though my younger brother is growing out of it now.' IR to GB, dated in GB's hand, '1.15 pm 25 Sept. 1917', *PHH*, p. 107. The photograph concerned is now at the IWM.

49 Amshewitz's widow, Sarah Briana Amshewitz, remembered that 'it was at Amshewitz's instigation that Michael Sherbrooke read [Rosenberg's] poems to a lady who, with two friends, afterwards enabled the young poet and painter to study art at the Slade'. Amshewitz, p. 17.

50 *Poems* (1922), p. 2.

51 GB to DH, 10 June 1936, Bristol.

52 *CW*, p. 276.

53 GB to DH, 10 March 1936, Bristol.

54 Interview with JC, 12 June 1960.

55 *CW*, p. 277.

56 ibid.

57 *CW*, p. 278.

58 *CW*, p. 281.

59 *CW*, p. 283.

60 JLD, 7 June 1911.

61 Silkin, p. 266.

62 *PPIR*, p. 22.

63 Mrs Henrietta Löwy wrote to DH on 22 November 1935 from 12 Ladbroke Terrace, London, in response to his request for material for the 1937 edition: 'I have no letters or fragments of prose from Isaac Rosenberg. I have a very charming small sketch of Kensington Gardens (oil painting by him 7 by 6 inches).' (Bristol) This has not been identified, but may be a.k.a. 'The Fountain'. She also showed him the '4 or 5 poems' she had of IR's, which included 'To Mr & Mrs Löwy, on their Silver Wedding', 'Summer in Winter: Six Thoughts' and 'L—— and M——'.

64 *School*, November 1933, p. 22.

65 It is clear both from the minutes of the JEAS and from IR's letters to Mrs Cohen that she was initially paying for the fees on her own (as well as supplying a living allowance) and was not helped by either Mrs Joseph or Mrs Löwy, as is sometimes suggested.

66 JL's interview with JC, 20 February 1960.

67 DM, p. 44.

68 Mrs Cohen (née Saloman) published *Rhythmic Waves* in 1916 under the pseudonym J.C. Churt. Her play *The Chain* was performed all round the country.

69 'Twilight', 'So Innocent You Spread Your Net', 'In the Woods' and 'My Songs' were the poems. The paintings were *London Park* (1911), *Landscape* (1911–12), *The Bridge, Blackfriars* (1911) and *The Murder of Lorenzo* (1912).

CHAPTER 7

1 *CW*, p. 191. I believe that this letter was written earlier than the September 1912 suggested by IP, since IR refers in it to poems returned to him by Austin Harrison, an event which had occurred by 25 December 1911 according to JLD.

2 *CW*, p. 300.

3 'Art', part II, *CW*, p. 294.

4 ibid.

5 e.g. Stanley Spencer, David Bomberg, Mark Gertler, William Roberts, C.R.W. Nevinson, Edward Wadsworth and Jacob Kramer.

6 Frank Emanuel to LB, 28 April 1921, *PHH*, p. 128.

7 'Art', part II, *CW*, p. 293.

8 Nash, pp. 92–3.

9 Joseph Hone, *The Life of Henry Tonks*, Heinemann, 1939, p. 103.

10 *CW*, p. 297.

11 *CW*, p. 295.

12 ibid.

13 Henry Tonks was born in 1862 and died in 1937, succeeding to the Chair at the Slade in 1918.

14 Nash, p. 89.

15 William Rothenstein, *Men and Memories*, vol. II, London, 1932, p. 166.

16 Sarah MacDougall relates this story in her biography of Mark Gertler (p. 33); it is taken from Gilbert Cannan's *Mendel*, a novel based firmly on Gertler's life.

17 George Charlton, 'The Slade School of Fine Art, 1871–1946', *The Studio*, October 1946, p. 6.

18 IR to WS, 1912, see note 1 of this chapter. *CW*, p. 191.

19 ibid.

20 Hone, op. cit., p. 272.

21 *CW*, pp. 295–6.

22 GB to DH, 25 June 1937, Bristol.

23 MacDougall, p. 39.

24 Among these awards were Best Painting from the Life, Best Drawing from the Life, Best Drawing from an Antique Figure, Best Composition from a Given Subject, and a prize for an examination in anatomy. Tonks awarded his own special award for Best Drawing of a Head, which Bomberg would win with his portrait of IR.

25 ibid.

26 MG, interview with JC, 12 June 1960, USC.

27 ibid.

28 *CW*, p. 300. The references that follow in this paragraph are from the same source.

29 DB to JL, 8 April 1957, Tate Archives.

30 Based on Kramer's interview with JC, 14 June 1960, USC.

31 Besides Gertler, Kramer, Bomberg and Rosenberg, there were Ruth Löwy, her cousin Gilbert Solomon, Clara Birnberg, Hubert Schloss, David Sassoon and (the half-Jewish) Adrian Allinson.

32 Quoted in MacDougall, p. 34.

33 Charlton, p. 203.

34 Interview with the author, 1973.

35 Gertler to William Rothenstein, *c.* May–June 1910, in Gertler, *Selected Letters*, ed. Carrington, p. 33.

36 Marcia Allentuck's 'Isaac Rosenberg and Gordon Bottomley: Unremarked Documents in the Houghton Library', *Harvard Library Bulletin*, vol. XXIII, no. 3, July 1975, in which she records her interview with Ruth Löwy.

37 'Isaac Rosenberg' by JL, almost certainly prepared in 1936 for the WAG IR exhibition of 1937, CZA. This would appear as an article in the Literary Supplement of the *Jewish Chronicle* (February 1936).

38 ibid.

39 JK interview with JC, 14 June 1960, USC.

40 Michael Reynolds, '*The Slade School of Art*' (read in TS at University College London's Special Collections), p. 207.

41 ibid.

42 IR to EM, ?Nov. 1915, *CW*, p. 225.

43 Quoted (from the *Jewish Chronicle* of May 1914) in Tickner, p. 158.

44 See 'Art', part II, *CW*, p. 296: 'In their anxiety . . . patterns of clear form.'

45 *CW*, p. 294.

46 ibid.

47 *Works by David Bomberg*, catalogue of DB's July 1914 exhibition at the Chenil Gallery, London.

48 Hassall, p. 281.

49 'Head of a Poet', now lost, was bought by the American collector John Quinn but sold on to the art dealer, Mr R. Chait after Quinn's death in the mid-1920s for $10. It was reproduced in *John Quinn 1870–1925: Collection of Paintings, Water Colors, Drawings and Sculptures* (New York, 1926).

50 Jacob Kramer (1892–1962).

51 Interview with JC, 14 June 1960, USC.

52 ibid.

53 ibid.

54 ibid.

55 JL interview with JC, 20 February 1960, USC.

56 JK interview with JC, 14 June 1960, USC.

57 See 'To J. Kramer', *PPIR*, p. 36.

58 JK interview with JC.

59 ibid.

60 Ruth Löwy would marry the publisher Victor Gollancz, eventually becoming Lady Gollancz. Gilbert Solomon was the son of the painter Solomon J. Solomon.

61 'Summer in Winter: Six Thoughts', *PPIR*, p. 19.

62 GB to DH, 25 June 1937, Bristol.

63 *PPIR*, p. 28.

64 Interview with JC, 1960, USC.

65 Marcia Allentuck, as cited in n.36 above, p. 258.

66 ibid.

67 *CW*, p. 186.

68 See 'Uncle's Impressions in the Woods at Night', *CW*, pp. 285–6.

69 *CW*, p. 186.

70 Letter of ?October 1916, *CW*, p. 247.

71 See IR's oil painting of Clara Birnberg, and CB's two pencil drawings of IR, one in the Prints and Drawing Dept. of the British Museum, the other in the Strang Collection at University College, London.

72 Cork, p. 28.

73 ibid.

74 Clara Birnberg (1894–1989) had three children by Stephen Winsten.

75 Quoted in 'The Whitechapel Boys' by Rachel Dickson and Sarah MacDougall, *Jewish Quarterly*, Autumn 2004, no. 195.

76 'Art', part II, *CW*, p. 297.

77 Interview with JC, 1960, USC.

78 'A Painter's Pilgrimage', unpublished memoir by Adrian Allinson, p. 18. TS at McFarlin Library, University of Tulsa, Oklahoma.

79 ibid., p. 28.

80 ibid., p. 20.

81 'Art', part II, *CW*, p. 297.

82 ibid.

83 LEC, p. 28.

84 'Art', part II, *CW*, p. 295.

85 Ecclesiastes, 12:5.

86 Cork, p. 27.

87 'The Pre-Raphaelite Exhibition', *CW*, p. 285.

88 ibid.

89 This is still in the IRFP.

90 This is dated 1911 and now in the possession of a private collector.

91 Quoted in Reynolds, p. 174.

92 Letter to DH, 13 July 1936, Bristol. All following quotations by Nevinson are taken from the same source.

93 Mark Gertler to William Rothenstein, *c*. May–June 1910, Gertler, p. 33. Gertler would break off his close friendship with Nevinson after only a year over rivalry for Dora Carrington.

94 Adrian Allinson, p. 18.

95 The 'Head Painting' could have been either of the two portraits in oils he painted of his father in 1911, or his *Head of a Woman. Grey and Red* in 1912. He also painted a self-portrait in oils in 1912.

96 Reynolds, p. 175.

97 DB to JL, 8 April 1957, Tate Archives.

98 ibid.

99 Letter of ?October 1912, *CW*, p. 194.

100 Charlton, p. 4.

101 *CW*, p. 196.

102 The drawing was named as 'Sanguine Drawing' in the NEAC catalogue, but is now lost.

103 IR to Alice Wright, ?October 1912, *CW*, p. 195.

CHAPTER 8

1 *CW*, p. 193.

2 IR to Alice Wright, postmarked 15 July 1912, *CW*, p. 187.

3 JC believes that 'Hark, Hark, the Lark' represents IR's initial sketch for 'Joy' and that he rejected it because it showed too much Cubist influence. However, it is fairly clear from IR's letter to EM of mid-1915 that 'Hark, Hark, the Lark', a drawing in charcoal and wash, was not executed by 1912. Even if the letter to EM has been

misdated as [?1915], IR did not meet EM until November 1913. See *CW*, p. 213.

4 Postmarked 6 August 1912, *CW*, p. 188.

5 ibid.

6 'Art', part II, *CW*, p. 293.

7 IR to Alice Wright, postmarked 10 August 1912, *CW*, p. 188.

8 IR to RL, ?August 1912, *CW*, p. 189.

9 Bernard Wynick also told me, during the same telephone conversation in July 2006, that the picture was in his mother, Annie Wynick's house until the end of the Second World War. An admirer of Rosenberg's, a conductor from the New York Symphony orchestra, he believed, had noticed that the glass of the painting was damaged and offered to have it restored. He took it away and the family never saw it again. The man concerned may have been Hugo Weisgall (1912–1997), a composer and conductor of Jewish Czechoslovakian descent who admired Rosenberg's poems and set one of them, 'The Dying Soldier', to music in his *Soldier Songs* cycle. I am grateful to his daughter, Deborah Weisgall, for information about her father.

10 IR to RL, ?August 1912, *CW*, p. 189.

11 IR to Alice Wright, prob. 26 September 1912, *CW*, p. 191.

12 IR to MHC, ?October 1912, *CW*, p. 193.

13 IR to MHC, December 1912, *CW*, p. 195.

14 IR to RL, ?October 1912, *CW*, p. 194.

15 Rem., p. 2.

16 IR to Alice Wright, prob. October 1912, *CW*, p. 194.

17 IR to MHC, ?December, *CW*, p. 196.

18 IR to MHC, prob. October 1912, *CW*, p. 193.

19 IR to MHC, prob. December 1912, *CW*, p. 195.

20 *Poems* (1922), p. 6.

21 ibid.

22 Minutes of JEAS, 24 July 1912, Parkes Library, University of Southampton.

23 IR stayed at what I have assumed to be Mrs Herbert Cohen's holiday home near Bournemouth between 20 February and 1 March 1914. (*CW*, p. 200)

24 IR to MHC, prob. Dec. 1912, *CW*, p. 196.

25 IR first found a room at 40 Ampthill Square, near Euston Station, in October 1912, but stayed there only one night, kept awake by the noise of the trains. (The original building has not survived.) His second attempt at 1 St George's Square (later renamed Chalcot Gardens) was more successful and he rented it until February 1914.

26 IR to RL, ?March 1912, *CW*, p. 185.

27 IR wrote two poems into the back of his first pamphlet of poems (*Night and Day*): 'To Michael Sherbrooke on Hearing his Recitation of "The Raven"' and 'Dust Calleth to Dust' (both *CW*, p. 42). His plea to Sherbrooke in the first of these – 'O master – take thought of our weakness, be not like God in his might; / He may forget – He is God, but why should you play with our hearts?' – suggests the power of the actor's hold over him at the start. It may be that Sherbrooke wanted more than friendship from Rosenberg. Sherbrooke's copy of *Night and Day* is now at the University Library in Jerusalem.

28 IR to MHC, prob. December 1912, *CW*, p. 196.

29 IR to Alice Wright, n.d., *CW*, p. 197.

30 IR also wrote a short prose piece, 'Joy', during this same period. (*CW*, p. 303)

31 IR to RL, prob. July 1912, *CW*, p. 188.

32 *PPIR*, p. 28.

33 *Poems* (1922), p. 7.

34 ibid., pp. 7–8.

35 'The Pre-Raphaelites and Imagination in Paint', *CW*, p. 298.

36 John Woodeson, London, 1972, p. 111. This must have occurred some time in 1911–12, which was Gertler's last year at the Slade.

37 IR to RL, ?August 1912, *CW*, p. 189.

38 IR to SS, *c.* August 1916, *CW*, p. 240.

39 ibid.

40 'Romance at the Baillie Galleries', *CW*, pp. 286–8.

41 *Poems* (1922), pp. 1–2. Laurence Binyon (1869–1943) was appointed to the Department of Prints and Drawings at the British Museum in 1895 and became Assistant Keeper in 1909.

42 IR to LB, 1912, his second letter to LB, *PHH*, p. 64.

43 Mr Bogdin to Mr Ward, 10 October 1957, Tower Hamlets Libraries.

44 See John Tytell, *Ezra Pound: the Solitary Volcano*, Bloomsbury, 1987, p. 102, and D.P. Corbett *Modernities and Identities in Modern Art*, Manchester UP, 2000, where Corbett discusses the links as well as the differences between Binyon's late Romantic aesthetics and early Modernism in Britain. I am indebted to Deborah Maccoby for this connection.

45 IR to LB, 1912, *CW*, p. 192.

46 ibid.

47 *Poems* (1922), p. 8.

48 ibid., p. 4.

49 Mr Bogdin to Mr Ward, 10 October 1957, Tower Hamlets Libraries.

50 Morris Robinson to DH, 5 February 1936, Bristol.

51 I am grateful to Marcia Allentuck, both for the quotations (from Binyon's *The Drawings and Engravings of William Blake*, London, The Studio Limited, 1922, p. 28) and for her insights into its bearing on Binyon's response to IR. See Allentuck, p. 254.

52 IR to EM, postmarked 17 August 1916, *CW*, p. 241.

53 IR to LB, 1912, *PHH*, p. 64.

54 IR to EM, postmarked 17 August 1916, *CW*, p. 241.

55 ibid.

56 Laurence Binyon, 'For the Fallen'.

57 IR to RL, ?March 1912, *CW*, p. 185. Piciotto was co-editing *A Piece of Mosaic Being the Book of the Palestine Exhibition and Bazaar* (London, 1912) and soliciting contributions.

58 *Poems* (1922), p. 3. IR wrote to LB in 1912: 'Among modem artists Rossetti appeals very much to me and also his poems.' (*PHH*, p. 63)

59 'Raphael', *PPIR*, p. 43.

60 *PPIR*, pp. 43–4.

61 *Poems* (1922), p. 9.

62 IR to LB, 1912, *PHH*, p. 64.

63 IR to EM, mid-May 1916, *CW*, p. 232.

64 ibid.

65 ibid.

66 I am indebted to DM's *God Made Blind* (pp. 40–2) for most of this information.

67 IR to SS, late August 1916, *CW*, p. 243.

68 *Scrutiny*, vol. VI, no. 2 (September 1937), pp. 229ff.

69 *PPIR*, p. 46.

70 ibid. IR explores the subject of twilight frequently in his early verse: e.g. 'Nocturne', 'Twilight' (I), 'Twilight' (II).

71 See *Poems* (1922), p. 3 and *PHH*, p. 63.

72 *PPIR*, p. 46.

73 IR to EM, postmarked 26 January 1918, Berg. Cf. also IR's 'Christ! end this hanging death' ('Chagrin') and 'O think! you reverend shadowy, austere, / Your Christ's youth was not ended when he died' ('Of Any Old Man').

74 Sowden, p. 23.

75 IR to EM, postmarked 15 May 1915, *CW*, p. 201.

76 IR to WS, before 1911, *CW*, p. 180.

77 *PPIR*, p. 48.

78 *PPIR*, pp. 52–3.

79 'Returning, We Hear the Larks', *PPIR*, p. 138. IR was already using a similar set of images as early as 1911 when he wrote in 'Knowledge': 'Yet midst his golden triumph a despair / Lurks like a serpent hidden in his hair' (*PPIR*, p. 30).

80 *PPIR*, pp. 57–8.

81 *PPIR*, p. 144.

82 *PPIR*, p. 51.

83 *PPIR*, p. 139.

84 Tomlinson, p. 6.

85 IR to LB (1912, since the letter is written from 32 Carlingford Road): 'The opening two stanzas especially appeal to me – and the second stanza about the moon as earth's mirror – and all the end part from "Peace is it peace". I like the whole poem but these especially appeal to me for the rapture they rise into. I like the restraint of

it as a whole and the metre.' See LB's 'The Mirror' (1903–13), *Collected Poems*, Macmillan, 1943, p. 175.
86 *PPIR*, p. 41.

CHAPTER 9

1 *PPIR*, pp. 62–3.
2 IR to Alice Wright, n.d. *CW*, p. 196.
3 JEAS minutes for 18 December 1912, Parkes Library, University of Southampton.
4 'Peace' (*PPIR*, pp. 63–4) was sent to Alice Wright in a letter postmarked 27 December 1912.
5 SCM, p. 2.
6 ibid.
7 He would keep this studio at 1 St George's Square until he left the Slade just over a year later.
8 The winner, Colin Gill, was a Slade student, though puzzlingly Tonks was reputed to be angry that a Slade student had not won.
9 JEAS minutes, 9 May 1913.
10 ibid.
11 IR to WS, Dec–Jan. 1912–13, *CW*, p. 198.
12 *PPIR*, p. 101.
13 This became 'The Poet' (II).
14 SCM, p. 3.
15 *PPIR*, p. 64.
16 *PPIR*, p. 106.
17 *PPIR*, p. 69.
18 *CW*, p. xix.
19 *PPIR*, pp. 108–9.
20 Interview with JC in 1960.
21 ibid.
22 ibid.
23 Anne Willett in an interview with the author, 2 February 2004.
24 SCM, p. 4.
25 DB described SC's action as 'going to live with a long, skinny poet in a slot meter [sic]' (SCM, p.4).
26 SCM, p. 4.
27 ibid.
28 ibid., p. 2.
29 Aldington's review of Amy Lowell's

Swordblades and Poppy-Seeds, *The Egoist*, 15 November 1914, pp. 422–3.
30 'A Retrospect', *Literary Essays of Ezra Pound*, Faber & Faber, 1954, p. 3.
31 *Poetry* (Chicago), vol. 6, no. 3, April–September 1915, pp. 156–7.
32 Apart from its founding members, Pound, Aldington and 'H.D.', other 'Imagist' poets would include F.S. Flint, Amy Lowell, William Carlos Williams, James Joyce and Ford Madox Ford.
33 IR to WS, 1912, or earlier, *CW*, p. 184. *In the Net of Stars* (London, Elkin Mathews, 1909), the first collection by F.S. Flint, includes 'Exultation' and 'The Heart's Hunger'.
34 *PPIR*, p. 169. Harding and Bottomley had classed 'Green Thoughts Are' as a fragment in their 1937 edition, but both the 1979 and 2004 editions treat it as a complete poem. Silkin (p. 259) has traced Imagist influence as late as 'Dead Man's Dump'.
35 IR to WS, 1912, or earlier, *CW*, p. 184.
36 ibid.

CHAPTER 10

1 *CW*, pp. 202–3.
2 Hassall, p. 252.
3 MacDougall, pp. 84–5.
4 IR to SS, August 1916, *CW*, p. 242.
5 Quoted by D. Hooker in *Nina Hamnett, Queen of Bohemia*, Constable, 1986, p. 72.
6 Quoted in MacDougall, p. 84.
7 SCM, p. 4.
8 Interview with JC.
9 Hassall, p. 254.
10 ibid., p. 23.
11 ibid.
12 MacDougall, p. 86.
13 Hassall, p. 244.
14 Marsh, *Ambrosia and Small Beer*, p. 53.
15 Marsh, *A Number of People*, p. 32. I am indebted to Jean Liddiard's examination of EM's position in poetry here.
16 JC, p. 89.
17 IR to EM, postmarked 17 August 1916, *CW*, p. 241.
18 ibid, ?November 1913, *CW*, p. 199.

19 Wilson, *Siegfried Sassoon*, p. 166.

20 John Rodker contributed an article on Yiddish Theatre to *Poetry and Drama* in 1913, which IR almost certainly read and which may have increased his own interest in the genre.

21 The contributors to *Georgian Poetry 1911–1912* were Lascelles Abercrombie, Gordon Bottomley, Rupert Brooke, G.K. Chesterton, W.H. Davies, Walter de la Mare, John Drinkwater, James Elroy Flecker, Wilfrid Gibson, D.H. Lawrence, John Masefield, Harold Monro, T. Sturge Moore, Ronald Ross, Edmund Beale Sargant, James Stephens and R.C. Trevelyan.

22 *CW*, pp. 199–200. IP suggests December 1913 for this undated letter, but since the copy EM presented and signed to IR (in my possession) is dated May 1914 this is the more likely date for the letter.

23 JEAS minutes for 22 December 1913, Parkes Library, University of Southampton.

24 ibid.

25 IR to MHC, presumably October 1912, *CW*, p. 193.

26 IR to EM, ?May 1914, *CW*, p. 201.

27 DM, pp. 34. This same line of argument could also be applied to the painter-poet David Jones.

28 DM, pp. 34–5.

29 *CW*, p. 193.

30 ibid.

31 IR to EM, ?May 1914, *CW*, p. 201.

32 See Hassall, p. 186. This is now in Eton College Library. IR contributed 'If You are Fire and I am Fire'.

33 There is some confusion over the dating of 'Hark, Hark, the Lark', which JC, who had such a work in his collection in 1975, claims was executed in 1912. But IR's letter to EM, probably of 1915 (see *CW*, p. 213), suggests that it was undertaken that year. A 'wash and pencil' drawing (as distinct, perhaps, from JC's 'charcoal and monochrome wash'?) was left to Christopher Hassall by EM and eventually sold by his estate to Messrs Charles, Rare Books.

There may have been two works of this title.

34 EM to DH, 14 December 1935, Bristol.

35 *CW*, p. xvi.

36 ibid. AW was fierce in her defence of EM, reacting strongly to charges of 'condescension': '[he] did everything he could to help him' (AW to JL, 12 September 1935. Joseph Leftwich Papers, CZA).

37 Silkin, pp. 257–8.

38 *CW*, p. 86.

39 ibid., p. 203.

40 Ian Parsons argues that though IR 'clarified and improved the poem in places', 'the original lines 7 to 11 were damagingly condensed to the new lines 7 to 9 inclusive'. Another typescript of a draft of the poem has 3 additional lines between lines 9 and 10:

> A rainbow smiling on a sodden wretch:
> Like those deaf cherubim whose bright shadows fell
> From Eden on the joy beleaguered waste

41 *PPIR*, pp. 71–3.

42 *PPIR*, p. 103. Line 15 is given as 'love-strange' in *Moses*, with a 'd' added in IR's own copy of *Moses*.

43 *JT* p. 205, note 38, has an interesting note on tree imagery in IR's work.

44 *CW*, p. xvi.

CHAPTER II

1 *CW*, pp. 200–1.

2 IR to EM, ?May 1914, *CW*, p. 201.

3 IR to Ernest Lesser, ?Spring 1914, *CW*, p. 200.

4 William Horvitch had been born in England on 13 May 1887, before emigrating to South Africa with his parents as a child. He died, shortly after returning to England, on 21 August 1961.

5 It is not clear whether IR intended to stay permanently in South Africa; his visit to the Emigration Office suggests he did, but a later letter to EM suggests that he did not.

6 IR to EM, postmarked 15 May 1914, *CW*, p. 201.

7 IR wrote two addresses on a fair copy of 'Wedded' (I): 'Eastbourne Municipal School of Art / H.W. Fovargue. Town Clerk & Sec. / Education Department / Town Hall Eastbourne' and 'The Director of Education / Education Offices / Municipal Buildings / Bournemouth', perhaps while he was convalescing in Bournemouth between 20 February and 1 March 1914. (*PPIR*, pp. 328–9)

8 There were five other Jewish artists from France – Modigliani, Pascin, Nadelman, Kisling and Pissarro. Jacob Epstein, who had studied in Paris before coming to England, was co-organizer of the Jewish section with Bomberg.

9 Both of these have since disappeared, though both are reproduced in *CW*, facing pp. 65 and 224 respectively. The Whitechapel Art Gallery Catalogue for 1914, *Twentieth-Century Art, May 8–June 20, 1914* (no. 260), gives the names of IR's three other works as *Head of a Girl, The Judgement of Paris* and *Portrait*.

10 'The Whitechapel Boys', *Jewish Quarterly*, autumn 2004, no. 195, p. 1.

11 *The Jewish Chronicle*, no. 2,354, 15 May 1914, p. 10. The reviewer signs him-/herself only 'L.K.'

12 See Lisa Tickner in *Modern Life and Modern Subjects*, where she explores the concept of 'Jewish' art and its possible links to Modernism and suggests further reading (e.g. p. 285, note 70).

13 *The Jewish Chronicle*, no. 2,354, 15 May 1914, p. 10.

14 'Art', part II, *CW*, p. 297.

15 ibid., p. 296.

16 Ian Parsons and others have claimed that IR visited St Helena in July 1911, but the postcard to his mother on which this is based is not clearly dated (see IWM) and the likelihood of such a long sea voyage in 1911 highly implausible. It is far more likely that the postcard was sent from St Helena when his ship put in there on his 1914 trip to South Africa.

17 *PPIR*, p. 109. The Jewish Book of Jubilee, or Leptogenesis, written in the century before Christ, gives a chronology of the lives of Adam and Eve and the names of their two daughters – Avan and Azura.

18 *PPIR*, p. 61. IP dates this poem 1914 but *PPIR* (p. 323) gives it as '?1912'.

19 *PPIR*, pp. 109–10.

20 IR to EM, early June 1914, *CW*, p. 203.

21 *PPIR*, p. 123. *CW* dates 'Significance' 1914–15, *PPIR* '?Summer 1915'. In either case this poem was written after IR arrived in Cape Town. Originally entitled 'Interest', it had only four verses, the present third verse ('Chaos that coincides', etc.) occurring in a later, holograph fair copy entitled 'Significance', as well as in an untitled BL draft of this verse which has an alternative version written above it.

22 *PPIR*, p. 98.

23 e.g. 'Dawn', 'The Mirror', possibly 'Dusk and the Mirror', also fragment XXX in *PPIR* (p. 159). 'In mingled skies of dark and red'.

24 IR to EM, postmarked 20 or 30 June 1914, *CW*, p. 203.

25 'Of all Eastern Europe's diasporas', Veronica Belling writes in "In Her Own Language" – Ozer Bloshteyn's Yiddish cookbook for Jewish Women (*Jewish Affairs*, Pesach 2006, p. 44), 'The Jewish Community of South Africa constitutes the most undiluted community, eighty per cent having immigrated from Lithuania, Belorus, and Latvia, in the Old Russian Empire, between 1890 and 1914.'

26 District Six would become a victim under Apartheid of the Group Areas Act of 1966, which would declare it a white area, though by then it would be inhabited mainly by non-Europeans and people of mixed race. The inhabitants would be moved out wholesale and dumped outside the city in an area known as the Cape Flats, and there is now no sign of District Six's once vibrant life. Only Beinkinstadt's Jewish Bookshop in Canterbury Street, being on the periphery of the area, has

escaped the bulldozer. A supplier not just of religious books and prayer shawls, but also of Jewish delicacies, such as Redelheim's potato flour and Passover sugar, Rokeach's Kosher Fish Oil, Manischewitz's Famous Matzos, and finest Dutch salted herrings, dill pickles and truffles, it would certainly have been a familiar landmark to Rosenberg on his daily walk down into the city centre. De Villiers Street itself has been renamed De Villiers Avenue.

27 Beatrice Horvitch was born on 27 July 1914.

28 IR's aunt, Mrs A. Rosenberg, is listed in the Juta guide to Cape Town for 1913 as living in Maynard Road, Wynberg, a suburb of Cape Town. She is also listed with the same address under 'Greengrocers and Fruiterers', so must have lived above her shop. While Maynard Road still exists, it is impossible to locate which shop IR visited, since the guide does not give a number for it, or her dwelling.

29 If IR's portrait of Peretz Rosenberg was painted in Cape Town, it would help to explain why its present whereabouts are unknown, since he would almost certainly have presented it to his sitter, who subsequently emigrated to Israel.

30 The Beth Hamidrash in Constitution Street, consecrated in 1897, had accommodation for approximately 300 worshippers. In 1939 it moved out of District Six to a more affluent area higher up the slope, Vredehoek, and amalgamated with the New Hebrew Congregation in 1983 to form the Beth Hamedrash Hachodosh (the United Orthodox Hebrew Congregation). The building still stands, though no longer an active synagogue, on the corner of Vredehoek Avenue and Rabbi Mirvish Avenue (named after its saintly leader, Rabbi M.C. Mirvish).

31 'Wolf' Horvitch was later promoted to Deputy Postmaster of the Caledon Square branch.

32 IR to EM, postmarked ?24 July 1914, *CW*, p. 204.

33 Quoted in DM, p. 54, from First and Scott, p. 200.

34 Isaac Horvitch in an account written for the author in 1974.

35 ibid.

36 *PPIR*, pp. 89–90. There are two pencil drafts and an ink fair copy of this poem, which both *CW* and *PPIR* follow. Line 4 originally read 'lark' for 'bird' and line 5 'watching her' for 'shrined in her'.

37 Ruth Farrington (Ruth had left Alexander for the non-Jewish Ben Farrington, a classics lecturer at the University of Cape Town, in the early Thirties, a daring act at the time) to DH, 20 February 1936, Bristol.

38 Edward Roworth (1880–1964).

39 DB to JL, 8 April 1957, Tate Archives.

40 Notes based on a seminar given by the author at the Kaplan Centre, the Institute of Jewish Studies, at the University of Cape Town on 7 February 2007 and several conversations with Professor Dubow.

41 Author's telephone conversation with Haydn Proud on 9 February 2007.

42 See Edward Roworth's introduction to *Famous Works of Art*, Cape Town, 1939.

43 Morris Robinson to DH, 5 February 1936, Bristol.

44 *PPIR*, p. 339, a pencil note written on the MS of 'A Flea Whose Body Shone like Bead'.

45 Professor Neville Dubow's words.

46 IR to EM, 20 or 30 June 1914, *CW*, p. 203.

47 Minnie Horvitch's memory of IR painting Sir Herbert Stanley's 'three daughters' (Rem., p. 4) cannot be true, since Stanley did not marry (Reniera Cloete) until 1918 when, in any case, they would have two daughters, not three. The commission must have been for a friend or acquaintance.

48 IR to EM, ?24 July 1914, *CW*, p. 205.

49 ibid.

50 Though more detailed than IR's South African self-portrait in a green hat in the opposite profile, there are strong similarities between the two. Whereas I have found no evidence that the National Por-

trait Gallery picture was painted in London, we do know that IR was painting himself frequently in Cape Town.

51 IR to EM, Oct.–Nov. 1914, *CW*, p. 206.

52 This self-portrait is reproduced on the cover of *Selected Poems of Isaac Rosenberg*, ed. Jean Moorcroft Wilson, Cecil Woolf Publishers, 2003.

53 LEC, p. 29. The final quotation is from IR's 'Art', part II, *CW*, p. 294.

54 IR to EM, Oct.–Nov. 1914, *CW*, p. 206.

55 IR to EM, ?July 1914, *CW*, p. 205.

56 Besides painting many landscapes himself, Roworth wrote an article on 'Landscape Art in South Africa', which was published in *The Saul* (date unknown) in an issue devoted to 'Art of the British Empire Overseas'.

57 IR to EM, ?24 July 1914, *CW*, p. 205.

58 ibid.

59 IR to EM, Oct.–Nov. 1914, *CW*, p. 206.

CHAPTER 12

1 *PPIR*, p. 76.

2 Tennent, p. 47.

3 ibid.

4 Undated letter from 'Scrappy' Van Hulsteyn to IR, Bristol.

5 Tennent, p. 48.

6 Morris Robinson to DH, 5 February 1936, Bristol.

7. JC interview with SC, 1960.

8 *CW*, p. xx.

9 *PPIR*, p. 91.

10 Letter from Gwen Ffrangcon-Davies to the author, 8 July 1974.

11 IRFP.

12 *PPIR*, p. 339.

13 Fragment XXXI, *PPIR*, p. 159. Another fragment XXXIII from South Africa which takes up the central image of 'If You Are Fire' is also about female fickleness (*PPIR*, p. 160). 'She kindles fire / Her icy flame is like the moon / She is like the moon / In her icy flame / As a giant turns in sleep.'

14 *PPIR*, pp. 92–3. IR originally wrote 'flame' for 'song' in line 11, linking it more

firmly to Margueretha Van Hulsteyn.

15 Ashbey's, bought by the Robinson brothers from its German founder, was situated in various premises in and around Greenmarket Square in the centre of Cape Town. It was probably in Long Street when IR frequented it between June 1914 and February 1915.

16 Morris Robinson to DH, 5 February 1936, Bristol.

17 Morris Robinson (1890–1947) married the schoolteacher Hettie Sandler, with whom he had three sons and one daughter. After his premature death his second son, Basil, took over the running of Ashbey's until his own death in 2002.

18 Dr Norman Robinson in an interview with the author, 9 February 2007.

19 Morris Robinson to DH, 5 February 1936, Bristol.

20 ibid. IR did, in fact, have two poems published in *South African Women in Council*, 'Beauty' (II) and 'The Dead Heroes', vol. 2, no. 3, December 1914.

21 This notebook is almost certainly the one now preserved in IWM.

22 Letter from Isaac Horvitch to the author, 30 September 1974.

23 This was situated in Burmeister Buildings, which I have been unable to locate.

24 Text of a lecture given at Birkbeck College, University of London, on 30 October 2000. IR evidently felt he needed help in broaching Marinetti, since he was reading *The Italian Futurist Painters*, on whose flyleaf he drafted a poem. (See *PPIR*, p. 381, for note on fragment XXXVIII.) This was discovered later by the South African writer William Plomer, but I have been unable to identify the book further.

25 *CW*, p. 290.

26 ibid.

27 ibid., p. 291.

28 IR to EM, ?24 July 1914, *CW*, p. 204.

29 ibid., postmarked 8 August 1914, *CW*, p. 205.

30 Tennent, pp. 46–7.

31 ibid., p. 46. The portrait-drawing of Madge Cook could be one of three female heads IR drew in 1914. One possibility is the sketch now in the Jewish Museum, Cape Town, though this is in chalk not pencil (monochrome plate 14 in *CW*, opp. p. 157). Another is monochrome plate 10 (b) (*CW*, opp. p. 161), which though described as 'chalk' by IP is titled 'Pencil Study of a Girl' by JC (present whereabouts unknown). The third possibility is definitely a pencil portrait, monochrome plate 6 (a) (*CW*, opp. p. 97), subject unidentified, though said by some critics to be IR's sister Minnie.

32 The Cooks were living at Camp's Bay by 1936, when Agnes Cook wrote to DH, but had also lived at Sea-Point, and may have been living there when IR wrote his poem 'At Sea-Point'. Their town apartment was at 38 Church Street, very central and very close to Ashbey's Galleries.

33 Agnes Cook to DH, 31 March 1936, Bristol.

34 Tennent, p. 51.

35 Agnes Cook to DH, 31 March 1936, Bristol.

36 ibid.

37 The quotation is taken from an account given to JC by AW and originally transcribed by Wolf Horvitch from Agnes Cook.

38 'Art', part II came out in *South African Women in Council* in January 1915, vol. 2, no. 4.

39 IR to his family, ?1914, *CW*, p. 342.

40 IR to Betty Molteno, ?May 1915, University of Cape Town Libraries.

41 Sandown House has since been demolished, after having been first turned into a nursing home, according to Betty Molteno's great-niece, Selina Cohen.

42 Late 1914, *CW*, p. 207.

43 'A Bird Trilling its Gay Heart Out', *PPIR*, p. 79.

44 IR to EM, spring 1915, *CW*, p. 210.

45 ibid.

46 IR to EM, Oct.–Nov. 1914, *CW*, p. 206.

CHAPTER 13

1 *CW*, p. 206.

2 IR to EM, postmarked 8 August 1914, *CW*, p. 205. The reference to the 'North Pole' is probably inspired by Ernest Shackleton's expedition of 1914.

3 See stanzas 60 to 66. The influence of 'Locksley Hall' is also evident in a poem written shortly after this letter, 'Under These Skies'.

4 IR to EM, ?24 July 1914, *CW*, p. 204.

5 ibid., Oct.–Nov. 1914, *CW*, 206.

6 IP reads IR's comment in this letter of Oct.–Nov. 1914 as 'This is the last thing I've written', whereas JC transcribes it 'This is the best thing I've written'.

7 DM, p. 135.

8 *PPIR*, pp. 85–6.

9 IR had shown his knowledge of Kabbalah in at least one of his earlier poems, 'Creation', where, as Vivien Noakes points out, line 81 reflects the 'Kabbalistic view of creation as an emanation, the coming into being of the universe through the unfolding in stages of the essence of God rather than *creatio ex nihilo*' (*PPIR*, p. 326).

10 Beth Ellen Roberts, 'The Female God of Isaac Rosenberg: A Muse for Wartime', *English Literature in Transition*, vol. 39: 3, 1996, p. 321.

11 ibid.

12 ibid.

13 Cf. IR's reference to Heine's poem 'Princess Sabbath' (IR to BR, received 11 August 1917, *CW*, p. 261).

14 'Like Some Fair Subtle Poison', *PPIR*, p. 40.

15 *PPIR*, pp. 83–4. *PPIR* gives the full title of this poem as 'On Receiving News of the War: Cape Town', and an MS at the Berg as 'News of the War in S.A.'.

16 Roberts, op. cit., p. 327.

17 Silkin, p. 275.

18 Samson, p. 33. The passage is from Isaiah 1: 18–20.

19 Bergonzi, p. 112.

20 DM, p. 155.

21 IR to MHC, prob. late Oct.–Nov. 1916, *CW*, p. 238.

22 *PPIR*, p. 130.

23 *PPIR*, pp. 86–7.

24 *PPIR*, p. 333.

25 *PPIR*, p. 84.

26 Rem., p. 3.

27 Reported by David Dainow in his 1960 interview with JC, USC.

28 *JT*, p. 112.

29 JC's notes of his 1960 interview with David Dainow, USC.

30 Mrs Ruth Swade in a telephone interview with the author, 30 October 2006.

31 IR to EM, 'Oct.–Nov. 1914, *CW*, p. 206.

32 IR noted down the addresses of two or three schools in Johannesburg during his stay, which suggests he may also have applied there: 'Roedean School, Miss Barber', and 'Johansberg [*sic*] S of Art St Margarets School roon Union Ground J.' (*PPIR*, p. 338)

33 Morris Robinson to DH, 5 February 1936, Bristol. It is most unlikely that IR refused to remove his hat on religious grounds.

34 *CW*, p. 204.

35 Morris Robinson to DH, 5 February 1936, Bristol.

36 DB to JL, 8 April 1957, Tate Archives.

37 Morris Robinson to DH, 5 February 1936, Bristol.

38 ibid.

39 *CW*, p. 205.

40 Dr Norman Robinson in an interview with the author, 9 February 2007.

41 IR to EM, ?24 July 1914, *CW*, p. 205.

42 Fragment XXXIX, *PPIR*, p. 162.

43 IR to Betty Molteno, ?May 1915, University of Cape Town Libraries.

44 ibid.

45 ibid.

46 ibid.

47 *PPIR*, p. 94.

CHAPTER 14

1 University of Cape Town Libraries.

2 Rodker, *Memoirs of Other Fronts*, p. 77.

3 Aldington and Gurney were rejected at first on medical grounds but accepted later when standards were lowered.

4 Litvinoff, p. 30.

5 IR to RCT, last week of May 1916, *CW*, p. 234.

6 MacDougall, pp. 100–1.

7 JL, who was born in Holland and still unnaturalized by 1914, could claim exemption as a 'neutral alien' and MGe was exempt to begin with because his parents had come from Austria and were therefore 'enemy aliens'. MG was not naturalized until the late 1940s.

8 JR described his experience at this time in *Memoirs of Other Fronts*, and SW in his 1920 collection of poems, *Chains*.

9 Rodker, *Memoirs of Other Fronts*, p. 111.

10 ibid.

11 IR to EM, late December 1915, *CW*, p. 227.

12 ibid.

13 *Daily Telegraph*, 13 June 1916.

14 Hibberd, *Harold Monro*, p. 148.

15 IR to SS, October 1915, *CW*, p. 218.

16 IR to Ezra Pound, apparently unfinished letter, 1915, *CW*, p. 214.

17 SC told her daughter Joan, born 1 May 1915, that this portrait was painted just before her birth.

18 *CW*, p. 211.

19 ibid.

20 IR to EM, Oct.–Nov. 1914, *CW*, p. 206.

21 I am grateful to Julia Weiner for this suggestion, made during her lecture on IR's art at Toynbee Hall, London, on 1 April 2006.

22 IR submitted to NEAC Winter Show and had hung: 'Drawing' (unspecified), 'Gray and Red' and 'The Family of Adam and Eve' (now lost).

23 JC, who owned this picture for some time, dates it 1912, perhaps relying on DB's dating '1912' in the 1937 WAG exhibition of IR's work. It is just possible that IR executed two different versions of the same title and that the one referred to in his letter to Marsh was either not finished or lost.

24 IR to EM, ?1915, *CW*, p. 213. Meredith's couplet has been misquoted by IR, its first

line should read: 'And every face to watch him raised'.

25 IR to EM, Spring 1915, *CW*, p. 210.

26 IR to WS, Dec.–Jan. 1912–13, *CW*, p. 198. Emile Verhaeren (1855–1916) was a Symbolist poet and was published in London by Lucille Pissarro at the Eragny Press in 1901. Eragny Press books were usually beautifully illustrated, an added appeal for IR.

27 IR to GB, postmarked 29 August 1916, *PHH*, p. 83.

28 GB to DH, 25 June 1937, Bristol.

29 *PPIR*, pp. 114–15.

30 GB to IR, 4 July 1916, IWM.

31 Spring 1915, 'You cleave to my bones ...', *CW*, p. 208.

32 IR to EM, March–April 1915, *CW*, p. 212.

33 See chapter 10, note 34.

34 IR to EM, Spring 1915, *CW*, p. 210.

35 IR to SS, 8 June 1915, *CW*, p. 216.

36 ibid.

37 Of the poems probably written between 1914 and 1915 the seven selected were 'None Have Seen the Lord of the House', 'A Girl's Thoughts', 'Love and Lust', 'Break in by Subtler, Nearer Ways', 'God Made Blind', 'The Dead Heroes' and 'The Cloister'.

38 These were 'Aspiration', 'In the Park / In the Woods', 'Desire Sings of Immortality', 'Noon in the City', 'Lady, You Are My God' and 'In the Workshop'. It is puzzling that IR decided *not* to include 'Sacred, Voluptuous Hollows Deep' and 'The Female God', both of which are powerful poems.

39 *PPIR*, pp. 97–8.

40 IR to EM, Spring 1915, *CW*, p. 210.

41 IR's use of two shorter lines at the centre of each 8-line stanza emphasizes the contrast between God's long-drawn-out malignancy and the narrator's short, sharp, sexual 'joy' and 'gleeful ecstasy'. His personification of love, with his 'heady valour', 'loved pain' and 'springing eagerness', conveys the physicality of the narrator's passion but also its power to make him

Godlike. And the contrasts set up throughout – between love and hate, God and his creature, openness and deceit, blindness and seeing – are mirrored in the imagery, in particular that of the last two lines of the opening stanza.

42 *PPIR*, p. 15.

43 DM, p. 139.

44 IR to EM, Spring 1915, *CW*, p. 211. IR's final arrangement would be:

Faith and fear: 'Aspiration', 'In the Park', 'Song of Immortality', 'Noon in the City', 'None Have Seen the Lord of the House', 'A Girl's Thoughts', 'Wedded', 'Midsummer Frost'. *The Cynic's Lamp*: 'Love and Lust', 'In Piccadilly', 'A Mood'. *Change and Sunfire*: 'April Dawn', 'If You Are Fire', 'Dim-watery-Lights', 'Break in by Subtler Ways', 'Lady, You Are My God', 'The One Lost', 'My Soul Is Robbed', 'God Made Blind', 'The Dead Heroes', 'The Cloister', 'Expression'.

45 i.e. Sydney Schiff, R.C. Trevelyan, Gordon Bottomley and Jacob ('Jack') Isaacs. Even before printing *Youth* IR's doubts about the middle section had made him cut two poems from it: 'The Cynic's Path' and 'Tess'.

46 IR to EM, March–April 1915, *CW*, p. 212.

47 Bonham's sale 15,230 – the library of the late Paul Betts, and other properties including MSS and photography, 27 March 2007. (Letter headed '87 Dempsey Street'.)

48 *Colour*, a middle-of-the-road publication which steered well away from the avant-garde, gave IR his first appearance in a London magazine when it printed three of his lyrics in its June, July and August numbers respectively: 'Heart's First Word' (II), 'A Girl's Thoughts' and 'Wedded' (II), each poem placed beneath a picture, in turn, a seascape by Sydney Pavière, a portrait of Frank Brangwyn by Joseph Simpson and a nude bending over

two swans by Maurice Langaskens. Though, as JC points out, 'few poets could have been more out of place' in the pages of this 'chic, bourgeois, coffee-table publication', the 'little romantic poems' IR submitted were 'well suited to the magazine's indulgence in polite fantasies'. (*JT*, p. 114)

49 Letter in the possession of JC (given him by AW).

50 Hassall, p. 329.

51 ibid., p. 346.

52 ibid., pp. 344–5.

53 Quoted in an unfinished piece on IR by JL, CZA.

54 IR to EM, April–May 1915, *CW*, p. 215.

55 Searle, p. 40.

56 IR to EM, April–May 1915, *CW*, p. 215.

57 Sydney Schiff (1868–1944).

58 Interview with JC, 1960, USC.

59 *The Apes of God* was published in 1930 and enraged many of its victims.

60 Lewis, p. 240.

61 ibid.

62 IR to SS, ?April 1915, *CW*, p. 213.

63 *CW*, p. 215.

64 *PPIR*, p. 120. Despite IR's description of the *Lusitania* as 'peace-faring' it emerged that she had been carrying small-arms ammunition as well as passengers on her journey across the Atlantic from America.

65 *PPIR*, p. 123.

66 Absalom, the favourite son of King David who nevertheless betrayed him, was killed while escaping on horseback when his long hair caught in the overhanging branches of a tree.

67 *PPIR*, pp. 103–4.

68 IR to EM, May–June 1914, *CW*, p. 202.

69 *PPIR*, pp. 104–5.

70 IR to RCT, postmarked 15 June 1916, *CW*, p. 235.

71 *CW*, p. 216.

72 ibid.

73 ibid.

74 IR to SS, July 1915, *CW*, p. 216.

75 IR to SS, September 1915, *CW*, p. 217.

76 IR to SS, July 1915, *CW*, p. 217.

77 IR to SS, October 1915, *CW*, p. 218.

78 ibid., p. 217.

79 This was almost certainly at the LCC Central School of Art and Crafts, Southampton Row, London, since IR jotted some lines of verse on the lower half of a printed letter from this address. The letter accompanied a prospectus for the 1915–16 session. (IWM)

80 IR to SS, October 1915, *CW*, p. 218.

81 ibid., ?October 1915, *CW*, p. 219.

CHAPTER 15

1 IR to SS, October 1915, *CW*, p. 218.

2 The Suffolk Regiment was amalgamated in 1959 with the Royal Norfolk Regiment as the 1st East Anglian Regiment.

3 Sorley, p. 195.

4 IR to EM, October 1915, *CW*, p. 219.

5 ibid.

6 IR to SS, October 1915, *CW*, p. 219.

7 ibid.

8 Letter to A.E. Hutchinson, 20 September 1914, Sorley, p. 189.

9 IR to SS, early 1916, *CW*, p. 229.

10 ibid.

11 IR to SS, October 1915, *CW*, p. 220.

12 ibid.

13 ibid.

14 Notes sent to the author in 1974. Waley was with a Trench Mortar Battery and IR was 'in the cookhouse' while serving under him.

15 IR to SS, early November 1915, *CW*, p. 220.

16 IR to SS, November 1915, *CW*, p. 222.

17 IR to EM, late December 1915, *CW*, p. 227.

18 IR to EM, Oct.–Nov. 1915, *CW*, p. 223.

19 IR to SS, October 1915, *CW*, p. 219.

20 IR to SS, November 1915, *CW*, p. 222.

21 Henry Morris in an interview with the author, 16 March 2006.

22 See 'Anti-Semitism in England at War, 1914–1916', *Patterns of Prejudice*, ed. Elkan D. Levy, London, 1970; 'An Embattled Minority: the Jews in Britain During the

First World War', article from *Immigrants and Minorities*, March 1989, reprinted in *The Politics of Marginality: Race, the Radical Right and Minorities in Twentieth-Century Britain*, London, 1990; 'Russian Jews in Britain During the First World War' by Asher Tropp, unpublished MA thesis for the University of London; *Die Hard, Aby!* by David Lister, Pen and Sword, 2005.

23 Sidney Allinson, p. 253.

24 ibid.

25 Interview with the author, 1974.

26 Notes sent to the author in 1974.

27 Interview with the author, 1974.

28 *PPIR*, p. 126.

29 IR to SS, early November 1915, *CW*, p. 221.

30 IR to EM, December 1915, *CW*, p. 225.

31 IR to EM, Oct.–Dec. 1915, *CW*, p. 223.

32 IR to SS, November 1915, *CW*, p. 221.

33 *CW*, p. 224.

34 IR to EM, Dec. 1915, *CW*, p. 225.

35 IR to SS, last week of May 1916, *CW*, p. 233.

36 IR to WS, December 1915, *CW*, p. 226.

37 IR to SS, November 1915, *CW*, p. 222.

38 IR to SS, early December 1915, *CW*, p. 224.

39 IR to WS, Spring 1916, *CW*, p. 331.

40 ibid.

41 Interview with the author, 1974.

42 ibid.

43 IR to SS, November 1915, *CW*, pp. 221–2.

44 IR to SS, early 1916, *CW*, p. 230.

45 Quoted by IR in a letter to SS, early December 1915, *CW*, p. 224.

46 LA to EM, postmarked 3 November 1915, Berg.

47 IR to WS, December 1915, *CW*, p. 226.

48 IR to EM, ?November 1915, *CW*, p. 224.

49 IR to EM, Spring 1915, p. 211.

50 i.e. 'The Sale of St Thomas' in *Georgian Poetry 1911–1912* and 'The End of the World' in *New Numbers*, vol. 1, no. 2, April 1914.

51 IR to EM, postmarked 10 October 1916, *CW*, p. 248.

52 IR to WS, prob. March 1915, *CW*, p. 208.

53 *CW*, p. xvi.

54 IR wrote to GB (letter postmarked 29 August 1916) about Abercrombie's verse plays: 'I always enjoy (especially out here) his work; and the wit in this play is strong and robust.' (*PHH*, p. 82)

55 IR to SS, November 1915, *CW*, p. 222.

56 IR to EM, postmarked, 1 December 1915, *CW*, p. 223.

57 ibid.

58 ibid.

59 IR to LA, 11 March 1916, *CW*, p. 230.

60 IR to SS, late December 1915, *CW*, p. 227. Cf. 'What If I Wear Your Beauty As This Present', ll. 11–12: 'I like an insect beautiful wings have gotten / Shed from you . . .' (*PPIR*, p. 78)

61 *PPIR*, pp. 123–4.

62 These were vol. II, no. 1 (April 1913), which contained Pound's 'Contemporania' and 'Tenzone – The Condolence – The Garret – The Garden – Ortus – Dance Figure – Salutation – Salutation the Second – Pax Saturni – Commission – A Pact – In a Station of the Metro', and vol. III, no. II (November 1913), in which the section containing Pound's poems ('Ancora – Surgit Fama – The Choice – April – Gentildonna – Lustra I, II III – Xenia I, II, III, IV, V, VI, VII') has either been removed or, less believably, fallen out. AW has marked the November 1913 copy 'IR's Library' (IRFP).

63 JR to Harriet Monroe, 25 February 1916, Chicago.

64 IR to EM, late December 1915, *CW*, p. 227.

65 See Cork, p. 115.

66 See the striking jacket of Sarah Mac-Dougall's *Mark Gertler* biography.

67 IR to EM, postmarked 29 January 1916, *CW*, p. 229. It has not been possible to establish whether 'Marching' as it stands incorporates the few extra lines IR sent to Marsh. (See *PPIR*, pp. 354–5, for a fuller discussion of this.)

68 JR to Harriet Monroe, 25 February 1916, Chicago.

CHAPTER 16

1 *CW*, p. 230.

2 IR was not to see *Georgian Poetry 1913–1915* until 1916. When the War Cabinet had been reconstituted in November 1915 and Churchill had not, as EM hoped, been recalled, Churchill enlisted in the Grenadier Guards (after arranging a secretaryship for Marsh which he did not want) and left for the Front immediately.

3 IR to EM, postcard postmarked 19 May 1916, *CW*, p. 232.

4 IR to SS, early December 1915, *CW*, p. 224.

5 There had been a large number of under-size volunteers still on the rolls of the South Lancashires' Warrington recruiting committee in September 1915. Lacking only a battalion able to accept them, the authorities had created the 12th (Service) Battalion, appointing Lt. Col. W.B. Ritchie, DSO as its Commanding Officer. This then formed part of the 120th Brigade of the 40th Division and was sent to Divisional Headquarters in Aldershot to prepare for the Front.

6 *CW*, pp. 228–9.

7 ibid.

8 IR to SS, ?March 1916, *CW*, p. 230.

9 IR to EM, postmarked 5 January 1916, *CW*, p. 229.

10 IR to EM, postmarked 29 January 1916, *CW*, p. 229.

11 Sorley, p. 212.

12 IR to SS, early 1916, *CW*, p. 230.

13 Lines 17–20 of what *CW* calls 'Sleep (another version)' and *PPIR* 'Sleep' (II) are incorporated into *Moses*, act 1, ll. 106–9.

14 'Sleep' (II), *PPIR*, p. 125.

15 'Sleep' (I), *PPIR*, pp. 119–20.

16 Note to 'Sleep' in *CW*, p. 97.

17 *PPIR*, p. 125.

18 GB notes to DH about their 1937 edition of IR's poems, Bristol. IR had written variously in different drafts 'the pink', 'pink neck' and 'vague pink'.

19 Carter, p. 4.

20 IR to WS, *CW*, p. 231.

21 Sidney Allinson, p. 138.

22 ibid., pp. 152–3.

23 IR to WS, Spring 1916, *CW*, p. 231.

24 ibid.

25 ibid.

26 IR to EM, October–November 1915, *CW*, p. 224.

27 IR to EM, *CW*, p. 228.

28 IR to WS, Spring 1916, *CW*, p. 231.

29 IR sent copies to all his friends and patrons, including EM, SS, RCT, GB, LA, WS and Lazarus Aaronson. He must also have given copies to JL and JR, and certainly sent one to Israel Zangwill, who replied (to IR's sister) on 12 June 1916: 'You can tell him from me that I think there are a good many beautiful and powerful lines, but that I hope his experiences of war will give his next book the clarity and simplicity which is somewhat lacking in this.' (IRFP)

30 These were 'Marching', 'Sleep', 'Spring 1916', 'In the Park' (pub. in both *Night and Day* and *Youth*), 'God', ['I Did Not Pluck At All'], 'Chagrin', 'Wedded', and 'Heart's First Word'.

31 Now at the IWM.

32 IR to Alice Wright, postmarked 10 August 1912, *CW*, p. 188. See *The Cenci*, act V, sc. IV, ll. 48–74.

33 Stephen Phillips (1864–1915) first came to public notice with his *Poems* (1898), which won him a literary award. There was a short-lived vogue for his 'sonorous poetic dramas' (*Cambridge Companion to English Literature*), of which Beerbohm Tree produced four: *Herod* (1900), *Ulysses* (1902), *Nero* (1906) and *Faust* (1908). George Alexander also staged what many consider to be his best effort in the genre, *Paolo and Francesca* (1902). Marsh, who saw at least one of his plays, *Ulysses*, was not impressed, but IR may have been referring to Phillips when he asked GB whether he knew the author of 'Erebus', a mistaken reference GB believed to Phillips's verse play *Eremus*. There was, however, a book of poetry called *Erebus* by Evangeline Ryves, pub. anon. in 1903 and reissued by Elkin Mathews in 1913.

34 IR also discarded some prose passages

describing Moses and the burning bush, and the final version is completely in verse.

35 *PPIR*, pp. 193–4.

36 Exodus 2:11–12.

37 *Jerusalem*, f. 10, l. 20.

38 IR to Israel Zangwill, late May 1916, *CW*, p. 233.

39 Scene II, ll. 326–8, *PPIR*, pp. 200–2.

40 *JT*, p. 140.

41 ibid.

42 *Moses*, ll. 347–51, *PPIR*, pp. 202–3. Cf. 'God', ll. 11–15, *PPIR*, p. 117.

43 See *Moses*, ll. 139–44, *PPIR*, p. 192.

44 *JT*, p. 142.

45 See *Moses*, IWM facsimile edition, 1990, ed. with an introduction by Martin Taylor.

46 *My Head! My Head!* by Robert Graves, Martin Secker, 1925, pp. 24–5. I am grateful to DM for this reference. (See DM, pp. 149–50.)

47 e.g. Silkin, pp. 301–7.

48 e.g. Lawson, pp. 19–43.

49 'Creation', l. 34, *PPIR*, p. 66.

50 Samuel Hynes, *The Auden Generation*, Bodley Head, 1976, p. 15.

51 ibid., p. 14.

52 Bergonzi, *Heroes' Twilight: A Study of the Literature of the Great War*.

53 IR to EM, prob. December 1916, *CW*, p. 250.

54 IR to JL, 8 Dec. 1917, *CW*, p. 267.

55 Hassall, pp. 401–2.

56 ibid.

57 IR to EM, postmarked 17 August 1916, *CW*, p. 192.

58 Allentuck, p. 65.

59 *PPIR*, pp. 188–9.

60 Sisson, p. 90.

61 Hassall, p. 402.

62 ibid. Hassall is quoting from GB's letter to Marsh.

63 See Dennis Silk, 'Isaac Rosenberg (1890–1918)', *Judaism*, xiv, No. 4 (Autumn 1965), pp. 562–74.

64 Sisson, p. 89.

65 ibid.

66 IR to SS, late July 1916, *CW*, p. 238.

67 GB to IR, 4 July 1916, IWM. IR had not read any of GB's verse plays before writing *Moses*, though he was able to do so afterwards and admire them.

68 Hassall, p. 402.

69 IR to EM, postmarked 12 July 1916, *CW*, p. 236. *CW* gives 'June 12', but GB did not write his first letter to IR until 4 July 1916.

70 IR to GB, postmarked 23 July 1916, *CW*, p. 238.

71 Cf. Lawson, p. 22: 'Rosenberg's theory of an "ungraspable" poetry relates both to the traditional Jewish conception of an unrepresentable God and to an "ineffable" or indefinable Jewish identity.'

72 Whitton, p. 12.

73 Carter, p. 5.

74 IR to EM, prob. 27 May 1916, *CW*, p. 234.

75 IR to SS, last week of May, *CW*, p. 232.

76 Quoted in *JT*, p. 136.

77 This is given as the SS *City of Benares* in Sidney Allinson, but SS *Clementine* in the Battalion history, which is confirmed by the KORL diary.

78 Sidney Allinson, p. 142.

79 Frank Kermode and John Hollander, *The Oxford Anthology of English Literature: Modern British Literature*, New York, 1973, p. 550.

80 *PPIR*, p. 126. IR sent 'The Troop Ship' to GB in his first letter to him, postmarked 12 July 1916. See *PHH*, pp. 21–2.

81 *PPIR*, p. 127.

CHAPTER 17

1 *PPIR*, pp. 136–7.

2 Sidney Allinson, p. 143.

3 ibid., p. 19; Whitton, p. 25.

4 IR to WS, June 1916, *CW*, p. 235.

5 *JT*, p. 148, based on AW's account to him.

6 *PPIR*, p. 131.

7 The one surviving MS of 'Wan, Fragile Faces' bears no title, though another MS or TS may have.

8 IR to EM, probably December 1916, *CW*, p. 250.

9 IR to WS, written in hospital, 15 November 1917, *CW*, pp. 265–6.

10 IR to GB, postmarked 22 October 1917, *PHH*, p. 112.

11 *PPIR*, pp. 131–2.

12 Carter, p. 5.

13 AW wrote in *Art & Letters* (summer 1919, London): 'The last work of his, which was done in the trenches, was a watercolour panel of himself, entitled by him "The New Fashion boiler hat" – the trench hat.'

14 GB to IR, 7 September 1916, IWM.

15 ibid.

16 IR to RCT, *c.* June 1916, *CW*, p. 245.

17 IR to WS, June 1916, *CW*, p. 235.

18 Arthur, *Last Post*, p. 84.

19 Foreword to *CWHB*, p. ix.

20 Apart from variations to the punctuation introduced almost certainly by the editor, there was an extra line following l.8 '(And God knows what antipathies)' and the American version printed four completely different lines between l. 19 and the final couplet: 'At the boom, the hiss, the swiftness, / The irrevocable earth buffet— / The shell's haphazard fury. / What rootless poppies dropping?' a quatrain that IR greatly improved in a later version, dated June 1916, in which he also deleted the line in parenthesis following l. 8. IR sent a version to GB (in a letter postmarked 23 July 1916) which was clearly later than the one sent to *Poetry* (Chicago), since he tells him: 'The poem "In the Trenches", I altered a little and have asked my sister to send on to you. I left a line out "a shell's haphazard fury" after "irrevocable earth buffet". I don't think I made my meaning quite clear that it is a shell bursting which has only covered my [*sic*] and the poppy I plucked at the beginning of poem still in my ear with dust' (*PHH*, p. 73). Another TS of the poem sent to GB substitutes 'It seems, odd thing, you grin as you pass' for 'It seems you inwardly grin as you pass'; like DH, who argued that IR's intentions were ambiguous in this respect (DH to IP, 31 January 1966), I prefer the latter version.

21 *PPIR*, p. 127.

22 IR enclosed 'In the Trenches' in an undated letter (*CW*, p. 245).

23 GB to IR, 19 July 1916, IWM. IR's probable response (postmarked 23 July 1916) enclosing a new draft of the poem shows that the ending has still not arrived at the perfection of his final choice, his last three lines of this version reading: 'A shell! / Safe. Again murder has overlooked us / Only white with powder and chalk.' (*PHH*, p. 75)

24 IR to EM, 4 August 1916, *CW*, p. 239.

25 *PPIR*, p. 128.

26 See *PPIR*, p. 359, which notes that the 'sanctity' was replaced by the less illuminating 'sense' in IR's letter to EM of 4 August 1916.

27 See note 20 for my choice of this alternate reading to *PPIR*.

28 See stanza 3 of 'A Flea Whose Body Shone Like Bead': 'A rat whose droll shape would dart and flit / Was like a torch to light my wit' (*PPIR*, p. 95).

29 Leone Samson and Diana Collecott both favour this view.

30 IR to EM, 4 August 1916, *CW*, p. 239.

31 Fussell, p. 250.

32 IR to EM, postmarked 30 June 1916, *CW*, p. 237.

33 IWM.

34 IR to GB, postmarked 23 July 1916, *PHH*, p. 74.

35 IWM.

36 IR to EM, *CW*, p. 241.

37 IR to GB, postmarked 15 August 1916, *PHH*, p. 81.

38 IR to SS, August 1916, *CW*, p. 242.

39 IR to JR, n.d., *CW*, p. 242.

40 *PPIR*, p. 133. IR sent a version of 'Pozières' to GB in a letter postmarked 29 August 1916 (*PHH*, p. 82), which differs only in two minor respects of punctuation and spelling (or rather *mis*spelling). It was written, he told GB, in mid-August 1916.

41 IR to GB, postmarked 29 August 1916, *PHH*, p. 80.

42 H.W. Massingham (1860–1924) edited the *Nation* from 1907 to 1923.

43 IR to SS, late August 1916, *CW*, p. 243.

44 See Wilson, *Siegfried Sassoon: the Making of a War Poet*, pp. 373ff.
45 IR to JR, n.d. *CW*, p. 251.
46 IWM.
47 IR to SS, late July 1916, *CW*, p. 239.
48 IR to SS, August 1916, *CW*, p. 242.
49 IR to SC, n.d. but prob. before August 1916, since IR includes 'In the Trenches' with his letter, *CW*, p. 245.

CHAPTER 18

1 IR to LB, *CW*, p. 248. The full text of the letter is in the BL.
2 *PHH*, p. 83.
3 Whitton, p. 38.
4 IR to EM, August 1916, *CW*, p. 243.
5 Whitton, p. 40.
6 IR to GB, postmarked 17 & 20 September 1916, *PHH*, pp. 83–4.
7 *PPH*, p. 86.
8 'The Destruction of Jerusalem by the Babylonian Hordes', *PPIR*, p. 137, was written just before 12 November 1916.
9 *PHH*, p. 86.
10 IR to GB, postmarked 5 December 1916, *PHH*, p. 87.
11 IR to LB, ?December 1916, *PHH*, p. 68.
12 Whitton, p. 42.
13 The Battalion diary records that 11th KORL relieved the 13th York Regiment, 121st Brigade, just north of Suzanne, and on 4 January 1917 relieved the 19th Royal Welch Fusiliers in the Rancourt Sector. IR was almost certainly transferred to the 40th Division's Works Battalion on 31 December.
14 IR to EM, probably December 1916, *CW*, p. 250.
15 IR to GB, postmarked 5 January 1917, *PHH*, p. 88.
16 AW wrote to EM on 2 January 1917: 'My brother has asked me to write you with a view to obtain your assistance in getting him leave. ... Please see what you can do' etc. Berg.
17 A.J. Creedy to EM, 8 January 1917, Berg.
18 IR to GB, postmarked 5 January 1917, *PHH*, p. 89.

19 ibid.
20 IR to EM, postmarked 18 January 1917, *CW*, p. 251.
21 Frank Waley, interview with the author, 1974. All subsequent quotes from Waley are taken from this interview and from letters sent to the author during 1974.
22 Letter to the author, 5 February 1975.
23 Frank Waley to Vivien Noakes, quoted in Liddiard, p. 215.
24 ibid.
25 See IR to GB, ?July 1917, *PHH*, p. 93. Gasmasks had replaced gas-helmets by 1917.
26 Whitton, p. 40.
27 IR to EM, postmarked 8 February 1917, *CW*, p. 252.
28 IR to GB, postmarked 8 April 1917, *CW*, p. 253.
29 GB to IR, 12 February 1917, IWM.
30 IR to LB, Autumn 1916, *PHH*, p. 66.
31 IR to EM, 4 August 1916, *CW*, p. 239. This survives only in a fragment of just over 30 lines (*CW*, p. 177).
32 Deborah Maccoby gives an excellent summary of *Adam and Lilith* and its legendary origins. (See DM, p. 203.)
33 *PPIR*, p. 235.
34 *PPIR*, p. 237.
35 ibid.
36 IR to GB, postmarked 23 July 1916, *PHH*, p. 73.
37 IR to LB, Autumn 1916, *PHH*, p. 66.
38 Alice Mayes quotes DB's letter in her unpublished TS 'The Young Bomberg', now in the Tate Archives.
39 See IR to GB, postmarked 23 July 1916, *PHH*, p. 73.
40 IR to SS, ?August 1916, *CW*, p. 244.
41 IR to LB, *CW*, pp. 248–9.
42 IR to GB, postmarked 8 April 1917, *CW*, p. 253.
43 IR to MHC, n.d., *CW*, p. 237.
44 IR to SS, August 1916, *CW*, p. 240.
45 IR to EM, prob. December 1916, *CW*, p. 250.
46 IR to GB, 5 December 1916, *PHH*, p. 87.

47 IR to EM, prob. December 1916, *CW*, p. 250.

48 IWM.

49 IR to GB, postmarked 15 August 1916, *PHH*, p. 81.

50 ibid.

51 IR to EM, postmarked 8 February 1917, *CW*, p. 252.

52 *PPIR*, pp. 133–4.

53 IWM.

54 IR to GB, postmarked 23 July 1916, *PHH*, p. 73.

55 *Poems* (1922), p. 40.

56 *PPIR*, pp. 134–6.

57 In this particular instance, however, one of Rosenberg's models for 'dynamic' form may have come from art. In 1914 Bomberg had sketched some scenes from Diaghilev's Russian Ballet, which was still holding London in thrall for reasons Bomberg tried to sum up in the brief text that accompanied the lithographs he later made from his drawings:

Methodic discord startles . . .

Insistent snatchings drag fancy from space,
Fluttering white hands beat – compel. Reason concedes.
Impressions crowding collide with movement around
Us – the curtain falls – the created illusion escapes.
The mind clamped fast captures only a fragment for new illusion. (Quoted in Cork, p. 125.)

Since Rosenberg was in frequent contact with Bomberg in 1914, before he left for South Africa, he would almost certainly have seen his ballet sketches and been reminded of them by Bottomley's reference to 'a naked ballet for the Russian dancers'. Parts of Bomberg's text sound like raw material for 'Louse Hunting'.

58 'The Jolly Beggars' appeared in an edition of Burns's *Poems and Songs* in the Harvard Classics Series, published between 1909 and 1914, when IR was reading a great deal of poetry. He may, however, have read 'The Jolly Beggars' when he met the Scotsmen of the Black Watch in June 1916.

59 IR to GB, 8 April 1917, *CW*, p. 253.

CHAPTER 19

1 *PHH*, p. 92.

2 IR to EM, postmarked 25 April 1917, *CW*, p. 254.

3 Whitton, p. 59.

4 IR to EM, *CW*, p. 254.

5 IR to EM, postmarked 25 April 1917, *CW*, pp. 253–4.

6 IR to EM, February 1917, *CW*, p. 253.

7 *PPIR*, pp. 138–9.

8 Connor, p. 6.

9 'Joy', *CW*, p. 303.

10 IR to GB, postmarked 23 July 1916, *CW*, p. 238.

11 IR to EM, 10 October 1916, *CW*, p. 248.

12 IR to EM, postmarked 27 May 1917, *CW*, p. 255.

13 IR to GB, postmarked 31 May 1917, *PHH*, p. 92.

14 IR to EM, postmarked 8 May 1917, *CW*, p. 254.

15 *PPIR*, pp. 139–42.

16 GB to IR, 29 June 1917, IWM.

17 In one draft to GB, IR had a few minor variants in the first three stanzas, then, after stanza 3 included 4 lines omitted in the final version: 'Now let the seasons know / There are some less to feed of them / That winter need not hoard her snow / Nor autumn her fruits and green.' After 'soul's sack' he omitted another 2 lines: 'Emptied of all that made it more than the world / In its small fleshy compass.' With regard to 'the swift iron burning bee', the protagonist in Scott Turow's *Ordinary Heroes*, set in the Second World War, says that 'the real sound of a round that misses is just a sinister little sizzle and a wake of roiled air, a bee farting as it passes'.

18 Tomlinson, p. 14. For 'Emptied of God-ancestralled essences' IR had originally written 'Emptied of all that made it more than the world' etc. (see note 17 above), a prime example of his ability to condense meaning.

19 ibid., p. 15.

20 *PPIR*, p. 130.

21 IR omitted a full stanza eventually after 'Dear things, war-blotted from their hearts'; 'Maniac Earth! howling and flying, / your bowel / Seared by the jagged fire, the iron love, / The impetuous storm of savage love. / Dark Earth! Dark heaven, swinging in chemic smoke / What dead are born when you kiss each soundless soul / With lightning and thunder from your mined heart, / Which man's self dug, and his blind fingers loosed.'

22 See *PPIR*, pp. 368–9.

23 DM, p. 180.

24 IR to EM, postmarked 27 May 1917, *CW*, pp. 254–5.

25 Sent home to his sister for typing, these drafts were IR's attempt to ensure that his work was not lost. AW duly sent EM a draft of 'Daughters of War' on 3 June 1917 (Berg).

26 Liddell Hart, p. 321.

27 Whitton, p. 82.

28 ibid.

29 Information based on the diary of the 229th Field Company, Royal Engineers.

30 IR to EM, *CW*, p. 257.

31 ibid.

32 ibid.

33 Whitton, p. 82.

34 ibid.

35 IR to GB, *CW*, p. 257.

36 IR to SS, ?July 1917, *CW*, p. 258.

37 IR to GB, *CW*, p. 257.

38 IR to EM, postmarked 30 July 1917, *CW*, p. 258.

39 IR to SS, *CW*, p. 258.

40 Fragment LXVII, *PPIR*, pp. 171–2.

41 IR to GB, postmarked 20 July 1917, *CW*, p. 257.

42 IR to EM, ?August, poss. July 1917, *CW*, p. 261.

CHAPTER 20

1 IR to GB, postmarked 23 July 1917, *PHH*, pp. 94–5.

2 IR told GB that his copy of Emerson's poems, which he had taken out with him to France, 'vanished', together with his copy of GB's *Chambers of Imagery*. Letter of October 1917, *PHH*, p. 116.

3 IR to EM, 19 June 1917, *CW*, p. 257.

4 IR to EM, postmarked 30 July 1917, *CW*, p. 260.

5 IR to GB, postmarked 5 January 1917, *PHH*, p. 89.

6 IR to EM, postmarked 27 May 1917, *CW*, p. 255.

7 GB to IR, IWM.

8 ibid.

9 GB to IR, 29 June 1917, IWM.

10 *PPIR*, pp. 143–5.

11 IR to EM, June 1917, *CW*, p. 257.

12 *CW*, p. 247.

13 *JT*, p. 159.

14 GB to IR, 21 December 1916, IWM.

15 *PPIR* has a break here, *CW* does not.

16 GB to IR, 21 December 1916, IWM.

17 GB to DH, 20 September 1934, Bristol.

18 Notes on 1937 edition from GB to DH, Bristol.

19 I have not discovered any reference to IR having read Gerard Manley Hopkins. Though the first edition of his works, *Poems*, edited by Robert Bridges was not published until 1918, however, IR may have read some of his verse in anthologies such as *Poets . . . of the Centuries* (1893) or *The Spirit of Man*, also edited by Bridges, in 1916.

20 GB to IR, IWM.

21 IR to EM, postmarked 29 May 1917, *CW*, p. 256. Though only two of the twenty-three Gotha bombers that set out on 25 May 1917 reached London, because of cloud, 95 people were killed and 192 injured. The next air raid came less than two weeks later on 4 June.

22 IR to EM, postmarked 29 May 1917, *CW*, p. 256.

23 GB uses 'terrene' twice in the final stanza of 'Atlantis', an unusual word which IR then repeats in 'Daughters of War'.

24 IR to GB, *CW*, p. 257.

25 IR to GB, postmarked 3 August 1917, *CW*, p. 261.

26 The diary of 229th Field Co., RE, records on 13 September 1917: '1 O[ther] R[ank] granted leave.'

27 IR to GB, *CW*, p. 262.

28 ibid.

29 IR to GB, postmarked 20 July 1917, *CW*, p. 257.

30 IR to RCT, 26 September 1917, *CW*, pp. 262–3.

31 *The Pterodamozels*, p. 2. The title may be a reverse echo of Rossetti's 'The Blesséd Damozel'.

32 IR to GB, postmarked 9 March 1918, *PHH*, p. 123.

33 IR to RCT, 18 October 1917, *CW*, p. 263.

34 'Isaac Rosenberg' (1939), CZA, A 330/595, p. 13.

35 *PPIR*, pp. 145–6.

36 *PPIR*, pp. 146–7.

37 Sorley, p. 229.

38 Jacob Isaacs (1896–1973) was Professor of English Literature at Queen Mary's College from 1952 to 1964. He gave the opening address when the Leeds Exhibition of IR's work transferred to the Slade.

39 Interview with JC, 1960, USC.

40 See *Sotheby's Catalogue of Modern First Editions and Presentation Copies* for 22 July 1981, Lots 144 & 145, and for 25 January 1982, Lot 12, respectively.

41 IR to JL, 8 December 1917, *CW*, pp. 266–7. AW told GB, in a letter of 23 July 1918: 'Isaac told me at the time, that Lieut. Isaacs' work was very ordinary' (IWM).

42 IR to GB, 25 September 1917, *PHH*, p. 108.

43 IR to GB, 28 September 1917, *PHH*, p. 110.

CHAPTER 21

1 *The Unicorn*, ll. 88–95, *PPIR*, p. 250.

2 IR to JL, 8 December 1917, *CW*, p. 266.

3 IR was still 'Attached to 229th Field Company, Royal Engineers' on 15 October 1917, when AW gives this as his address to RCT, and IR gives it as his address until at least 18 October 1917.

4 Carter, p. 19.

5 The Battalion diary gives a figure of 11 killed, wounded or missing for September, compared with 91 for November 1917.

6 To commemorate the 40th Division's achievement at Bourlon Wood, General Headquarters granted permission for an acorn and oak leaves, representing Bourlon Wood, to be added to the divisional sign of a diamond superimposed on a bantam cock.

7 IR to JL, *CW*, p. 266.

8 IP interprets the 'S.A.H.A.' as 'South African Horse Artillery', but such a unit did not exist. The initials must stand for the 'South African Heavy Artillery', part of which served in France in the First World War and to which several British units were 'attached'.

9 IR to RCT, ?late October–early November 1917, *CW*, p. 265.

10 ibid. The final sentence of this extract is almost certainly a pun on one of Shakespeare's comedies, *All's Well That Ends Well*.

11 H.G. Wells, *Mr Britling Sees It Through*, Book II, ch. 4.

12 IR to EM, postmarked 26 January 1918, *CW*, p. 267.

13 *The Men Who March Away*, ed. Ian Parsons, Chatto & Windus, 1965, p. 26.

14 DH had written tactfully in his letter of encouragement and suggestion to Sassoon that he supposed most people would agree 'that he possessed a certain integrity and was developing further and further away from sham of any kind, that he was sensitive and vigorous, that he was extraordinarily interested in seeing what could be done with language, and probably that he represents one fruitful form of fusion between Hebrew and English culture', all phrases that would be echoed, even repeated, in Sassoon's Foreword. (See DH to Sassoon, 28–29 May 1937, Bristol.)

15 IR to WS, 18 March 1918, *CW*, p. 270.

16 AW to RCT, 15 October 1917, IWM.

17 IR to JR, early March 1918, *CW*, p. 269.

18 IR to GB, postmarked 22 October 1917, *PHH*, p. 112.

19 *PPIR*, p. 130. 'The Dying Soldier' was sent to GB in a letter postmarked 26 February 1918, with the comment 'but since I left the hosp[ital] all poetry has quite gone out of me', *CW*, p. 268.

20 IR to WS, 8 March 1918, *CW*, p. 270.

21 IR to GB, postmarked 26 February 1918, *CW*, p. 268.

22 GB to IR, 12 February 1917, IWM.

23 GB to IR, 4 July 1917, IWM.

24 IR to LB, Autumn 1916, *CW*, p. 249. On the one hand Flaubert's novel *Salammbô*, set in ancient Carthage, convinced him that it was good – 'It decides the tone of the work.' But he could also see that it might make it more difficult to give 'the human side' and to make it 'more living'.

25 *PPIR*, p. 240.

26 IR to EM, postmarked 29 May 1917, *CW*, pp. 255–6.

27 *PPIR*, p. 270, ll. 101–3.

28 IR to EM, *CW*, p. 257.

29 IR to GB, postmarked 3 August 1917, *CW*, p. 260.

30 GB to IR in his last surviving letter to him of 7 August 1917, IWM.

31 *PPIR*, pp. 171–2 (Fragment LXVII).

32 *PPIR*, pp. 254–5 (ll. 181–96).

33 IR to GB, postmarked ?October 1917, *PHH*, p. 116.

34 *PPIR*, p. 273.

35 *PPIR*, p. 253.

36 GB to DH, 27 March 1936, Bristol. (Referring to the revision IR sent GB towards the end of 1917, which GB returned to the trenches, and agreeing to place *The Unicorn* with the war poems): 'If the version before the latest one (mine) were to turn up, you would find it much more of a play, and with so much more kinship with "Moses" than with anything else that I think you would feel bound to put them together. But I suspect he destroyed it in the trenches when he had put together his latest revision for me ...

he always insisted he had nowhere he could keep anything.'

GB to DH (15 April 1936). GB still felt it might be somewhere in the 'loose sheets ... if only one could reconstruct it' – but he can't finally accept that IR 'destroyed it'. '"The Amulet" is more like it than anything else: but it went on further than that piece does ... I hold for certain that "The Tower of Skulls" was a part of "The Unicorn" – for it came in its place in that complete version (I mean complete *pro tem.*) which he showed to me and then destroyed.'

GB to DH, 14 April 1937, Bristol. (Concerning his regrets at having criticized the fuller version of *The Unicorn* that IR sent him on leave in September 1917, since he pruned it too drastically): '... the previous stage was much fuller, and the version represented by my typescript represents a severe pruning of that – following my criticism of its starting too many hares at once. This pruning was only done in the last weeks of Rosenberg's life. Now, of course, I would give a good deal for that earlier fuller version which I criticized: for he pruned it too much, and the lost version would give us a better idea of his intentions than we have now.'

37 Denys Harding, *Isaac Rosenberg*, Compact Poets Series, Chatto & Windus, 1972, p. 7.

CHAPTER 22

1 Censored extract from a letter of IR to EM, postmarked 26 January 1918, *CW*, p. 267 (Berg).

2 Ruth Swade to the author in a telephone interview of 30 October 2006.

3 Only when he had left London for South Africa did he begin to appreciate it. IR wrote to WS from France in defence of London also (IR to WS, 15 November 1917, *CW*, p. 265).

4 IR to EM, postmarked 26 January 1917, *CW*, p. 267.

5 IR to JR, early March 1918, *CW*, p. 269.

IR may be thinking of *Père Goriot*.

6 Quoted by DM, p. 118, and taken from Martin Gilbert's translation of an article in a front-line newspaper of 26 March 1917, *First World War*, p. 313.

7 IR to SS, ?July–September 1917, *CW*, p. 258.

8 Aldington, p. 333. I am indebted to DM for this reference.

9 IR to WS, 14 February 1918, *CW*, p. 268.

10 IR to JR, ?23 February 1918, *CW*, p. 268.

11 IR to GB, postmarked 26 February 1918, *CW*, p. 268.

12 In a letter clearly misdated '1917 ?November', which must have been written in February 1918, IR writes: 'I applied for a transfer about a month ago [to the Jewish Battalion] but I fancy it fell through. I shall apply again.' (*CW*, p. 264)

13 There are no letters of application from IR in the Jewish Battalion Archives at the Parkes Library, University of Southampton. This may indicate that Jabotinsky was right to suspect that someone at the War Office was preventing applications reaching him. (Jabotinsky to Mr Landa, 15/11/17, Parkes Library, University of Southampton.)

14 IR to GB, postmarked 9 March 1918, *PHH*, p. 122. See also IR to EM, 7 March 1918: 'I have put in for a transfer to the Jewish Batt – which I think is in Mesopotamia now.' (*CW*, p. 271)

15 Hassall, pp. 437–8: '[IR]'s devoted sister Annie had begun urging Marsh either to get him transferred to a Jewish battalion in Mesopotamia or brought home on sick leave. Marsh put the former scheme in train, but for once was too busy to write to Rosenberg himself. The problem of the moment was again Sassoon. He had decided after all to consult Eddie about his war poems.'

16 Whitton, p. 158.

17 IR to JR, early March 1918, *CW*, p. 269.

18 IR to GB, 7 March 1918, *CW*, p. 269.

19 *PPIR*, p. 147.

20 Frank Waley's MS notes sent to the author.

21 IR to WS, *CW*, p. 270.

22 Letter dated ?November 1917, *CW*, p. 264, but clearly written later, probably in February 1918.

23 ibid.

24 ibid.

25 IR's two letters to his brother have, I believe, been placed in the wrong order in *CW*, since his letter of 28 March to Marsh also clearly gives his address as '6th Platoon'.

26 *PPIR*, pp. 147–8.

27 *CW*, p. 272.

28 e.g. *JT*, pp. 1–3, DM, pp. 216ff, Lloyd, pp. 34–5. Martin Lloyd, for instance, points out that it was written only four days after the Balfour Declaration committed the British to providing a homeland for the Jews in Palestine, and draws attention to the fact that it was quoted by Israel's Minister of Defence, Shimon Peres, at the inauguration of a Chair of Zionism at Haifa University in 1976. (Lloyd, p. 34) There is a puzzling reference in a letter to Joseph Leftwich from Professor Joseph Nevada of Haifa University, dated 6 August 1976 (preserved at School of Asian and Oriental Studies, London), about ten lines he believed were missing from the version in IR's *Collected Works* (1937) but which he had heard quoted by Shimon Peres.

29 IR to EM, 28 March 1918, *CW*, p. 272.

30 Leone Samson has pointed out the striking number of contrasts set up in the poem – 'pale/dark', 'dark/blonde', 'cold/burn', 'living/dead' and emphasizes 'the extremity of the conditions in which Rosenberg found himself, where there were only polar opposites: existing or dying'. (Samson, p. 31)

31 Allentuck, p. 264.

32 IR to EM, 28 March 1918, *CW*, p. 272.

33 AW to EM, 24 April 1918, Berg.

34 RCT to AW, 'May 1918', IWM.

35 'Shorter Fragments of Prose', I, *CW*, p. 298. IR wrote 'imaging' but almost certainly meant 'imagining'.

Bibliography

A: Works by Isaac Rosenberg published during his lifetime

1 'The Wharf' (i.e. 'In the Workshop'), in *A Piece of Mosaic being the Book of the Palestine Exhibition and Bazaar*, edited by Cyril Picciotto and C.M. Kohan (London: William Clowes and Sons Limited [?for the editors], 1912), printed on the recto only of a plate between pp. 38 and 39.

'The Wharf', the first appearance of a poem by Rosenberg in print, was published in *A Piece of Mosaic*, a booklet issued to accompany the Palestine Bazaar in London on 13 May 1912. One of the editors, Cyril Picciotto KC, was the husband of a first cousin of Ruth Löwy, Rosenberg's friend and fellow student, and daughter of his patron Mrs Henrietta Löwy. In a letter to Ruth Löwy (dated '1912, ?March' by Parsons), Rosenberg discusses poems and prose which have been shown to Picciotto, expressing his elation at Picciotto's appreciation of the poems and asking 'whether the poem I sent you would do for the publication' (*CW*, pp. 185–6); however, the cuts in the poem which Rosenberg notes – 'the two or three verses about the parents and brother should be left out' – indicate that he is most probably referring to 'A Ballad of Whitechapel' and not 'In the Workshop' (cf. *PPIR*, 9, footnote, which notes the cancellation of stanzas 10–11 by Rosenberg in the typescript of 'A Ballad of Whitechapel'). 'In the Workshop' was printed beneath a reproduction of a drawing by Rosenberg depicting a group of three men on a dockside with the caption 'THE WHARF. BY ISAAC ROSENBERG.' at the foot of the plate. Apart from the title and variations in the punctuation, the text is the same as that printed in *PPIR*, with one exception: in the fifth line 'Filling the room' is amended to 'Filling the place'.

2 'At the Baillie Galleries. The Works of J.H. Amschewitz and the late H. Ospovat', *The Jewish Chronicle*, no. 2,251, 24 May 1912, p. 15.

A review of an exhibition of works by Rosenberg's friend and mentor John H. Amshewitz and the illustrator and draughtsman Henry Ospovat (1877–1909) at the Baillie Gallery, London; the greater part of the review discusses Amshewitz's work and Ospovat's is only considered in the final paragraph.

3 *Night and Day* ([London: Israel Narodiczky for I. Rosenberg, 1912]).

Rosenberg's first separate publication, issued in an edition of about 50 copies printed for him in late spring or early summer 1912. The cost of printing was £2, which was lent to Rosenberg by Mrs Herbert Cohen and later repaid from the sale for £4 of a drawing exhibited at the New English Art Club 1912 Winter Exhibition. FACSIMILE: *Night and Day* (Oxford: The Grove Press for Quarry Books, 1979). A facsimile edition of 25 copies.

4 'Our Dead Heroes', in *South African Women in Council*, vol. II, no. 3, December 1914, p. 20.

The magazine *South African Women in Council* was edited by Mrs Agnes Cook, the mother of the artist Madge Cook, at whose studio Rosenberg may have delivered his lectures on art, which were later published in two parts in the magazine (cf. A5 and A6).

5 'Art' [part I] prefaced by the poem 'Beauty' [II], in *South African Women in Council*, vol. II, no. 3, December 1914, pp. 13–15.

6 'Art [part II]' in *South African Women in Council*, vol. II, no. 4, January 1915, pp. 15–17.

7 *Youth* (London: I. Narodiczky [for I. Rosenberg], 1915).

An edition of about 100 copies printed for Rosenberg at a cost of £2.10s and published at 2s.6d a copy in April 1915; the publication expenses were paid for by the sale of three drawings to Edward Marsh. The three poems that comprise 'The Cynic's Lamp' (pp. 11–12) were cancelled by Rosenberg in his own copy and the leaf bearing them was torn out of the copy which he sent to Sydney Schiff, amongst others; Rosenberg's postscript to the covering letter accompanying the volume commented that, 'The poems were very trivial and I've improved the book by taking them out' (*CW*, p. 215).

8 'Heart's First Word' [I], in *Colour*, vol. II, no. 5, June 1915, p. 164.

The magazine *Colour* was first published in August 1914 (whilst Rosenberg was in South Africa), with the remit of reporting on contemporary art in Britain and overseas, and producing high-quality, colour-printed reproductions of paintings. Shortly after his return to Britain in March 1915, Rosenberg sent three poems to the magazine, which were published in this and the following two issues (A10 and A11).

9 'Art.' Part I, *The Jewish Standard*, no. 1, 1 July 1915, pp. 2–3.

The Jewish Standard was edited by Reuben Cohen and printed by Israel Narodiczky, for whom Cohen worked; only this, the first issue of the magazine, was published. 'Art.' Part I comprises the first part (approximately half) of 'Art' [part I] previously published in *South African Women in Council* (cf. A5).

10 'A Girl's Thoughts', in *Colour*, vol. II, no. 6, July 1915, p. 203.

11 'Wedded' [II], in *Colour*, vol. III, no. 1, August 1915, p. 7.

12 *Moses. A Play* (London: The Paragon Printing Works [for I. Rosenberg], 1916).

Printed for Rosenberg by Reuben Cohen of Narodiczky under the name 'Paragon Printing Works' on Narodiczky's presses during Rosenberg's embarkation leave in London in May 1916 and published on 19 May 1916. (Paragon's address, '8, Ocean Street, Stepney Green, E', was also given for Cohen as editor of *The Jewish Standard*.) The work was issued bound in wrappers at 1s and bound in cloth by Mendel at 4s.6d; although

Rosenberg did write to R.C. Trevelyan in May 1916 that '3/6 [i.e. 3s.6d] will do' as payment for a cloth-bound copy (*CW*, p. 234), he appears to have quoted both Israel Zangwill and Edward Marsh the full price during the same month (cf. *CW*, pp. 233–4). FACSIMILE: *Moses*, Arts and Literature Series, no. 2 (London: Imperial War Museum, 1990). A facsimile edition of the first edition and the Imperial War Museum's manuscripts and proofs of *Moses*.

13 'Marching – As Seen from the Left File' and 'Break of Day in the Trenches', in *Poetry: A Magazine of Verse* (Chicago), vol. IX, no. 3, December 1916, pp. 128–9.

John Rodker sent 'Marching – As Seen from the Left File' to *Poetry*'s editor Harriet Monroe in early 1916. Rosenberg then wrote to Monroe, sending her 'Break of Day in the Trenches' and 'The Troop Ship' for publication (cf. *CW*, p. 247). The two poems that Monroe accepted were published under the heading 'Trench Poems'.

14 '"Ah, Koelue ..."', in *Georgian Poetry 1916–1917*, edited by Edward Marsh (London: The Poetry Bookshop, 1917), p. 53.

The third of this series of anthologies edited by Rosenberg's patron Marsh, which was issued in September 1917. Rosenberg sent Marsh both '"Ah Koelue ..."' (extracted from Scene I of Rosenberg's verse play *Moses*) and 'Daughters of War' for inclusion, but only the former was accepted.

B: PRINCIPAL POSTHUMOUS PUBLICATIONS OF WORKS BY ISAAC ROSENBERG

1 *Poems ... Selected and Edited by Gordon Bottomley. With an Introductory Memoir by Laurence Binyon* (London: William Heinemann, 1922).

The first collected edition of Rosenberg's poems, prefaced by a 'Bibliographical Note' (pp. xi–xii) and Binyon's 'Introductory Memoir', which contains extensive quotations from Rosenberg's letters (pp. 1–50). Although important as the first attempt to collect Rosenberg's writings, Bottomley was constrained in the scope of the work by commercial concerns. This edition erroneously attributes 'Killed in Action', Joseph Leftwich's elegy for Rosenberg, to its subject; the poem was omitted from subsequent collections.

2 *The Collected Works ... Poetry, Prose, Letters and Some Drawings. Edited by Gordon Bottomley & Denys Harding. With a Foreword by Siegfried Sassoon* (London: Chatto & Windus, 1937).

The first collected edition of Rosenberg's poems, letters, and paintings and drawings; the text is prefaced by Sassoon's 'Foreword' (published here for the first time, pp. ix–x), a 'Biographical Note' (p. xi), and an 'Editorial Note' with bibliographical details of the three volumes published in Rosenberg's lifetime and Bottomley's edition of the *Poems* (pp. xiii–xv). 'Notes' follow the text on pp. 383–9. Eight drawings and paintings by Rosenberg are reproduced in monochrome. The spine of the volume is titled 'THE / COMPLETE / WORKS OF / ISAAC / ROSENBERG' (rather than 'The Collected Works'), possibly due to the difficulty of fitting the longer word across the spine's breadth.

3 *The Collected Poems ... Edited by Gordon Bottomley & Denys Harding. With a Foreword by Siegfried Sassoon* (London: Chatto & Windus, 1949).

A revised edition of the poems published in Bottomley and Harding's *The Collected Works*, reprinting Sassoon's 'Foreword' (pp. vii–viii) and the 'Biographical Note' (p. viii), and a revised 'Editorial Note', which omits references to the letters and prose included in the previous work (pp. 1–2). The 'Notes' of *The Collected Works* are also omitted.

4 Silkin, Jon, and Maurice de Sausmarez, *Isaac Rosenberg 1890–1918. A Catalogue of an Exhibition Held at Leeds University May–June 1959 Together with the Text of Unpublished Material* (Leeds: University of Leeds with Partridge Press, 1959).

The catalogue publishes for the first time four poems by Rosenberg ('Uncollected Verse Fragments', pp. 4–6) and 34 letters by him, comprising 30 to Sydney Schiff, two to his mother, one to his father, and one to John Rodker ('Unpublished Letters', pp. 7–20). Four paintings and drawings are reproduced in monochrome.

5 *The Collected Works ... Poetry, Prose, Letters, Paintings and Drawings. With a Foreword by Siegfried Sassoon. Edited with an Introduction and Notes by Ian Parsons* (London: Chatto & Windus, 1979).

A revised and augmented edition of *The Collected Works*, extensively annotated and prefaced by Sassoon's reprinted 'Foreword' (p. ix), a 'Chronological Summary of Rosenberg's Life' (pp. x–xiv), an Introduction (pp. xv–xxvii), and an 'Editor's Note' (pp. xxxi–xxxii). Twenty-three paintings by Rosenberg are reproduced in colour and 33 paintings and drawings by Rosenberg are reproduced in monochrome.

6 *The Selected Poems of Isaac Rosenberg. Edited and with an Introduction by Jean Moorcroft Wilson* (London: Cecil Woolf, 2003).

7 *The Poems and Plays ... Edited by Vivien Noakes* (Oxford: Oxford University Press, 2004).

A comprehensive, extensively annotated variorum edition, with an 'Introduction' describing the bibliography of Rosenberg's works, the manuscripts, and the editorial conventions employed (pp. xv–xxxiv), a 'Chronological Summary of Isaac Rosenberg's Life' (pp. xxxvii–xlviii), 'Accidental Variants' (pp. 277–98), 'Commentary' (pp. 299–416), and appendices on 'Contents of Volumes Published by Rosenberg' (pp. 417–18) and 'The Large Black Notebook' (pp. 419–20).

8 *Poetry Out of My Head and Heart. Unpublished Letters & Poem Versions* (London: Enitharmon Press in association with The European Jewish Publications Society, 2007).

The text of a group of manuscripts including letters and poems by Rosenberg used in the preparation of the 1922 edition of his *Poems*, previously either partially or wholly unpublished.

C: Select bibliography of secondary works

Adler, Rev Michael (ed.) *British Jewry Book of Honour*, Caxton, 1922
Akers, Geoff *Beating for Light*, Juniper Books, 2006

Aldington, Richard *Death of a Hero*, Chatto & Windus, 1930

Allentuck, Marcia, 'Isaac Rosenberg and Gordon Bottomley: Unremarked Documents in the Houghton Library', *Harvard Library Bulletin*, vol. XXIII, no. 3, July 1975.

Allinson, Adrian 'A Painter's Pilgrimage', unpub. autobiography at McFarlin Library, University of Tulsa

Allinson, Sidney *The Bantams: the Untold Story of World War I*, Howard Baker, 1981

Amshewitz, Sarah Briana *The Paintings of J.H. Amshewitz*, B.T. Batsford, 1951

Arthur, Max *Forgotten Voices of the Great War*, Ebury, 2003

—— *Last Post*, Weidenfeld & Nicolson, 2005

Aughton, Peter *Bristol: a People's History*, Carnegie, 2000

Barham, John E. *Alice Greene: Teacher and Campaigner, South African Correspondence 1887–1902*, Troubadour Publishing, 2007

Battalion Diary of 11th King's Own Royal Lancasters, King's Own Royal Regiment Museum

Bergonzi, Bernard *Heroes' Twilight: a Study of the Literature of the Great War*, Constable, 1965

Black, Gerry *Jewish London: an Illustrated History*, Breedon Books, 2003

Booth, Charles *Charles Booth's London*, Penguin, 1971

Brodetsky, Selig *Memoirs; from Ghetto to Israel*, Weidenfeld & Nicolson, 1960

Carter, William *Bantams at War: the Story of the 11th (Service) Battalion, the King's Own Royal (Lancaster) Regiment*, King's Own Royal Regiment Museum, 2002

Charlton, George 'The Slade School of Fine Art 1871–1946', *The Studio*, London, October 1946

Cohen, Joseph *Journey to the Trenches: the Life of Isaac Rosenberg 1890–1918*, Robson Books, 1975

Cohen, Sonia, Unpublished Memoir in the possession of her daughter, Joan Rodker.

Collecott, Diana 'Isaac Rosenberg (1890–1918): a Cross-Cultural Case-Study', in Aubrey Newman (ed.), *The Jewish East End*, Jewish Historical Society of England, 1981

Connor, Steven, 'Isaac Rosenberg: Birkbeck's War Poet', text of a lecture delivered at Birkbeck College, University of London, on 30 October 2000, http://www/bbk/ac/uk/english/skc/rosenberg.

Cork, Richard *David Bomberg*, Yale UP, 1987

Cowper, J.M. *The King's Own: the Story of a Royal Regiment 1914–1950*, vol. III, Aldershot, 1957

Davin, A. *Growing Up Poor: Home, School and Street in London, 1870–1914*, Rivers Oram Press, 1996

Deutscher, Isaac *The Non-Jewish Jew and Other Essays*, Oxford UP, 1968

Donnelly, Peter *The History and Traditions of The King's Own Royal Border Regiment*, King's Own Royal Regiment Museum, 2000

First, Ruth, and Ann Scott *Olive Schreiner*, Rutgers UP, 1990

Fishman, William J. *The Streets of East London*, Duckworth, 1979

Fussell, Paul *The Great War and Modern Memory*, Oxford UP, 1977

Gartner, Lloyd P. *The Jewish Immigrant in England 1870–1914*, 3rd (updated) edition, Vallentine Mitchell, 2001

Gertler, Mark *Selected Letters*, ed. Noel Carrington, Rupert Hart-Davis, 1965

Gilbert, Martin *The First World War*, Weidenfeld & Nicolson, 1994

—— *Jewish History Atlas*, Weidenfeld & Nicolson, 1969

Goldsmith, S. J. (ed.), *Leftwich at 85: a Collective Evaluation*, pub. by the Federation of Jewish Relief Organization, the Association of Jewish Writers and Journalists and the World Congress Yiddish Committee, London, January 1978

Graves, Robert *Contemporary Techniques of Poetry*, Hogarth Press, 1925

Graves, Robert & Laura Riding *A Survey of Modernist Poetry*, London 1927

Harding, Denys *Experience Into Words*, Penguin, 1974

Hassall, Christopher *Edward Marsh, Patron of the Arts: a Biography*, Longmans, 1959

Hibberd, Dominic *Harold Monro: Poet of the New Age*, Palgrave, 2001

—— *Wilfred Owen: a New Biography*, Weidenfeld & Nicolson, 2002

Hirson, Baruch *The Cape Town Intellectuals*, Witwatersrand UP, 2001

Holmes, Richard *Tommies*, Harper Perennial, 2005

Horvitch, Minnie, Reminscences of her brother, Isaac Rosenberg, IRFP

Isaacs, Jack *The Background of Modern Poetry*, Bell, 1951

Jabotinsky, Vladimir *The Story of the Jewish Legion*, London, 1945

Johnston, John *English Poetry of the First World War*, Oxford UP, 1964

Jones, David *In Parenthesis*, Faber and Faber, 1937

Lawson, Peter *Anglo-Jewish Poetry from Isaac Rosenberg to Elaine Feinstein*, Vallentine Mitchell, 2005

Leavis, F.R. *New Bearings in English Poetry*, Chatto & Windus, 1932

Leftwich, Joseph *Along the Years: Poems 1911–1937*, Robert Anscombe, 1937

Lewis, Percy Wyndham *The Apes of God*, Black Swan, 1930

Liddell Hart, B.H. *History of the First World War*, Papermac, 1992

Liddiard, Jean *Isaac Rosenberg: the Half-Used Life*, Victor Gollancz, 1975

Litvinoff, Emanuel *Journey Through a Small Planet*, Michael Joseph, 1973

Lloyd, Martin 'Poets and Patriotism – Three Experiences of the Great War', MA thesis for University of Southampton, 2001

London, Jack *The People of the Abyss*, Isbiter & Co., 1903

McArthur, Kathleen 'The Heroic Spirit in the Literature of the Great War', PhD thesis for the University of Cape Town, 1989

Maccoby, Deborah *God Made Blind: Isaac Rosenberg: His Life and Poetry*, Symposium Press, 2000

MacDougall, Sarah *Mark Gertler*, John Murray, 2002

Manning, Frederic *Her Privates We*, with an Introduction by Edmund Blunden, Peter Davies, 1964

Marsh, Edward *Ambrosia and Small Beer*, Longmans, 1964

—— *A Number of People*, Heinemann, 1939

Nash, Paul *Outline*, Faber and Faber, 1949

Nevinson, C.R.W. *Paint and Prejudice*, Methuen, 1937

Pimlott, J.A.R. *Toynbee Hall: Fifty Years of Social Progress 1884–1934*, Dent, 1935

Quinn, Patrick *British Poets of the Great War: Brooke, Rosenberg, Thomas: a Documentary Volume, Dictionary of Literary Biography, no. 216*, Gale Group, 2000

Reynolds, Michael 'The Slade: the Story of an Art School, 1871–1971', typescript in Special Collection, University College, London, 1974

Rocker, Fermin *The East End Years*, reprint Freedom Press, 1998

Rodker John *Memoirs of Other Fronts*, Putnam, 1932

—— *Poems and Adolphe*, Carcanet, 1996

Rosenberg, Barnett, Autobiographical fragment, translated into English by Joseph Cohen and his father, IRFP (copy).

Ross, Robert H. *The Georgian Revolt*, Faber and Faber, 1967

Russell, C. & H.S. Lewis, *The Jew in London*, London, 1900

Samson, Leone 'Isaac Rosenberg: Selected War Poems', unpublished dissertation for the University of Hertfordshire, 2005

Searle, Chris 'Spanning Two Languages: the Legacy of Isaac and Jacob', *Race and Class*, xxviii, 1 (1986)

Seymour-Smith, Martin *Who's Who in Twentieth Century Literature*, London, 1976

Shain, Milton *Jewry and Cape Society*, Historical Publication Society of Cape Town, 1983

Shain, Milton & R. Mendelsohn (eds) *Memories, Realities and Dreams*, Jonathan Ball, 2002

Silkin, Jon *Out of Battle: the Poetry of the Great War*, Oxford UP, 1972

Simkins, Peter *Kitchener's Army*, Manchester UP, 1988

Sims, George *Living London*, Cassell, 1902

Sisson, C.H. *English Poetry 1900–1950: an Assessment*, Carcanet, 1981

Sorley, Charles Hamilton *The Collected Letters*, ed. Jean Moorcroft Wilson, Cecil Woolf, 1990

Sowden, Dora, 'Isaac Rosenberg, the Anglo-Jewish Poet', *Jewish Affairs*, vol. 7, no. 12, December 1952

Tennent, Madge (née Cook) *Autobiography of an Unarrived Artist*, Columbia UP, 1948

Tickner, Lisa *Modern Life and Modern Subjects: British Life in the Early Twentieth Century*, Yale UP, 2000

Tomlinson, Charles *Isaac Rosenberg of Bristol*, Bristol Branch of the Historical Association, 1982

Van Emden, Richard *The Trench*, Bantam Press, 2002

Walker, Henry *East London: Sketches of Christian Work and Workers*, pub. by the Religious Tract Society, 1896

Whitton, F.E. *History of the 40th Division*, Gale & Polden, 1926

Wilson, Jean Moorcroft *Charles Hamilton Sorley: a Biography*, Cecil Woolf, 1985

—— *Siegfried Sassoon: the Making of a War Poet, 1886–1918* and *Siegfried Sassoon: the Journey from the Trenches, 1918–1967*, pub. by Duckworth, 1998 and 2003 respectively

Winstone, Reece *Bristol in the 1890s*, Bristol, 2nd ed., 1965

Woodeson, John, *Mark Gertler: Biography of a Painter, 1891–1939* (London, Sidgwick & Jackson, 1972)

Zangwill, Israel *Children of the Ghetto*, first pub. in 3 vols by Heinemann, 1892 (page references to White Lion Publishers ed. of 1972)

A Checklist of Paintings and Drawings by Isaac Rosenberg

Abbreviations used

AACE   Aberystwyth Arts Centre Exhibition of the Arts of the 1914–1918 War, 1979

AJE   Anglo-Jewish Exhibition, 1951

BGL   Bluecoat Gallery (Liverpool) Exhibition: Tribute to Edward Marsh, 1976

BU   Ben Uri Gallery, London Jewish Museum of Art, 2008. (Whitechapel at War: Isaac Rosenberg and his Circle)

IWM   Imperial War Museum

IWM (1974)   Exhibition of Poets of the First World War at the Imperial War Museum, 1974–5

IWM (1980)   Exhibition of Rosenberg Material Recently Acquired by the Imperial War Museum, 1980

JC, USC   The Joseph Cohen Collection of World War I Literature/the Joseph M. Bruccoli Great War Collection, Thomas Cooper Library, University of South Carolina

LEC   Leeds University Rosenberg Exhibition Catalogue, 1959

NBL   National Book League Exhibition of Rosenberg's Works, 1975

WAG   Whitechapel Art Gallery Memorial Exhibition of Paintings and Drawings by Isaac Rosenberg, 22 June–17 July 1937

All sizes are given in millimetres, height by width.

1 Caxton and Edward IV
Date: 1901
Medium: Pen and watercolour on canvas
Size: 270 x 370
Owner: Mrs Gerda Horvitch
Exhibitions: NBL no. 6, BU

2 Self-portrait (in left profile)
Date: 1906
Medium: Pencil on card
Size: unspecified
Owner: Joseph Cohen
Exhibitions: NBL cat. no. 7

3 Copy of a Madonna and Child (possibly Correggio's *The Virgin of the Basket*, c. 1524)
Date: early
Medium: oil on canvas
Size: 355 x 254

Owner: Mrs Gerda Horvitch
Exhibitions: NBL no. 12

4 Two Studies of Nude Children
Date: *c.* 1908
Medium: Sanguine Drawing on paper mounted on board
Size: 184 x 292
Owner: Imperial War Museum [IWM] 6368
Exhibitions: LEC no. 32, British Council Fine Arts Dept: 'Pen as Pencil', no. 60B, IWM (1980), no. 16

5 Head of a Monk – Birkbeck Art School Study
Date: 1908 (IWM dates it *c.* 1911)
Medium: carbon chalk, or pencil on board
Size: 488 x 400
Owner: IWM 6369
Exhibitions: WAG no. 38, LEC no. 33, BU

6 Landscape with Three Figures
Date: 1910
Medium: oil on canvas
Size: 360 x 260
Owner: Mrs Betty Silver
Exhibitions: WAG no. 13 ('Shanklin' 1910), LEC no. 1, NBL no. 10

7 Sea and Beach (sometimes known as 'Seashore')
Date: 1910
Medium: oil on canvas
Size: 234 x 342
Owner: IWM 6365
Exhibitions: LEC no. 4, NBL no. 17

8 Self-portrait
Date: 1911 (often dated 1910)
Medium: oil on canvas
Size: 495 x 387
Owner: The Tate Gallery, presented by David Burton, 1972
Exhibitions: WAG no. 18, ICA 20th Century Poetry Catalogue (M) May 1951, AJE no. 66, LEC no. 12, NBL no. 13, BU

9 Head of a Barrister
Date: 1910
Medium: red chalk
Size: 178 x 147
Owner: JC, USC
Exhibitions: NBL no. 14, BU

10 Seascape (sometimes known as 'People on the Seashore')
Date: 1910
Medium: oil on wood panel
Size: 215 x 368
Owner: unknown, formerly Mrs Victor Gollancz
Exhibitions: ?WAG?, LEC no. 7, NBL no. 41

11 Two Figures at a Table
Date: *c.* 1910
Medium: pen, Indian ink and wash
Size: 152 x 101
Owner: Tullie House Museum and Art Gallery
Exhibitions: LEC no. 40, NBL no. 15

12 Family Group at a Meal (sometimes known as 'Figures Seated Round a Table')
Date: *c.* 1910
Medium: pen, Indian ink and grey wash on paper
Size: 139 x 178
Owner: Tullie House Museum and Art Gallery
Exhibitions: LEC no. 41, NBL no. 16, BU

13 Copy of Correggio's *Venus, Cupid and Mercury*
Date: *c.* 1910
Medium: oil on canvas
Size: 737 x 445
Owner: Bernard Wynick
Exhibitions: NBL no. 11, BU

14 Self-portrait (in profile facing left)
Date: *c.* 1910–11, possibly 1912
Medium: pencil
Size: 190 x 146
Owner: unknown, formerly David Burton
Exhibitions: ?WAG no. 4?, ?NBL no. 9?

15 (Landscape) – The Road
Date: 1911
Medium: oil on board
Size: 266 x 361
Owner: IWM 6359
Exhibitions: WAG (?no. 19?), LEC no. 3,
  NBL no. 21

16 The Fountain
Date: 1911
Medium: oil on board
Size: 158 x 260
Owner: IWM 6366
Exhibitions: WAG no. 24, LEC no. 6,
  NBL no. 18, BU

17 London Park
Date: 1911
Medium: oil on wood panel
Size: 216 x 279
Owner: unknown
Exhibitions: WAG no. 21, AJE no. 67,
  LEC no. 8, NBL no. 25

**18 Kensington Gardens (there are two
  paintings of this name)**
Date: 1911
Medium: oil
Size: unknown
Owner: unknown
Exhibitions: WAG nos 15 and 22

19 Chingford
Date: 1911
Medium: oil on canvas
Size: 190 x 298
Owner: unknown
Exhibitions: WAG no. 27, LEC no. 9

20 The Bridge, Blackfriars
Date: 1911
Medium: oil
Size: 229 x 330
Owner: Mrs Janet Lawson
Exhibitions: WAG no. 25, LEC no. 11,
  NBL no. 19, AACE no. 2

21 The Artist's Father
Date: 1911
Medium: oil on cardboard

Size: 412 x 305
Owner: Mrs Betty Silver
Exhibitions: WAG no. 36, LEC no. 13
  (incorrectly described as WAG no. 34),
  NBL no. 30, BU

22 The Artist's Father
Date: 1911
Medium: oil on canvas board
Size: 609 x 508
Owner: unknown
Exhibitions: 20th Century Art – A.
  Review of Modern Movements, WAG
  1914 Cat. no. 260, WAG no. 12, LEC
  no. 14, NBL no. 32 (photograph)

**23 'Sing Unto the Lord' (sometimes
  known as 'The Song at Sea')**
Date: 1911
Medium: oil on board
Size: 165 x 260
Owner: the Garson family
Exhibitions: WAG no. 11, LEC no. 17

24 The Artist's Mother
Date: 1911
Medium: black chalk and pencil on paper
  mounted on board
Size: 254 x 206
Owner: Mrs Betty Silver
Exhibitions: WAG no. 37 (incorrectly
  described as 'pencil'), LEC no. 34, NBL
  no. 31, BU

25 The Pool of London
Date: 1911
Medium: oil
Size: 320 x 210
Owner: Mrs Betty Silver
Exhibitions: WAG no. 16, LEC no. 52,
  NBL no. 22

26 Highgate
Date: 1911
Medium: oil
Size: 315 x 215
Owner: Mrs Betty Silver
Exhibitions: WAG no. 26, LEC no. 53,
  NBL no. 23

27 Landscape (?Springfield Park)
Date: 1911–12
Medium: oil on canvas board
Size: 222 x 317
Owner: Mrs Janet Lawson
Exhibitions: WAG, either no. 1 (1912) or no. 19 (1911), LEC no. 5, NBL no. 40

28 The Wharf
Date: *c.* 1911
Medium: line drawing / etching
Size: unknown
Owner: unknown
Exhibitions: None – but reproduced in *A Piece of Mosaic*, a booklet pub. for the Palestine Bazaar, London, 13 May 1912 (ed. C. Picciotto and C.M. Kohan) with lines from 'In the Workshop' / 'Day'.

29 Landscape with Flowering Trees
Date: 1911–12
Medium: oil on board
Size: 152 x 260
Owner: IWM 6361
Exhibitions: WAG (either no. 1 (1912) or no. 19 (1911)), LEC no. 10, NBL no. 26

30 Sacred Love
Date: 1912
Medium: pencil and oil on board
Size: 475 x 610
Owner: private collection
Exhibitions: WAG no. 6 (incorrectly described as 'watercolour'), LEC no. 20, NBL no. 49, BGL (photograph), BU (reproduction in cat. only)

31 Self-portrait
Date: 1912
Medium: pencil
Size: 360 x 285
Owner: JC, USC
Exhibitions: WAG no. 3, LEC no. 35, NBL no. 56, BU

32 Landscape with River
Date: 1911–12
Medium: oil on canvas board
Size: 288 x 349
Owner: IWM 6360

Exhibitions: ?IWM (1974), NBL no. 24, AACE no. 3

33 Trees
Date: 1912
Medium: oil on board
Size: 266 x 355
Owner: IWM 6363
Exhibitions: WAG (no. ?), LEC no. 2, NBL no. 39, BU

34 Head of a Woman 'Grey and Red'
Date: 1912
Medium: oil on board
Size: 419 x 304
Owner: IWM 6362
Exhibitions: New English Art Club 1915, no. 130, WAG no. 17, LEC no. 15, IWM (1974), NBL no. 42, BU

35 Self-portrait (with raised right hand)
Date: 1912
Medium: oil on board
Size: 450 x 400
Owner: Mrs Betty Silver
Exhibitions: WAG no. 29, LEC no. 16, NBL no. 38, AACE no. 4, BU

36 Hilarities
Date: 1912
Medium: oil on cardboard
Size: 253 x 190
Owner: unknown
Exhibitions: WAG no. 9 (incorrectly described as 'watercolour'), LEC no. 18

37 The Murder of Lorenzo
Date: 1912
Medium: oil on board
Size: 304 x 248
Owner: unknown, formerly Ben Uri Society
Exhibitions: 20th Century Art, WAG 1914 cat. no. 273, WAG no. 5, AJE no. 68, LEC no. 19, NBL no. 48

38 Joy
Date: 1912
Medium: oil – Slade Summer Competition entry 1912

Size: Approx. 1830 x 1220
Owner: unknown, formerly Annie Wynick
Exhibitions: WAG no. 35

39 La Belle Dame Sans Merci
Date: *c.* 1912
Medium: unknown
Size: unknown
Owner: unknown
Exhibitions: None – but referred to in a letter to Winifreda Seaton *(CW,* p. 185)

40 Ruth Löwy as the Sleeping Beauty
Date: 1912
Medium: red chalk
Size: 267 x 349
Owner: private collection
Exhibitions: WAG no. 30, LEC no. 36, NBL no. 50

41 Hark, Hark, the Lark (possibly the same as 'Larks Ascending')
Date: 1912? 1915?
Medium: charcoal and monochrome wash
Size: 385 x 330
Owner: JC, USC
Exhibitions: WAG no. 2 (described as 'pencil'), LEC no. 37, NBL no. 53, BGL (photograph), BU

42 Head of a Woman, in profile, looking left
Date: 1912
Medium: red chalk
Size: 181 x 155
Owner: private collection
Exhibitions: WAG no. 40, NBL no. 34

43 Three Nude Drawings
(a) Study of a Nude Woman (seated with knee raised)
Date: 1915 (?1912)
Medium: charcoal on grey paper
Size: 358 x 326
Owner: British Museum
Exhibitions: BU
(b) Study of a Nude Woman (seen from behind walking)
Date: 1915 (?1912)

Medium: charcoal on grey paper
Size: 481 x 276
Owner: British Museum
Exhibitions: BU
(c) Study of a Nude Figure
Date: 1915 (?1912)
Medium: charcoal on grey paper
Size: unknown
Owner: British Museum
Exhibitions: BU

44 Head of a Woman, full face
Date: *c.* 1912
Medium: black chalk
Size: 206 x 200
Owner: British Museum
Exhibitions: None – but reproduced *CW,* plate 15(b), opp. p. 288

45 The Artist's Father
Date: *c.* 1913
Medium: pencil
Size: 241 x 203
Owner: private collection
Exhibitions: None

46 The Judgement of Paris
Date: 1914, or earlier
Medium: unknown
Size: unknown
Owner: unknown
Exhibitions: 20th Century Art, WAG 1914, no. 279

47 Self-portrait, hand in jacket lapel
Date: ?1914
Medium: oil
Size: 765 x 510
Owner: private collection
Exhibitions: ?WAG no. 33, LEC no. 21, BU

48 Cape Coloured Woman
Date: 1914
Medium: oil on board
Size: 406 x 304
Owner: the Garson family
Exhibitions: WAG no. 20, LEC no. 22, NBL no. 59 (photograph)

49 Cape Coloured Man
Date: 1914
Medium: oil on cardboard
Size: 406 x 304
Owner: the Garson family
Exhibitions: WAG no. 23, LEC no. 23, NBL no. 58

50 South African Coloured Girl
Date: 1914
Medium: oil on canvas
Size: 508 x 406
Owner: Mrs Gerda Horvitch
Exhibitions: LEC (noted only in Addendum)

51 Self-portrait in a Red Tie
Date: 1914
Medium: oil on canvas
Size: 412 x 310
Owner: Mrs Betty Silver
Exhibitions: WAG no. 10, LEC no. 24, NBL no. 74, BU

52 Self-portrait in a Pink Tie
Date: 1914
Medium: pencil on board
Size: 400 x 323
Owner: IWM 6372
Exhibitions: WAG no. 32, LEC no. 25, NBL no. 80, IWM 2007, BU

53 Self-portrait (with rounded shirt collar)
Date: 1914
Medium: oil on canvas
Size: 508 x 457
Owner: private collection
Exhibitions: LEC no. 29 (photograph), NBL no. 73, BU

54 Wolf Horvitch (the artist's brother-in-law)
Date: 1914
Medium: oil on canvas
Size: 406 x 305
Owner: Mrs L. Kellman
Exhibitions: LEC no. 30 (photograph), NBL no. 64

55 Minnie Horvitch (the artist's sister)
Date: 1914
Medium: oil on board
Size: 406 x 305
Owner: private collection
Exhibitions: LEC (noted only in Addendum), NBL no. 65 (photograph)

56 The Artist's Father in a Straw Hat
Date: 1914
Medium: oil on canvas
Size: 305 x 330
Owner: private collection
Exhibitions: LEC no. 31 (photograph), NBL no. 67, BU (reproduction in cat. only)

57 Portrait of Marda Vanne
Date: 1914
Medium: pencil on board (both LEC no. 38 and NBL no. 69 describe it as 'black chalk')
Size: 400 x 323
Owner: IWM 6367
Exhibitions: New English Art Club 1915, cat. no. 62, WAG no. 31, LEC no. 38, IWM (1974), NBL no. 69

58 Head of a Woman (possibly same as no. 61)
Date: 1914
Medium: probably chalk
Size: unspecified
Owner: Mrs L. Kellman
Exhibitions: LEC no. 51 (photograph)

59 The Artist's Father (possibly the same as No. 45)
Date: 1914
Medium: probably chalk
Size: unspecified
Owner: not known, formerly the Horvitch family
Exhibitions: LEC no. 50 (photograph)

60 Head of a Woman (said to be Minnie Horvitch, but could be Madge Cook)
Date: *c.* 1914
Medium: pencil on cardboard
Size: 381 x 279
Owner: Mrs Gerda Horvitch
Exhibitions: NBL no. 71

61 Head of a Woman, full face, with plaited hair
Date: *c.* 1914
Medium: Conté drawing
Size: 308 x 241
Owner: Jewish Museum, Cape Town
Exhibitions: NBL no. 70

62 Head of a Woman, in profile, looking right
Date: 1914
Medium: probably chalk
Size: 160 x 165
Owner: private collection
Exhibitions: ?20th Century Art, WAG 1914, no. 268, BU

63 Self-portrait, in green hat, looking left
Date: 1914–15
Medium: oil on board
Size: 304 x 228
Owner: Mrs Gerda Horvitch
Exhibitions: LEC (noted only in Addendum), NBL No. 61, BU (reproduction in cat. only)

64 Peretz Rosenberg (the artist's uncle)
Date: ?1914
Medium: oil
Size: unknown
Owner: unknown
Exhibitions: LEC no. 2 (photograph)

65 Self-portrait (in felt hat, looking right)
Date: 1915
Medium: oil on panel
Size: 295 x 222
Owner: National Portrait Gallery
Exhibitions: WAG no. 34, LEC no. 27, IWM (1974), NBL no. 90, AACE no. 1 (photograph), BU

66 The Artist's Father
Date: 7 March 1915
Medium: pencil on cardboard
Size: 228 x 152
Owner: Tullie House Museum and Art Gallery
Exhibitions: LEC no. 39, NBL no. 93

67 Sonia Cohen (later Joslen)
Date: 1915, shortly before May
Medium: oil on canvas
Size: 610 x 460
Owner: Joan Rodker
Exhibitions: LEC no. 26 (described as 'unfinished'), NBL no. 106 (also described as 'unfinished'), BU

68 Clara Birnberg (later Clare Winsten)
Date: ?1915 (Strang Collection gives it as 1916)
Medium: oil
Size: 610 x 510
Owner: UCL Art Collections, University College London
Exhibitions: BU

69 Lazarus Aaronson
Date: 1915
Medium: pencil (drawn on last page of Francis Thompson's *Poems*)
Size: unknown
Owner: unknown, formerly Lazarus Aaronson
Exhibitions: LEC no. 42

70 The Family of Adam
Date: by 1915
Medium: unknown
Size: unknown
Owner: unknown
Exhibitions: New English Art Club, 1915

71 The First Meeting of Adam and Eve
Date: *c.* 1915 (WAG gives 1912)
Medium: charcoal on paper
Size: 245 x 270
Owner: Tullie House Museum and Art Gallery
Exhibitions: WAG no. 7 (incorrectly described as 'pencil' and title given as 'Adam and Eve'), LEC no. 43, NBL no. 92, BU

72 Compositional Studies
Date: 12 April 1915
Medium: pen and wash (on reverse of letter from Edward Marsh)
Size: 224 x 127

Owner: private collection
Exhibitions: LEC no. 47, NBL no. 88

73 Self-portrait in a Steel Helmet
Date: 1916
Medium: black chalk and gouache on brown wrapping paper
Size: 240 x 195
Owner: private collection
Exhibitions: WAG no. 14 (incorrectly described as 'watercolour'), LEC no. 45, NBL no. 142, BU

74 Christmas Card Design ('*Pozières*')
Date: 1916
Medium: ink over pencil
Size: unknown
Owner: British Library
Exhibitions: NBL no. 120 (copy), BU

75 Self-portrait Sketch in steel helmet (knees drawn up, in dugout)
Date: 1916
Medium: pencil (in a letter to R.C. Trevelyan)
Size: unknown
Owner: IWM
Exhibitions: IWM (1980), no. 12, BU

76 Self-portrait Sketch, full face, wearing steel helmet
Date: after 1916 (in a letter to Gordon Bottomley)
Medium: pencil (drawn on back of a letter to Gordon Bottomley)
Size: 114 x 91
Owner: IWM
Exhibitions: LEC no. 44, BGL, IWM (1980), no. 22, BU

77 Self-portrait Sketch, in profile, looking left, in peaked cap
Date: July 1917
Medium: pencil

Size: unknown
Owner: IWM
Exhibitions: IWM (1980), no. 17, BU

UNDATED WORKS

78 Studies – Two Figures and a Head and Shoulders
Medium: pencil on page of an exercise book
Size: 203 x 164
Owner: private collection, formerly Annie Wynick
Exhibitions: LEC no. 46

79 Studies – Figure Composition
Medium: pen and pencil on notebook leaf
Size: 190 x 127
Owner: private collection, formerly Annie Wynick
Exhibitions: LEC no. 48

80 Drawing for a Figure Composition
Medium: pencil on tracing paper
Size: 304 x 228
Owner: private collection, formerly Annie Wynick
Exhibitions: LEC no. 49

81 Sanguine Drawing
Date, dimensions and whereabouts unknown
Exhibitions: New English Art Club 1912

82 Figures on a Beach
Medium: oil on board
Size: 190 x 230
Owner: unknown (sold at Sotheby's 1973)

83 Head of a Male Figure
Date: *c.* 1911
Medium: graphite on paper
Size: 253 x 203
Owner: British Museum
Exhibitions: BU

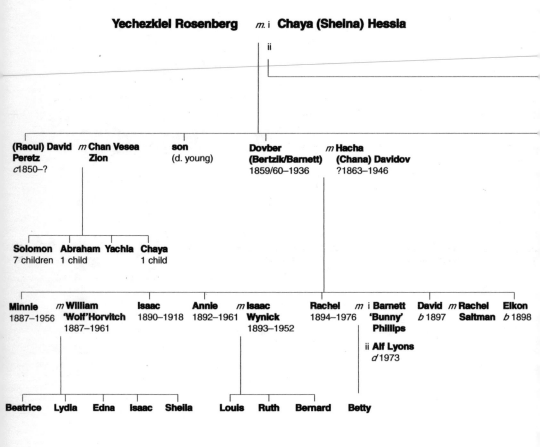

Yechezkiel Rosenberg *m.* i **Chaya (Sheina) Hessia**

ii

(Raoul) David *m* **Chan Vesea**   **son**   **Dovber** *m* **Hacha**
Peretz   **Zion**   (d. young)   **(Bertzik/Barnett)** **(Chana) Davidov**
*c*1850–?   1859/60–1936   ?1863–1946

Solomon **Abraham** **Yachia** **Chaya**
7 children 1 child   1 child

Minnie *m* **William**   **Isaac**   **Annie** *m* **Isaac**   **Rachel** *m* i **Barnett**   **David** *m* **Rachel**   **Elkon**
1887–1956   **'Wolf'Horvitch** 1890–1918   1892–1961 **Wynick**   1894–1976   **'Bunny'**   *b* 1897 **Saltman**   *b* 1898
            1887–1961   1893–1952   **Phillips**

                                                                       ii **Alf Lyons**
                                                                          d 1973

Beatrice **Lydia** **Edna** **Isaac** **Sheila**   **Louis** **Ruth** **Bernard**   **Betty**

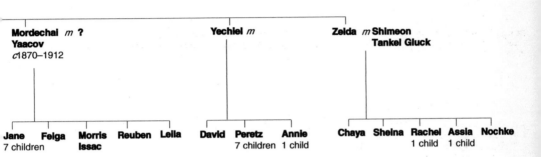

Bryna   Ita Leah

Mordechai *m* **?**
Yaacov
*c*1870–1912

Jane   Felga   **Morris**   Reuben   Leila
7 children   **Issac**

Yechiel *m*

David   **Peretz   Annie**
            7 children 1 child

Zelda *m* **Shimeon**
            Tankel Gluck

Chaya   Shelna   Rachel   Assia   Nochke
                      1 child   1 child

Acknowledgements

My first thanks must go to the family of Isaac Rosenberg for their help in writing and illustrating this book: to the late Isaac Horvitch and his wife Mitzi for their initial encouragement and allowing me free access to the family papers; to Bernard Wynick and his wife Armelle for continuing that access and giving me permission to quote work still in copyright, as well as helping with family photographs; to Betty Silver and her daughter Janet, the Garson family and Doron Swade for permission to reproduce Rosenberg's paintings and drawings in their possession; and to Ruth Swade, Mickie Loeb and Lilian Rosenberg for filling in details of the South African branch of the family.

I should like too to thank Joan Wheelton, Mark James (who also helped greatly with the bibliography), Jorje Pringle and Morgan Merrington for their invaluable assistance in the more elusive areas of research; and Joseph Cohen, Martin Lloyd, Leone Samson, Sarah MacDougall and Rachel Dickson for their willingness to share their own work on Rosenberg.

In the course of writing this book I have received help, advice, encouragement and great hospitality from so many other people, both here and in South Africa, that I have been forced simply to list them alphabetically. They are John Barham, Clive Bettington, Selina Cohen, Stanley Cohen, Cyril Dainow, Linda Dobbs, Neville Dubow, Rhona Dubow, Pat Fisher, Raymond Francis, Luke Gertler, Rita Gold, Brian Johnson-Barker, Ivor Kamlish, Robbie Kirsner, Amanda Leslie, Alison Light, Emanuel Litvinoff, Edward Maggs, Robert Molteno, Judith Perle, Christopher Peters, Cyril Prisman, Norman and Libby Robinson, Joan Rodker, Louis Shachat, Daphna Shakked, David Stern, Georgina Stuttaford, Stephen Watson, Deborah Weissgall, and Anne Willett.

In addition I should like to thank the staff at the following libraries and archives in Britain, America and South Africa: Isaac Gewirtz, Stephen Crook and Philip Milito at the Berg Collection, New York Public Library; Michael Boggan at the Department of Western Manuscripts, British Library; Rochelle Rubinstein at the Central Zionist Archives, Jerusalem; Bonita Bennett at the District Six Museum, Cape Town; Uta Ben-Joseph at the Gitlin Library, Cape Town; Martin Bolton and staff at the Hyman Kreitman Research Centre, Tate Britain; Roderick Suddaby, Simon Offord and staff in the Library, and Sara Bevan in the Prints and Drawings Department of the Imperial War Museum; Henry Morrison at the Jewish Military Museum, London; Shea Albert at the Jewish Museum, Cape Town; Peter Donnelly at the King's Own Royal Regiment Museum, Lancaster; staff at the London Metropolitan Archives; Mr Bennett, headmaster of St Paul's School, Wellclose Square, London; Haydn Proud at the South African National Gallery; Malcolm Barr-Hampton at the Tower Hamlets Local History Library (Bancroft Road); Katharine Bradley at Toynbee Hall; Melanie Gardner at the Tullie House Museum and Art Gallery, Carlisle; staff of the Archive Department at the University of the Arts on the South Bank; M.T. Richardson at the Arts and Social Science Library, University of Bristol; Milton Shain and Veronica Belling in the Kaplan Institute, and Lesley Hart in the Manuscript and Archives Department at the University of Cape Town; Christine Terry and Elaine Pankhurst at Birkbeck College, University of London; Helen Beer in the Department of Hebrew and Jewish Studies; Dalia Tracz in the Jewish Studies Library, and staff of the Special Collections at University College, University of London; Patrick Scott at the Thomas Cooper Library, University of South Carolina in Columbia; staff at the Parkes Library, University of Southampton; Nayia Yiakoumaki at the Archive Research Centre, Whitechapel Art Gallery.

I am also grateful to my editor, Alan Samson, his Personal Assistant, Carole Green, and my more-than-typist, Gertrud Watson, for their encouragement, patience and forbearance.

But the warmest thanks of all must go to my family for supporting me in so many ways through yet another literary pilgrimage: my children, Kate, Philip, Emma, Alice and Trim and, above all, my husband, Cecil Woolf.

The author and publisher are grateful for permission to reproduce illustrations. While every effort has been made to trace copyright holders, if any have been inadvertently overlooked, the publisher will be happy to acknowledge them in future editions.

Index